KNOWLEDGE

As we move through our modern world, the phenomenon we call knowledge is always involved. Whether we talk of know-how, technology, innovation, politics or education, it is the concept of knowledge that ties them all together. However, despite its ubiquity as a modern trope, we seldom encounter knowledge in itself. How is it produced, where does it reside, and who owns it? Is knowledge always beneficial, will we know all there is to know at some point in the future, and does knowledge really equal power? This book pursues an original approach to this concept that seems to define so many aspects of modern societies. It explores the topic from a distinctly sociological perspective, and traces the many ways that knowledge is woven into the very fabric of modern society.

Marian Adolf is Professor of Media Culture at Zeppelin University in Friedrichshafen, Germany. His research interests revolve around the interface of media and social change, communication and cultural theory. He has held appointments as Visiting Professor at Quest University and Alpen-Adria-University Klagenfurt, and currently serves as chair of the German Communication Association's section for Media Sociology.

Nico Stehr is Karl Mannheim Professor of Cultural Studies at Zeppelin University in Friedrichshafen, Germany. He formerly held professorships at the University of Alberta, Edmonton, the University of British Columbia, Ludwig Maximilians University in Munich, and was Paul F. Lazarsfeld Guest Professor at the University of Vienna. He has published widely on the topic of knowledge and is one of the proponents of Knowledge Society, a term that has acquired widespread currency not only in academia.

KEY IDEAS
SERIES EDITOR: PETER HAMILTON

Designed to compliment the successful Key Sociologists, this series covers the main concepts, issues, debates, and controversies in sociology and the social sciences. The series aims to provide authoritative essays on central topics of social science, such as community, power, work, sexuality, inequality, benefits and ideology, class, family, etc. Books adopt a strong 'individual' line, as critical essays rather than literature surveys, offering lively and original treatments of their subject matter. The books will be useful to students and teachers of sociology, political science, economics, psychology, philosophy, and geography.

Culture – second edition
Chris Jenks

Human Rights
Anthony Woodiwiss

Childhood – second edition
Chris Jenks

Cosmopolitanism
Robert Fine

Nihilism
Bulent Diken

Transnationalism
Steven Vertovec

Sexuality – third edition
Jeffrey Weeks

Leisure
Tony Blackshaw

Experts
Nico Stehr and Reiner Grundmann

Happiness
Bent Greve

Risk – second edition
Deborah Lupton

Social Identity – fourth edition
Richard Jenkins

Renewable Energies
Matthias Gross and Rüdiger Mautz

Sustainability
Thomas Pfister, Martin Schweighofer and André Reichel

Knowledge – second edition
Is knowledge power?
Marian Adolf and Nico Stehr

KNOWLEDGE

Is knowledge power?

Second edition

Marian Adolf and Nico Stehr

LONDON AND NEW YORK

Second edition published 2017
by Routledge
2 Park Square, Milton Park, Abingdon, Oxon OX14 4RN

and by Routledge
711 Third Avenue, New York, NY 10017

Routledge is an imprint of the Taylor & Francis Group, an informa business

© 2016 Marian Adolf and Nico Stehr

The right of Marian Adolf and Nico Stehr to be identified as authors of this work has been asserted by them in accordance with sections 77 and 78 of the Copyright, Designs and Patents Act 1988.

All rights reserved. No part of this book may be reprinted or reproduced or utilised in any form or by any electronic, mechanical, or other means, now known or hereafter invented, including photocopying and recording, or in any information storage or retrieval system, without permission in writing from the publishers.

Trademark notice: Product or corporate names may be trademarks or registered trademarks, and are used only for identification and explanation without intent to infringe.

British Library Cataloguing in Publication Data
A catalogue record for this book is available from the British Library

Library of Congress Cataloging in Publication Data
Names: Adolf, Marian, author. | Stehr, Nico, author.
  Title: Knowledge : is knowledge power? / by Marian Adolf and Nico Stehr.
  Description: Abingdon, Oxon ; New York, NY : Routledge, 2016. | Includes bibliographical references and index.
  Identifiers: LCCN 2016009864| ISBN 9781138685673 (hardback) | ISBN 9781138685680 (pbk.) | ISBN 9781315543093 (ebook)
  Subjects: LCSH: Knowledge, Sociology of.
  Classification: LCC HM651 .A26 2016 | DDC 306.4/2–dc23
  LC record available at https://lccn.loc.gov/2016009864

ISBN: 978-1-138-68567-3 (hbk)
ISBN: 978-1-138-68568-0 (pbk)
ISBN: 978-1-315-54309-3 (ebk)

Typeset in Bembo
by Taylor & Francis Books

Dedicated to all we love.

CONTENTS

List of tables   x
Preface   xi

Introduction   1

1 Classical sociological conceptions of knowledge   6

2 Knowledge about knowledge   10

    2.1 Attributes of knowledge 11
    2.2 Knowledge as a capacity to act 18
    2.3 Knowledge and information 21
    2.4 Practical knowledge 31
    2.5 Additional knowledge 33
    2.6 The uneven development of knowledge 38
    2.7 The limits of the growth of knowledge 41
    2.8 A sociological concept of knowledge and its context 42

3 The knowledge of the powerful   47

3.1 Knowledge is power and power is knowledge 48
3.2 The iron law of oligarchy 50
3.3 Knowledge/power 54
3.4 The global class 63

4 Non-knowledge   69

4.1 Sigmund Freud and Friedrich August von Hayek 70
4.2 Observing non-knowledge 72
4.3 Non-knowledge as a myth? 74
4.4 Lack of knowledge 79
4.5 Ignorance 82
4.6 The division of knowledge and information 88
4.7 Knowledge gaps 91
4.8 Non-knowledge about non-knowledge 93

5 Policing knowledge   100

5.1 The self-realization of knowledge 102
5.2 The self-protection of knowledge 106
5.3 Superfluous knowledge 111

6 Forms of knowledge   114

6.1 Everyday knowledge 115
6.2 The power of everyday knowledge 121
6.3 Indigenous or traditional knowledge 132
6.4 Tacit knowledge 136

7 Global knowledge   142

7.1 Basic reflections on global knowledge 143
7.2 Global knowledge worlds 146
7.3 Structures of global knowledge spaces 150
7.4 Forms of global knowledge worlds 152
7.5 Attributes of knowledge that promote globalization 156

7.6 Limits to the globalization of knowledge 157
7.7 The project of worldwide worlds of knowledge, and the doubts about its likelihood 164

8 Digital worlds and knowledge/information 175

8.1 Information, communication and technology 176
8.2 Societal communication and shared knowledge 177
8.3 Analyzing the ubiquity of media: mediatization 178
8.4 New media, old media and the hybrid media system 180
8.5 ICTs, surveillance and knowledge 181
8.6 Communication, media and knowledge 185

9 Functions of knowledge 188

9.1 Knowledge as power and authority 190
9.2 The power of ideas 191
9.3 Knowledge and the economy 196
9.4 Knowledge as property and public good 199

10 The price of knowledge 207

10.1 Human capital 210
10.2 Symbolic and knowledge capital 214
10.3 Patents 219
10.4 Taxation 227

11 The benefits of knowledge 237

11.1 The distribution of knowledge 240
11.2 Knowledge, power and participation 245
11.3 Knowledge societies 247

Bibliography 257
Index 306

TABLE

10.1 Inter-nation technology trade 225

PREFACE

In our conception and exploration of knowledge about knowledge, its social role as a capacity to act, its various forms and carriers, and the social division of knowledge in modern societies we have taken cues from a variety of our previous work, both taken on board and elaborated. Relevant discussions, in which especially Nico Stehr was involved, now range over a period of more than four decades. The theoretical and empirical work on the social role of knowledge is reflected in a series of monographs, anthologies and journal articles including our earlier volume on *Knowledge* (Adolf and Stehr, 2014). Many of these past efforts were published in German. References to these initial publications can be found in the relevant sections of the text and, of course, in our bibliography.

What unites these works on the societal role of knowledge is a *sociological* concept of knowledge. Our discussion, therefore, is not primarily based on the post-positivist unease, increasing since the 1960s, towards a positivist philosophy of science that is constrained by a narrow understanding of the scientific method. Undoubtedly, the critique of positivism has brought forth perspectives that also play a part in the sociological study of knowledge. These include, for example, the concepts of tacit knowledge and situation-specific knowledge or the notion of "bounded rationality." On the other hand, the sociology of knowledge has contributed a valuable extension to modern philosophy of science.

The discourse on the concept of knowledge and the societal function of knowledge were initially explored in a comprehensive manner in the study *Knowledge Societies* (Stehr, 1994). The preceding publication, dating from 1986, by Gernot Böhme and Nico Stehr on the theory of modern society as a knowledge society turned out to be one of the publications that substantially co-determined the research field of knowledge and contemporary social relations (Böhme and Stehr, 1986).

In the meantime, the issue of the social role of knowledge has on various occasions been repeatedly taken up, often in collaboration with Marian Adolf. Fundamental questions such as the cultural foundations of innovation and the role of the media in the knowledge society have been examined together, as well as current societal developments and problems such as, for example, the importance of moral convictions for modern markets or the consequences of the digital media revolution and the re-assertion of social physics.

In all of these discussions, new aspects and perspectives were added to the concept of knowledge and information while approaches that had already been elaborated were rarely discarded entirely. This is also the case in our present examination of the fundamental metaphor (with a question mark) *Knowledge: Is Knowledge Power?* In other words, this study is also a summary and an extension, not accomplished so far, of the discourse on knowledge found in publications in different locations and at different times, all dealing with the role of knowledge and cognition in social relations.

The sociological definition of knowledge as a form of "collective consciousness" (see Durkheim, [1955] 1983) and as a capacity to act continues to be conceived of in sharp contrast to the philosophical and everyday conception of knowledge as fact-oriented, "certified information" ("knowledge is authenticated information"; e.g. Dretske, 1983) or "true belief" ("knowledge as a justified belief"; e.g. Huber, 1991; Nonaka, 1994: 15). The present English version of our initial German monograph *Ist Wissen Macht?* (Stehr and Adolf, 2015) includes five new, additional chapters on the following topics: 1 the alleged idea of non-knowledge, 2 the assertion of the phenomenon of global knowledge, 3 reflections on digital worlds and knowledge/information, 4 a discussion of the price of knowledge, and 5 comments on the knowledge of the powerful. In addition, the chapters that were already part of the German edition were comprehensively updated.

Given the long-term examination of the question of knowledge, and exemplifying our notion of knowledge as an essentially social phenomenon, it is appropriate to refer to important intellectual as well as personal debts at this point. Individuals and institutions have over the years provided a significant social context for the task of developing our understanding of the role of knowledge in human affairs. The universities of Oregon, Alberta, Munich, Vienna, the University of British Columbia and Zeppelin University should be mentioned. While it is impossible for us to establish a complete list of all the persons whose advice and critical interventions have been helpful at this point, we would like to acknowledge our special thanks and huge intellectual debt to, as well as considerable appreciation of, Gernot Böhme, David Kettler and Volker Meja. We are grateful to Hella Beister, Dustin Voss and Jan Morgenstern for their diligent and editorial advice. We also thank Anders Blok, Albert Borgmann, Thomas Brante, Dennis Deicke, Sven Eliaeson, Steve Fuller, Yves Gingras, Reiner Grundmann, Horst J. Helle, Marcus Kleiner, Wolfgang Krohn, Charles Lemert, Cyril Levitt, Amanda Machin, Jason Mast, Scott McNall, Richard Münch, Sebastian Nestler, Theresa Richardson, Alexander Ruser, Daniel Sarewitz, Martin Schulte, Hermann Strasser, Stephen Turner, Ulrich Ufer, Jay Weinstein and Helmut Willke for their constructive cooperation, editorial assistance and helpful notes concerning different parts of this study of knowledge and its power.

INTRODUCTION

"Among the innumerable observations at which we have ceased to be amazed," the philosopher Hans Blumenberg wrote, "are the fact of the existence and the extraordinary exertion of science that affects our consciousness and conditions our life; in fact, makes it possible in the first place." Even in the early 1970s this insight had become so self-evident that "[one] can easily be reproached for making a trivial observation if one suggests that the modern era is the age of science," as he goes on to say (Blumenberg, [1973] 1983: 229). His observation refers to the extraordinary importance of scientific knowledge for our very existence and the ways we live *today*. Moreover, Blumenberg's statement resonates strongly with our own definition of knowledge. We would like to characterize knowledge not as something *that is so* but as a generalized capacity to act on the world, as a model *for* reality, or as the ability to set something in motion (Stehr, 1994). Knowledge represents a *capacity to act*, a capacity that becomes increasingly important in modern societies. Although we recognize that knowledge is both a product of the *past* and a factor that determines the *future*, our conception of knowledge as a capacity to act is intended to stress our theoretical and practical emphasis on the social role of knowledge. If defined in an even broader sense and not restricted to scientific knowledge, following Georg Simmel (1906: 441), for example, knowledge is an anthropological constant: "All relationships of people to each other rest, as a matter of course, upon the precondition that they know something about each other." Knowledge in the broad sense as employed here is not restricted to any particular social system in modern societies. Knowledge is everywhere (see Luhmann, 1990: 147). More about our definition of knowledge later.

The notion of knowledge is one of the most widely used concepts in everyday life, in scientific discourse, in policy discussions, and in reflections about science and technology. Put more formally, the term knowledge typically performs the speech-act of commending what it describes (cf. Sartori, 1968). Knowledge in the English-speaking world often has a meaning approaching that of "truth." Knowledge therefore becomes a species of true belief.

The idea that we are living in a knowledge society is gaining acceptance, as is the notion that the modern economy is knowledge-based, and that the worlds of work, politics and everyday life are transformed by and based on knowledge and information. By the same token, Ulrich Beck, Scott Lash and Anthony Giddens's concept and theory of reflexive modernization is a knowledge-based theory of modern society that is, in one sense, "bound in essence […] to knowledge (reflection) on foundations, consequences and problems of modernization processes" and, in another sense, "to the unintended consequences of modernization" (Beck, [1996] 1999: 109; Beck, 1996), or to the idea that we are living in "an age of side effects" (Beck, 1994: 175). There is no clear-cut distinction between the two meanings of reflexive modernization, the focus being on knowledge and reflexivity in both cases.

Hans Blumenberg's observation that our identity and our existential conditions are profoundly affected by knowledge is as apt as is his observation that our consciousness and our life represent realities made by our knowledge. If, for the time being, we restrict the concept of knowledge to scientific knowledge, then Blumenberg's statement means that human reality is one that is dependent on science.

However, especially in our age when the idea prevails that society *and* nature have to be apprehended as accomplishments of active human subjects, Blumenberg's remark about the nature and the social role of knowledge also raises skepticism from those who are concerned about the science dependence of the modern world and who therefore would echo Jean-Jacques Rousseau's ([1762] 1979: 10) early and general admonition in *Émile, or On Education*: "Everything is good as it leaves the hands of the author of things, everything degenerates in the hands of man." According to Rousseau, who was obviously a skeptic when it came to the role of scientific knowledge in society, knowledge loses its innocence once it is implemented or used to "get things done."

However, precisely what knowledge is and how it differs from information, cognitive categories, classification, expertise, ideology, rumors, power, human or symbolic capital, ideas and other intellectual skills and competencies is a contentious matter. It is self-evident therefore that one needs to devote time and care to examine the central notion of the term of knowledge itself. This requires, as we will try to argue, a *sociological* conception of knowledge, which is not only concerned with its social bases as was traditionally the case but also with the kind of "work" knowledge performs in the context of social action. Hence, the emphasis in this volume will be on the role knowledge plays in society rather than on the ways knowledge is produced. Nonetheless, a few remarks about the more traditional treatment of knowledge and what changed it are in order.

However, before turning to a more extensive discussion of the major *attributes* of knowledge, we will in the next part of our analysis refer to some of the central classical sociological conceptions of knowledge.

Traditionally it has been the role of philosophy to ponder the nature of knowledge. In Plato's *Theaetetus* a scientific approach to knowledge and cognition is laid out, and his dualistic ontology rests on epistemological foundations. Subsequently, the philosophers of the French and Scottish Enlightenments recognized that all social differences had *social* origins and were thus subject to human control. They were aware that a wide range of social, economic and political factors shapes the genesis, structure and content of human consciousness. They thus anticipated one of the major presuppositions of the modern *sociology of knowledge*, namely that existing societal conditions co-determine, if not outright determine, our consciousness.

In general, however, philosophers have attempted to demonstrate that a sociology of knowledge is neither possible nor desirable. Immanuel Kant thus argued that while there could be no perception without conception, the constitutive components of cognition remained *a priori*. Similarly, empiricists of various persuasions have maintained that *scientific* knowledge is warranted by direct experience unaffected by social conditions. At most, these philosophies concede that extra-theoretical factors may influence the genesis of ideas (that is, the context of discovery), but not the structure and the content of thought (the context of justification). Otherwise quite different philosophies of thought have shared an often explicit rejection of what they saw as a case of sociological relativism, and attempted to overcome doubt by placing knowledge on a firm foundation, even outside the realm of socio-historical experience.

Further questions investigated by philosophy and its branch, the philosophy of science, are the relation between knowledge and belief (or ideology), the validity and reliability of knowledge claims pertaining to the external world and based on sense perception, the presuppositions required for the production of knowledge, and the use of language in the construction of knowledge claims. Knowing, in the philosophical tradition, has often been reduced to the relationship between the individual subject – the knower – and the object or referent – the known.

The systematic idea that our knowledge is a social construct and that an empirical analysis of the production of knowledge including the politics of the generation of scientific knowledge could be of interest is of more recent origin (see Jasanoff, 2012; Knorr-Cetina, 2005). Since the early 1920s, the various traditions of the *sociology of knowledge* have been concerned with the social forces and processes that affect knowing and knowledge claims. Similarly, the by now rapidly growing interest in the study of the social distribution and the impact of knowledge on social relations (cf. Schütz, 1946) can be linked much less directly – if at all – to any philosophical traditions concerned with the secure foundations of knowing.

More recently, with the emergence of the sociology of *scientific* knowledge in the 1970s and early 1980s (see Shapin, 1995; Bloor, 2004), the earlier, apparently rock-solid images of scientific knowledge have been questioned: that is, a sociology of scientific knowledge is not possible (Ben-David, 1971: 11–13; Stehr, 2004a).

The sociology of scientific knowledge can of course trace its lineage to the philosopher Immanuel Kant, who stresses the crucial role of the subject in any cognitive process. In his *Critique of Pure Reason* Kant insists that "we ourselves bring into the appearances [of things] that order and regularity in them that we call nature" (Kant [1781] 1998: A125). Interest in science and technology studies (STS) is now centered on knowledge as practice, on knowing and thinking as a social process and accomplishment; that is, on the interior, specialized socio-cultural systems of science that serve as the basis for the creation and warranting of (scientific) knowledge. These developments need not be reiterated here; they have been extensively documented (e.g. Meja and Stehr, 2005).

Developing almost concurrently, the *economics* of knowledge (e.g. Boulding, 1966; Forey, 2006), including the issue of human capital and the knowledge-based economy (e.g. Drucker, 1993a; Stehr, 2002), can for the most part be bracketed out for the purposes of our analysis. Today a strong and growing scholarly interest has shifted toward an analysis of the effects of knowledge on social relations, for example, the social distribution of knowledge and, even more generally, the idea that modern societies are knowledge societies (Böhme and Stehr, 1986; Stehr, 1994). These perspectives, along with the more doubtful notion of knowledge *management* (Prusak, 1997), have gained prominence not only in the social sciences – in particular in sociology, economics, political science, business administration and management studies (e.g., Machlup, 1962; Drucker, 1986; Bell, 1973; Stehr, 1994, 2001) – but also in the political system – for instance, in the programmatic pronouncements of political parties, in policy statements of national governments and transnational organizations, or in the growing role of experts, advisors and counsclors in modern societies (Grundmann and Stehr, 2011). Questions pertaining to the role of knowledge for social organization are also, if less visibly, inherent in research that focuses on the diffusion and adoption of information or technological innovations, such as, for example, studies investigating the "knowledge gap" (Tichenor et al., 1970) or the "digital divide" (Norris, 2001).

1
CLASSICAL SOCIOLOGICAL CONCEPTIONS OF KNOWLEDGE

The idea that all of our knowledge is a social construct is of recent origin. As a matter of fact, sociology itself could only arise after the dogma of the congruence between natural and social inequality had fallen into disrepute. It was one of the great accomplishments of the pioneers of social thought that shapes our societies until today, namely that *social differences* were also of *social origin* rather than God-given. From there the social sciences went on to explore how social, economic and political factors shape the genesis, structure and content of human consciousness. However, these early reflections on the effect of social conditions on consciousness did not result in a more systematic examination of the questions that later became a focus of the sociology of knowledge, in particular. Nevertheless, some of these early writings, which either denied or represented first tentative steps in the direction of a sociological examination of knowledge, must be acknowledged as intellectual precursors of such an analysis. At this point, we will make but brief references to the classical social scientific conception of knowledge; however, we will refer to the more specific positions taken by its core representatives, especially Max Weber, Karl Marx, Max Scheler, Karl Mannheim or Georg Simmel, throughout our discussion.

A prominent place in this list must be granted to Karl Marx whose famous sub- and superstructure scheme – i.e. his assertion that there is, at least under certain historical conditions, a primacy of economic realities, a determination of the "ideological superstructure" by socio-economic processes – has been particularly influential. Perhaps the sociology of knowledge even today represents, as has occasionally been argued, a struggle with this Marxist assertion. Marx's conception of a close affinity between *social structure* and *culture* continues to constitute the primary theme of the sociology of knowledge. The distinctly Marxist response to the central sociology-of-knowledge assertion has resulted in some outstanding sociological analyses of problems of cultural production, for example in the work of Georg Lukács.

The classical French sociologist Emile Durkheim, too, may be regarded as a pioneer of the sociological analysis of knowledge even though he failed to develop a general model of the classificatory process from his assertions about the basic categories of perception and the ordering of experience (space, time, causality, direction), which he saw as derived from the social structure of simpler societies.

Emile Durkheim and Marcel Mauss, but also Lucien Lévy-Bruhl, examined the forms of logical classification prevalent in "primitive" societies and concluded that the basic categories of cognition have social origins. They were not prepared, however, to extend this kind of analysis to more complex societies. Their inquiry into the social foundations of logic generated considerable criticism of their guiding assumptions, and much of this criticism has withstood the test of time and continues to be invoked against a sociologically informed inquiry into knowledge (cf. Crick, 1982). Moreover, Durkheim (e.g. [1955] 1983: 48) developed a pragmatic conception of the social origins or the basic motivations that prompt the search for knowledge as a capacity to act, in the first place: "At the origin of the process of knowledge, the idea to be checked is the idea of something to be *done*."

Although Max Scheler in the early 1920s first used the term *Wissenssoziologie* (translated as "sociology of knowledge"), it was Karl Mannheim who, only a few years later, provided the most elaborate and ambitious programmatic foundation for a sociological analysis of cognition, even though Edward Shils (1982: 8), in his typical dismissive sense of others who just do not know, rated this project as something

Mannheim had carried out "with half his mind." Max Scheler extended the Marxist notion of substructure by claiming that different "real factors" (*Realfaktoren*) conditioned thought in different historical periods and in different social and cultural systems in specific ways. Karl Mannheim, like Scheler, extended the Marxist concept of substructure by referring to the possibility that biological elements (such as race), psychological elements (such as a "drive for power"), and spiritual or even supernatural phenomena, among others, may take the place – provided they were conceived of as contexts of meaning – of primary economic relations (Mannheim, 1971). However, Mannheim's contribution to the sociology of knowledge also represents exemplary research into the social conditions associated with different forms of knowledge.

Even today, Mannheim's analyses of competition as a cultural form, of conservative thought, of the problem of generations, and of economic ambition, among others, remain examples of the kind of firstrate analysis that the sociological analysis of knowledge has to offer. For Mannheim, the sociology of knowledge is destined to play a considerable role in the intellectual and political life of society, particularly in an age of dissolution and conflict, by sociologically examining the very conditions that gave rise to competing ideas, political philosophies, ideologies and diverse cultural products. According to Mannheim, the sociology of knowledge must also be a *diagnosis of its time* and provide practical solutions in an age of disenchantment and disorientation. Other sociological traditions, even those without any direct link to the sociology of knowledge, which pursue similar – often explicitly critical – goals, also feature the (implied) importance of the foundations of knowledge and its significant role in and for social relations. This applies, for example, to the current critique of consumerism that rests on the assumption of the overwhelming power of marketing and advertising (or, more generally, on the power of the media) to tell people what to think, want and desire.

Mannheim's project, while achieving considerable critical acclaim, nevertheless also foreshadowed the subsequent reception and transformation of the sociology of knowledge. The latter developed into a sociological specialty, as sociology itself evolved increasingly into a professional activity clearly differentiated from philosophy, history, anthropology, economics and linguistics, and was transplanted into other societies and reflected the commitments of disciplinary traditions that differed considerably from those found in Germany at the time when its intellectual and political mission had first been formulated.

After this review of some of the classical conceptions of knowledge, the next part of our examination of the nature of knowledge must deal in greater depth with the core concept of our analysis, namely "knowledge." We therefore offer a range of observations concerning the knowledge about knowledge.

2
KNOWLEDGE ABOUT KNOWLEDGE

As we have stressed already, the concept of knowledge is one of the most widely used concepts in everyday life and in scientific discourse. This applies even more specifically to contemporary conditions. The notion that modern economy is irrevocably based on knowledge and that the world of work is both transformed by and based on knowledge and information has become textbook reality and is widely accepted in society.

By the same token, the idea that knowledge generated in the sciences is a *producer* of many *of the problems* with which modern society has to deal is gaining currency. Thus, Max Scheler (1960 [1925: 17]) emphasizes that our identity and our existential conditions are profoundly affected and produced by knowledge.

Although the idea that knowledge is of crucial and growing importance in social, political and economic relations in contemporary societies is increasingly accepted in the social sciences and in society in general, the most serious theoretical deficiency of present-day theories of knowledge and theories of modern society that assign a central role to knowledge, for example the theory of modern society as a network society or the idea of contemporary society as a risk society, is their still rather undifferentiated and ambivalent treatment of the concept of (scientific) knowledge (and information).

The important role that knowledge plays in these theories has not yet been matched by an extended and enlightened discussion of the concept and the social role of knowledge. As a result, we will start our inquiry into knowledge with an examination of our knowledge about knowledge, and of various significant and often unique attributes of knowledge.

2.1 Attributes of knowledge

Precisely what knowledge is and how it may differ from information, human capital and other cognitive skills and social competencies is an essentially contested matter (Gallie, 1955–56). As we have noted, the concept of knowledge, let alone its production, distribution and consequences, cannot be taken for granted – at least by the scientific observer. Thus, it is almost self-evident that one needs to devote time and care to examine the central notion of the term of knowledge. This requires, at least from our perspective, as we will try to argue, a genuinely *sociological* conception of knowledge.

A sociological approach does not treat knowledge as rules that "reduce environmental uncertainty through connections between ideas and facts" (Tywoniak, 2007: 53), or, as is more common, as *justified* or *true* (incontestable) knowledge, as would be the case, for example, in the philosophy of science, but conceives of it as a deeply social, a human-made category. In addition, we will discuss the difference between knowledge and information, acknowledging the fact that the two concepts are routinely conflated and contested in everyday as well as scientific discourse (cf. Ancori et al., 2000).

A sociological conception of knowledge as opposed to a philosophical or epistemological notion of knowledge is about social actors who *share* knowledge rather than about referents or warrants of knowledge that certify that knowledge claims are valid or objective, for example. A sociological conception of knowledge is not only concerned with its social bases, as is the case in the sociology of knowledge, but also with the kind of "work" knowledge performs in the context of social action in general; that is, with the real impact knowledge cultures and forms of knowledge have on social, cultural and economic processes. A sociological conception of knowledge furthermore includes reflections on where knowledge resides. All of this of course involves consideration of issues such as at what point knowledge acquires a function in social action, that is, becomes connected to different fields of practices, how knowledge may assimilate to power and how it is distributed as well as accessed.

What is it, then, that we know, and what does knowing mean that we know? Some examples, taken from the *Oxford Dictionary of Current English*, are: "Every child knows that two and two make four." "He knows a lot of English." "Do you know how to play chess?" "I don't know whether he is here or not." These examples show that knowledge is always the knowledge of *someone* and that knowing is *a relation* to things and facts, but also to laws and rules. In any case, knowing is some sort of personal *participation*: knowing things, facts and rules means to "appropriate" them in some manner, to include them in our field of orientation, competence and skills.

Rather than suggesting that knowledge is something that people have in their possession or are able to obtain with relative ease – a notion that may be more appropriate for the term of "information," as we will see, or for the fact that knowledge refers to the relation between the knower and the referent (object) of knowledge – we will describe knowing as an activity, as something that individuals *do*. Knowledge can be treated, using a term John Dewey (1948: 197) employs in an even more general sense, as a *transaction*, that is, as a *collective* entity that does not exist apart from human participation. In this sense, different forms of knowledge can be distinguished on the basis of the kind of participation that happens to be involved.

Knowledge can, of course, be objectified. The crucial innovation of recording knowledge first occurred some 4,000 years ago in China, India, Egypt and Mesopotamia, and later in classical Greece. As Donald (1991: 344) observes, "for the first time in history complex ideas were placed in the public arena, in an external medium, where they could undergo refinement over the longer term, that is, well beyond the lifespan of single individuals." In short, the intellectual appropriation of things, facts and rules can be established and articulated symbolically, so that in order to know, it is not necessary to get into direct contact with the things themselves, but only with their symbolic representations. This is the social significance of language, writing, printing, data storage and the Internet – of the media in general.

Modern societies have made dramatic advances in the intellectual appropriation of nature and society. Knowledge may be embedded and objectified in materials, equipment, apparatuses, instruments and other artifacts. Capital goods represent embedded knowledge on how to produce such commodities (see Baetjer, 2000). As Giovanni Dosi and Marco Grazzi (2009: 1) therefore suggest, it is useful "to begin by thinking of a technology as something like a 'recipe' entailing a design for a final product which, much like a cookbook recipe, concerns a physical artifact together with a set of procedures for achieving it. The recipe specifies a set of actions that need to be taken to achieve the desired outcome and identifies, if sometimes implicitly, the inputs that are to be acted on and any required equipment."

There is an immense stock of such *objectified knowledge* that mediates our relation to nature, society and to ourselves. In a general sense, this advancement used to be called, in earlier contexts, modernization or rationalization and, more recently, globalization, allegedly leading to a "unity of civilization."[1]

This secondary nature is overgrowing the primary nature of humans. The real and the fictional merge and become indistinguishable; theories become facts, but not vice versa. Facts, for example, cannot police theories. In other words, as Emile Durkheim emphasizes in his classical *The Elementary Forms of Religious Life* (1965 [1912]), the world out there does not name and classify itself (cf. Barnes, 1995: 96). A sociological concept of knowledge has to accept the intrinsic "impurity" of knowledge, its rootedness in all social institutions (including science) and cultural processes, its entanglement with power and interests, its enormous variability and its lack of zero-sum attributes.

It is only after a sense of the societal significance of such opposites and oppositions has been acquired that the full sociological significance of knowledge begins to emerge. Such a perspective leads to the realization that knowledge is increasingly not only the foundation of authority but also of resistance, and that access to knowledge becomes a major societal resource and an occasion for political and social struggles.

Although knowledge has always had a social function, it is only recently that scholars have begun to examine the structure of society and its development from the point of view of the production, distribution and application of knowledge to knowledge itself (e.g. Malinowski, 1955; Machlup, 1962, 1981, 1984; Drucker, 1993b: 53). Applied to present-day society, the question is whether knowledge can provide the principle for social hierarchies and social inequality, for the distribution of opportunities of social and political influence, for societal conflicts and for the nature of personal life; and, finally, whether knowledge may also prove to be a normative principle of social cohesion and integration, even though the variations and alterations in the reproduction of knowledge appear to be considerable. Paradoxically, efforts to entrench necessity in history, or to eliminate chance from history, have produced its opposite, at least at the collective level. The role of chance, ambiguity and – as we will stress – "fragility" at the collective level continues to be an increasingly important part of the way society comes to be organized.

One of the first comprehensive sociological analyses of societies in which the knowledge-producing sector attains decisive importance for the dynamics of social relations is Daniel Bell's *The Coming of Post-Industrial Society* (1973; also Lasch, 1992). Radovan Richta et al.'s (1969) theory of the scientific-technical revolution, formulated at roughly the same time, constitutes the then "socialist" counter image to Bell's theory of modern society as a post-industrial society. It is worth noting that Bell (1973: 212) argues that post-industrial society is a *knowledge society* for two major reasons: 1 "the sources of innovation are increasingly derivative from research and development (and more directly, there is a new relation between science and technology because of the centrality of theoretical knowledge)"; and 2 "the weight of the society – measured by a larger proportion of Gross National Product and a larger share of employment – is increasingly in the knowledge field." The pace and scale of the translation of knowledge into technology provide the basis for the possibility of modernity. Thus, if there is a "radical gap between the present and the past, it lies in the nature of technology and the ways it has transformed social relations and our ways of looking at the world" (Bell, 1968: 174).

Science has been the site where most of the currently circulating concepts of knowledge originated during the past centuries, but in its attempt to elaborate and come to a shared understanding of knowledge, scientific discourse has developed a taken-for-granted attitude toward its own knowledge. The number of well-explicated categories of knowledge has therefore been limited. We have not moved far beyond the different forms of knowledge proposed by Max Scheler (1960 [1925]) in his essays on the sociology of knowledge in the 1920s: namely, the distinction between: 1 knowledge of salvation (*Erlösungswissen*); 2 cultural knowledge, or knowledge of pure essences (*Bildungswissen*); and 3 knowledge that produces effects (*Herrschaftswissen*).

Even those scholars who, like Daniel Bell, have elevated knowledge to some kind of new axial principle of modern society actually treat knowledge as a *black box*, and more particularly as a disembodied phenomenon. Bell and many sociological theorists before him saw every reason, typically in polemically charged circumstances, to defend positive knowledge as non-problematic: inherently practical, uncontested, efficient, truthful, objective, powerful and even ethical. Many of the past discussions of knowledge in science have limited their assessment of the reasons for the legitimacy and the societal power of scientific knowledge by simply noting that such knowledge has been successfully utilized in practice.

However, knowing is *grosso modo* participation in the cultural resources of society. Knowledge represents *partaking* in the affairs of society, but this participation is subject to stratification. Life chances, lifestyles and the social influence of individuals as well as their capacity to affect contingencies depend on their access to the social stock of knowledge as well as other resources of social action, for instance, energy, power or language.

Under present conditions we possess an enormous inventory of objective knowledge that mediates between nature and humans. Nature cannot be experienced other than as a human product or as a part of human products; social relations are increasingly generated and embedded in a network of administrative, legal or technological systems. The emerging social structure imposed on nature and social relations is nothing but objectified knowledge or, in other terms, a *realization* of what we know. Knowledge therefore is, as we will discuss in greater detail below, a model *for* reality.

The individual and collective appropriation of society proceeds in an analogous fashion, namely through the process of rule production. As for the production, dissemination and reproduction of knowledge we may, then, initially propose a purely quantitative diagnosis for contemporary society: the superstructure of society has become so immense that the majority of social action is not production but reproduction, in particular *reproduction of knowledge*. That reproduction predominates is mainly due to the fact that much of scientific knowledge is treated as a form of universal knowledge.

Knowledge is a most peculiar entity, with properties generally unlike those of commodities or secrets, for example. A secret that is known to everyone is a secret no longer, but knowledge, when revealed, does not lose its influence. Knowledge known to all still performs its function. If sold, knowledge enters other domains and yet remains within the domain of its producer. Knowledge does not have zero-sum qualities. On the contrary, knowledge represents a positive-sum game. Knowledge grows and apparently has no limits to its growth (cf. Weber, [1919] 1922b: 534–535).[2] Everyone is able to win. However, there is no guarantee that everyone will win to an equal extent; nor is there any assurance that the *practical* gains some actors may be able to realize will not result in the contraction of resources or utilities other actors command. Moreover, commanding a volume of knowledge similar to or better than that of an opponent or competitor, for example, is not the sole prerequisite for influence and competent conduct.

While it has been understood for some time that the "creation" of knowledge (for a history, see Carlsson et al., 2009) is fraught with uncertainties, the conviction that its application is without risks and that its acquisition reduces uncertainty has only recently been debunked (cf. Downer, 2011). Unlike money, property rights and symbolic attributes such as titles, knowledge cannot be transmitted more or less instantaneously. The acquisition of knowledge does not take place in a vacuum; it takes time and is typically based on intermediary cognitive capacities and skills (transaction costs). However, acquisition can be unintended and can occur almost unconsciously. Both the acquisition and the transmission of knowledge are typically not easily visualized. Once knowledge has been "mastered," it is difficult to arrest and return it. The development, mobility and reproduction of knowledge are difficult to regulate. To *protect knowledge* from others is much more difficult than to *restrict* others from gaining access to capital or weapons (see Elias, 1984). Therefore, it is "troublesome" to censor and control knowledge.

Knowledge is typically seen as a *public good* or communal commodity par excellence; for example, the ethos of science demands that it be made available to all in the scientific community as a collective good, at least in principle, but is the "same" knowledge available to all? Is scientific knowledge, when transformed into technology, still subject to the same normative conventions? The answer provided by one economist is that technology must be considered a "private capital good." In the case of technology, disclosure is uncommon, and rents for its use can be privately appropriated. However, the potentially unrestricted availability of knowledge to all makes it, in peculiar and unusual ways, resistant to private ownership.

At times, knowledge may be a positional good. The value of positional goods, as Fred Hirsch (1977) argues, is conditional on the failure of others to gain access to them. The value of knowledge is tied to its scarcity. As we will discuss as part of this section, the proposition that scarcity of knowledge determines its exchange value already signals that at least some forms of knowledge (not subject to scarcity and depletion) must have properties that place such knowledge (at least in terms of economic reasoning) close to the attributes typically shared by public goods.

Modern communication technologies ensure that access to knowledge and information becomes easier and may even subvert remaining proprietary restrictions. The so-called transaction costs have significantly declined in recent years. However, the ease with which knowledge and information become available engenders fears, such as the fear of bioterrorism. Concentration, rather than dissemination, of knowledge is also distinctly possible and is certainly a worrisome development to many observers (see Ginsberg, 1986: 127). It is equally possible to surmise, however, that the increased social importance of knowledge will in the end undermine its exclusiveness. Yet the opposite appears to be the case, which again raises the question of the persisting basis of the power of knowledge. Despite its reputation, knowledge is virtually never uncontested. Unlike the conviction displayed by the classical functionalist theory of social differentiation, science is in many instances incapable of offering cognitive certainty. This is to say that scientific discourse has been de-pragmatized: that it cannot offer definitive, or even true, statements (in the sense of proven causal chains) for practical purposes, but only more or less plausible and often contested assumptions, scenarios and probabilities (see Stehr, 1992). Instead of being the source of reliable trustworthy knowledge, science becomes a source of contestation and uncertainty. The uncertainty linked to scientific findings is not an expression of ignorance, or of a (temporary) deficit of knowledge. Uncertainty is a constitutive feature of knowledge, as it is of the contexts in which knowledge must operate.

Contrary to what rational scientific theories suggest, this problem cannot be comprehended or remedied by differentiating between "good" and "bad" science (or between pseudo-science and correct, i.e. proper, science). In the context of some philosophies of science, the contestability of scientific claims is seen as one of its foremost virtues. In practice, the contested character of knowledge is often repressed by, or conflicts with, the exigencies of social action.

2.2 Knowledge as a capacity to act

We would like to characterize knowledge as a generalized *capacity to act* and as a model *for* reality. Knowledge enables us to "set something in motion" or prevent something from occurring, such as the onset of an illness. Knowledge creates, sustains and changes existential conditions. Social statistics, for example, are not merely mirrors of societal reality; they problematize social reality by showing that it could be otherwise, suggesting and representing capacities for action (see Durkheim, [1955] 1983: 45–49; Canguilhem, 1978; Hunter, 1996: 154).[3]

In 1948, Claude Shannon published a small volume entitled *The Mathematical Theory of Communication*. In it he explains how words, sounds and images can be converted into blips and sent electronically. While Shannon's communication model has been surpassed by ever more complex models in communication theory, it might be argued that he foretold the digital revolution in communications. Knowledge as a symbolic "system" enables people to act on the world. Based on the same general definition of knowledge, a *software program* as a protocol for organizing "information" constitutes a form of knowledge. How to capture water power, how to smelt iron and craft tools, how to increase the output of heavy soils, how to structure a state and markets (cf. Goldstone, 2006: 276–279), all of this constitutes knowledge that made up the core of the emergence of modernizing societies.

Our definition of the term "knowledge" is indebted to Francis Bacon's famous observation that *knowledge is power*, a somewhat misleading translation of Bacon's Latin phrase: *scientia est potentia*. Bacon suggests that knowledge derives its utility from its capacity to set something in motion. More specifically, Bacon asserts at the outset of his *Novum Organum* (I, Aph. 3) that "human knowledge and human power meet in one; for where the cause is not known the effect cannot be produced. Nature to be commanded must be obeyed; and that which in contemplation is the cause is in operation the rule." The success of human action can be gauged from changes that have taken place in social and natural reality (Krohn, 1981, 1988: 87–89), and knowledge acquires *distinction*, last but not least because of its apparent ability to transform reality. Knowledge is discovery. The added value of knowledge should be seen as a capacity to illuminate and to transform reality. Knowledge as an effective or productive model *for* reality, of course, requires knowledge *of* reality. Our definition of knowledge as a capacity to act, as *enabling* knowledge, resonates with the conception of the term "know-how" by Daniel Sarewitz and Richard P. Nelson. Sarewitz and Nelson (2008: 101) define know-how as knowledge, "some articulated and some tacit, that guides the actions of skilled agents who aim to achieve a particular practical objective."[4] Hence *technical* or practical knowledge, perhaps most frequently associated with the metaphor "knowledge is power," refers, in concert with our conception of knowledge, to the ability to change, build, manufacture or fashion an "object" (cf. Popitz, 1986: 115). We should not neglect, as is often the case, the fact that knowledge represents the concomitant ability *to resist*, using, for example, technical means (e.g. Hobsbawm, 2007: 102, 103; Stehr, 2016: 243–335).

Our conception of knowledge as a capacity to act also resonates with Barry Barnes's (1988: 57) inventive notion of social power as a capacity for action in society. However, there are significant differences. Central to his idea of power as a capacity for action is the general model that a "society is a distribution of knowledge […] social power, must be an aspect or a characteristic of a distribution of knowledge." Despite Barnes's emphasis that power is an *aspect* of the distribution of knowledge and resides in rights to exercise discretion, the conflation of knowledge and power is evident. In linking knowledge as closely as he does to social power, perhaps making it indistinguishable from power as a resource of social action, Barnes reiterates the well-worn metaphor that knowledge is power. As we will indicate, our definition of knowledge as a capacity to act does not imply that knowledge is immediately performative. Problems we are confronted with, for example environmental problems, *are not directly* "scientific or technological, but social, political, and cultural" (Lowe, 1971: 569). For example, climate scientists and other impatient observers concerned with the impact of global warming on society fail to see that "decisions of public concern have to be made according to a time table established within the political sphere, not the scientific or technical sphere" (Collins and Evans, 2002: 241).

Put another way, the realization and implementation of discoveries may, for example, require an entrepreneur, as Joseph Schumpeter ([1912] 1934) argued; an entrepreneur who is able to raise the financial capital, perhaps form a company, find the necessary personnel and develop the new commodity, in short, "to get the job done" (cf. Phelps, 2013). More generally, actors independently need power to convert a capacity for into a practice of social action. The societal distribution of knowledge and that of power do not necessarily converge. There is power without knowledge and knowledge without power. Yet "knowledge and society are inseparable" [and] "cognitive order is social order" at all levels of society (Barnes, 1988: 170).

Science is not merely the solution to the mysteries and miseries of the world, as was once widely thought; it is, rather, the coming-into-being of a world. The idea that knowledge is a capacity for action that transforms, or even creates, reality is perhaps almost self-evident in the case of social science knowledge, but less persuasive in the case of the natural sciences. In the case of contemporary biology, however, one is prepared to acknowledge that biological knowledge extends to the fabrication of new living systems. Biology does not simply study nature. Biology transforms and produces novel natural realities. Biology and biotechnology are closely linked. As a result, (most of) the reality we confront in modern societies arises from and embodies knowledge, and does so to an ever-increasing degree. Thus, knowledge is not power (in the usual sense of the word) but, at best, represents *potential power*. It is necessary, as a result, to distinguish between the possession of knowledge as a capacity to act and the ability to exercise or implement knowledge.

The *ownership* of knowledge, and thus the power to dispose of knowledge, is as a rule not exclusive. This exclusivity, however, is required by jurisprudence as the definition of property or of the institution of ownership. Formal law, as is well known, recognizes owners and proprietors; in particular, it recognizes individuals who ought to possess, but do not. In the eyes of the legal system, property is indivisible. It is also of no importance what concrete material or immaterial "things" are at issue. Likewise, the sociological significance of knowledge lies primarily in the actual ability to dispose of knowledge as capacity for action.

Not everybody knows everything; therefore capacities to act are stratified, that is, not equally distributed throughout society; the social mechanisms of the distribution of knowledge therefore form a core subject matter of any sociological analysis of knowledge (cf. Schütz, 1964: 121). However, whether knowledge always flows to the powerful or whether the powerful tend to be the most likely stratum to exploit the social control attributes of knowledge should not be determined *a priori* but be subjected to theoretical and empirical analysis.

2.3 Knowledge and information

In the context of an examination of some of the important properties of knowledge, it is unavoidable to take up the contentious question of the relation/difference between knowledge and information. Before attempting to differentiate and explore the relations between knowledge and information, the initial puzzle that has to be addressed is whether it is possible and sensible, given the currently much more typical insistence on their close affinity, to distinguish between them, in the first place. It would appear to be extremely difficult, if not impossible, to sustain any difference between the two notions in light of the fact that both concepts are frequently employed as virtual equivalents (for example, Stewart, 1997; Faulkner, 1994: 426).

We would like to argue in favor of the need for and benefits of making this differentiation. It would be misleading to argue that there is *a single* distinction between information and knowledge. However, we would like to suggest that the dissolution of the unity of knowledge and information is of value. It is our contention that the substance of information primarily concerns the properties of *products or outcomes* while the stuff of knowledge refers to the qualities of *processes or inputs*. It is equally important to stress from the outset that knowledge and information have attributes in common. The most important common trait is that neither information nor knowledge is self-evident and free of context. However, before we attempt to explicate the distinction between information and knowledge as the distinction between attributes of product and attributes of process, a discussion of the various alternative ways of *linking* the two concepts is in order.

Many dictionaries and scholarly treatises simply define information as a certain kind of knowledge[5] or refer to the apparent ease with which knowledge is converted into information. A similar symmetry between information and knowledge is evident if one defines information as "knowledge reduced and converted into messages that can be easily communicated among decision agents" (Dasgupta and David, 1994: 493). In other definitions of information and knowledge, information is simply conceptualized as a subspecies, an element or the raw material of a number of knowledge forms.

For example, information is codified knowledge as well as indirect knowledge (see Borgmann, 1999b: 49), or knowledge is defined as the cumulative stock of information (Burton-Jones, 1999: 5), or "information is always only information in the light of certain knowledge" (Abel, 2008: 17); similarly, knowledge in general is seen to extend to "tacit knowledge" (cf. Polanyi, 1958, 1967: 204–206) and other categories of knowledge (Dosi, 1996: 84). Is there such a phenomenon as "tacit" information? The outcome of many efforts to define knowledge and information appears always to remain the same: knowledge and information become indistinguishable (see Wikström and Normann, 1994: 100–111).

Treating information "as a cause, measure and product of power," the historian Jeremy Black (2014: 3) in his all-encompassing examination of how information and technology made the modern world – that is, a world made by the West – suggests that "the relationship between [… the] global power of the West and the Western ability *to impose information systems* on the rest of the world seems clear" (Black, 2014: x, our emphasis). Information, he adds, "covers the spectrum from raw 'data' to systems of 'knowledge'." His sweeping and porous concept of information, designed to accommodate different historical notions of information and technologies, not only liberally conflates knowledge and information but also transforms information into the handmaiden of power. Information, for the author, covers "flows of information *and* the media of information exchanges, such as the printing presses, telegraphs and the Internet, as well as categories and uses of information. The latter are frequently discussed in terms of 'know-how', technical knowledge and scientific knowledge" (Black, 2014: 3, our emphasis). Last but not least, "information expands and changes with use" (ibid.: 3). Such a limitless concept of information results in tautological accounts; everything is information and information is immediately performative – for example, it directly establishes and ensures authority and power in societies.

It would therefore seem that the extent to which such widespread indiscriminate usage of the terms of information and knowledge has made them indistinguishable, raises, finally, the problem of the futility of any alternative effort that aims not to conflate but to distinguish their meanings and referents (cf. Malik, 2005).

Nonetheless, from time to time efforts have been made to differentiate between information and knowledge. Starbuck (1992: 716), for example, suggests that knowledge refers to a stock of expertise and not a flow of information. Thus, knowledge relates to information in the way that capital or assets relate to income. Kenneth Boulding (1955: 103–104) warns that we should not regard knowledge as a mere accumulation of information. Knowledge, in contrast to information, has a structure: sometimes it is a loose network, sometimes a quite complex set of systemic interrelations. Fritz Machlup (1983: 644) refers to the possibility that one may acquire new knowledge without receiving new information. Summing up the distinction between knowledge and information, Machlup (ibid.) prefers to claim that "information in the sense of telling and being told is always different from knowledge in the sense of knowing. The former is a process, the latter a state. Information in the sense of that which is being told *may* be the same as knowledge in the sense of that which is known, but *need* not be the same." The act of delivering (information) is one side of the coin, the "object" that is being delivered (knowledge) the other (see also Machlup, 1979a: 63–65).

Brown and Duguid ([2000] 2002: 119–120) stress that knowledge, in contrast to information, has at least three distinctive attributes. First, knowledge usually entails a knower; second, knowledge is harder to detach than information; and third, knowledge requires a greater effort of assimilation: "knowledge is something we digest rather than merely hold." However, only rarely does one find, in definitions designed to differentiate between information and knowledge, any reference to practical usefulness or correctness as the salient characteristics of knowledge and information.

If there is another side to the ledger, it is the *unease* with the practice of liberally conflating information and knowledge both in everyday life and in scholarly reflections and of reducing or extending them to an all-inclusive "mental material." It is true, of course, that in public places such as airports, shopping centers or train stations one rarely finds a counter or booth marked "Knowledge," rather than "Information." It is likely, however, that prevailing practices of conflating knowledge and information, for example in legal discourse (cf. Easterbrook, 1982), will prove more persuasive than efforts designed to distinguish between them. After all, who is able to distinguish clearly between the information and the knowledge society?

An equally formidable barrier to any new or renewed attempt to sociologically separate knowledge and information (and/or point to their commonalities) is the almost insurmountable mountain of competing conceptions of knowledge and/or information that are embedded in and indebted to multiple epistemological perspectives or pragmatic purposes. Knowledge and information may be distinguished on the basis of economic considerations or other social points of reference: the different ways in which they are produced, stored, diffused, consulted and applied, their typical carriers and the distinct social consequences they may be seen to have in society. We will refer to some relevant conceptions of knowledge *and* information, thereby recognizing the tremendous difficulties faced by efforts to sustain and codify differences between them.

One of the more traditional distinctions among knowledge forms is the opposition between *knowledge of acquaintance* and *knowledge-about* (in theory). Though these terms appear to be somewhat clumsy in English, they signify an asymmetrical dichotomy available in many languages as indicated, for example, by the terms *connaître* and *savoir*, *kennen* and *wissen* or *noscere* and *scire*. As William F. James (1890: 221) observes with respect to this opposition of forms of knowing, "I am acquainted with many people and things, which I know very little about, except their presence in the places where I have met them. I know the color blue when I see it, and the flavor of a pear when I taste it; I know an inch when I move my finger through it; a second in time, when I feel it pass; an effort of attention when I make it; a difference between two things when I notice it; but *about* the inner nature of these facts or what makes them what they are, I can say nothing at all."

The difference between knowledge of acquaintance and knowledge-about as described by William James in turn resonates with Gilbert Ryle's ([1949] 2000) distinction between *knowing-that* and *knowing-how* or, even earlier, with Aristotle's knowledge taxonomy that distinguishes between *épistème* (that is, "know-why") and *techné* (that is, "know-how").

Knowing-that encompasses knowledge that one is able to articulate, while knowing-how, in addition, includes what is best described as tacit knowledge, and therefore the volume of the latter is more extensive than that of the former (e.g. Ryle, [1949: 41]). The distinctions made by James and Ryle also suggest a possible difference between information and knowledge where information becomes less penetrating and consequential, a more superficial and fleeting cognizance of the attributes of a process or the instructions about an object.[6]

Knowledge of acquaintance or knowledge of attributes (World Bank, 1999: 1) – for example, the quality of a product, the diligence of a worker or the profitability of a company – refer to the presence or absence of information among market participants about relevant economic "data." In this sense, economic discourse has always made reference to the importance of information, but also to incomplete information and its function in pricing mechanisms or market transparency, for instance. The attributes and instructions information in this sense conveys indicate that information plays an instrumental role in social conduct.

However, the distinction between knowledge and information, even in its most elementary sense, is not only an asymmetrical dichotomy but also a difference that is supposed to have its dynamic, even progressive, elements. For what might be called acquaintance-with becomes knowledge-about as knowledge develops, matures or becomes more explicit and articulate. James (1890: 221) indicates as much when he observes that the two kinds of knowledge are, "as the human mind practically exerts them, relative terms." As a result, the distinction moves closer to the dichotomy of scientific knowledge in the sense of formal, analytic, rational and systematic knowledge, and "information," as later interpretations of James (for example by Park, 1940) show as well.

Given the general attention paid to Daniel Bell's (1979) theory of post-industrial society and the extent to which knowledge for Bell is constitutive of such a society, it is worth giving some thought to the definitions of information and knowledge articulated within the context of his theory of modern society. Bell refers to what is an anthropological constant, namely that knowledge has been necessary for the existence of any human society. In other words, knowledge is a basic provision for social relations and social order.

What, therefore, is new and distinctive about knowledge in the post-industrial society? It is "the change in the character of knowledge itself. What has now become decisive for the organization of decisions and the control of change is the centrality of *theoretical* knowledge – the primacy of the theory over empiricism, and the codification of knowledge into abstract systems of symbols that can be utilized to illuminate many different and varied circumstances. Every modern society now lives by innovation and growth and by seeking to anticipate the future and plan ahead" (Bell, 1968: 155–156).

However, the distinction between forms of knowledge that have run their course because they "informed" industrial society and theoretical knowledge constitutive of post-industrial society does not necessarily affect Bell's general differentiation between information and knowledge, to which we will now turn.

By information, Bell (1969: 168) suggests, "I mean data processing in the broadest sense; the storage, retrieval, and processing of data becomes the essential resource for all economic and social exchanges (in post-industrial society)." Bell's conception of information is indistinguishable from the technical conception of communication in which the meaning, exchange and transfer of a piece of information are independent of the carriers (source and receiver) of information. By knowledge, in contrast, he means "an organized set of statements of fact or ideas, presenting a reasoned judgment or an experimental result, which is transmitted to others through some communication medium in some systematic form" (Bell, 1979: 168).[7]

It would appear that the technical conception of communication applies to knowledge as well, although Bell makes implicit reference to the distinct epistemological status (or value) of knowledge and information, which results in a hierarchical and asymmetrical gradient between knowledge and information. As a result, information is easily dubbed "mere" information, while knowledge is methodically generated, sorted and judged.

Manuel Castells ([1996] 2000a: 17) in his widely appreciated observations about *The Rise of the Network Society*,[8] offers identical, *objectivist* conceptions of information and knowledge (cf. Bourdieu, [1972] 1977: 3). As a matter of fact, Castells defers to Daniel Bell and his conception of knowledge and joins Marc Porat (1977: 2) in his definition of information as "data that have been organized and communicated." Castells sees no reason to improve on these definitions.

An additional prominent theory of modern society, Ulrich Beck's (e.g. [1996: 110) theory of reflexive modernization, relies on the essential assertion that the modernity of a society is linked to the volume of knowledge it possesses, and the more knowledge "it has available about itself and the more it applies this, the more emphatically a traditionally defined constellation of action within structures is broken up and replaced by a knowledge-dependent, scientifically mediated global reconstruction and restructuring of social structures and institutions." Not only is the implicit definition of the authority of knowledge asymmetrically linked to scientific knowledge but the conception also strongly implies the immediate productivity of such forms of knowledge which in practice *forces* "decisions and opens up contexts for action."

Nonetheless, the dichotomies or linkages offered between the concepts of knowledge and information by Bell and Castells but also the theory of reflexive modernization by Beck, Giddens and Lash, have strong disembodied strains. That is, there is no reference to the contingent character of information and knowledge; science does not speak with one voice or to the need to interactively render knowledge and information intelligible and negotiate whether they are valuable or appropriate. At least implicitly, the concepts depict innovation and fabrication of incremental knowledge as a fairly smooth, well-behaved process. Objectivity is a social product that the objectivist conception of knowledge and information fails to take into consideration.

Given Bell's scientist and technological conception of the communication and acquisition of knowledge and information, the strong assumption is that both knowledge and information are generated unobstructed and then travel virtually unimpeded. In addition, the linkages, if any, that may exist between information and knowledge remain ambivalent. At best, it would seem that Bell's conception of knowledge and information contains the claim that information is the handmaiden of knowledge. Moreover, this notion tends to be overly confident about the authority, trustworthiness and power of information and knowledge. According to Bell, knowledge is primarily abstract, disembodied, formal, individual – and aspires to be universal (or knowledge in space). It seems to us that Bell's interpretation raises more questions than it answers.

Nonetheless, a discussion of the interrelation between knowledge and information provides an opportunity to summarily repeat some of the comments we have made about the role of knowledge in social affairs. Knowledge, as we have defined it, constitutes a capacity for action. Knowledge is a model for reality. Knowledge enables an actor, in conjunction with control over the contingent circumstances of action, to set something in motion and to (re-)structure reality. Knowledge allows an actor or actors to generate a product or some other outcome. Knowledge is ambivalent, open, and hardly blind to the specific meaning knowledge claims contain. However, knowledge is only a necessary, and not a sufficient, capacity for action. As indicated, in order to set something in motion or generate a product, the circumstances within which such action is contemplated to take place must be subject to the control of the actor. Knowledge that pertains to moving a heavy object from one place to another is insufficient to accomplish the movement. In order to accomplish the transfer, one needs control over some medium of transportation that can be used for moving heavy objects, for example. The value that resides in knowledge, however, is relational in the sense that it is linked to its capacity to set something in motion. Yet knowledge always requires some kind of attendant interpretive skill and a command of the situational circumstances. In other words, knowledge – its acquisition (see Carley, 1986), dissemination and realization – requires an active actor; a knower who "has a particular history, social location and point of view" (Oyama, 2000: 147). Knowledge involves appropriation and transaction rather than mere consumption or assimilation. It demands that something be done within a context that is relevant beyond being the situation within which the activity happens to take place. Knowledge is conduct. *Knowing*, in other words, is (cognitive and collective) *doing* and the active accomplishment of multiple actors.

In contrast, the function of information as we would see it is both more restricted and more general. Information is something actors have and get. It can be reduced to "taking something in." Information can be condensed into quantifiable forms. It is therefore possible and sensible to conclude that someone has more information than someone else. It is much more difficult and contentious to conclude that someone commands more knowledge than someone else.

In its compacted form, information can migrate more easily. Information does require sophisticated cognitive skills, but places fewer intellectual demands on potential users. Information is often immediately productive but not necessarily politically neutral (Burke, 2000: 116–148). This applies, for example, to a map, a timetable, legal records, charts, bibliographies, a census questionnaire, a directory, etc. In many instances, and contrary to knowledge as a capacity for action, there is no need to be the master over the conditions of its implementation. Information is more general. Information is not as scarce as knowledge. It is much more self-sufficient. Information travels and is transmitted with fewer context-sensitive restrictions. Information is detachable; it can be detached from meaning. It tends to be more discrete than knowledge. In addition, the access to and the benefits of information are not only (or not as immediately) restricted to the actor or actors who come into possession of information. Information is not as situated as knowledge.[9]

Information, in comparison to knowledge, can have a very high depreciation rate over time. The information that share X is a good buy rapidly loses its value. The information about the value of purchasing the share quickly decreases in value, and does so not only as a result of its wide communication and the possibility that many will follow the advice. In other words, the marginal utility of information can be quickly reached. If, however, one wants to ensure that information quickly depreciates, one should act and encourage others to act according to the information. For example, having been informed about a share price that may decline, acting on the information is likely to prompt the price to fall even further, depending, of course, on the extent to which such shares are sold.

The use of knowledge can also be quite restricted and limited in its use value, however, because knowledge alone does not allow an actor to set something in motion. Information may be a step in the acquisition of knowledge. The acquisition of knowledge is more problematic. In general, a simple and quite straightforward model of communication is appropriate for the purposes of tracing the "diffusion" or transfer of information. Whether it is even possible to speak of a transfer of knowledge is doubtful. Knowledge does not disseminate by itself; it has to be "transmitted and received, and there are barriers at both ends," as Joseph Stiglitz and Bruce Greenwald (2014: 74) note. The "transfer" of knowledge is part of a learning and discovery process that is not necessarily confined to individual learning. Knowledge is not a reliable "commodity." It tends to be fragile and demanding, and has built-in insecurities and uncertainties.

Good examples of information are price advertising and other market information, such as the availability of products (*signaling* function). Such information is easy to get, unproblematic to have, often robust, and can certainly be useful. In the context of the modern economy, it is very general and widely available, but the consequences of having this information as such are minimal. From a consumer's point of view, price information combined with knowledge about the workings of the marketplace may constitute a capacity to realize some savings, but information about prices does not enable that consumer to generate insights into the advantages or disadvantages of different economic regimes within which such prices are generated. A comparative analysis of distinct economic systems and the benefits it may have for different groups of actors requires special economic knowledge.

Not unlike language, information has attributes, especially on the supply side, which ensure that it constitutes, certainly to a greater extent than is the case for knowledge, a public good. It is not enabling, in the sense of allowing an actor to generate a product. Information merely reflects the attributes of products from which it is and can be abstracted. In the economic context – more specifically in the context of market relations – information concerns characteristics of the commodities or services being transacted (see also Stiglitz, 2000b: 1447). The information of interest to the consumer or producer is, of course, by no means limited to the price of a product or service. Interest on the demand side of the transaction extends to many characteristics of the commodity as well as to the (often hidden) behavior of the item paid for.

As we suggested at the outset of this chapter, knowledge refers to and specifies attributes of a *process* or input, whereas information refers to attributes of a *product* or output (state). It might now be clearer why we distinguish between knowledge and information in this manner. As Charles Lindblom (1995: 686) explains with respect to the attributes of commodities and services and the decisions consumers make about them, in many instances in the market place, "how and where the refrigerator was made, whether the work force was well treated, whether the process produced harmful wastes, and the like, you have no control over and little knowledge of." The consumer is typically informed about the price of the fridge, its energy efficiency, life expectancy, warranty, colors, the volume it may hold, its size and so on. None of the information provided will enable you to know anything about the process of building the refrigerator, let alone convey the ability to construct it yourself. In general, however, as Ikujiro Nonaka (1994: 16) underlines, "a genuine theory of information would be a theory about the content of our messages, not a theory about the form in which this content is embodied."

2.4 Practical knowledge

Knowledge, as a generalized capacity for action, acquires an "active" role in the course of social action *only* under circumstances where such action does not follow purely stereotypical patterns or is strictly regulated in some other fashion. Knowledge assumes significance under conditions where social action is, for whatever reasons, based on a certain degree of freedom in view of the courses of action that can be chosen. For this reason alone, there will always be, although of course not with respect to all fields of action and problems, a surplus of knowledge. We often know more than we can influence, control or manipulate (cf. Borgmann, 1999b).

The circumstances of action we have in mind may also be described as the capacity of actors to alter, transform or change a specific reality, a kind of "creative leeway" of social life, a "discretion to create" (*Gestaltungsspielraum*). The capacity to alter and affect reality is not symmetrical with respect to the capacity to act (knowledge). Knowledge may be present, but for a lack of the capacity to transform, knowledge cannot be employed. On the other hand, actors may have the necessary authority, power or material resources to change reality, yet lack the capacity to act.

In our conceptual approach, the social phenomena and processes of knowledge and power are treated as distinct entities. Barry Barnes (1988: 58) in his discussion of the *Nature of Power* assimilates knowledge and power much more closely; power is an aspect of the distribution of knowledge or, as he observes, "social power *is* the capacity for action in a society." Additional power is never equally distributed throughout society: "Social power is *possessed* by those with discretion in the direction of social action [...] to gain power is to gain such discretion." In this sense, our notion of the "*Gestaltungsspielraum*" of actors is close to Barnes's conception of discretion. However, we would maintain that knowledge and discretion are not quite the same. *Gestaltungsspielraum* refers to the ability of actors to get things done because they control relevant circumstances of action. In order to get things done, you need the power to command specific resources of action. Thus, the *deployment* of knowledge in particular social contexts cannot be detached from the *relations of power* in that context.

Karl Mannheim ([1929] 1936) defines, in much the same sense, the range of social conduct in general, and therefore the contexts in which knowledge plays a role, as restricted to spheres of social life that have not been completely routinized and regulated. For, as he observes, "conduct, in the sense in which I use it, does not begin until we reach the area where rationalization has not yet penetrated, and where we are forced to make decisions in situations which have as yet not been subjected to regulation" (Mannheim, [1929] 1936: 102).[10] Concretely to the point, as Mannheim notes, the:

> action of a petty official who disposes of a file of documents in the prescribed manner or of a judge who finds that a case falls under the provisions of a certain paragraph in the law and disposes of it accordingly, or finally of a factory worker who produces a screw by following the prescribed technique, would not fall under our definition of "conduct." Nor for that matter would the action of a technician who, in achieving a given end, combined certain general laws of nature. All these modes of behavior would be considered as merely "reproductive" because they are executed in a rational framework, according to a definite prescription entailing no personal decision whatsoever.
>
> *(Mannheim, [1929] 1936: 102)*

For Mannheim, the question of the relation of theory to practice is, then, restricted precisely to situations that offer a measure of discretion in social conduct, and which have not been reduced to a corset of strictly ordered and predictable patterns of social action. It cannot be ruled out, however, that even under circumstances where situations are repeated with routine regularity, elements of "irrationality" (that is, openness) remain. The ability to deploy *new* knowledge (in the sense of additional knowledge or, in more conventional terms, invention and innovation) is just as crucial as is the process of finding knowledge for the evolution of society.

2.5 Additional knowledge

Additional knowledge enlarges our capacity to act; thus, it is unavoidable that knowledge has *political as well as economic* attributes. Knowledge as a capacity to act contributes to what is constitutive for politics: to change or to preserve and perpetuate. In general, therefore, knowledge is a medium of social control because once *deployed* it may structure and restructure social formations. In the context of the knowledge-based economy in modern societies (cf. Stehr, 2002), knowledge becomes a steering mechanism, a force of production, displacing the forces of production typical of industrial society, namely property and capital, and therefore a source of additional value, economic growth and productivity including, of course, the possibility of a transition to a sustainable economic system.

The science system in modern societies is by definition a core part of the innovative set of societal institutions. The prestige, the exceptional social, economic and intellectual importance of scientific knowledge, is firmly associated with the capacity of the social system of science within which it is embedded to fabricate *additional knowledge* claims. In modern societies, scientific and technical knowledge is of unique importance because it produces *incremental* capacities for social and economic action, or an *increase* in the ability of "how-to-do-it" that may, at least temporarily, be "privately appropriated." In social institutions other than science, routinized, habitual conduct and the interpretation and defense of established intellectual perspectives are constitutive. In science, invention and therefore the production of knowledge beyond what already exists is the prime function of the social system of science.

In the case of the economic importance of knowledge in general, and additional knowledge in particular, contrary to neoclassical assumptions, the unit price for knowledge-intensive commodities and services decreases with increased production, reflecting a "progress down the learning curve" (cf. Schwartz, 1992; see also the economic implications of learning by doing; Arrow, 1962b). Incremental knowledge is just as heterogeneous as is socially widely accessible knowledge. Thus it is entirely conceivable that among incremental knowledge there may, at any given time, be "key findings" that prove especially valuable in many respects, as for example in economic, military or political contexts. Which knowledge will become key knowledge can only be determined empirically (see Stehr, 2000).

Knowledge constitutes *a* basis for power. Knowledge excludes. As John Kenneth Galbraith ([1967] 1971: 67) stresses with justification, power "goes to the factor which is hardest to obtain or hardest to replace [...] it adheres to the one that has greatest inelasticity of supply at the margin." However, knowledge as such is not a scarce commodity, though one feature of some knowledge claims may well transform knowledge from a plentiful into a scarce resource: What is scarce and difficult to obtain is not access to knowledge *per se*, but access to *incremental knowledge*, to a "marginal unit" of knowledge. The greater the *tempo* with which incremental knowledge ages or decays, the greater the potential influence of the social system within which additional knowledge is produced and the greater the social importance and prestige of those who manufacture or augment knowledge; and correspondingly, of those who transmit (moderate) such increments to other social systems.

If sold, knowledge enters the domain of others; yet it remains within the domain of the producer, and can be spun off once again. This signals that the transfer and the absorption of knowledge do not necessarily include the transfer of the cognitive ability to generate such knowledge; for example, the theoretical apparatus, the technological regime or the required infrastructure that yields such knowledge claims in the first place, and on the basis of which they are calibrated and validated. Cognitive *skills* of this kind, therefore, are scarce. It is often taken for granted by economists that the fabrication of knowledge is expensive, whereas the dissemination is virtually without costs. This view is further supported by the common conviction that technological knowledge is nothing but a blueprint that is readily usable at nominal cost to all.

However, the acquisition of the kinds of cognitive skills needed to comprehend knowledge and technology can be quite expensive. For example, in many cases only the rough outlines of technical knowledge are objectified or codified by non-personal means of communication (cf. Berrill, 1964). As a result, some economists suggest that the dissemination and absorption of knowledge, at least of some forms of knowledge, are more costly than its production (see Stigler, 1980: 660–641). Such a conclusion, as well as evidence supporting the observation (Teece, 1977), raises the question of whether the fabrication and the dissemination, in the sense of reproduction, of knowledge can really be easily separated at all.

The progressive elimination of time and space as relevant elements in the production of knowledge has paradoxically injected the importance of time and location into the interpretation and use of (objectified) knowledge. Since mere understanding and the validation process of knowledge cannot refer back, except in rare circumstances, to the original author(s) of the claim, the separation between social roles makes the interpretive tasks carried out by "experts" more crucial. Knowledge must be made available, interpreted, and linked to local, contingent circumstances. The complexity of the linkages and the volume of resources required to enact capacities for action delineate the limits of the power of scientific and technical knowledge. Such limits are an inevitable part of the fabrication of scientific knowledge (cf. Downer, 2011 for a case study), and explain why the knowledge work performed by the stratum of experts in knowledge-based occupations, generally speaking, attains greater and greater centrality in an advanced society. The social prestige, authority and influence of experts are heightened, moreover, if their claim to expertise is uniquely coupled with access to additional knowledge (see Grundmann and Stehr, 2012).

The centrality of knowledge-based occupations or, to use a narrower term, experts in knowledge societies does not mean that we are on the way, as social theorists have feared in the past, to a technocratic society or a technical state. A technocratic model of society and its major social institutions, which "sees technicians dominating officials and management, and which sees the modern technologically developed bureaucracies as governed by an exclusive reliance on a standard of efficiency" (Gouldner, 1976: 257), be it a nightmare or a utopia, is a counterintuitive scenario. It is doubtful whether the crucial choices that modern societies will be forced to make are more about the technical means and less about the competing ends of social action.

Quite a number of arguments can be deployed to demystify the threat of technocracy and a new ruling class made up of faceless experts. The most persuasive argument is social reality itself, which has failed to support the transformation of society in this direction. The long-predicted emergence of technocratic regimes has not materialized. The diagnosis of an imminent and menacing technocratic society was greatly overdrawn.

Michel Crozier offers a less obvious argument about the limits of the power of experts, counselors and advisors in his study of the bureaucratic phenomenon. Crozier ([1963] 1964: 165) argues that the power of an expert is self-curtailing and self-defeating:

> The rationalization process gives him power, but the end results of rationalization curtail his power. As soon as a field is well covered,

as soon as the first intuitions and innovations can be translated into rules and programs, the expert's power disappears. As a matter of fact, experts have power only on the front line of progress – which means that they have a constantly shifting and fragile power.

The objectification and routinization of incremental knowledge curtails the power of knowledge. Yet knowledge assimilated to power is most likely incremental knowledge. Crozier's vision of the "natural" limits of the power of experts, however, is still animated, if only implicitly, by the idea that experts – temporarily and exclusively – command uncontested knowledge, that their clients fully trust expert knowledge, and that experts therefore do not get enmeshed in controversies.

However, the growing importance of knowledge-based occupations in modern society does not mean that the trust of the public in experts, advisors and consultants (cf. Miller, 1983: 90–93) is growing at the same pace or is not contingent on relationships (Wynne, 1992). On the contrary, we believe less and less in experts, although we employ them more and more. Yet without some element of trust exhibited by ordinary members towards experts, expertise would vanish.

Nonetheless, experts today are constantly involved in a remarkable number of controversies. The growing policy field of setting limits to the presence of certain ingredients in foodstuffs, of safety regulations, risk management, and the control of hazards, has had the side effect of ruining the reputation of experts. As long as an issue remains a contested matter, especially a publicly contested matter, the power and influence of experts and counter-experts is limited (see Mazur, 1973; Nelkin, 1975); once a decision has been made and a question settled, the authority of experts becomes almost uncontested as well. The work required to transform a contested matter into an uncontested issue is linked to the ability of experts to mobilize social and cultural resources in *relevant* contexts (see Limoges, 1993).

How knowledge and its role are defined in a particular context is determined by individual actors as well as by the legal, economic, political, or religious constructs that have gained authority. Moreover, the nature of the interaction, whether private or public (see van den Daele, 1996), the issue or practices at hand, and the audiences concerned are crucial in deciding what knowledge is mobilized and how it is enacted. Increasingly it is the job of experts, counselors and advisors to define the role of knowledge. The group of occupations designated here as experts, counselors and advisors is required to mediate between the complex distribution of the changing knowledge and the seekers of knowledge. Ideas tend to travel as the baggage of people, as it were, whereas skills, in the sense of know-how and rules of thumb, are embodied or inscribed in them. Studies of innovation processes have shown how important the close coupling of social networks is for the transfer of knowledge, as well as for the ultimate success of innovations in economic contexts. These studies indicate that the traffic of *people* within and among firms, for example, is crucial to the transfer process of knowledge (e.g. Miller, 2007). By the same token, nonmarket organizations such as regulatory agencies or intergovernmental organizations can facilitate the transfer of knowledge within societies or across borders (cf. Jandhyaia and Phene, 2015).

A chain of interpretations must come to an "end" in order for knowledge to become relevant in practice and effective as a capacity for action. This function of ending reflection, or healing the lack of immediate practicability of scientific and technical knowledge as it emerges from the scientific community for the purpose of action, often even before scientific consensus is achieved, is largely performed by various groups of experts in modern society. Their societal prominence today is intimately related to the central role of knowledge for contemporary society.

Aside from the question of the nature of practical and additional knowledge, it is important to reflect briefly about what can only be called the uneven development of knowledge, for example, in light of pressing social, political or health issues that remain unsolved due to our lack of knowledge while we could well have a surplus of knowledge in other fields such as bioengineering, weapons know-how, or psychological knowledge designed to manipulate and persuade based on hidden means.

2.6 The uneven development of knowledge

The apparently comprehensive provision of intersubjectively accessible knowledge in objectified form, especially in the current digital world of the Internet, supports the mirage that knowledge is more or less evenly produced, that it is democratically available and that all knowledge represents a benefit to society.

On the other hand, it has long been acknowledged that the development of knowledge is uneven and varies with respect to epistemological attributes used by scientists to judge the adequacy of knowledge and the subjects or objects about which knowledge is produced but also with respect to a variety of societal indicators, human ambitions, wants and needs. Moreover, the ability to translate knowledge successfully into action varies across scientific fields. The development of knowledge is uneven, especially when judged with respect to its efficacy to have solved troubling problems or contributed to pressing human objectives.

In some fields, such as modern physics, information and communication technology, or in specific fields of the treatment of diseases, knowledge appears to be extraordinarily powerful while the contribution of knowledge to objectives such as the prevention of violence and war have been limited (cf. Nelson, 2003). In short, it can hardly be disputed that knowledge in the eyes of many practitioners, advisors, experts and scientists, but also the public at large, develops at different tempi. Why is the development of knowledge uneven? The answers vary depending on the points of reference.

First, let us examine the unevenness of knowledge in tackling troubling problems and human wants. Richard Nelson (2000: 120) points to two factors that could account for the failure or the rapid advance of "know-how." For him, know-how rather than knowledge constitutes "enabling (or practical) knowledge." Enabling knowledge or know-how denotes the "wide range of techniques and understandings human societies have acquired over the years that enable them to meet their wants" (Nelson, 2003: 909). Know-how incorporates that which is commonly defined as *technology* or techniques. Techniques are embedded in specialized apparatuses, substances and other artifacts. In addition, effective know-how also involves a body of practices and skills embodied in the practitioners of the techniques. Importantly, knowledge also incorporates what Nelson terms a tacit or explicit (articulated) "body of understanding" – that is, "how it is done knowledge." For example, the surgeon has a broad understanding of the human body, the circumstances that make for the success or failure of surgery, and the various embedded and embodied surgical techniques, substances and instruments. An important part of the how-it-is-done knowledge involves information about how to gain access to and coordinate such knowledge in order to utilize it for an objective.

Nelson speculates that there are two cognitive processes that enhance the rapid advance of know-how in a particular field (including technological advance): one is "a strong body of understanding"; the other is the ability of experimentally oriented scientific fields to get "relatively sharp and quick feedback from efforts to advance the art regarding whether the departure is a success, or at least promising, or not, preferably on the basis of probes that are less expensive and time consuming than full scale trial" (Nelson, 2000: 120). Both processes are enhanced by a "strong science" that offers guidance as the path to be taken to advance know-how. Nelson also treats the two processes that accelerate the development of know-how as variables in their own right which stimulate the evolution of a strong science. This applied, for example, to the invention of the transistor which offered both puzzles and challenges for science.

Aside from considerations that would link the uneven advance of knowledge to the volume and quality of the intellectual and material "resources" mobilized to tackle an obstacle or serve an ambition or want, the uneven development Nelson examines focuses on technologies or knowledge that is enabling. Excluded from inspection are intellectual or cognitive advances in different fields of knowledge less readily quantified and priced. Yet, such advances could have powerful societal consequences. The discovery of global warming is a case in point.

Similarly, the uneven development of knowledge within the field of science may be tied to intrinsic attributes that differentiate co-existing forms of knowledge and where the hierarchy of forms of knowledge or their "force" depends on attributes that are overwhelmingly internal to science. Such attributes may refer to the logical coherence of claims, the conformity of propositions with facts, the truthfulness of statements, the reproducibility of assertions or the extent to which hypotheses may be falsifiable.

In addition, the unbalanced development of knowledge in science may be seen to be a reflection of that nature of the subject with which different scientific fields are confronted, such as the difference between social and natural processes including the greater likelihood that social scientists are in competition with other "meaning producers" outside science. The exact ways in which the relationship to the objects and the nature of the objects may be responsible for the uneven development of knowledge can differ. We will emphasize one of several possibilities.

Knowledge involves, as we have emphasized, the relationship of participation to what is known. If the relationship of participation to what is known involves "natural" conditions or "social" conditions, it makes a great deal of difference whether the relationship is one of empathy or one of domination (cf. Böhme, 1992: 60). Since the prevailing view of what makes science-generated knowledge properly scientific regularly refers to the desirability of maintaining the distance of participation in order to ensure that neither the object of knowledge is influenced by the subject of knowledge nor the subject of knowledge is influenced by the object of knowledge, it is perhaps more difficult to abstain from feelings of empathy when social phenomena are concerned. The uneven development of knowledge could in this sense, therefore, be the outcome of the differential relation of participation to the object of knowledge. Relations to social phenomena are less easily based on instrumental attitudes, attempts to dominate and exploit, and personal views of coldness. Closely linked to considerations about the unbalanced development of knowledge is the issue of the possible limits to the growth of knowledge, especially within the field of scientific knowledge.

2.7 The limits of the growth of knowledge

The assertion that the growth of knowledge is without discernible limits is by no means without dissenting voices, at least when it comes to the growth of basic (natural) scientific knowledge. In 1872, Emil du Bois-Reymond, in a lecture entitled "On the limits of our knowledge of nature" (du Bois-Reymond, 1974 [1872]), offered widely discussed ideas about the limits of science. It is with respect to the limits of the growth of basic scientific knowledge that a few contemporary scientists – to the dismay of many other scientists – have voiced the opinion that science will no longer grow significantly, or has only limited room for additional growth. The narrative that speaks of a lack of limits to the growth of scientific knowledge fails to see, as the proponents of the existence of a law of diminishing returns in science argue, that we have uncovered the major secrets of nature; that science has solved its main problems. Science *works*, they say; it mirrors reality well (Stent, 1969; Glass, 1971).

Moreover, "given how far science has already come, and given the physical, social, and cognitive limits constraining further research, science is unlikely to make any significant additions to the knowledge it has already generated. There will be no great revelations in the future comparable to those bestowed upon us by Darwin or Einstein and Crick" (Horgan, 1996: 16).[11]

In addition, there may also be limits to the growth of scientific knowledge brought about by socio-economic constraints, due to increasingly expensive future research endeavors (Rescher, 1978: 193–207). The contentious issue evidently involves, first and foremost, the question of the growth of *basic* knowledge. Even if one limits the discussion to the difference between basic and applied knowledge, proponents of the thesis that the growth of scientific knowledge is not immune to the law of diminishing returns concede that applied science will continue to grow for a long time.

2.8 A sociological concept of knowledge and its context

Let us summarize our argument thus far, and conclude the chapter with an argument for a sociological concept of knowledge. The definition of knowledge as a capacity for action has a number of advantages. It implies that knowledge for action always has multi-faceted implications and consequences. The term *capacity* for action signals that knowledge may be left unused, may be employed for irrational ends or cannot be mobilized to change reality. The thesis that knowledge is invariably pushed to its limit in the absence of friction, that it is realized and implemented almost without regard for its consequences (as argued, for instance, by C.P. Snow; cf. Sibley, 1973), represents a view that is not uncommon among observers of the nature of technological development, for example. However, the notion that science and technology inherently and inevitably force their own realization in practice fails to give proper recognition to the context of implementation by assuming such automaticity in the realization of technical and scientific knowledge. Any conception of the immediate practical efficacy of scientific and technological knowledge (for example, in the sense "there is nothing as practical as a good theory") overestimates the "built-in" or inherent practicality of knowledge claims fabricated in science. As we have tried to show, the implementation of knowledge as a capacity for action relies upon existing frameworks of social action.

It would be equally misleading to conclude that the conception of knowledge as a capacity for action — and not as something, using the most traditional contrasting image, that we know to be true — thereby supports a reversal of the metaphor "knowledge is power" into "power equals knowledge." Indeed, the implementation of knowledge requires more than knowing how to put something into motion. The realization of capacities of action and power, or better, control over some of the circumstances of action, are allies. The relation is not symmetric. Knowledge does not always lead to power. Power does not lead to knowledge and power does not always rely on knowledge. To put it differently, the deployment of abstract capacities to act depends for its *success* on the (possible) development (unless such conditions are already in place) and maintenance of "complex networks of forces" (cf. Latour, 1998).

If one refers to "society as a laboratory," as Wolfgang Krohn and Johannes Weyer (1989: 349) do, in order to capture the idea that research processes and the risks associated with them are moved outside the established boundaries of science into society — for example, in the case of nuclear technology, the planting of genetically modified seeds, or the use of chemicals with certain undesirable side effects — this also alerts us to the necessity that the replication of laboratory effects outside the laboratory requires as a basic pre-condition the ability to control the conditions under which the effect was produced or was observable in the first instance. It is only then that the initial observation of an effect can be duplicated. This also means that every "realization" of knowledge, not only of major experiments, requires the ability to control the circumstances of action. Put differently, the "application" of scientific knowledge in society demands an adjustment to the existing conditions of action, otherwise social conditions have to be transformed according to the standards set by science (Krohn and Weyer, 1989: 354). In much the same sense, Gernot Böhme (1992: 59) remarks, "not that science is valid under *all* conditions, but it is valid under definite conditions." One must, for example, introduce certain conditions in developing countries before the technology of the developed world can be introduced effectively.

In the sense of our definition of knowledge, *scientific and technical* knowledge clearly represent "capacities for action," but this does not mean that scientific knowledge should be seen as a resource that is incontestable, is not subject to interpretation, travels without serious impediments (for example, as in the sense that knowledge travels even more effortlessly than money and spreads instantly), can be reproduced at will and is accessible to all; nor that scientific and technical knowledge primarily convey unique and generally effective capacities for action. What counts in modern societies – especially in the sense of gaining advantages in societies that operate according to the logic of economic growth and are dependent on the growing wealth of significant segments of the population – is access to and command of the *marginal additions to knowledge* rather than the generally available stock of knowledge (cf. Kerr, 1963: vii).

In the following chapters, we will discuss those properties of knowledge that make it a unique and contentious element of modern social relations and the resulting questions pertaining to its creation, deployment and subsequent role as a social entity – and the kind of protection and regulation it requires.

Notes

1 Cf. Arnold Toynbee's (1946: 36–41) critique of the superficial nature of the thesis of the unity of civilization.
2 Max Weber ([1919] 1989: 12) in his famous lecture "Science as a vocation," delivered to students at the University of Munich in 1917, compares the commonalities and differences of the products of artistic and scientific work. Whereas in the case of a work of art nobody "will ever be able to say of a work which involves genuine 'fulfillment' in an artistic sense that it has been made 'obsolete'," scientific work "is harnessed to the course of *progress*." Weber solemnly adds that "every scientific 'fulfillment' means new 'questions': it asks to be 'surpassed' and made obsolete […] To be overtaken in science is, however […] not only the fate of everyone of us but also our common goal […] Such progress is in principle infinite."

Knowledge about knowledge 45

3 Peter Drucker (1993b: 52–53) argues that there has been a radical change in the global meaning of the term knowledge: "In both the West and Asia knowledge had always been seen as applying to *being*. Almost overnight, it came to be applied to *doing*. It became a resource and a utility." We are not able to follow Drucker's differentiation of historical periods. Knowledge has always had the function of doing. What has happened and has been transformative is that the volume of knowledge as a capacity to act has increased immeasurably in recent decades.

4 In their paper "Progress in know-how. Its origins and limits," Daniel Sarewitz and Richard Nelson (2008) attempt to explain why the evolution of know-how is uneven, and what factors make progress in some areas of human activity particularly difficult while in other human affairs the improvement of know-how has been much more rapid. According to Sarewitz and Nelson, the answer is linked to the differential capability, in the development of know-how, to generate standardized procedures at the level of management and policy making for the purposes of implementing technological know-how (see also Nelson, 2003).

5 A couple of references as examples of the widespread conflation and the idea of an essential unity of information and knowledge may suffice: "Information evolved as a category of knowledge […] by comparison with knowledge it has been usually more detached from the theoretical context in which it was produced […] Information is characteristically more restricted to the technical practical surface of knowledge […] Information is often but thin knowledge" (Ezrahi, 2004: 257; also Urry, 2003: 64–65; Narayanaswamy, 2013: 1067–1068).

6 However, Gilbert Ryle ([1949] 2000: 56) stresses that knowing-that does not necessarily entail or typically result in knowledge-how.

7 Bell (1973: 175), in addition, offers an "operational" definition of knowledge when he indicates that knowledge "is that which is objectively known, an intellectual property, attached to a name or group of names and certified by copyright or some other form of social recognition."

8 The term of network society also appears at about the same time in an article by Peter Drucker in *The Wall Street Journal* ("The Network Society," March 29, 1995) about the future of the typical organization of firms that likely will outsource all those activities supporting "rather than revenue-producing and all activities that do not offer career opportunities into senior management."

9 If we are not mistaken, the description of the resource that information typically conveys and that is explicated here resonates with Gregory Bateson's (1972: 482) definition of information as "news of a difference." Elsewhere, Bateson (1972: 381) indicates that information is that which "*excludes* certain alternatives." That is, according to classical information theory, as Bruner (1990: 4) also stresses, "a message is informative if it reduces certain alternatives." Pre-existing codes allow for the reduction of possible alternative choices. However, by defining information as pertaining to "any difference which makes a difference in some later event," Bateson

moves the idea of information, it seems to us, closer to the notion of knowledge as a capacity for action, especially if one adds the questions about what and for whom information makes a difference. Niklas Luhmann's (1997: 198) central conceptual platform (see Bechmann and Stehr, 2002) allows him to follow Bateson's definition of information as a difference that makes a difference, inasmuch as the "news" – which could be an increase in the population or a change in climatic conditions – alerts a system and thereby triggers new system conditions. However, as Luhmann ([1984] 1995a: 67) therefore also stresses, "a piece of information that is repeated is no longer information [...] The information is not lost, although it disappears as an event. It has changed the state of the system and has thereby left behind a structural effect; the system then reacts to and with these changed structures."

10 Similar conceptions may be found in Friedrich Hayek's 1945 essay on "The use of knowledge in society." Hayek's essay is in fact a treatise in praise of decentralization, the importance of knowledge of local circumstances for action (knowledge in place), and the price system as an agency that communicates information and constitutes the answer to the question of coordinating local knowledge. Hayek ([1945] 1948a: 82) goes on to emphasize that "as long as things continue as before, or at least as they were expected to, there arise no *new problems* requiring a decision, no need to form a new plan" (our emphasis).

11 Speaking (of course) from the vantage point of a systems-theoretical position, Niklas Luhmann ([1981] 1987: 57) argues that differentiated and largely autonomous social systems cannot in principle control their own growth; as a result, there are no scientific grounds why science should not continue to grow and produce more and more knowledge claims. Luhmann concedes, however, that the growth of systems may be limited; for example, due to a lack of resources supplied by other systems.

3

THE KNOWLEDGE OF THE POWERFUL[1]

If there is, in addition to the frequent conflation of knowledge and scientific knowledge, any common trait one encounters in observations about knowledge – both in much of common sense and in science – it is the almost inescapable bond that is seen to exist between knowledge and the powerful in society.

In the following section we will engage in a critical examination of the typical association between power and knowledge in much of social theory where affirmative observations about the knowledge of the *powerless* are indeed rare. Our discussion proceeds as follows: We will begin by discussing Robert Michels's classic study of the *oligarchic* tendencies in large, formal organizations, especially in antioligarchic organizations that publicly aspire to, and fight for, democratic goals.[2] We will then, at some length, discuss the apparently inescapable bond between knowledge and power in the work of Michel Foucault, at least if judged by many of the reflections of commentators of his work. Finally, we will take a closer look at the idea of the emergence of a *global class* whose power is based on knowledge, as developed by Ralf Dahrendorf.

By way of introduction, our attention first turns to a (festive) lecture by Wilhelm Liebknecht,[3] one of the founders of the German Social

Democratic Party, given before an audience of members of the *Arbeiterbildungsvereine* (Workers' Education Association) in early 1872 in Dresden and Leipzig. In his lecture, banned from publication in Germany for a dozen years until 1890, Liebknecht stresses the empowerment function of knowledge and the differences in the culture of the working class and the bourgeoisie in nineteenth-century imperial Germany. The major task Liebknecht sets himself in his lecture is to draw a most critical picture of the dominant political, economic, social and work conditions in class-based imperial Germany.

3.1 Knowledge is power and power is knowledge

In the introduction to his lecture, Liebknecht strongly affirms the idea that knowledge is power but also that the powerful strata of society throughout history have always attempted to monopolize knowledge and continue to keep it away from the powerless: A "caste, an estate, a class appropriated knowledge and used it as a means of power for the oppression and exploitation of other castes, estates and classes" (Liebknecht, 1891 [1872: 11]). Knowledge is for the powerful and ignorance for the powerless. Anyone teaching a slave to become literate, he relates, was threatened with the death penalty in the slave societies of the southern United States.

Liebknecht stresses that "there has never been a ruling caste, a ruling state, a ruling class that uses their knowledge and power to enlighten those not in control, to educate the powerless and not, in contrast, systematically exclude them from real education, from education that liberates" (Liebknecht, 1891 [1872]). From a political point of view it is not so much the ability to read and write that is decisive but the economic and political information and knowledge about society, rights and responsibilities and the constitution of the country as well as the moral stance of citizens. The non-political bourgeois education accomplishes but the opposite, namely docile workers and citizens.

Not surprisingly, the social democratic politician Liebknecht is a strong proponent of social and economic equality and the importance of the equitable distribution of knowledge in society as well as among the members of his party (but see Robert Michels's critical examination of the power structure of the German Social Democratic Party we will discuss next). Liebknecht recognizes the importance of education for the political culture of a country and sees the function of leaders of the workers' movement also to focus on the cultural and educational emancipation of the working class (cf. Ritter, 1978: 166). The Social Democratic Party, he stresses, is in a most eminent sense the party of education (*Bildung*).

Since Liebknecht is unable to discern such equality in access to and command of knowledge in Germany, his interest shifts toward an analysis of the foundations and consequences of the lack of an equitable distribution of knowledge in the society of his day. Moreover, his appeal to a more equitable distribution of knowledge is a plea for adult education.

From a contemporary historical point of view, Liebknecht argues, it is more than questionable that education and the education of the educated in light of the multitude of brutal wars in Central Europe could lay claim to the idea that education truly confers any civilizational virtues. As a matter of fact, Liebknecht suggests that such education carries within itself the seeds of corruption. Militarism and clericalism are champions of superstition and ignorance desiring to attain and retain their status of exclusive moral and political authority. As a matter of fact, state expenditures for education of his day dwarf spending of the state for the military. However, equality in educational opportunities ought to be a cultural desideratum. In a free nation, education is a resource of liberation; in an authoritarian state or class-based society, education is a means of servitude. Thus in the modern class-based society, education produces but a special form of "intelligence," a servient kind of intelligence suited to be molded and employed for the benefit of the rulers, for example, in the shape of recruits for the military machine. Well-educated youth, Liebknecht is convinced, cannot in contrast be turned into cannon fodder.

Liebknecht describes the typical curriculum of Prussian schools as characterized by a blind memorizing – the sibling of blind obedience – of irrelevant names and dates, the acquisition of nationalism through hatred and lies about other countries and an emphasis on the alleged virtues of one's own nation. Upon completion of an elementary school education, the students are barely literate. Next to the school and the military, the third significant educational establishment is the media.

Once again, Liebknecht is unimpressed by their educational function since the media are far from being free. The bottom line is the really existing tripartite education system: The schools, the military barracks and the press offer but system-reproducing knowledge and information. State and society operate hand in hand, "forming the mind as well as the body in a one-sided manner, unfolding subordinate skills in an unnatural way, suffocating or crippling the most important capacities. Thanks to the division of labor and machinery work, work is more and more void of cognitive demands" (Liebknecht, 1891 [1872: 38]).

In short, Karl Liebknecht is convinced that the workers in his audience and beyond are the victims of a most successful campaign of the state and its rulers to subordinate workers by withholding "genuine," emancipating educational skills, and hence are most effective in assuring that the reigning system of inequality is perpetuated. The powerful are knowledgeable in keeping knowledge from the powerless and do so at least partly by destroying those intellectual capabilities that would make the acquisition of knowledge capacities possible. If, however, the entire nation were educated, "we would quickly have reasonable social and political conditions" (Liebknecht, 1891 [1872: 52]), but for the time being that is just an impossibility to presuppose. Liebknecht emphatically concludes: "Without power no knowledge!"

3.2 The iron law of oligarchy

Robert Michels ([1911] 1949: 93), in his classic analysis of undemocratic or oligarchic tendencies in large, formal organizations that are devoted to combat and negate oligarchic tendencies,[4] is also concerned with the relationship between knowledge and power, or the lack thereof: Following Gaetano Mosca and other theorists of the early twentieth century, Michels refers to an almost "natural" state of incompetence, immaturity and passivity found in the mass of people in modern democracies. Since the rank and file are incapable "of looking after their own interests, it is necessary that they should have experts to attend to their affairs" (ibid.). Seldom are the people willing to shake off the authority of the expert leaders and dismiss them from control. Party politics, for example, becomes the business of the full-time, professional politician, a condition that holds true for present-day politics in many democratic countries equally well. Democratic control is reduced to a minimum or is a sham (Michels, [1908] 1987: 154).

Michels ([1915] 1970: 86–87) further argues that among the complex social tendencies that act as a barrier against the realization of democracy *organizations* play a crucial role. Insofar as organizations form a strong structure, they engender differentiations (bureaucratization). Aside from the size of a social organization, be it a democratic state, a political party or a labor union, it is the nature of the tasks an organization is expected to fulfill that generates extensive structures around the division of labor within the organization. Any division of labor automatically generates specialists, and specialists enjoy authority. Expertise dominates and, as Michels ([1911] 1949: 401) formulates succinctly: "Who says organization says oligarchy"; every organization *as such* enables oligarchy (Michels, [1908] 1987: 158).

Although the function of the "leaders" of the organization is formally subjected to control by those led, "this control is condemned, as the organization grows, to a pseudo-existence [...] The sphere of democratic control is restricted to ever smaller circles." The emerging differentiations are of a hierarchical nature and stem from "technical needs" as well as practical circumstances. Michels ([1915] 1970: 75) observes that even "the radical tendency in the social democratic party [...] does not object to this regression. Democracy is nothing but a form, they say. And form must not dominate content."

Leadership positions in growing organizations are filled on the basis of competence, which results in a considerable gradient, in terms of formal instruction, between the ordinary members of the organization and its leaders. In proletarian political parties, the "deserters from the bourgeoisie become the leaders of the proletariat, not in spite of, but because of, that superiority of formal instruction which they have acquired in the camp of the enemy and have brought with them thence" (Michels, [1915] 1970: 87).

These steep differences in competence and experience count not only within the party organization, but also in other political contexts such as, for example, in parliament. The outcome is that the elites become indispensable. Technical competence implies authority and oligarchies within oligarchies are formed. The negation of democratic principles is complete. On the basis of these observations, as indicated,

Michels ([1911] 1949: 55) reaches the conclusion that the Social Democratic Party is not practicing democracy but a party *fighting to attain* democracy. The meta-conclusion for Robert Michels ([1915] 1970: 96), and therefore for the relationship between knowledge and democracy as practiced by the organizations he observed, is that democracy ends up becoming a form of governance of the best, and that means an aristocracy.

Robert Michels's *Political Parties* emerged from a *case study* inquiry into the nature of the Social Democratic Party at the beginning of the last century. This would justify the question whether Michels, with the iron law of oligarchy, has indeed discovered a timeless, general "sociological law." One of the foremost answers to the limits of the generalizability of Michels's iron law of oligarchy comes from a study by Seymour Martin Lipset, Martin Trow and James S. Coleman ([1956] 1962). In their now equally classic study *Union Democracy*, they examine, inspired by Robert Michels, democratic processes in an American labor union in the postwar era, the International Typographical Union (ITU).

Lipset, Trow and Coleman conclude that the democratic control by ordinary members of the union leadership is possible in principle.[5] According to Lipset et al. the social context that is responsible for their specific observation and, therefore, for a possible revision of Michels's iron law is that the ITU typically has had two internally *competing parties*. However, Lipset and his colleagues consider their effort a *deviant case study* that does not topple Michels's *general* theory but rather clarifies and amplifies the iron law of oligarchy.

Even Robert Michels ([1908] 1987: 172) is not without a slight but severely restrained hope and praise for democratic governance when, at the conclusion of his observation about the immanent tendencies of social aggregates to generate oligarchies, he remarks, "it is in the nature of democracy, and therefore also the labor movement, to strengthen and inspire the individual ability to criticize and to control, although on the other hand it must be admitted that bureaucratization undermines this capacity to a large extent."

Lack of information, passivity, and lack of concern of rank and file members in the affairs of an organization is in the interests of the powerful and supports their capacity to perpetuate power advantages.

As Lipset and his colleagues ([1956] 1962: 402) therefore emphasize, "the less the members know or desire to know about policy, the more secure the leaders are. The single-party organization in a trade union consequently acts to dampen participation, while in the ITU, membership interest and activities are the lifeblood of the party."

In the context of interpretations of the extraordinary asymmetry and highly stratified nature of the social distribution of knowledge, the thesis of the emergence of modern society as a knowledge society may run the risk of acquiring a peculiar elitist taint, since the proportion of those who feel secure in their own ability to competently command knowledge resources, or who anticipate that they will benefit from the features of the emergent society, must be small and cannot possibly extend to the "masses" of citizens. Everywhere, it seems, the already powerful have understood the effective utility of knowledge advantages and the exclusive use of technical innovations.

However, the powerful, or interpretations that stress the "naturally" stratified consequences of serious deficits and astonishing surpluses in access to knowledge, have usually also overestimated both the security and the permanence of their knowledge advantage. Major societal institutions that assumed that their power base was secured had to discover that their authority and influence over time has in fact been fragile and seriously eroded.

Aside from the apprehension that there is a tendency to a concentration of knowledge and a lack of equitability in the distribution of its socioeconomic benefits, another concern about the acceleration of knowledge advances and its decisive impact on social relations becomes visible in the phrase that knowledge is somehow "frightening." At the turn of the millennium, the so-called Y2K bug became the reason for a widely shared unease that "society is growing dependent on a lattice of technology that is now so far-reaching, interconnected and complex that no one completely understands it, not even the priesthood that writes its digital code."[6] Michel Crozier ([1979] 1982: 126) alludes to similar *psychological* reasons why people may be scared and dismayed by knowledge advances: "Knowledge implies the risk of change. It confronts people without concern for their wants or what they believe are their needs. It throws the established intellectual and social world into turmoil." However, does it do so universally?

The claim that knowledge advances pose a risk to established patterns of social stability and may threaten traditional belief systems is obviously associated with the conviction and expectation that scientific-technical knowledge is highly subversive of the status quo and most effective in dislodging and ultimately displacing such traditions. This claim is a corollary of the thesis that knowledge naturally flows to the powerful, that it has *conserving* consequences when examined from the point of the view of the powerful, and a *destabilizing* impact on those without power. The ways in which knowledge becomes an intimidating and frightening force is attributed to its ability to negate traditional forms of knowledge and mainly to enlarge and strengthen the power of the already influential social groups. It follows that knowledge is not only seen as distributed in a highly stratified manner but also as presenting a zero-sum phenomenon that virtually displaces and eliminates the conventional knowledge mostly found and relied on in non-privileged segments of society. In the final analysis, knowledge and knowledge advances affirm the centralization of cognitive authority in the hands of a few.[7] We will turn our attention next to one of the most prominent modern-day proponents – at least in the eyes of many of his interpreters – of the symmetry of knowledge and power: Michel Foucault.

3.3 Knowledge/power

Niklas Luhmann once affirmatively observed: "The ownership of knowledge confers authority. This person can teach the others. The individual who claims authority, must therefore base it on knowledge. The knowledge function and political function cannot be separated, in the final analysis" (Luhmann, 1990: 149).[8] In this observation, he is not alone. Just as much as Liebknecht's and Michels's writings, Michel Foucault's (e.g. [1975: 32]) major work is designed to display the complicity of knowledge in disciplining, governing and repressing people. Knowledge and power, it would appear, are like Siamese twins: "Power produces knowledge; [...] power and knowledge directly imply one another; [...] there is no power relation without the correlative constitution of a field of knowledge, nor any knowledge that does not presuppose and constitute at the same time power relations." Furthermore, one should not expect, Foucault goes on to explain, that the conflation of power and knowledge can somehow be disentangled one day: "Knowledge and power are each an integral part of the other, and there is no point in dreaming of a time when knowledge will cease to be dependent on power [...] It is not possible for power to be exercised without knowledge, it is impossible for knowledge not to engender power" (Foucault, 1977b: 15).

The question Foucault's statement leaves open is, of course, who is exercising power? Is it in fact the case that knowledge and political authority are inseparable and always benefit only a particular social stratum, namely that of the powerful? In spite of his critical reflections and the critical stance Michel Foucault assumes toward the powerful segments of society, he takes for granted, in his archeology and genealogy of social problems and topics – such as madness, clinical medicine, the penal system and sexuality, which blend the problems of power and knowledge – that each of the disciplinary sciences associated with these organized activities is "successfully" implicated in modern society's attempt to control and shape its citizens ("*gouvernementalité*").[9] Although Foucault enlarges more traditional conceptions of power to encompass all social relations, more often than not the addressees of his critical interventions seem to be the large social institutions representing the loci of power.

What on the surface had been primarily a political and legal matter becomes invested with newly fabricated dimensions of scientific knowledge. Practical or political knowledge, like power, is a context-specific phenomenon. One needs to examine the socio-political practices in which knowledge is embedded. Consequently, Foucault ([1969] 1972: 194; see also Foucault, [1975] 1977a: 305) formulates his "knowledge-guiding interests" as follows:

> Instead of analyzing this knowledge – which is always possible – in the direction of the episteme that it can give rise to, one would analyze it in the direction of behavior, struggles, conflicts, decisions, and tactics. One would thus reveal a body of political knowledge that is not some kind of secondary theorizing about practice, nor the application of theory [...] It is inscribed from the outset, in the field of different practices in which it finds its specificity, its functions, and its networks of dependencies.

Practical knowledge embedded in various discursive activities within different institutional settings is successively described by Foucault as a "political anatomy, a political economy, a discursive formation, a discursive disposition, and a political technology. Repressions and prohibitions, exclusions and rejections, techniques and methods bring individuals under surveillance" (Lemert and Gillan, 1982: 60).

However, the power joined to knowledge and exercised by the modern state as "the political form of centralised and centralising power" (Foucault, 1981: 227) in labeling, masking, censoring, segregating, prohibiting, normalizing, surveying and oppressing (for example, Foucault, [1975] 1977a: 304) its subjects by the powerful state is not total, but not quite enabling either. The conditions for the possibility of recalcitrance shown by the subject are not completely displaced; as a result, there are limits to the power exercised by state agencies (cf. Foucault, 1980: 119). Although overly efficient, the knowledge/power axis, according to Foucault, is more complex and leaves room for enabling results among those that are oppressed. However, resistance as a *reaction* to the seemingly well-functioning social controls remains a blind spot in Michel Foucault's approach.

The primary impression of Foucault's theorizing is that of the enormous authority of knowledge embedded in the discursive practices of the state. Such a conception of the omnipotence of the state resonates strongly with much of the historical literature on empire that portrays the "overwhelming power of the early modern state in its relationship with subject people, be they members of lower social classes, bureaucrats, and administrators, or indigenous populations" (Edwards et al., 2011: 1399). This impression cannot be set aside. Emphasizing, as Foucault does, the efficacy of knowledge attached to power and the extent to which it works by forcing its imprints on subjects and society, it is difficult, if not impossible, to allow or account for the possibility of societal discontinuities. How does social change come about? Power is enabling, if only because it has unanticipated consequences, but its agency for those who are subject to power appears to pale against the background of its productivity in stabilizing social figurations.

In the face of this conception of the overwhelming power of normalization, Alain Touraine ([1992] 1995: 168) asks with good reason:

"Why reduce social life to the mechanism of normalization? Why not accept that cultural orientations and social power are always intertwined, and that knowledge, economic activity and ethical conceptions therefore all bear the mark of power, but also the mark of opposition to power?" (see also Megill, 1985: 140–252).

Let us take a brief look at the genealogy of Foucault's thinking about the relationship between knowledge and power, domination and agency. In 1966, Michel Foucault published a book that was to become a philosophical bestseller in France, *Les mots et les choses* (translated as *The Order of Things* in 1970). In this book he examined biology, economics and medicine, noting a fundamental transformation of each of them toward the end of the eighteenth century: "A monetary reform, a banking custom, a commercial practice can be rationalized, developed, maintained or dissolved each according to its appropriate form; they are always founded upon a certain knowledge: a dark knowledge that does not appear in itself in a discourse, but the necessities of which are precisely the same for abstract theories and speculations without any seeming connection to reality" (quoted in Paras, 2006: 23).

This "dark knowledge" that informed all discourses he was to call *épistème*, something that was unique to a historical period. During the eighteenth century the dominating *épistème* was a tabular representation of reality. Anything that existed could be represented in tables.[10] However, there is no trace of the subject who assembles these tables, a practice Immanuel Kant was to ridicule as "tabular reason" (*tabellarischer Verstand*). Foucault's conclusion was that there was no place for "man" in such an *épistème*. Only with the advent of the modern discourse did "man" move to the center of the discourse. The implication was, at least for Foucault, that with the end of the modern discourse man will again disappear, "like a face in the sand at the edge of the sea," as he famously put it in the last sentence of *The Order of Things*.

In his next book, *The Archaeology of Knowledge* ([1969] 1972), Foucault develops a programmatic statement about the analysis of what he calls *discursive formations*: "Whenever one can describe, between a number of statements, such a system of dispersion, whenever, between objects, types of statement, concepts, or thematic choices, one can define a regularity […] we will say […] that we are dealing with a discursive formation […]" (Foucault, [1969] 1972: 41). Here he outlines his understanding of how knowledge and power, and discourses and objects, in society relate to each other.

Drawing on the example of madness he asks what it is that makes a discourse unified. He rejects the idea that there are objects out there that could be described more or less accurately through scientific language, as there cannot be "madness itself, [with] its secret content, its silent, self-enclosed truth." Rather, "mental illness was constituted by all that was said in all the statements that named it" (Foucault, [1969] 1972: 35). One cannot, therefore, speak of a discourse "concerning madness."

The same logic applies to specific instances of madness such as neurosis or melancholia, so that it does not make sense either to speak of a "discourse concerning neurosis," or a "discourse on melancholia." These objects *come into being* only through the discursive activities around the objects – the objects are in turn constituted by the discourse. Again, as in the above statement about human subjects, it is discourse that gives rise to something called objects.

Consequently Foucault rejects the idea that there could be a "prediscursive subjectivity," or experienced subjectivity that is "murmuring beneath the surface" and then taken up by scientific observation and research. Very much in agreement with the structuralists who were dominant in France at the time, Foucault asserts, "before all human existence, all human thought, [...] there must already be a knowledge, a system, that we are rediscovering" (quoted in Paras, 2006: 29). For him, the history of knowledge was "the unfolding of an anonymous process; a process of the formation and transformation of bodies of *statements* according to isolable rules" (Paras, 2006: 34–5).[11]

Foucault points out that this choice of terminology is for heuristic reasons, convenience, and to demarcate against the connotations of other established terms, such as science, ideology, theory or domain of objectivity (cf. Foucault, [1969] 1972: 41). One of the crucial tasks is to map the surface of the emergence of an object of discourse. It should be noted that it is not an object that is stable and therefore gives rise to a stable or unified discourse. It is the discursive *practice* that constitutes the object. Such a mapping will "show where these individual differences [...] will be accorded the status of disease, alienation, anomaly, dementia, neurosis or psychosis" (Foucault, [1969] 1972: 45). He continues: "These surfaces of emergence are not the same for different societies, at different periods, and in different forms of discourse."[12] There are two more elements that are necessary for a discursive formation: specialized institutions (Foucault designates them "authorities of delimitation"), and what he calls grids of specification (for example, the body, soul or life history).

In the early 1970s Foucault took on board several political and theoretical concerns of some of his neo-Marxist friends and colleagues. The resulting orientation was described as a move from *archeology* to *genealogy*. Here he fully engages with the problem of power on a theoretical level. In a discussion with his inspirator and interlocutor Gilles Deleuze, he told him: "We still don't know what power is [...] And Marx and Freud are perhaps insufficient to help us to know this deeply enigmatic thing, at once visible and invisible, present and hidden, invested everywhere that is called power. The theory of the State and the traditional analysis of the State apparatus do not, undoubtedly, exhaust the field of exercise of power's functioning" (quoted in Paras, 2006: 64).[13]

Discourses are linked to power and depend on knowledge. Foucault tried to escape a traditional conceptualization which interpreted power either in terms of violence or in terms of persuasion and ideology: "Now, power is not caught in this dilemma: either to be exercised by imposing itself by violence, or to hide itself, and to get itself accepted by holding the chatty discourse of ideology. In fact, every point of exercise of power is at the same time a site of transformation: not of ideology, but of knowledge. And on the other hand, every established knowledge permits and assures the exercise of power" (quoted in Paras, 2006: 113).

What we see here is a concept of both power and knowledge that acknowledges their *generative potential* (for good or bad). Foucault says that it does not make sense to see power as separate from or opposed to knowledge. Knowledge enables power to be exercised and power transforms knowledge. There is no basis for a distinction between knowledge and ideology; there is no *true* knowledge behind the veil of ideology.

One of Foucault's central theses was that modern industrial society emerged alongside the social and human sciences. These provided the knowledge base for disciplining the workforce into a system that depended on their collaboration. The prison and the hospital, surveillance and madness were the crucial places and issues to analyze. The books, entitled *Birth of the Clinic* (*Naissance de la clinique*, 1963) and *Discipline and Punish* (*Surveiller et punir: Naissance de la prison*, 1975), are programmatic. The term discipline is understood in a double sense: on the one hand, it is the practice of *disciplining* workers and citizens; on the other hand, it is the *discipline-based knowledge* that enables power holders to discipline workers, which means that it does not make sense to separate knowledge and power. Both are fused; one cannot be exercised without the other. There is no truth that speaks to power, only knowledge that has been created by the powerful to serve their purposes. Admittedly, this is a slight overstatement not necessarily borne out by Foucault's texts, although he did make statements to this effect in comments and interviews. Foucault preferred to speak of the simultaneous emergence of concepts and practices, or discourses. Nevertheless, the constellation he describes by the knowledge/power nexus has strong functionalist overtones, something he would later abandon.

Eventually Foucault was to replace the concept of power/knowledge with the concept of government, a move that, according to some observers, was connected to a more general reorientation towards recognizing subjectivity and agency (Paras, 2006). Using the power/knowledge terminology during the early 1970s, Foucault was led to an "extremist denunciation of power [...] hence the question of government – a term Foucault gradually substituted for what he began to see as the more ambiguous word, 'power'" (Pasquino, 1993: 79, quoted in Dean, 2001: 325).

Thus he came to see power as a *creative force* that enables subjects to act upon each other in flexible relationships. He reserves the term *domination* for the repressive, unidirectional and rigid form of power. Domination leads to a limitation of possible action since the margin of liberty is extremely narrow. What Michel Foucault now calls domination is akin to what Max Weber and others had called power.

In an interview with Paul Rabinow we find a description by Foucault of his own work. He says that to a certain extent he tries to analyze the relations among science, politics and ethics or, more precisely, "how these processes may have interfered with one another in the formation of a scientific domain, a political structure, a moral practice" (Foucault, [1984] 1987: 386). Once again he refers to the example of psychiatry:

> I have tried to see how the formation of psychiatry as a science, the limitation of its field, and the definition of its object implicated a political structure and a moral practice: in the twofold sense that they were presupposed by the progressive organization of psychiatry as a science and that they were also changed by this development. Psychiatry as we know it could not have existed without a whole interplay of political structures and without a set of ethical attitudes.
>
> *(Foucault, [1984] 1987: 386–387)*

He then goes on to explain that he followed the same methodological principle in his studies on madness, delinquency and sexuality, i.e. "the establishment of a certain objectivity, the development of a politics and a government of the self, and the elaboration of an ethics and a practice in regard to oneself" (Foucault, [1984] 1987: 387). He calls these three dimensions "fundamental elements of any experience" – namely 1 a game of truth, 2 relations of power, and 3 forms of relation to oneself and to others. Foucault makes the point that prevailing accounts were emphasizing only one dimension while the other two were screened out. With psychiatry the organization of knowledge took center stage, crime was seen as a problem for political intervention, and sexuality was designed above all as an ethical problem. "Each time I have tried," Foucault says, "to show how the two other elements were present, what roles they played, and how each one was affected by the transformations in the other two" (Foucault, 1994: 387–388).[14]

A further transformation in Foucault's interpretation of the relation between knowledge and power occurs in his later work, specifically in his 1977 lectures at the Collège de France, and under the influence of the work of the *nouveaux philosophes* and his observations about the revolution in Iran. Michel Foucault's reflections now center on the subject and the changing forms of subjectivity in modern societies (see Foucault, 1982: 211–212). The self-determining subject that has gained in significance also for him as a person now influences his professional point of view and thus allows him to let go of the strict symbiosis of power and knowledge (see Paras, 2006: 105–116).

However, contrary to what many commentators continue to say about Foucault's reflections on knowledge and power – that is, treating them as an essential *identity* in Foucault's work (e.g. Kusch, 1991) – it is exactly the nature of the *linkage* between knowledge and power that remained his decisive research problem up until a year before his death, as his response in an interview reveals:

> You have to understand that when I read – and I know it has been attributed to me – the thesis "Knowledge is power," or "Power is knowledge," I begin to laugh, since studying their *relation* is precisely my problem. If they were identical, I would not have to study them and I would be spared a lot of fatigue as a result. The very fact that I pose the question of their relation proves clearly that I do not *identify* them.
>
> *(Foucault, in Kritzman, 1988: 43)*

So how can we summarize Foucault's theorization of knowledge and power, their relationship, and the development of his thinking about these terms? For Foucault, power is a productive force, a force that shapes subjects and subjectivity. It is virtually everywhere, and "reaches into the very grain of individuals, touches their bodies and inserts itself into their actions and attitudes, their discourses, learning processes and everyday lives" (Foucault, 1980: 30).

The productivity of power rests on knowledge, and Foucault, too, stresses the capacities that are conveyed through knowledge. Knowledge is thus depicted as a deeply social – and only social – entity, as something that shapes and emerges from discourse, not as that which corresponds to an objective truth. Truth is nothing but a tool for the interest-driven execution of power. It is easy to see how such a conception would lead many observers to conclude that there is in fact an intimate conceptual bond between knowledge and power, as they are functions of the social, of the will to power, and always already political. To govern means to "structure the potential field of the actions of others" (Foucault, 2007: 97).

Still, the close connection of knowledge, power and government is by no means a clear-cut process or confined to governmental agencies or the large institutions. In any society, there are "multiple forms and loci of governing" (Foucault, 2007: 101, our translation), ultimately suggesting that power and domination reside "outside the institutions" (ibid.: 99).

What emerges in his later writings is that Foucault eventually acknowledges the different ways in which knowledge-as-power may be used, hinting towards the agency inherent in employing what one knows for purposes beyond "normalization":

> I don't see where evil is in the practice of someone who, in a given game of truth, knowing more than another, tells him what he must do, teaches him, transmits knowledge to him, communicates skills to him. The problem is rather to know how you are to avoid in these practices – where power cannot not play and where it is not evil in itself – the effects of domination.
>
> *(Foucault, 1984: 129)*

Relations of power may thus still be emancipatory occurrences. The phrase "knowledge is power" is, then, as much Foucaultian as it is Baconian, but holds a quite distinctive meaning; rather than supposing that those who wield power do so by their privileged knowledge of the truth, this relation is inverted, rendering knowledge a deeply social category: those who have the capacity to claim what is true (knowledge), have a claim to power. (In this light, Foucault may be read not only as an historian and philosopher, but fundamentally as a proponent of the sociology of knowledge.) Knowledge and power mutually create each other, are intimately tied up, but can, for exactly this reason, never be the same.

Judging by the gradual, if decisive, change in the development of his theory, the statement that in modern societies, liberty is a daughter of knowledge may no longer be seen as a utopian idea for Foucault, either (cf. Stehr, 2016).

3.4 The global class

Ending this section dedicated to the relation between knowledge and power, we want to return briefly to the concept of class, albeit in a new setting. In one of his later works, Ralf Dahrendorf warns us of the emergence of a new kind of powerful stratum of capitalist societies, that of the global class.

The origins of the emergence of the global class, as Dahrendorf (2000) describes it using the term in the classical sense of the concept of social class, are to be found among the profound social, political and economic consequences of the end of the Cold War in the late decades of the twentieth century. It is not that these events, or the bipolar world they displaced, represent the forces that allowed for the emergence of the new global class, but the end of the Cold War permitted them to evolve manifestly and more rapidly. The processes Dahrendorf has in mind are of course usually described by the concept of globalization (see Stehr, 2009). In concurrence with Dahrendorf's reputation as a conflict theorist, he stresses the contradictions and antagonisms of the economic and social forces brought about by globalization.

The decisive new forces are informational assets and the technologies (computerization, digitization, miniaturization, satellite communication, the Internet and fiber optics) that in principle ensure worldwide access to these resources. The proper designation of the society that is evolving therefore is that of an *information society*, and those who form the power elite of the information society exert the social, political and economic control. New forces create new interests. The globalization process brings about the new global class with its unique class-specific consciousness,[15] its optimistic outlook and message of hope. Although the dominance and victory of the global class is not assured, neo-liberal economic policies with their distinct emphasis on deregulation, define and promote the interests of the global class. The emphasis on personality traits extends especially to creativity, flexibility, initiative, education and innovation.

The power of global classes due to the control exerted by them over the resources of the information society is immense. The global class "has turned us into hostages, and the more 'advanced' countries are, the less resistance they meet" (Dahrendorf, 2000: 1039). Our society is a slave to the global class. Although the ruling class is not omnipotent, they definitely set the tone in many areas of the world community since 1989. With the rise of the global class and the dominance the class exerts in the knowledge economy, there will be a momentous change in the amount of socially necessary labor (see also Stehr, 2002).

Dahrendorf (2000: 1064) calls it the age of capital without work. The work society (*Arbeitsgesellschaft*) disappears.

New forms of inequality are central to emerging forms of social conflict in a society that runs out of work. However, the premise manifest in the ambivalence of these observations, namely that the societal monopolization of knowledge proceeds just as easily as that of capital or of the instruments of violence, should be questioned. The question we therefore want to raise is: Is it really much more difficult to withhold knowledge from others than it is to withhold access to capital or the means of violence from the powerless?[16]

So, in concluding this chapter, there are two relevant issues that we would like to take up in response to the widespread assumption that knowledge invariably is commanded by the powerful in a society. First, why is it that knowledge is appropriated by the politically powerful, but not by the weak? Second, why is this knowledge powerful and very effective, even though it really only represents, as defined here, the *capacity* to act?

The answer to the first question is relatively simple: It needs power to monopolize knowledge and effectively deploy it. The transaction costs for the acquisition of knowledge, let alone the resources needed to deploy knowledge, are simply too high to reach for vulnerable populations, who are unable to afford the fruits of knowledge.

The answer to the second question, on the conditions that make for the power of knowledge, refers to a related line of argument that points out that the special social significance of scientific findings is a function of the unique reliability, objectivity, reality and conformity of the incontrovertible knowledge claims articulated in the scientific community. In short, it is about the *scientificity* ("*Wissenschaftlichkeit*") of scientific knowledge.

This thesis of the special characteristics of scientific knowledge has, in the meantime, been greatly demystified. The differences between everyday knowledge and scientific discoveries are not as dramatic as is often assumed, and scientific findings are themselves often essentially contested assertions. Their development and interpretation is influenced by non-scientific or political judgments. We are thinking, for example, of climate determinism as a more or less common belief in everyday life that is by no means absent from climate research (cf. the article by

Hsiang et al., 2011, in *Nature* on civil conflicts and global climate change). In short, scientific knowledge is fragile, and this fragility may be described, from the perspective of democratic governance, as one of the virtues of scientific knowledge claims.

In any case, it is evident that whatever conditions are responsible for the power of knowledge, different social constraints affect the dissemination of knowledge in society and impede or enhance the role that knowledge plays in a democracy.

Notes

1 The next section makes use of a discussion of various theoretical perspectives on the power of knowledge in Stehr (2016), which deals explicitly with the question of the relation between knowledge and democracy.
2 Robert Michels ([1908] 1987: 134) stresses, however, that an "ideal democracy" – still pursued by socialist political "schools" – based on nothing less than full social equality is impossible to realize under existing, massive socio-economic dependencies in society.
3 After Wilhelm Liebknecht had been released from prison while legal proceedings against him continued, he had to promise to abstain from "political agitation"; hence he became a "festive lecturer" (cf. Liebknecht, 1891 [1872]: 4).
4 Robert Michels ([1908] 1987: 144) notes that oligarchic tendencies in conservative political parties occur with an almost taken-for-granted regularity and are accepted as part of their general political strategy. Evidence showing that oligarchic social processes occur in anti-oligarchic organizations demonstrates, according to Michels, that we are dealing with an immanent, inevitable tendency in society; moreover, Michels ([1908] 1987: 142–143) adds, "like all sociological laws, the law that pronounces the immanent tendency of all human aggregates to form cliques and subclasses, is an assertion that is neither good nor evil."
5 By the same token, Robert Alford (1985: 295) suggests that Athens in the late fifth and early fourth centuries BC represents another case that mitigates Michels's iron law: "Athens' success is related to its practice of universal male citizen participation in the administration of the city." Similarly, the optimistic discussion in the 1960s and 1970s of the possibility of *industrial democracy* within the confines of modern-day factories sought to reconcile either capitalist ownership of the means of production with democracy or state ownership of the means of production and democratic governance in state-owned factories.
6 "Computers and year 2000: A race for security (and against time)," *The New York Times*, December 27, 1998, partners.nytimes.com/library/tech/98/12/biztech/articles/27millennium.html.

7 Michel Crozier ([1979] 1982: 128) describes some of the emerging convictions and relations – which he does not see as unique to our age, however, and which he goes on to reject – as follows: "The fact is that we do not seem to control anything anymore. Experts are everywhere, imposing limits, making people recognize their limitations, determining the right options. All important decisions are made by different technicians, who have no consideration for what people are going through. Some people think that eventually computers will be able to make all decisions without us."

8 Our translation.

9 Nikolas Rose and Peter Miller (1992: 175) sum up Foucault's thesis of governmentality as follows: "Government is the historically constituted matrix within which are articulated all those dreams, schemes, strategies and maneuvers of authorities that seek to shape the beliefs and conduct of others in desired directions by acting upon their will, their circumstances or their environment [...] Knowledge is [...] central to these activities of government and to the very formation of its objects, for government is a domain of cognition, calculation, experimentation and evaluation."

10 Compare, for example, the contemporary works of one of the pioneers of social science, Adolphe Quetelet.

11 Eric Paras's reading of Foucault is based on Foucault's lectures at the Collège de France during the early 1980s. There he traces the development of Foucault's thinking in the context of his intellectual and social relations. The early dispute with Sartre, the events of 1968 and French left-wing politics, the Iranian Revolution, the closeness to Deleuze, the long stays in San Francisco, and the rise of the *nouveaux philosophes* all had an important, even direct impact on his thinking. Foucault would go so far as to admit that his oeuvre lacked consistency, the only consistency being provided by his *biography* (see Paras, 2006: 146). Paras argues that each decisive conceptual turn in Foucault's work was provoked by the inadequacy of his theoretical framework vis-à-vis the political climate that surrounded his intellectual activities (Paras, 2006: 11).

12 There is an interesting parallel to Otto Neurath's program of physicalism in sociology (see section 7.4). Social scientists should investigate (and *only* investigate) events in space and time, look at statements that describe and classify them, and look for consistency between statements.

13 By the late 1970s Foucault's sympathy for neo-Marxist analysis had vanished, largely after he aligned himself with the *nouveaux philosophes* who had forcefully attacked the Marxist legacy in Stalinist Russia.

14 Elsewhere Michel Foucault admits that all three elements of any experience were present only in *Madness and Civilization*, and even there in a "somewhat confused fashion." Truth was prominent in *The Birth of the Clinic* and *The Order of Things*, while power was studied in *Discipline and Punish* and ethics in *The History of Sexuality* (Foucault, 1984: 352).

15 Rosabeth Moss Kanter (1991) refers in her study of the emergence and attributes of the *World Class* to the *consciousness* of a new cosmopolitan stratum rich in concepts, competence and contacts.

16 Norbert Elias (1984: 251–252) supports the view that it is knowledge that is more difficult to withhold from those who aspire to gain it than it is to deny access to capital or means of violence, but why is it less difficult to monopolize knowledge, "thus endowing a group or person with a higher power ratio in relation to others"? Elias (1984: 253) observes in apparent contradiction that "even in the more advanced countries this expansion [of knowledge] and democratization of knowledge to the urban masses is still in the early stages, for there are many countercurrents. But even the present expansion of knowledge, the rise of educational standards reached so far, has been enough to increase noticeably the power potential of a country's population." Nonetheless, as Elias (1984: 254) also notes, "the staggering growth of humanity's fund of knowledge as a whole, which consists to a considerable extent of highly specialized technical and scientific knowledge, is usually accessible only to limited groups of experts, to the oligarchs of knowledge, who thus have a kind of monopolistic grip on it."

4
NON-KNOWLEDGE[1]

We would like to preface our observations about non-knowledge with two perceptive quotations from Alfred Schütz and Georg Simmel. Both of these much-invoked observers of social action emphasize that there is more at stake here than the plain difference between knowledge and non-knowledge. Alfred Schütz (1946: 463) points out that "[t]he outstanding feature of a man's life in the modern world is his conviction that his life-world as a whole is neither fully understood by himself nor fully understandable to any of his fellow-men." Georg Simmel ([1922] 2009: 309), in turn, emphasizes: "Our knowledge of the whole being on which our actions are grounded is marked by characteristic limitations and diversions" (see also Schütz, 1959).

This, first of all, raises the elementary question of precisely what the reference point is for the concept of non-knowledge. There are *non*-members of a club, there are *non*conformists, etc., but are there *non*-knowers? Is non-knowledge an historically specific form, an historically specific phenomenon? Or is so-called non-knowledge something like an anthropological constant? Whose non-knowledge is at issue, and in relation to what form of knowledge? Is non-knowledge an individual phenomenon, i.e. a phenomenon that is attributable to an individual? Or can only collectives be carriers of non-knowledge? What intellectual tradition can help clarify the concept? Could the difference between knowledge and non-knowledge be the decisive one? Does knowledge grow out of non-knowledge? Is the implicit bias in favor of knowledge that underlies reflections on non-knowledge justified? Can you really imagine such a thing as a "knowledgeless social group"? That is rather unlikely (see also Elias [1987] 2006a: 309). Finally, is non-knowledge perhaps even a virtue and a source of strength?

Our thesis will be that there can be no such thing as non-knowledge. Put in a nutshell, the thesis about the alleged phenomenon of non-knowledge can be described in reference to a phrasing by economist Joseph Stiglitz (2005: 133) regarding the *invisible hand* that is said to operate in the markets: Why is the invisible hand invisible? Because it does not exist. Why is non-knowledge so difficult to conceive? Because there is no such thing as non-knowledge.

However, since we refuse to capitulate already at this point, we will in this chapter focus on scientific discourses which claim that something like non-knowledge indeed exists, and therefore also an "anti-epistemology" dedicated to the exploration of non-knowledge (cf. Galison, 2004: 237). In many of these affirmative discourses on the difference between knowledge and non-knowledge, the knowledge/non-knowledge dichotomy is framed as a performative speech act that, however, recommends only one side of what it describes, namely knowledge. At the same time, and in a more constructive vein, we will draw attention to other terms that we deem empirically and theoretically more fruitful than the bare reference to the difference between knowledge and non-knowledge. Finally, we will point to a number of fascinating but rarely studied topics that have to do with the question of the societal function of apparently insufficient knowledge, that is with the way societies will deal with such knowledge. These questions are of practical as well as theoretical relevance and can best be subsumed under the socio-theoretical concept of a *division of knowledge*. [2]

4.1 Sigmund Freud and Friedrich August von Hayek

It seems obvious, or so one would think, that there can be no such thing as non-knowledge, an assertion to which prominent theorists would readily subscribe. Yet even these observers have been fascinated by the alleged phenomenon of non-knowledge, disavowing their own statements, however logically grounded. Sigmund Freud's and Friedrich August von Hayek's approaches to the issue of non-knowledge are typical examples of this contradictory discourse about knowledge. They acknowledge that there can be no such thing as non-knowledge as a research theme in its own right – whether relating to individuals or to societal formations such as markets – only to proceed, unfazed, with their attempts to explore what does not exist.

Freud's theory, set forth in "A General Introduction to Psychoanalysis," of the dream as a psychic phenomenon is essentially based on the idea that "[t]he dreamer himself [...] is to tell us the meaning of his dream" (Freud, [1917] 1920: 85). This, however, apparently comes up against a fundamental obstacle, for the dreamer is, as a rule, firmly convinced that he does not know what his dream means: "the dreamer always says he knows nothing," Freud notes (ibid.). Given his aim to develop a scientific and methodical interpretation of dreams, Freud thus faces a seemingly dead-end situation. "Since he knows nothing and we know nothing and a third person surely knows nothing, it looks as though there were no possibility of discovering anything" (Freud, [1917] 1920: 85).

However, instead of accepting these findings and resigning himself to working on some topic that lends itself more readily to scientific elucidation, Freud considers another possibility: "For I assure you, it is very possible, in fact, probable, that the dreamer does know what his dream means, but does not know that he knows, *and therefore believes he does not know*" (Freud, [1917] 1920: 85).

This interpretation seems to be as confusing as it is contradictory; Freud himself even wonders whether his thesis, "that there are unconscious things in man which he knows without knowing that he knows" (Freud, [1917] 1920: 85), might be a *contradictio in adjecto*: "Where, in what field of observation shall we seek the proof that there is in man a knowledge of which he is not conscious, as we here wish to assume in the case of the dreamer? That would be a remarkable, a surprising fact, one which would change our understanding of the psychic life, and which would have no need to hide itself. To name it would be to destroy it, and yet it pretends to be something real, a contradiction in terms" (ibid.: 85).

From this it would seem to follow that this approach to dream interpretation had best be abandoned, but not so Freud. The knowledge does not hide at all. One only has to keep digging. Freud writes that the assumption "that there is also present in the case of the dreamer a knowledge of his dream, a knowledge which is so inaccessible that he does not believe it himself, does not seem to be made out of whole cloth. [The] question is, how to make it possible for him to discover this knowledge, and to impart it to us?" (Freud, [1917] 1920: 88).

Friedrich von Hayek, confronted with a similar dilemma, decides, just like Freud, to ignore it. In an essay entitled "The creative powers of a free civilization" and dealing with the distribution of knowledge in markets, he starts out by saying that any progress in civilization is due to an increase in knowledge. However, Hayek ([1960] 1978: 22) argues, it is equally true that in the real world "the individual benefits from more knowledge than he is aware of," and adds: "This fundamental fact of man's unavoidable ignorance of much on which the working of civilization rests has received little attention […] our knowledge is, in fact, very far from perfect" (Hayek, [1960] 1978: 22–23).[3]

The relevant key passage in Hayek's analysis of the difference between what he calls the boundaries of ignorance, that is "man's unavoidable ignorance," and "conscious knowledge" is: "It must be admitted, however, that our ignorance is a peculiarly difficult subject to discuss […] We certainly cannot discuss intelligently something about which we know nothing" (Hayek, [1960] 1978: 23). Hayek then takes recourse to something like a "Münchhausen manoeuver": "We must at least be able to state the questions even if we do not know the answers […] Though we cannot see in the dark, we must be able to trace the limits of the dark areas" (Hayek, [1960] 1978: 23). Yet, Hayek insists, "[i]f we are to understand how society works, we must attempt to define the general nature and range of our ignorance concerning it" (ibid.).

4.2 Observing non-knowledge

Our action is knowledge-guided. Knowledge of others and knowledge of self are a prerequisite of sociation. Just as you are not naked without a scarf, an individual or a system "without" knowledge is not ignorant. A society where there are no secrets is unrealistic. A society where there is total transparency of behavior is equally impossible. It is, therefore, questionable whether a human *non*-knowledge society exists at all. It would not be a *human* society. Yet the discourse about non-knowledge is virulent.

We live in a complex society with a highly developed division of labor, where all members are ignorant of almost all the knowledge and information that exists. The individual knows that his or her knowledge is limited. There is no comprehensive knowledge; one cannot know everything. Acting under conditions of uncertainty is commonplace. Knowledge of these apparent "knowledge gaps" is knowledge; especially as we know, or at least can find out, who may have the knowledge that will fill this gap (Stehr and Grundmann, 2010). On the other hand, there are many things (almost) everyone knows (almost everyone is *informed* about), such as, for instance, how to build a fire, or that almost every human being has two eyes, or that there is such a thing as weather, or climate.

We will therefore argue that it is *sociologically* unproductive to refer to knowledge as the opposite of non-knowledge.[4] This specific static contrast only leads right into the abyss of the arbitrary and no doubt tiresome dichotomy of rational and irrational, as when saying, for instance, that any (new rational) knowledge gives rise to new irrational non-knowledge (e.g. Jischa, 2008: 280).[5] Knowledge represents a continuum that cannot be divided just like that. Knowledge is a total social phenomenon (a "*fait social total*," as defined by Marcel Mauss, 1966). Rather than insisting on the dichotomy of knowledge and non-knowledge it would seem to be more productive, on a theoretical as well as a practical level, to highlight the variable relation between *knowledge* and *lack of knowledge*. As a consequence, we will draw on the concept of the societal *division of knowledge* to account for the fact that knowledge and information are variably distributed among societal roles and institutions. The division of knowledge, thus, becomes something like an anthropological constant that can be found in any form of society and in any functional societal system.

4.3 Non-knowledge as a myth?

Why, then, has the term *"non-knowledge"* even become something of a fashion in the cultural and social sciences? Why is the category of non-knowledge (as the alleged dark side of knowledge) increasingly singled out as the prominent monetary unit also in the media and the public discussion? Is the difference between knowledge and non-knowledge[6] an example of the static polarity typical of the concepts of earlier philosophy (cf. Elias, [1984] 2006b: 41–42)? Or is it essentially just the well-known criticism-of-culture lament[7] that the individual, given the enormous, and growing, volume of existing objectivated knowledge in present-day societies, and the new and uncomplicated technical ways of accessing it (cf. Earl, 2009), can master only a tiny (and probably diminishing) share of the total stock of knowledge? Does the concept of non-knowledge basically refer to nothing but the societal *distribution* of knowledge, as we suggest, or to the widespread existence of "pseudo-opinions" (see Sturgis et al., 2008)? Or could it even be that the term of non-knowledge primarily refers to the future about which we have only limited information, or know little (cf. Zimmerli, 1999; cf. also section 9.4)?

It is certainly not a coincidence that the discussion about non-knowledge is gaining momentum in the context of the thesis, more and more prominent in politics and science, that modern societies are being transformed into knowledge societies. So, what comes to be expressed this way are manifest doubts about the theory of the knowledge society (e.g. Ungar, 2008). It is evident, at any rate, that rhetorical references to the societal relevance of non-knowledge are increasingly associated with the knowledge society and that the latter is, then, characterized as *"alleged, so-called, or self-proclaimed"* (Wehling, 2008: 17; Wehling, 2009: 95). Another interpretation could be that the interest in non-knowledge is only another way of deploring the more and more frequent association of knowledge and uncertainty and, thus, the loss of legitimacy of the mechanisms of securing knowledge that can be observed in recent times. After all, well into early modernity and even up to the present day knowledge has been closely linked to the expectation that it be *certain*. Only knowledge that has shed the attribute of "uncertain" could pass as stringent knowledge.

Precisely who or what is the reference point when non-knowledge or the knowledge/non-knowledge relation is invoked?[8] Is it the individual or is it a social collective? For how long must or can non-knowledge be observable or "palpable" to be qualified as non-knowledge? Can there be ignorance that lasts but a few seconds, for instance? Does one refer to individual forms of knowledge (or information) that the isolated individual (as a scientist, for instance) does not have and cannot have because one always proceeds by selection, or has to rely on screening (e.g. Weber, [1904] 1922a; Fleck, [1935] 1980)? The common discussion about non-knowledge adheres to a static view. The adverse attributes of non-knowledge make us overlook the fact that while we know nothing about the future, we still have to act.

The economist John Maynard Keynes (1937: 213–214) refers to our "'uncertain' *knowledge*" (our emphasis) of the future and explains that it does not absolve us from acting: "Nevertheless, the necessity for action and for decision compels us as practical men to do our best to overlook this awkward fact and to behave exactly as we should if we had behind us a good Benthamite calculation of a series of prospective advantages and disadvantages, each multiplied by its appropriate probability, waiting to be summed."

Keynes (1937: 214) points out three techniques in this context, on which we rely when dealing with uncertain action conditions:

1. We assume that the present is a much more serviceable guide to the future than a candid examination of past experience would show it to have been hitherto. In other words we largely ignore the prospect of future changes about the actual character of which we know nothing.
2. We assume that the *existing* state of opinion as expressed in prices and the character of existing output is based on a *correct* summing up of future prospects, so that we can accept it as such unless and until something new and relevant comes into the picture.
3. Knowing that our own individual judgment is worthless, we endeavor to fall back on the judgment of the rest of the world which is perhaps better informed. That is, we endeavor to conform with the behavior of the majority or the average. The psychology of a society of individuals each of whom is endeavoring

to copy the others leads to what we may strictly term a *conventional* judgment.

While forms of behavior and judgment such as these are supposed to make up for uncertain knowledge, the basis they provide is no doubt rather fragile and may collapse or be invalidated at any time.

At any rate, it is a paradoxical situation for us to want to "discuss intelligently something about which we know nothing" (Hayek, 1960: 22) and, thus, at the same time, to reflect on the allegedly *disproportionate* non-linear increase in non-knowledge (Ravetz, 1986: 423; Luhmann, 1997: 1106; Wehling, 2008: 31; Roberts and Armitage, 2008: 346),[9] as well as on the possibility of a (scientific) analysis of "how, why and by whom non-knowledge" is generated (e.g. Wehling, 2009: 95). Remarkably, the discussion of non-knowledge is as a rule not accompanied by any *explicit* attempt to provide a precise definition of this concept *or* of the concept of knowledge and its form.[10]

This lack of conceptual precision also holds for the problematic question of whether it makes sense to distinguish between information and knowledge. Is knowledge conceived of as scientific knowledge only? If the discussion about the non-knowledge of individual members of society were based on its contrast to scientific knowledge alone, the insights thus gained would be modest indeed; that the stock of knowledge in modern societies is not confined to scientific knowledge alone is a truism. What is more to the point, if problematic, is Hayek's (1960: 24) observation that "the scientific methods of the search for knowledge" do "not exhaust even all the explicit and conscious knowledge of which society makes constant use." Hayek thus refers, among other things, to the limits of the societal power of scientific knowledge (cf. Stehr, 1991).

This reiteration of the more or less unspecified concept of non-knowledge, along with the typical conflation of the concepts of information and knowledge (e.g. Urry, 2003: 64–65; Ungar, 2008: 311–312; Proctor and Schiebinger, 2008: 2–3),[11] as well as a variety of other concepts,[12] or long lists of the most diverse properties of non-knowledge, including the idea of "relative non-knowledge" (Beck, 1996: 289), ultimately amount to the unsatisfactory conclusion that the phenomenon under scrutiny seems to be nothing but a murky *mixture* of knowledge and non-knowledge (Wehling, 2008: 18), if not a multitude of *shades* between knowledge and non-knowledge (Jischa, 2008: 280). Revealingly, Niklas Luhmann (2002: 97) indeed emphasizes "demarcating between knowledge and non-knowledge [...] or, more concretely, information is possible *only in very general terms*" (our emphasis), only to voice his strong skepticism regarding the theoretical function of the knowledge/non-knowledge difference by adding: "which doesn't help much."

So, a suspicion is beginning to grow within us: could one reason for the boom of observations about non-knowledge be that there is overestimation of the societal role of scientific knowledge and underestimation of its social risks? Are not there other, more adequate concepts for capturing the social phenomena that suggest the existence (and construction?) of forms of "non-knowledge" – provided we can specify them at all – on both the theoretical and the practical levels? At any rate, *one* key to an understanding of the myth of non-knowledge is the very concept of knowledge itself, and the question of how to distinguish between information and knowledge.

One of the first theses we would like to go into in more detail in this context is the observation that the knowledge/non-knowledge dichotomy seems to go with certain normative ideas, if not ressentiments, and quite often these reservations are raised against that side of the dichotomy which is associated with the concept of non-knowledge, or with a special form of knowledge. Thus, in the case of C.P. Snow's Two Cultures thesis, for instance, the real ignoramuses are the carriers of "literary" or "traditional" knowledge, i.e. the "Luddites" (the technophobes). Similarly, if conversely, in the very German dichotomy of culture and civilization (see Elias, 1978: 1–64), the ignoramuses are the unfortunate technicians and natural scientists as the driving forces of a purely civilizational "progress," while the humanities-based ideas and traditional worldviews of the "carriers of culture" are privileged by this distinction.

So it could be worthwhile, in the context of the discussion about so-called non-knowledge, once more to highlight the important elements of our understanding of knowledge, as well as the difference between information and knowledge. In this special context, too, we often find a liberal conflation of the terms of knowledge and information. Another remarkable fact is the frequent use of an *everyday* concept of knowledge ("everyday knowledge") which in turn can hardly hide its proximity to the concept of information. Exemplary exponents of this liberal conflation of knowledge and information are the communication researcher Phillip Tichenor and the sociologists George A. Donohue and Charles N. Olien (1970: 159), with the latter counting among the discoverers of the phenomenon of the "knowledge gap" since their publication of an article on "Mass media flow and differential growth in knowledge" in the journal *Public Opinion Quarterly*. Taking up the thesis of the growing knowledge gap in modern societies, and following his American colleagues, the Swiss communication researcher Ulrich Saxer (1978: 35–36), in turn, proposes another wording of the phenomenon: "When the flow of information from the mass media into a social system increases, those segments of the population that have a higher social status tend to more quickly assimilate this *information* than the lower-status segments do, with the result that the *knowledge* gap between these segments tends to grow rather than diminish" (our emphasis). So, an information gap is also a knowledge gap (also Wirth, 1997).[13]

In contrast, we assume, as stated, that the concept of information should be carefully demarcated from that of knowledge, however hard it may be to maintain this distinction in practice. Lack of information is not "non-knowledge."[14] Precisely what knowledge is and how knowledge differs from information, human capital, or other intellectual or cognitive properties is an *essentially controversial issue*, as we have emphasized.[15] Neither the concept of knowledge nor the way knowledge is produced, distributed and used, nor the consequences this may have, can be taken for granted – at least not by the scientific observer.[16]

Rather than defining knowledge as something a person may count among his or her qualities or can easily acquire – an idea that rather holds for the concept of information – the process of knowing and the knowledge relations should be perceived in terms of action, of something a person does. Knowledge can be described – following an idea of John Dewey (1948) – as a *transaction*,[17] as a phenomenon that does not exist independently of social interactions.[18] Based on this observation, forms of knowledge can therefore be distinguished by the type of participation they involve.

4.4 Lack of knowledge

The term *lack of knowledge* is often used instead of that of non-knowledge, with no discernable difference made between them. Therefore, we will pursue our discussion about non-knowledge under the umbrella term of lack of knowledge.

One of the significant points of the above discussion of the social role of "non-knowledge" and "lack of knowledge" are their primarily *individualized* points of reference, or their privileging the individual. This one-sided reversion to actors as non-knowers, however, can hardly be decisive for an understanding of so-called non-knowledge. Rather, the relevant reference here would be to the social structure under conditions of cultural differentiation. As it is, referring to the difference between knowledge and non-knowledge, and thus to the existence of non-knowledge, raises a lot of questions, in spite of the implicit belief that it will help clear the issue.

One difference can be ruled out from the very start: non-knowledge can*not* be the opposite of objective knowledge, knowledge that is consistent with reality, or true knowledge (even though the term knowledge is in many contexts and many languages closely linked to the idea of true knowledge). Just as there is no complete or true knowledge, there is no complete error or complete non-knowledge (see also Fleck, [1935] 1980: 31). On the other hand, from a theory-of-society perspective, knowledge in this *absolute* understanding is, in the everyday life of modern societies, rather reserved for the knowledge of the *stranger* and is, thus, a manifestation of cultural conflicts (cf. Schiebinger, 2008).

In contrast, knowledge that actors in everyday life accept in good faith (see also Simmel, [1908] 1992a: 389) – as opposed to the knowledge of the stranger, which they cannot verify – is the knowledge of *other* actors. In many of our most important practical decisions and actions we build on the knowledge of others, on the trust we have in the knowledge of these others, but not on their non-knowledge; i.e. we know that others know (Akerlof, 1970; Dulleck and Kerschbamer, 2006). Someone who is supposed to know nothing cannot be trusted.

Furthermore, "non-knowledge" has different functional meanings in different societal institutions. In an institution such as, for instance, science, it is a state to be overcome – a state that, in science, functions as an incentive. In a heavily stratified social institution, for instance in so-called "total" institutions, different stocks of knowledge are a constitutive characteristic (a functional necessity) of the institution, defended by all available means.

The category of knowledge is as a rule positively connoted. So-called non-knowledge, therefore, indicates a *problem* of a very special type. At the very least, the state of alleged non-knowledge points to something like a societal norm violation. The common condemnation of non-knowledge thus not least reveals the societal valuation and functionality of (one's own) knowledge. In their classical functionalist discussion of the societal functions of "ignorance," Wilbert Moore and Melvin Tumin (1949: 787) therefore highlight the widespread, as they see it, phenomenon that ignorance is understood to be the natural enemy of a society's stability and of the possibility of ordered social progress. This is complemented by the opposite belief that any increase in knowledge will automatically benefit the welfare of humanity. However, it can be observed that a generally positive valuation of new knowledge, which could still be found in the first post-World War II decades, is today giving way to growing skepticism towards new scientific-technical knowledge (see Stehr, 2003). In the range of attitudes toward ignorance vs. knowledge gains, the weighting has shifted. Yet it is rather unlikely that this should have substantially changed the valuation of ignorance.

Even this adverse function of and dismissive perspective on non-knowledge as a problem is not uncontroversial. There is a lot of convincing evidence for the supposed virtues of non-knowledge, lack of knowledge, or non-transparency. This primarily includes everyday sayings such as "ignorance is bliss," "what I do not know cannot hurt me," or "no-one can (must) know everything." Even the Bible suggests that "blessed are the poor in spirit, for theirs is the kingdom of heaven" (Matthew 5:3).

"Ignorance" is, then, conceived of as a form of emancipation (see also McGoey, 2012: 4–7). In this context, the discussion about one of the moral principles formulated by Hans Jonas (1974: 161–163), namely the individual's "right to ignorance," is of fundamental importance. This principle is invariably complemented by the no less momentous ethical call for a "right to knowledge." The call for a right to knowledge no doubt particularly applies to the collective or macro level (cf. Sen, 1981; Stiglitz, 1999). On the level of the individual, there is a variant form of the right to knowledge, i.e. his or her right to "private knowledge," that is the right to privacy of personal data. The biochemist Erwin Chargaff, a vehement opponent of genetic engineering and its promise to make human life more transparent, joins Jonas in affirming: "Ignorance is a blessing. Uncertainty is the salt of life."[19]

The thesis of, or rather the warning against, radically "transparent" man is a similar example (cf. Tangens, 2006). However, in the case of this general condemnation of transparent man as something undesirable it remains an open question whether the issue is primarily about mutual transparency or about the transparency of the powerless for the powerful. A society where there is full transparency is "fiendish" (Merton, [1957] 1965: 345).[20] As for the likelihood of a mutually transparent, complex society, it is unrealistic (Popitz, 1968: 18).

Resistance to having one's own behavior as well as that of other actors made overly transparent is a consequence of certain structural properties of social groups, as Robert Merton ([1957] 1965: 343), for instance, points out. These properties include the institutionally sanctioned but of course also limited negligence in dealing with, or enforcing, existent social norms, but also the psychologically induced, variable resistance to maximal behavioral transparency (see Popitz, 1968: 8). Along with these conditions of resistance, our society provides a range of technical and legal barriers that preclude an unrestricted screening of the behaviors and beliefs of individual actors who happen to become the target of a desire to know everything about them. Whether the thought police are supposed to be benevolent or malevolent is irrelevant. New opportunities to elude technologically mobilized surveillance, for instance, will always arise.

In his reflections in "Über die Präventivwirkung des Nichtwissens" ("On the preventive effect of non-knowledge"), Heinrich Popitz (1968), in turn, highlights the *disburdening* function that limited behavioral information has for the system of penalties. Limiting the available or sought for behavioral information – which at the same time means relinquishing sanctions – is thus something like an "uncertainty principle of social life" and "opens up a sphere where it is possible for the system of norms and penalties to not be taken at face value and yet not patently relinquish its claim to validity" (ibid.: 12).

Finally, there is another (primarily cognitive) function of non-knowledge, reflected in the claim that knowledge grows out of non-knowledge, or that non-knowledge can be converted into knowledge (e.g. Petersen and Faber, 2004). Precisely how this is supposed to happen, however, is not discussed in any detail. The thesis that knowledge will grow out of non-knowledge, out of nothing, as it were, completely ignores the social genealogy of knowledge, for instance the close relation or even affinity between scientific and practical knowledge.[21] The emergence of a scientific discipline is not a virgin birth. The thesis that non-knowledge can be converted into knowledge privileges certain kinds of knowledge simply by negating their very genealogy.[22]

4.5 Ignorance

In his study *The Easternization of the West*, Colin Campbell joins a number of other observers of modern society in highlighting the discrepancy between the existing stock of scientific knowledge and the science proficiency of a great majority of the population. Campbell (2007: 371) summarizes this fact by saying that for most people, the contents of science constitute "hidden" ("occult") knowledge. This knowledge is hidden in a double sense: it remains hidden for a majority of the population, on the one hand, and it is knowledge of phenomena that are hidden in everyday life, on the other. Campbell adds that except for cases where corporations, the state or other powerful institutions succeed in monopolizing knowledge and in keeping it from the public, the state of hiddenness is by no means the result of a conscious strategy by scientists to produce secret knowledge.

The existence of hidden knowledge thus calls attention to the fact that knowledge is a relational concept. A person from whom existing knowledge is hidden is not "ignorant," let alone permanently so. It is a state that can be reversed. What loses its hiddenness is absent knowledge, not ignorance. The interesting critical questions that arise in this context therefore relate to the conditions under which knowledge loses the attribute of hiddenness for someone, which is a permanent, ongoing process, and a process that may be consciously induced or happen more or less by accident.

In what follows, we will discuss the concept of *ignorance*, which is often used as an equivalent of "non-knowledge." Ignorance is a rather ambivalent term: "It may mean that people have no image at all about something where such an image is possible, or it may mean that they have images which are false or untrue" (Boulding, 1966: 1; also Poser, 2011; McGoey, 2012). Often ignorance does not imply a blank mind.

The term is no doubt most frequently used – often with disparaging intent – in relation to the ignorance of an "opponent," to his or her deficient cognitive state, and thus to the superior information or the superior knowledge of the person who circulates this diagnosis. This tactical use, however, does not enter into the following evaluation of the function of ignorance.

In the research literature, discussions of the phenomenon of ignorance (either in everyday life or in the scientific community) primarily start by asserting that the widespread social role of ignorance is either ignored or marginalized (e.g. Smithson, 1985: 151; Stocking and Holstein, 1993; Ungar, 2008: 313; Proctor and Schiebinger, 2008; Dilley, 2010; McGoey, 2012: 3).[23] As a consequence, a sociology of ignorance is called for as the necessary complement of, for instance, a comprehensive sociology of knowledge. Aside from this, however, the term of ignorance, provided it is not confounded with that of non-knowledge, is used in various and contradictory ways in the literature.[24]

For Karl Popper ([1960] 1962: 30), one of the epistemological results of his study on the foundations of knowledge and ignorance is the thesis that "[t]he more we learn about our world, and the deeper our learning, the more conscious, specific, and articulate will be our knowledge of what we do not know, our knowledge of our ignorance. For this, indeed, is the main source of our ignorance – the fact that our knowledge can be only finite, while our ignorance must necessarily be infinite" (see also Hayek, [1960] 2005; Hobart, 1993: 20). The discovery or production of new knowledge is, thus, supposed to involve always both the insight that it will only potentiate our lack of knowledge (Luhmann, 1992: 190–191) and – at least implicitly – something like a sincere acknowledgement of what remains unknown (see Bataille, 2001: 201).

The term of ignorance may signalize, as for instance in the theses about the societal division of knowledge, a seemingly inescapable constitutive feature of modern societies and their highly developed division of labor (e.g. Roberts and Armitage, 2008). Knowledge and ignorance get mixed up. In much the same spirit Hayek (1960: 25), for instance, argues: "The more civilized we become, the more relatively ignorant must each individual be of the facts on which the working of his civilization depends. The very division of knowledge increases the necessary ignorance of the individual of most of this knowledge."[25]

Following the philosopher of technology Hans Poser (2011), ignorance has a *trigger* function in thought processes, in general, and in research, in particular. Every piece of research starts with the insight into, or the admission of, ignorance. Ignorance, i.e. the recognition of a non-existent solution of a problem, can be framed as a question and thus trigger the work of finding a solution to this problem. Referring to technology experts, Poser (2011: 373) emphasizes that "an engineer's ignorance is characterized by a *problem* as the cognitive starting point," i.e. as the incentive to search for a solution. Thus, the search for a solution by no means starts out from a state of *tabula rasa*. The solution to the problem may be found in reference to existing opportunities for action. Moreover, the problem does not necessarily arise from the awareness of a non-existing solution, or non-existing knowledge, but may also be due to the fact that one disagrees with an existing solution, judging it to be deficient, obsolete or one-sided.

In contrast to this broadly affirmative, since inescapable, existence of societal ignorance, a much less positively connoted concept of ignorance,[26] namely as a substitute for the concept of non-knowledge, keeps turning up – especially in more recent times – in the laments by scientists and the media about the allegedly growing "stupidity" or narrow-mindedness of large parts of the public (such as students, consumers, young people, patients, etc., as the case may be). Unsurprisingly, at the same time, a new age of ignorance is being evoked.[27]

This observation of the supposedly limited knowledge – and limited scientific knowledge, in particular (see Stocking and Holstein, 1993; Stocking, 1998: 173–174) – of large parts of humanity often goes along with a warning against the domination of a new class. At present, this warning primarily relates to the domination of experts that is said to increasingly determine the way of living of a large majority of people (cf. also section 2.7).

In addition, there are other conceptions of the societal function of ignorance: Gunnar Myrdal (1944: 40–42), for instance, refers to the "convenience of ignorance" in his famous study on racial discrimination in the United States, *An American Dilemma. The Negro Problem and Modern Democracy*. What is meant by this is the striking information deficit of large parts of the white population of the United States in the 1930s and 1940s with respect to the conditions of life of the black population. For Myrdal, it is quite clear that the information deficit is not "natural" or otherwise to be taken for granted but part of an *opportunistic* defense mechanism. Myrdal (1944: 42) emphasizes that in the case of the population of the American South, "[t]he ignorance about the Negro is not, it must be stressed, just a random lack of interest and knowledge. It is a tense and highstrung restriction and distortion of knowledge, and it indicates much deeper dislocations within the minds of the Southern whites."

One of the early systematic sociological reflections on the concept of ignorance and its possible social *functions* can be found in Wilbert Moore and Melvin Tumin's essay "Some social functions of ignorance" (1949). Moore and Tumin, relying on an approach that is codetermined by a functionalist perspective, conceive of their observations of the role of ignorance in social life as a means of balancing and criticizing the "rationalistic" bias of the sociological discourse.

From Moore and Tumin's (1949: 788) definition it follows without doubt that for them, ignorance is just another term for non-knowledge: "Ignorance is to be taken here as simply referring to 'not knowing,' that is, the absence of empirically valid knowledge." The contrast between empirically valid knowledge and the absence of such knowledge – i.e. not a mere *disregard* of parts of the collectively available knowledge – clearly shows that Moore and Tumin bank on the difference between true and untrue knowledge. As a consequence, they employ terms such as "genuine ignorance" and "perfect" or "complete" knowledge (ibid.), even though they point out that perfect knowledge is impossible and ignorance inescapable. Then again, Moore and Tumin self-critically refer to a *continuum* where knowledge and ignorance represent the "polar antipodes." This view finally prompts

Moore and Tumin (1949: 794) to question the very contrast between ignorance and knowledge: "This continuous distribution of knowledge and ignorance makes many of the observations in this paper reversibly viewable as functions of *limited* knowledge rather than of ignorance" (our emphasis).

Robert K. Merton (1987: 1; see also Merton, 1971: 191) refers to a special and useful – as opposed to dysfunctional – ignorance in the cognitive and social practice of scientific work: this higher form of "manifest" ignorance can be described as a (temporary and future-oriented) "specified ignorance" (that is, recognized ignorance), i.e. as "the express recognition of what is not yet known but needs to be known in order to lay the foundation for still more knowledge." Far from seeking to remain in this state, this form of ignorance as an incentive results in definitive research questions by highlighting fields of deficient knowledge and detailing the reasons why research in these fields would make sense in view of overcoming ignorance: "In workaday science, it is not enough to confess one's ignorance; the point is to specify it. That, of course, amounts to instituting, or finding, a new, worthy, and soluble scientific problem" (Merton, 1987: 8; see also Merton, 1981; Moore and Tumin, 1949: 794; Luhmann, 1995a: 177).[28]

Specified ignorance at the same time symbolizes the very openness of knowledge claims that is constitutive of scientific work, if only in the form of making public one's knowledge deficit and emphasizing that scientific achievements are *contributions* to the enhancement of scientific knowledge (Merton, 1987: 10; Japp, 2000). However, from the viewpoint of the sociologist Robert Merton, momentary acknowledgments by eminent scientists of the more or less comprehensive knowledge gaps of their disciplines (primarily) represent "the living up to a normative expectation of ultimate humility in a community of sometimes egocentric scientists" (Merton, 1987: 7).

Merton's thesis concerning the public acknowledgement, by many scientists, of knowledge gaps that are not easy to fill – today ritually reiterated in almost every scientific publication – can be interpreted as relating to the four social norms of the scientific community worked out by Merton ([1942] 1973b) as the ethos of science: universalism, "communism," organized skepticism, and disinterestedness. Merton's framing of the ethos of science has drawn a lot of criticism, but the norm of disinterestedness referred to in the above quotation has as a rule been exempt from it.

Specified ignorance is opposed to another form of ignorance, namely "willful ignorance," or the deliberate editing-out of apparently known information. Linsey McGoey (2012) describes the case of the passengers of a Royal Caribbean International cruise ship moored off Haiti at the time of the devastating 2010 earthquake, who had to decide whether to stay on board or to participate in a heavily guarded shore leave only a few kilometers away from the site of the catastrophe. This and a number of similar situations of a socially induced "suppression" of information that was definitely known to the people involved perfectly illustrate that what is at issue here is not a lack of relevant information but a weighting of existing information in view of future conduct.[29]

Another question that keeps arising in this context is, of course, whether the increase in the volume of manifest ignorance is proportionate to the increase in the volume of provisional, uncertain knowledge. The answer, shared by many, is that the increase in manifest ignorance is indeed proportionate, if not over-proportionate, to the increase in knowledge (e.g. Moore and Tumin, 1949: 794). In contrast, the observation that the increase in knowledge goes along with an increase in the "burden of knowledge" for the individual is no doubt less controversial: "[I]f one is to stand on the shoulders of giants, one must first climb up their backs, and the greater the body of knowledge, the harder this climb becomes" (Jones, 2009: 284).

Thirty-five years after Moore and Tumin, Michael Smithson (1985) proposes a theory of ignorance that takes account of the intellectual developments that have occurred in the meantime. For Smithson, ignorance is a social construct that hides a comparative judgment by an individual or a group about another individual or group. Furthermore, Smithson (1985: 168) emphasizes that "[i]gnorance is made possible by the very nature of social interaction and language; and it is embedded in a variety of social norms, occasions, settings, roles, scripts, and identities. Ignorance also is negotiable and may be strategically created or manipulated." Given the systemically unequal distribution – rather than absence – of knowledge and information in every form of society, it seems reasonable to describe this state as the *distribution of knowledge and information* (see also Luckmann, [1982] 2002: 83–85). As we have emphasized, the division of knowledge is thus a concept that was framed in analogy to the societal division of labor, with Hayek being the first to do so.

Unsurprisingly, an analysis of such literature as refers to a social division of knowledge, or information, leads to the conclusion that when referring to their unequal distribution, knowledge and information are hardly ever clearly distinguished. Here, again, asymmetry of information and stratification of knowledge are liberally conflated. In the following analysis of the division of knowledge and information we, too, cannot completely steer clear of this equal treatment of information and knowledge.

At any rate, analyzing the division of information and knowledge is of relevance not only for the issue of the non-knowledge that is supposed to exist in society. Highlighting the societal division of knowledge and information leads up to the very questions that need to be asked as a consequence of having diagnosed the idea of non-knowledge as dubious in substance: like other forms of social stratification or a division of labor among societal institutions, a division of information and knowledge is a typical feature of differentiated societies. Exploring the genealogy as well as the consequences of the division of information and knowledge is, therefore, highly relevant for our understanding of modern societies. In the next chapter we will, therefore, first of all give a more detailed description of the fact that a societal division of information and knowledge exists and is an important topos, while the societal functions and consequences of the changing division of knowledge will be discussed separately.

4.6 The division of knowledge and information

The concept of a *division of knowledge* relates (see Hayek, 1937; Helmstädter, 2000a, 2000b) to the societal knowledge that is broadly dispersed among multiple carriers of knowledge, and thus to the elementary social fact that the stock of knowledge and information in society as a whole is variously and unequally distributed. It thus turns out that even in simple societies knowledge is stratified by, for instance, the actors' age or gender-specific position.

In modern societies this division of knowledge is found both *between* and *within* all social institutions and functional societal systems. The division of knowledge includes the specialization of knowledge and information for different social roles as well as the concomitant fragmentation of knowledge across persons and institutions. There is no societal role or institution capable of accessing the totality of knowledge. Consolidating disparate knowledge therefore suggests specific social activities.[30] For Hayek, it is the *market* or, more precisely, the competition among the agents of competition in the functional system of the economy, that fulfills this function of consolidating disparate forms of knowledge and information (information processor), which, in turn, leads to more transparency with respect to the division of knowledge:

> The price system is just one of those formations which man has learned to use (though he is still very far from having learned to make the best use of it) after he had stumbled upon it without understanding it. Through it not only a division of labor but also a co-ordinated utilization of resources based on an equally divided knowledge has become possible.
>
> *(Hayek, 1948a: 88)*

Especially in view of the unproductive discussion about the phenomenon of non-knowledge it would seem reasonable to extend the relevance of the fact of the division of knowledge beyond the *economic* sphere envisaged by Hayek and Helmstädter.[31] In doing so, both the division of knowledge and its social consequences and potential problems (fragmentation, non-transparency, diffusion, consolidation, opportunities for innovation) have to be taken into account. The societal division of knowledge can, then, be conceived of as an anthropological constant. In the different functional systems of modern society various social processes have taken root that account for the consolidation of knowledge, on the one hand, and ensure the perpetuation of the division of knowledge, on the other.

In an influential 1970 essay, "The market for 'lemons',"[32] economist and Nobel laureate-to-be George Akerlof proposed an exemplary analysis of the *information* held by buyers and sellers, respectively, of second-hand cars, paving the way for a systematic analysis of *asymmetric information*. From the viewpoint of one of the parties involved in social interactions, asymmetric information may be intended or unintended. Intended asymmetric information raises issues about the power and the ethos of social relations; this also goes for accidentally obtained information one may profit from on the stock market.[33]

Asymmetric levels of information are at any rate one of the fundamental characteristics of the different groups involved in the second-hand car market (see also Kurlat and Stroebel, 2014; Chinco and Mayer, 2014; Hellwig and Veldkamp, 2009).[34] Akerlof's observations illustrate a thesis that is not unfamiliar also to the sociological perspective on the societal differentiation of knowledge: thus, the study, referred to above, by Wilbert Moore and Melvin Tumin (1949: 788–789) calls attention to the role-specific knowledge of, for instance, the consumer and the specialist, and to the privileged status of people who due to their roles have more knowledge as well as control over this knowledge. It can therefore generally be said that social actors act on the basis of incomplete information even though they think of their actions as highly rational (see also Geanakoplos, 1992).

The owner and driver of the used car that is up for sale is usually much better informed on the reliability of the car, or its history of mechanical conditions, than the potential buyer is. In the context of negotiations for a credit agreement the person who takes out the loan is guided by certain intentions of paying it back – or not. The lender usually has no access to this information. Moreover, the lender cannot be sure that the investment contemplated by the borrower will really be profitable. Generally speaking, asymmetric information of market participants should actually lead to "market failure." In other words, from a perspective of economics, asymmetric or incomplete information results in inefficient choice behavior in market actors.[35]

Buyers and sellers, lenders and borrowers are often aware that there is, or may be, asymmetric information. As a consequence, both sides tend to look for indicators capable of minimizing their distrust in the available information, or of enabling them to rate it as more or less reliable. Since the transaction costs bound up with the "acquisition" of the relevant information may be considerable, information on the social *reputation* of the seller or the borrower, which is easier to obtain, becomes an important proxy indicator for the buyer or the lender to rely on.

For our analysis of the contrast between information, or knowledge, and non-knowledge, the reflections offered by Akerlof and other economists warrant the following general conclusion: since societal knowledge is asymmetrically dispersed rather than equally distributed, the assumption should be that there is a *cognitive societal division of labor* between and within *all* societal institutions. In other words: what makes sense, rather than talking about knowledge and non-knowledge, is to talk about a continuum of the knowledge held by groups of actors, its range extending to the pole of asymmetric (bounded) knowledge (see also Wang, 2012).

In the sciences, for instance, this fact is not only taken for granted but usually also understood to be a functional property of scientific work. Not every scientist can work on the same problem, and the role of each scientist cannot be determined in relation to him or herself but only in relation to other scientists.

4.7 Knowledge gaps

In various studies in empirical sociology, for instance medical sociology, analyzing the fact of asymmetric information or (relational) "knowledge gaps" is a standard research topic. In medical sociology, Talcott Parsons's (1951, 1975) analyses, based on a functional approach, of the social roles of doctor and patient, of layman and expert, were among the first studies in this field of inquiry.

The central premise of Parsons's theoretical perspective is that the expert (doctor), committed to disinterested and impartial action based on his complex theoretical knowledge and having in mind his client's best interests, faces a patient who is unable to understand, let alone question, the doctor's professional opinions, but who nevertheless accepts the diagnosis and follows the recommended treatment.

Subsequent studies of the patient–doctor interaction have primarily focused on analyzing the dynamics of the processes of knowledge gap formation and development (for instance, the increasing symmetry of information achieved in the course of contemporary consultations; see Pilnick, 1998), and have conceived of these processes as a *mutually* interactive realization. References to Akerlof's perspective, however, are rarely found in these studies.

One of the research interests derived from Parsons's perspective is the question of whether the knowledge gap between doctor and patient is increasingly narrowing – for instance, due to widespread access to relevant medical information on the Internet – and what this may imply for doctor–patient interaction patterns. The sociological analysis of the developmental dynamics of knowledge gaps between experts and laymen in modern societies, however, should be centered on the change it may bring about for the power and domination wielded by big societal institutions such as, for instance, the state, the sciences, or the Church. In developed societies, the levels of deference, humility or respect shown to institutions in everyday life (or in extraordinary situations) have considerably diminished in recent decades. These overall societal transformations have, of course, a significant impact on a society's division of information and knowledge.

Generally speaking, however, it is true that in modern societies whose knowledge structure is based on the division of labor, the fact that individuals, social groups or social institutions have long since given up wishing (or hoping) for knowledge to be autarchic is accepted and sanctioned as a matter of course. It is very easy, as Heinrich Popitz (1968: 6) notes, "to demonstrate the [various] limits of what we know of each other." Knowledge is not equally distributed; moreover, bounded knowledge is disburdening. Managers usually lack the technological knowledge of the lab workers, engineers or assembly-line workers they employ. They get to be managers in spite of this lack of knowledge (cf. Turner, 1990: 187). Knowledge gaps or non-comprehensive forms of a distribution of knowledge, rather than *non-knowledge*, are constitutive of societies that are based on the division of labor. Asymmetric stocks of knowledge do not lead to societal collapse.

A society lacking this limitation is inconceivable. Knowing everything is not essential. Once again, Georg Simmel's ([1922] 2009: 309) insight that our knowledge "is marked by characteristic limitations and diversions" comes to mind.[36] This elementary fact alone is decisive for the very mode of being of a society and rules out any conclusion to the effect that the counterpart of knowledge is non-knowledge. A being that is permanently mired in non-knowledge cannot exist.

Rejecting the possibility of an autarchy of knowledge, and in particular the possibility of an *individual* self-sufficiency of knowledge, or believing that knowledge is fundamentally *bounded knowledge*, comes with both costs and benefits. Knowledge gaps between individuals, groups, larger collectives, or whole regions of the world no doubt have significant consequences in terms of serious moral, cultural and economic disadvantages. Since knowledge is a resource for action, knowledge gaps inevitably immobilize people, make them incapable of warding off imminent danger. As an illustration, just think of the privileged access to an experimental serum (ZMapp) that seems to be capable of successfully fighting the otherwise fatal outcome for an Ebola virus-infected person (lethality rate of 60% to 90%). In August 2014, two Americans out of thousands of infected patients were the only ones to be treated with the serum developed by the American biotechnology company Mapp Biopharmaceutical.

Yet the loss of autarchy, provided such a state existed at all in traditional societies, is never to be conceived of as a form of non-knowledge. Societal innovations such as the market, science, the media or political systems ensure the coordination of knowledge gaps.

Relevant scales of knowledge differ in terms of era, type of society, interests or dominant worldview. In modern complex societies the scale of knowledge has a wider range than in traditional societies. There is a great distance from the sources of knowledge – there is no longer any need to know the bearer of knowledge in person. Only in exceptional cases does the knowledge one lacks but can acquire include the knowledge that was necessary for producing, legitimating and diffusing the knowledge acquired.

4.8 Non-knowledge about non-knowledge

The difference between knowledge and non-knowledge is an ancient European dichotomy whose lineage dates back to pre-modern cultures. The tradition is particularly manifest in the *attribution* of persons or groups to one of these two categories (see also Burke, 2000: 13). Those who are non-knowing or, more generally, the non-knowing stratum/class, are not only subjected, defenseless, to the power of other people's knowledge about prevailing conditions, but they are also stigmatized as a pitiful and backward social class (cf. Schiller, 1996). Inasmuch as non-knowledge is observed in one's relations to other societies and cultures, it is always the knowledge of these others that is non-knowledge – never one's own. Ludwik Fleck ([1935] 1979: 22) describes this fact as follows: "Whatever is known has always seemed systematic, proven, applicable, and evident to the knower. Every alien system of knowledge has likewise seemed contradictory, unproven, inapplicable, fanciful, or mystical."

With respect to the dilemma set out by Niklas Luhmann (1992: 154), however ("Is the commonly shared opinion still justified that more communication, more reflection, more knowledge, more learning, more participation – that more of all this would effect something good, or at any rate not something bad?"), the reflections set out above do not bring us any closer to a solution. This is the very dilemma the emergent political field of knowledge policies needs to dedicate itself to, as will be discussed in the next chapter (see also Stehr, 2003).

Before going into this, however, our résumé for the present topic of non-knowledge would be that we should reject the false dichotomy of knowledge and non-knowledge. There is only less or more knowledge but not non-knowledge. There are knowers who know something, and knowers who know something else. A person is not knowing *or* non-knowing. A person has *more* knowledge in one context and *less* knowledge in another. A person may know a great deal about tax regulations and next to nothing about golf. A functional social system is not non-knowing. The social differentiation between information and knowledge within a functional social system is a constitutive property of the system. The really interesting questions, therefore, are those concerning the *consequences for society* of the division of knowledge (cf. Dilley, 2010: 179–180). After all, a *bon mot* often attributed to Will Rogers says, "the trouble isn't what people don't know; it's what they know that isn't so."

Actors (including those in the sciences) respond to complex forms of society by devising simplifying mental constructs of them. These mental constructs are incomplete insofar as they fail to describe reality in its full complexity. These simple models change, they react to the unforeseen, but they are hardly something like non-knowledge. It is one of the constitutive virtues of liberal democracies to be aware that omniscience can be dangerous and that the protection of privacy must remain a sanctioned form of ignorance.

Notes

1 This chapter was translated from German by Hella Beister. Our discussion of non-knowledge has benefited from papers published, in a somewhat abridged version, in *Kursbuch* (Stehr, 2013b) and in the journal *Politik und Zeitgeschichte* (Stehr, 2013a).
2 Although Ulrich Beck ([1996] 1999: 109–110) and some of his colleagues frequently invoke the concept of "Nichtwissen" in their German writings, he clearly recognizes in an English translation of an originally German essay that it might be preferable not to translate Nichtwissen as "non-knowledge." The translation rather would be "*unawareness*," and the justification comes with the observation that "talk of a century of unintended consequences [in the context of a theory of reflexive modernization] cannot appeal to absolute, only to relative, unawareness *without contradicting itself*, and the interesting issue is the type of relativity" (our emphasis).
3 The German translations, chosen by Hayek, of key concepts of his essay – which was originally written in English – are of interest in this context and, as we see it, fully adequate: "the boundaries of his ignorance" and "man's unavoidable ignorance" (Hayek, 1960: 21) were translated as "Grenzen seines Unwissens" and "unvermeidliche Unkenntnis des Menschen." In other words, "*non-knowledge*" was not at issue.
4 It may in contrast be "reasonable," if hardly very productive, to ask *ontologically* whether there might be a dialectic relation of negation between knowledge and non-knowledge, mediating both phenomena in a new form that embraces both knowledge and non-knowledge; or whether there actually is nothing but a semantic duplication of the world in positive and negative terms, with each entity being assorted with a non-entity. However, is the non-entity not also something that exists, something that is present?
5 Nor do we believe that knowledge becomes non-knowledge *ex post facto*: it is not uncommon, in science, for the theories of eminent scientists to be subsequently falsified. Darwin or Einstein were the authors of theories that were later rejected by the scientific community (see Livio, 2013), but theories like these do not mutate to non-knowledge for all that. Rather, they often play a constructive role in the further development of scientific knowledge.
6 For the genealogy and the cultural or even biological relevance of opposites, see Ginzburg (1976).
7 This may even be more generally true – namely in the Enlightenment tradition – in view of the prevalent appraisal of ignorance as a negative, deficient phenomenon that must be overcome as a matter of principle.

8 As the contributions of natural scientists are in a minority in this discussion of non-knowledge, one is no doubt justified in saying that the phenomenon of non-knowledge is nothing to do with the concept of the "unknowable" in quantum physics (see Plotnitsky, 2002: 9–10, 98–99).
9 In an essay on the ignorance economy they had discovered, Roberts and Armitage (2008: 346) emphasize, for instance, that "the knowledge economy is necessarily engaged in the speedy obsolescence of knowledge and thus in the expansion of ignorance." The increasing division of intellectual labor "opens up areas of ignorance that can be exploited for commercial purposes" (ibid.: 347).
10 Drawing on Talcott Parsons's so-called pattern variables, Gernot Böhme (1992: 57) distinguishes between the following types of knowledge: "(1) personal or impersonal, (2) conservative or progressive, (3) diffuse or specific, (4) implicit or explicit, (5) particular or universal, and (6) empathetic or dominant."
11 For instance, is not the "right to non-knowledge" rather a right to be uninformed?
12 To name but a few of them: lack of knowledge, irrelevance, ignorance, the unknown, blind spots, error, cluelessness, uncertainty, the hidden, not-yet-knowledge, prejudice, etc.
13 Our aim here is not to call into question the longstanding research on the informative function of mass communication and, in particular, the journalistic production of information. This being said, the statements quoted above perfectly illustrate the typical conflation of concepts, which has serious consequences for theory. Moreover, communication research itself regularly highlights the low "recall" of media-provided content (cf. Gunter, 1987; Graber, 1988). Information is clearly more volatile than knowledge.
14 Peter Wehling (2009: 99) characterizes, for instance, the insufficient information, "Will the announced guest arrive at 5 pm or 6 pm?" as a case of "non-knowledge." This example is at best vague information, as we will show in more detail.
15 Cf. Walter B. Gallie's (1955–56) analysis of the properties and functions of *essentially controversial concepts* in the scientific discourse.
16 The differentiation, otherwise obvious, that distinct properties of knowledge cannot be assumed as self-evident refers to the often-invoked definition by Peter Berger and Thomas Luckmann (1969: 1) that knowledge relates to the taken-for-granted reality of everyday life (i.e. that in everyday social contexts, knowledge is "the certainty that phenomena are real and have determinable properties"), on the one hand; and that it is, therefore, "the task for the sociology of knowledge to analyze the social construction of reality" (ibid.: 3), on the other.
17 In the context of a definition of the concept of knowledge as a social phenomenon, the concept of social *performance* is also appropriate. For instance, patents incorporate knowledge and therefore "are a *performance*, in both their creation and subsequent enactions. They require skill, tacit/ embodied knowledge, and practice if they are to be successfully enacted" (Carolan, 2008: 295). In a similar vein, Barry Barnes (1995: 179) points out

that inasmuch as knowledge refers to social transactions, talking about knowledge is talking about persons.
18 Social theories that are based on individualistic premises, such as, for instance, Talcott Parsons's theory, favor individualistic theories of knowledge (see also Barnes, 1995: 94–95).
19 Interview with Erwin Chargaff, "Die wollen ewiges Leben, die wollen den Tod besiegen – das ist teuflisch" ("They want eternal life, they want to vanquish death – that's diabolical"), *Stern*, 47, November 2001.
20 Robert K. Merton ([1957] 1965: 345) describes and sizes up a society of unlimited transparency as a social formation where chaos would ensue: "[F]ull visibility of conduct and unrestrained enforcement of the letter of normative standard would convert a society into a jungle. It is this central idea which is contained in the concept that some limits upon full visibility of behavior are functionally required for the effective operation of a society." Against the backdrop of current developments in the process of digitizing and informationalizing society ("Big Data"), this warning gains renewed topicality (cf. Adolf, 2014). See also section 8.6 of this book.
21 Peter Burke (2000: 101–102, see also 15–17), for instance, describes the genealogy of economics and political science in his informative study on the societal history of knowledge.
22 A pertinent example can be found in Niels Brimnes (2004). Brimnes describes the conflicts of British colonial doctors who wanted to introduce a comprehensive anti-variola vaccination campaign in India and in the process attempted to deny the established practice of variolation its character of (culture-specific) knowledge.
23 Roy Dilley (2010: 176–177) describes the coupling of knowledge and ignorance, which he deems essential, by stressing that "[t]o talk of knowledge without recognition of the potential of ignorance is like speaking of velocity without a conception of distance [...] knowledge and ignorance must be regarded as mutually constituting, not simply in terms of an opposition by means of which one is seen as the negation of the other, but also in terms of how a dialectic between knowledge and ignorance is played out in specific sets of social and political relations; indeed, how, too, moral value is placed upon knowledge and ignorance in various ways."
24 Philip Kitcher (2010) works out different forms of ignorance in persons: with a particular view to scientific knowledge, he distinguishes between a mild degree of ignorance, a "directly remediable ignorance," an "indirectly remediable ignorance" and an "irremediable ignorance," the latter relating to persons who not only lack the capacity of acquiring elementary knowledge in a relevant scientific domain but also a well-founded power of judgment that would enable them to question the judgment of experts. Kitcher (2010: 41) further argues that the latter state of irremediable ignorance may grow into hostile resistance to and alienation from expertise.
25 Daniel Dennett is also interested in an historicization of ignorance but differs from Hayek in the conclusion he draws. Moreover, Dennett (1986: 144) considers ignorance in relation to virtuousness: "Our ancestors [...]

were [...] *capable* of living lives of virtue – of a virtue that depended on unavoidable ignorance. Modern technology has robbed us of the sorts of virtue that depend on such ignorance, for ignorance is all too avoidable today. Information technology has multiplied our opportunities to know, and our traditional ethical doctrines overwhelm us by turning these opportunities into newfound obligations to know" (Dennett, 1986: 144; cf. also Jean-Jacques Rousseau's praise of ignorance in his *Discours sur les sciences et les arts*, as well as Leo Strauss's [1947] interpretation of Rousseau).

26 In an essay on the economics of knowledge and the knowledge of economics, Kenneth Boulding (1966: 1) points out that the notion of ignorance is an essentially controversial term: "It may mean that people have no image at all of something where an image is possible, or it may mean that they have images which are false or untrue."

27 See Tim Adams, "The new age of ignorance," *The Observer*, July 1, 2007. Diagnoses of society of this provenience usually go hand in hand with a lament about an exponential growth of the volume of existent information and the individual's incapacity to "process" them (e.g. Lukasiewicz, 1993; 122). From this it follows that ignorance, in this sense, is seen as a deficit that needs to be filled: "Ignorance is most commonly seen [...] as something in need of correction, a kind of natural absence or void where knowledge has not yet spread" (Proctor and Schiebinger, 2008: 2).

28 In his description of open research fields Robert Merton (e.g. 1981: v–vi) quite deliberately refers to Kuhn's concept, virulent at the time, of paradigms as a research field where both open and closed research topics are at least temporarily involved.

29 The conduct of both the Royal Caribbean International and the passengers of their ship in 2010, right after the Haiti earthquake, clearly shows, as Linsey McGoey (2012: 2–3) notes, that this incident, rather than an issue in terms of a politics of knowledge, is a problem of a "politics of ignorance, [...] the mobilization of ambiguity, the denial of unsettling facts, the realization that knowing the least amount possible is often the most indispensable tool for managing risks and exonerating oneself from blame in the aftermath of catastrophic events." McGoey (2012: 4 and 13) points out that the description of the social role of ignorance clearly shows that "[i]gnorance *is* knowledge [...] knowledge and ignorance exist on an ever-changing continuum."

30 Ernst Helmstädter (2000a: 123) describes the analogy between the division of labor and the division of knowledge as follows: "The division of labor boosts the productivity of labor and the division of knowledge promotes the use of existing and the generation of new knowledge as well as its profitable implementation in economic practice."

31 Economists treat imperfect or asymmetric information as an *externality* (where someone is informed about something relevant to a market transaction that the other is not aware of; cf. Stiglitz, 2012: 32–34) that "distorts" efficient market outcomes.

32 "Lemons" in this context signify severely flawed products.

33 The question of the ethics of using accidentally obtained information was also discussed in an article in one of the more recent numbers of *The New York Times* (April 1, 2015, "Can I profit from accidentally obtained information?").
34 In their empirical study, Pablo Kurlat and Johannes Stroebel (2014: 35) highlight the relevance, for the market, of asymmetric information held by buyers and sellers in housing markets. Their findings show that "home owners have superior information about important neighborhood characteristics, and exploit those to time local market movements." Alex Chinco and Christopher Mayer (2014) show that real estate bubbles in cities may become even more inflated due to the asymmetric information of buyers (strangers) and sellers (locals).
35 In an experimental study on incomplete information in electricity rate payers, Katrina Jessoe and David Rapson (2014) show that even a small amount of low-cost information, for instance on variations in prices, that is made available to clients at frequent intervals will sway consumers' market behavior.
36 Elsewhere, Georg Simmel ([1922] 2009: 308) notes: "Because one can never know another *absolutely* – which would mean the knowledge of every individual thought and every attitude – because one forms for oneself in fact a personal unity of the other from the fragments in which the other is solely available to us, then the latter depends on that part of the other that our standpoint vis-à-vis the other allows us to see."

5
POLICING KNOWLEDGE

It is undoubtedly the case that the knowledge communicated by the scientific community to the public is rarely acknowledged to be problematic, partial, contingent, uncertain or conflicting. If knowledge is *not* contingent, then attempts to police knowledge – that is, restrict access to it, regulate its use or even outlaw its application (restrictive knowledge politics) – are bound to be futile. The restriction of the use of and access to knowledge occurs in one of many ways, including cultural taboos, but the main modern "weapons" are restrictions such as granting patents to additional knowledge, copyright limitations, secrecy provisions or property rights. However, we will not focus on these "conventional" ways of policing knowledge; instead, we focus on what are allegedly "iron" features that knowledge acquires in the course of its genesis or of social processes that ensure that most, if not all, attempts to police knowledge are redundant because of knowledge's almost automatic practical realization, or unnecessary because knowledge tends to protect itself.

Similarly, if a social collectivity *treats* knowledge *in toto* as a pure public or collective good, which means that its enjoyment cannot be denied to anyone, or that its use is open to all *insiders* (assuming that there are legitimate ways of excluding outsiders), it would only be *logical* to infer that knowledge politics would be unnecessary or not required (see Cerny, 1999: 95–102). Indeed, the discussion about public goods is often dominated by neo-classical economic discourse and commercial interests (see Ostrom and Ostrom, 1977). In this instance, arguments are advanced that justify regulations designed to ensure that information or knowledge mimics the commodity features of tangible goods. From a normative or political point of view, public goods are those that citizens and their representative institutions believe *ought* to be treated as collective property. As a matter of fact, however, knowledge has not only properties that resemble public goods but also attributes that ally it to commodities with the rivalry and excludability of typical economic goods.

In the following sections, we will therefore focus on various attributes of knowledge, information and technology that appear to deny *a priori* that knowledge and technological artifacts *can be* or, for that matter, *need to be* controlled. Any discussion of the emergence of efforts to police knowledge, for whatever reasons, in modern societies is based on one fundamental premise. The possibility of the control of knowledge relies, aside from allowing for the difference between knowledge and action, on the notion that evolving knowledge cannot automatically realize itself, is not self-protecting, and can only be exploited by the powerful in society, especially those actors who control large rationalized organizations. The anxieties that find expression in the formula that the economic (and other) fruits of science and technology almost automatically benefit only rich and powerful individuals and corporate actors in society also hint at another concern: namely, that we are witnessing a growing concentration of the ownership of the right to knowledge, and therefore a switch in the nature of knowledge from a "public good" to a private resource.

Knowledge politics in general, not only in the restrictive sense, require the ability to limit or enlarge the opportunities for the use of knowledge as a capacity for action. However, if one is persuaded that the realization of knowledge is guaranteed in principle, or perhaps is even inevitable because such a "fate" is part and parcel of emergent, additional knowledge, then the notion of knowledge politics makes no sense whatsoever. The only meaningful response to knowledge as a capacity for action that knows no limits is adaptation to the social, economic and political consequences that knowledge invariably produces. A second perspective, which rules out the need to control incremental knowledge, would be directly related to the assertion that knowledge and information are largely *self-protecting*. The third view, which denies the possibility of knowledge politics, relies on the underlying assumption that the use of knowledge invariably benefits the powerful and sustains the status quo in society.

5.1 The self-realization of knowledge

As far as we can see, there are two basic pathways, one immediate and the other indirect, that lead to the expectation that knowledge – quite independent of the context – cannot really be stopped from realizing itself. The immediate trajectory that invariably assures the realization of knowledge, and therefore defeats any efforts to control it, is seen as being built right into the very structure of knowledge itself. In other words, there is an essential, necessary coupling of theory and practice that already occurs, or is added, in the production process of knowledge itself. The fabrication of knowledge implies its realization. The less immediate route to the self-realization of knowledge points to the possibility, as Brave (2001: 3) does with respect to new genetic knowledge, that "no matter what roadblocks might be placed in the way, the human genome is now and forever in our midst, and its manipulation will be difficult to simply prohibit. Neither the relatively small-scale technology required nor the individual or societal belief in biological benefits will be easily reined in by a regulatory body." Thus, as Richard Dawkins[1] argues in this context, the discovery of the code of the human genome ought to be considered a triumph of the human spirit, and as the benefits of the genome project will become increasingly evident during our lifetimes (which will be extended), the practicalities of the genome persuasively speak for themselves. Any calls for a social regulation of the genome knowledge are likely to be viewed with suspicion.

In the case of technical artifacts, a species of determinist logic prevails in the imagery of technological developments that ensure from the beginning that the technological objects have a built-in destiny (i.e. technical necessity) that disallows ambiguous, or even alternative, paths of elaboration and therefore any "interpretative flexibility" (Pinch and Bijker, 1984: 419–424) of technical objects. Among the major arguments in favor of the view that discovery already implies its practical use are:

First, the fact that science is pursued in a self-realizing fashion is evident, for example, from the once widely discussed notion of different knowledge-guiding *interests* that prevail in science (Habermas, 1964). The different, quasi-transcendental knowledge-constitutive interests are anchored in the nature of the human species. From the beginning, we are engaged in the dual project of relating to our fellow human beings (social interaction) and providing for the physical necessities of life (work). The category of a *technical knowledge-guiding interest* – aside from the *practical* and the *emancipatory* (and literally innate) cognitive interests scientists pursue – suggests that it constitutes a form of knowledge that literally has a built-in urge to be applied, namely as knowledge that is useful or instrumental in practice. At least our interpretation of Habermas's ([1965] 1971: 309) own characterization of the nature of the technical knowledge-guiding interest leaves no other conclusion: "Theories of the empirical science disclose reality subject to the constitutive interest in the securing and expansion, through information, of feedback-monitored action. This is the cognitive interest in technical control over objectified processes." No other kind of (natural) science and technology is possible.[2] The boundaries between theory and practice disappear. The "decisions" made in the course of the development of technical devices are hidden, and as long as they remain invisible, the image of a technologically constrained and determined social order – for example, in the sphere of production – is projected and justified.

Knowledge generated under the auspices of a particular knowledge-guiding interest remains, of course, hostage to that interest and to the ways in which alone it can be realized. A kind of self-reinforcing spiral is set in motion: The rationalization of social contexts with the help of knowledge claims constituted on the basis of a technical interest lead, according to this perspective, to an increasing neutralization of social action, and thereby an increase in the demand for knowledge produced as the result of instrumental knowledge-guiding interests. In the end, society resembles a laboratory or a technical state.

The idea that knowledge is invariably pushed toward practical implementation is certainly a time-honored conception, and not merely an invention of the postwar era. The premise that knowledge carries within itself a kind of built-in pressure toward utilization is encountered in efforts to *legitimate* the very enterprise of science. Karl Dunkmann (1926: 7), for example, refers to the legitimation of *applied* sociology in the following terms: "It is impossible to point to theoretical research that is *solely* carried out on its own terms and that does not at the same time imply its own practical realization. As a matter of fact, one can go one step further and suggest that all theory originates with the motive of achieving some practical end" (see also Lynd, 1939: ix). Theory and practice are "now fused in the very heart of science itself, so that the ancient alibi of pure theory and with it the moral immunity it provided no longer hold" (Jonas, [1976] 1979: 35).

The philosopher Hans Jonas justifies the case for the fusion of theoretical and practical knowledge on the following grounds: 1 much of scientific knowledge now "lives" on the intellectual feedback it receives from its technological application; 2 the impetus for research stems from practical problems that need to be solved; 3 science uses advanced technology to generate new knowledge – the interlocking of technology and science is symmetrical; and 4 the costs of the science infrastructure must be underwritten by external sources that expect a return on their investment.

In sum, these arguments over the necessary fusion of theoretical and practical knowledge imply that any effort by civil society, the state or corporations to control and regulate knowledge becomes impossible once scientific discoveries have been made. It does not matter much whether new scientific knowledge proves irresistible to the marketplace or some other interests; the built-in utility of knowledge ensures that what can be shown, will be done.

Second, a less immediate trajectory, centering not on epistemological or methodological considerations or endogenous attributes of knowledge itself, and implying that attempts to police knowledge are bound to be futile, refers to social, economic or cultural processes or exogenous reasons that ensure the realization of knowledge despite resistance. For example, as one observer relates, "this is an age of consumption – if it can be bought, it will be" (Appleyard, 1998: 10).

We will focus initially on a number of assertions that center attention on what are seen as necessary, even inevitable, trajectories leading from the production of knowledge to its implementation. Assertions that knowledge will realize itself through a kind of automaticity are by no means indistinct, marginal reflections on the future role of knowledge in society. Therefore, reference is made to the peculiar powers of knowledge itself, due to its fruits realized in practice, which exempt it from regulation: Not only is the enlargement of knowledge boundless, but the application of the "knowledge explosion," too, has no apparent limits.[3] Part of those considerations that imply the almost automatic practical realization are prospective, utopian views of the future of modern society.

For example, Edward O. Wilson (1975: 574–575) was one of the first contemporary scholars who expected, well before the fall of the Soviet Empire, an end to history. Dramatic knowledge advances, designed to ensure the survival of humankind, are paradoxically bound to destroy that which has been demystified. Wilson closes his lengthy and controversial treatise on sociobiology with a few guardedly ambivalent thoughts about the future. He speculates about the completion of social evolution, probably by the end of the twentieth century.[4] By that time, humankind will have achieved an ecologically steady state, and the "internalization of social evolution" will be accomplished.

What does he mean? Reference is made to rapid intellectual advances, a kind of knowledge explosion in biology and sociology. However, the state of affairs Wilson (1975: 575) has in mind is by no means restricted to a perfection of the sciences. He envisions the evolution of a "planned society, the creation of which seems inevitable in the coming century." In the planned society, as far as we can see, the contribution of evolutionary biology offers not only the foundations for monitoring the genetic basis of social behavior, but also for the deliberate intervention in the gene pool of humankind to *steer* the world's population past "those stresses and conflicts that once gave the destructive phenotypes [aggression, dominance, violence] their Darwinian edge," in which case "the other phenotypes [cooperativeness, creativity] might dwindle with them." And in this "ultimate genetic sense, social control would rob man of his humanity" (Wilson, 1975: 575). The "evolution" of knowledge achieves a kind of solipsistic "completion," according to Wilson, since the new neurobiology that yields enduring first principles for sociology offers us, at the same time, efficient ways of intervening in our "cognitive machinery."

More specifically, social evolution is complete and, as Wilson maintains, has to be consummated by applying the advances of our knowledge to ourselves. The principle of natural selection becomes social selection. There is little ambiguity in his scenario. As Wilson (1975: 575) stresses, the results might be difficult to accept, but "to maintain the species indefinitely we are compelled to drive toward total knowledge, right down to the levels of the neuron and gene" (cf. Keller, 1992). Human agency is empowered to eliminate humanity, and under such utopian – or rather dystopian – circumstances it hardly makes sense to discuss the notion of knowledge politics.

Another perspective that might also be counted among the string of views that argue for a kind of automaticity in the realization of knowledge concerns speculations about the disappearance of any significant time-lag between processes of fabricating knowledge and its practical implementation. More specifically, interpretation and transformation of reality literally merge, denying that the famous Marxian metaphor about the need to change rather than merely interpret the world is still meaningful and applicable in the modern world. Francis Fukuyama's observations about the end of history resonate with similar notions: If history does not repeat itself, and if there is, as a result, a singular directionality to social evolution, then there must be a universal mechanism that accomplishes this goal. For Fukuyama (1992: 72), the only mechanism among the range of human endeavors that could ensure such directionality is modern, cumulative natural science: "Scientific knowledge has been accumulating for a very long period, and has had a consistent if frequently unperceived effect in shaping the fundamental character of human societies." In such a setting, the unfolding and realization of modern natural science occurs driven by an automatic, irrepressible process.

5.2 The self-protection of knowledge

The fundamental theoretical breakthrough in the economics of information (and knowledge) can be traced to the "recognition that information was fundamentally different from other 'commodities'" (Stiglitz,

2000b: 1448). Economists therefore have been concerned with the issue of the difficulties of appropriating as private profits any of the direct and indirect (social) benefits that the inventor and disseminator of knowledge generates, because knowledge is not consumed by its use and may be transmitted almost without cost. Kenneth Arrow (1962a: 614–615) alludes to the now conventional economic perspective of the fragile nature of the value of knowledge and information by emphasizing that "the cost of transmitting a given body of information is frequently very low [...] In the absence of special legal protection, the owner cannot, however, simply sell information on the open market. Any one purchaser can destroy the monopoly, since he can reproduce the information at little or no cost." We will set aside the questionable conflation of information and knowledge already discussed; instead, we refer to features of knowledge that are absent from neo-classical economic discourse concerned with knowledge as a commodity but protect knowledge without instituting special devices of protection.

One feature of knowledge that tends to protect it from being easily appropriated and disseminated in market transactions, or actually from being stolen, pertains to the issue of the *divisibility* of knowledge in distinction to the presence of this attribute of ordinary commodities involved in economic exchange and legal considerations. In contrast to money, for example, knowledge is akin to goods that are not divisible. Conflicts involving non-divisible goods have the character of either/or conflicts that are difficult to solve. Divisible goods more or less imply conflicts that tend to be solved more easily (Hirschman, 1994: 213). Non-divisible goods, moreover, are very difficult to distribute; for example, according to the principle of equality. Equal distribution is extremely difficult to achieve, not only because knowledge cannot be dismantled into an infinite number of pieces, but also because every transaction that has as its goal a more equal distribution demands both time and preconditions that cannot simply be provided by decree. A significant range of knowledge therefore enjoys a measure of built-in protection.[5] The idea of knowledge as self-protecting indicates also that the frame often employed by economists in their analysis of commodities as exclusive and non-rival phenomena has to be extended to *social contexts*, such as market transactions or firms in which knowledge is embodied.

Fabricating additional knowledge and enjoying the economic advantages that flow from such knowledge is, of course, a stratified and contingent process. Within technological regimes, techno-economic networks (cf. Freeman, 1991; Callon, 1992), or theoretical "paradigms," the advantage goes to those who command incremental knowledge. Technological regimes or paradigms may be embedded within a company, or in a network of firms, research institutes, etc. In analogy to Robert Merton's (1968) observations about the operation of the Matthew principle, that is, the process of accumulating reputation and prestige in science depending on the amount of symbolic capital already acquired, it is possible to stipulate a similar principle for the stratification of incremental knowledge.

Additional knowledge is most likely obtained by those who are able to benefit from what they already know. Both the notion of knowledge as a productive force ("input") and tacit knowledge further testify to the idea that knowledge (or information) is, under most circumstances, easy to transmit and reproduce. The competitive advantages that may accrue to individuals or firms that generate and manage to control incremental knowledge are limited. As Starbuck (1992: 716) stresses, it is "exceptional and valuable expertise," not the possession of knowledge per se, that is constitutive of successful knowledge-intensive firms. Such companies must continuously strive to stay ahead in the fabrication of knowledge: "Once they are imitated and their outputs standardized, then there are downward wage and employment pressures" (Storper, 1996: 257; also Donaldson, 2001), as well as a decline in profitability.

In addition, the material base in which knowledge or information is inscribed, and which restricts the non-competitive consumption or non-excludability of knowledge, affects the kinds of possible relations and transactions involving knowledge/information. For economists, the attributes of non-rivalrous consumption and non-excludability of knowledge/information are critical features of knowledge. Such attributes of knowledge make it a prototypical example of an (even global) public good (Samuelson, 1954). If at least some of the profits of knowledge can be appropriated, using trade secrets or patents, for example, it becomes an *impure* public good. Given these special characteristics of knowledge, the World Bank (1999: 17) reiterates the conventional premise of neo-classical economic discourse that "public action is sometimes required to provide the right incentive for its creation and dissemination by the private sector, as well as to directly create and disseminate knowledge when the market fails to provide enough." In contrast to the dominant economic justification for ways of fencing in knowledge, the idea that knowledge (or information) is self-protecting in yet another sense summons a very different perspective on knowledge and efforts to police knowledge. The idea that knowledge is self-protecting involves a supply and demand side argument, as Kitch (1980: 711–715) outlines. On the *supply* side, the point would be that knowledge is difficult to steal, or that no one has an interest in stealing knowledge because it is difficult to profit from stolen knowledge. That knowledge is difficult to transmit should be familiar to a teacher, for example, whose students fail to grasp most of what has been taught, or to an author who has the suspicion that his readers do not comprehend his argument.

The most common notion that knowledge does not travel well is, of course, the notion of the "tacitness" of knowledge properties, as first explicated by Michael Polanyi (1958, 1967). The "stickiness" of information/knowledge (von Hippel, 1994) is related to the ways in which knowledge is organized: "Managers can avoid increasing the ease with which information can be transmitted by resisting the temptation to assemble the information in organized written form" (Kitch, 1980: 712). On the supply side, the self-protection of knowledge would also be associated with the extent to which the command of *scarce cognitive competencies* is required for the appropriation of knowledge, the extent to which knowledge is *embedded* in specific socio-technical contexts or knowledge infrastructures (such as the ability to learn how to learn; see Stiglitz, 1987) that are not freely mobile or easily reconstituted; or the ability to mobilize capacities to effectively generate *access* to desired knowledge.

On the *demand* side, self-protective features of knowledge are related to a high depreciation rate, which means that knowledge, once it is acquired, has become worthless in relation to the cost of acquisition and to future benefits that may be derived from such knowledge. Moreover, in the case of some forms of knowledge, at least, the proprietary nature of such knowledge, not unlike a famous painting, can be easily identified by others and is therefore worthless except to its lawful owner. The exigencies that make it difficult to steal knowledge also protect it from unlawful distribution, since the thief may have difficulty establishing the necessary competence to offer any credible warranty of its efficacy and authenticity. Finally, the value of knowledge is related to its scarcity. Any dissemination or anticipation of dissemination of knowledge may reduce its value and therefore deter the incentive to obtain such knowledge. Such a depreciation of the value of knowledge occurs with greater likelihood among actors who compete in the same market or context. One can accelerate the depreciation of knowledge and information if one acts according to it and encourages others to do so. In short, a high depreciation rate means, "by the time someone steals the information it is worthless which in turn means there is no incentive to steal it" (Kitch, 1980: 714).

The sum of the exigencies enumerated amount to self-protecting attributes of knowledge, indicating that knowledge is embedded in a "network" of cultural and structural attributes that affect the ease of its mobility and migration. The idea that knowledge is self-protecting, or can be "serviced" or protected in such a fashion that travel is bound to be difficult (e.g. avoiding its organization in written form), has implications for the very project of formulating knowledge policies. If a stringent case can be made for the existence of significant self-protecting features of knowledge, then restrictive knowledge policies would not have to be put in place, since the more or less unencumbered dissemination of knowledge is unlikely.

However, rising voices, especially in the developing world, which see efforts by Western commercial interests to appropriate (traditional) public knowledge for private gain as a form of the theft of such knowledge would obviously oppose the notion that knowledge cannot be stolen and cannot be privatized easily. Vandana Shiva (2001: 284–285), for example, defines "biopiracy" as "based on a false claim of creativity. It involves the appropriation of the cumulative, collective creativity of traditional societies and projects the theft as an 'innovation'." The appropriation and translation of public knowledge in traditional societies into forms of knowledge protected by patents signals that knowledge – although, in this case, devalued by treating it as a form of indigenous or even invisible knowledge – can move, can be transported into different social contexts while the original context is unable to protect its migration.

5.3 Superfluous knowledge

In the context of a discussion of the protection of knowledge there is another, although very different, consideration that also expresses doubt about the need to exercise restrictive knowledge politics. Knowledge as a resource cannot be depleted (Max Weber's ideas can be used over and over again without being used up, as is the case for a scarce resource). Knowledge is therefore not subject to Garrett Hardin's (1968) famous "tragedy of the commons" – but it may become *superfluous*.

We are referring to the probability that knowledge becomes redundant as it is replaced by knowledge that supersedes earlier capacities to act and practices (cf. Schumann, 2003). The volume of available knowledge already consists of many forms of knowledge that have become obsolete in light of more effective forms of knowledge; for example, in the fields of transportation or medicine. Indeed, it is noteworthy how quickly intensively discussed and highly contested debates over efforts to police particular knowledge claims can recede into the background or disappear from public attention altogether. Such a change in the visibility of an issue may be the result of many factors, including successful regulatory politics, which remove the matter from the agenda, or the ability of proponents of the use of specific knowledge and techniques to persuade opponents that their fears about the impact are misplaced. For example, Susan Wright (1986) describes the emergence of a consensus among molecular biologists in the 1970s on minimal potential hazards of recombinant DNA technology. The organized defense of recombinant DNA work by molecular biologists contributed much to appease both the government and the public, and was instrumental in avoiding external regulation.

While the obsolescence of knowledge would not by definition require any further intervention in order to regulate and control its use, a kind of passive knowledge politics, which relies on the likelihood that knowledge is bound to become obsolete, is hardly an effective form of knowledge politics. In addition, one might anticipate a kind of planned obsolescence of knowledge, accomplished by way of agreements or social arrangements that voluntarily or by law rule out the utilization of specific capacities to act; for example, an agreement that outlaws the use of certain weapons in warfare. However, a planned strategy employed to ensure that knowledge becomes unnecessary represents only another definition of knowledge politics. Reliance on the inevitable "death" of knowledge is hardly a strategy that suggests itself in an era in which the political and economic ramifications of novel capacities to act are enormous.

Our discussion of the nature of knowledge as a capacity to act, and of knowledge as a self-realizing or self-protecting phenomenon, obviously has varied implications for the governance of knowledge. The discussion raises the general question of the importance of intellectual content and the institutional factors involved in the realization of knowledge, and therefore the possibility, and possible methods, of regulating knowledge in society. In a way, this question renews the much-reiterated issue of the power of ideas, and of what exactly accounts for the power of ideas.

Notes

1 Richard Dawkins, "The word made flesh," *The Guardian*, December 27, 2001.
2 As Jürgen Habermas ([1968] 1970: 87) explains, "technological development [...] follows a logic that corresponds to the structure of purposive-rational action regulated by its own results, which is in fact the structure of *work*. Realizing this, it is impossible to envisage how, as long as the organization of human nature does not change and as long as therefore we have to achieve self-preservation through social labor and with the aid of means that substitute for work, we could renounce technology, more particularly *our* technology, in favor of a qualitatively different one."
3 Compare the much more skeptical and hesitant stance that Georg Simmel ([1911/12] 1968: 44) takes toward the knowledge explosion or the incessant enlargement of the objective culture: "The infinitely growing supply of objectified spirit places demands before the subject, creates desires in him, throws him into total relationships from whose impact he cannot withdraw, although he cannot master their principal content. Thus, the typically problematic situation of modern man comes into being: his sense of being surrounded by an innumerable number of cultural elements which are neither meaningless to him nor, in the final analysis, meaningful. In their mass they depress him, since he is not capable of assimilating them all, nor can he simply reject them, since after all, they do belong *potentially* within the sphere of his cultural development."

4 For an analysis of the elective borrowing and blending of the rhetoric of sociobiology and its semantic relations to population genetics, molecular genetics and biometrical genetics, see Howe and Lyne, 1992.
5 Georg Simmel ([1900] 1907: 439–440) must have had in mind the fragile relations between principles of justice and the distribution of knowledge when he stressed that "the apparent equality with which educational materials are available to everyone interested in them is, in reality, a sheer mockery. The same is true for other freedoms accorded by liberal doctrines which, though they certainly do not hamper the individual from gaining goods of any kind, do however disregard the fact that only those already privileged in some way or another have the possibility of acquiring them. For just as the substance of education – in spite of, or because of its general availability – can ultimately be acquired only through individual activity, so it gives rise to the most intangible and thus the most unassailable aristocracy, to a distinction between high and low which can be abolished neither (as can socio-economic differences) by a decree or a revolution, nor by the good will of those concerned."

6

FORMS OF KNOWLEDGE

The British historian Eric Hobsbawm (1996 [1994]: 534) once made the observation that "[s]ome time during the Age of the Empire [1875–1914] the links had snapped between the findings of scientists and the reality based on, or imaginable by sense experience; and so did the links between science and the sort of logic based on, or imaginable by common sense." Hobsbawm's dating of the origins of the break between what may be part of ordinary sense experience and what is *not* accessible to ordinary sense experience, as well as what is imaginable by the logic governing common sense and science, vividly reminds us that categories of knowledge are socio-historical constructs.

One of the most prominent distinctions among forms of knowledge and probably the most frequent one in use is the demarcation between scientific and everyday knowledge. Most often this distinction is based on epistemological considerations. Knowledge produced through scientific research is not only of superior quality, closer or conforming to reality, lacking irrational qualities, and truer than everyday knowledge, but it is much more efficient in practice as the success of technology, based on scientific knowledge, is seen to objectively demonstrate.

In the meantime, the dichotomy between everyday and scientific knowledge has become taken for granted; as a result, non-scientific knowledge is at best a residual category. This has the consequence that the social sciences have hardly dealt systematically with the peculiarities and the status of everyday knowledge,[1] especially as, at least in the context of classical sociological theories of society, the assumption prevails that traditional and conventional forms of knowledge will sooner or later be displaced by scientific forms of knowledge.

The premise of such a widely held view among social scientists, past and, to a lesser extent, present, is, as Peter Weingart (1983: 228) perceptively points out, that our primary means of action orientation are being replaced "in more and more spheres of life, by the production and application of systematic knowledge," and that this process of replacement occurs as different aspects of life become successively the object of scientific scrutiny. Concretely, the displacement in dominant forms of knowledge implies that, on the basis of scientific knowledge, "different frames of reference and modes of attribution are established for social action and/or existing orientations are proven to be irrational or erroneous with respect to accepted purposes." The result is, according to Weingart, that "reflective reasoning, in light of competing components of systematic knowledge, takes the place of the internalization – on which its taken for granted status depends in the first place – of norms and values."

6.1 Everyday knowledge

As indicated, the differentiation between common sense or everyday knowledge and expert or scientific knowledge is typically thought to be asymmetrical, that is, the relations between these types of knowledge are described, as noted by Gernot Böhme (1992: 56), in terms of the *dominance* of scientific knowledge in modern society. The flow of influence can therefore only be unidirectional.

Max Weber ([1920] 1978: 11–12) stresses that rationalization processes take place in all societies and cultures and at all times, and that the rationalization of occidental cultures, or modern rationalization, occurs in response to the societal power of science and technology. Max Weber's views about the vital omnipotence of modern science can be found in the "*Zwischenbetrachtung*" in his *Gesammelte Aufsätze zur Religionssoziologie* (Weber, [1920] 1978: 564). Although he emphasizes that there is a distinctive limit to the societal influence of scientific knowledge, since modern science is incapable of offering any advice and insight into the meaning of the world, he also argues that despite this limit to the power of science, the basic attributes of modern nomological knowledge unquestionably imply that humanity "by means of calculation – in principle – can *dominate* all things" (Weber, [1919] 1922b: 139) and that such power and calculability therefore are not limited in principle. For Parsons (1937: 752), Weber's work culminates precisely in his "conception of a law of increasing rationality as a fundamental generalization about systems of action."

Emile Durkheim's discussion, in *The Elementary Forms of Religious Life*, of the conflict or reciprocal relations between science and religion, proceeds from the premise that science will displace religion, although Durkheim ([1912] 1965: 477–480) is prepared to grant a continual, if limited, role to religious knowledge in modern society. Of course, not all sociological classics assign to science such an uncontested function in the structure and culture of modern society. Vilfredo Pareto celebrates the societal function of illogicality (as a capacity for action), though he attempts to do so on the basis of strictly logical reasoning. In spite of such exceptions, an overwhelming majority of the classical social scientists anticipate with either fear or disillusionment an age of science and technology and an increasing rationalization of irrational forces.

Everyday knowledge that resonates with such terms as local and indigenous forms of knowledge is thought to be widely dispersed throughout particular societal contexts and extends to all routine activities of everyday life such as simple business transactions and familiarity with the ways of the natural environment and the "otherworldly" sphere. Everyday knowledge is frequently seen as superficial, if not unreflective and often false. Given these enormous deficiencies, one must of course wonder why common sense knowledge has not been radically displaced but has managed to survive in modern societies. In response, we do not want to dispense with the difference between everyday and scientific knowledge altogether (see Shapin, 2001), but ask what social functions common sense knowledge performs that ensure its "survival."

Whether there is in fact, as these observations would indicate, a kind of linear relation between common sense and scientific knowledge is an open question. Russell Hardin's (2002) concept of street-level epistemology — that is, a theory of knowledge of the ordinary person — indicates that the relation between scientific knowledge with its own distinctive epistemology and everyday knowledge may be non-linear. A theory of the knowledge of the ordinary person stresses unique attributes of such forms of (personal) knowledge as, for example, its messy and disorganized structure, its focus on the knower rather than on what is known, and its inefficacy in meeting standard philosophy of science criteria for its justification. Hardin (2002: 214) suggests that "street-level epistemology is not about what counts as knowledge in, say physics, but rather about what counts as your knowledge, my knowledge, the ordinary person's knowledge."

Nonetheless, one can hardly dispute the observation, even as scientific knowledge today is increasingly perceived as fragile and lacking closure and is often highly contested — and therefore is without some of its once taken-for-granted forceful, reliable and robust attributes — that everyday knowledge is increasingly influenced by scientific knowledge. Everyday knowledge has become robustly implicated in forms of scientific knowledge in the sense of a "scientification" of common sense knowledge. If this indeed is the case, it becomes more difficult, if not impossible, to distinguish reliably between the realities of scientific and non-scientific knowledge.

However, everyday or common sense knowledge continues to be made up of forms of knowledge that have to some extent at least resisted the process of scientification. It is therefore of particular interest to attend to some of these forms of common sense knowledge, especially those considered by many observers to be errors, irritations or manifestations of superstition, yet widely traveled in everyday life, in order to specify why such forms of knowledge have resisted displacement by more rational forms of knowledge.

As some observers will note, "harmless" but also widespread cognitive mindsets in modern society include superstition, occultism, belief in miracles, or the general conviction of the influence of supernatural events of all kinds on everyday life and on the course of individual lives. In developed countries most newspapers carry a daily astrology column. The success of fundamentalism, the survival of the Hutterites or the Amish, traditional explanations of natural events such as birth, illness, diet, death, weather patterns, natural catastrophes and all other recurring situations and processes of everyday life, strongly indicate that traditional knowledge is not pushed to the margins of modern society, let alone in danger of imminent extinction.

On the contrary, the distribution and relevance of "unconventional" knowledge has been underestimated by the scientific community, in the social sciences in particular, as the lack of empirical work in this area would indicate. Systematic studies designed to map the distribution and function of traditional knowledge in developed societies are virtually non-existent, but such neglect is understandable in light of the fact that everyday knowledge is, at best, considered a residual category in most theoretical schemata[2] and lives a most precarious existence in the scientific community. What we do have are episodic analyses, such as studies among US university students indicating that almost half of those interviewed reject the biological-evolutionary account of the origin of the species and the universe (cf. Almquist and Cronin, 1988). Characteristically, however, these results are used by the authors as an appropriate occasion to issue dire warnings about the lack of rational thought among "enlightened" segments of the population and to speculate about the reasons for such cognitive "backwardness."

Even more widespread in everyday life is a relatively transitory, perhaps "trivial" knowledge, bound closely to particular actors and situations. The knowledge John may have about his pet, for example, and the unique patterns of behavior he claims to have observed, is of little relevance to anyone else. This contrasts with everyday knowledge that is fairly widely shared and is of considerable social relevance, such as, for instance, everyday accounts of social inequality, deviant behavior or conceptions about other cultures. That such knowledge continues to be of importance in everyday life often goes unrecognized, especially in the scientific discourse about knowledge. The typical assumption made is that such knowledge is somehow defective and continues to lose its pertinence to social action. Less trivial, but equally widespread are strong, even vicious prejudices with regard to ethnic, class, national, religious, generational and gender divisions in modern societies. The once widespread optimism of social scientists who promised the imminent end of prejudices by way of an application of social scientific knowledge (e.g. Allport, 1958) has been replaced today by skepticism, even fatalism about the possibility of eradicating forms of prejudice, soon.

The question remains: What are the social and cognitive features of scientific knowledge that could account for the persistent presence of traditional knowledge in modern society? We therefore propose to examine the question of the systemic conditions for the apparent limits of the social power of scientific knowledge, insofar as these limits are attributes of scientific forms of knowledge. At the same time, one must consider the complementary question of the social conditions that may be associated with the apparent "survival" of traditional means of orientation manifest, for example, in the resistance shown in everyday life to scientific knowledge and technical artifacts.

We are not, however, concerned with allegedly inevitable or even "natural" limits of the power of scientific knowledge – for example, limits that are attributed to the *nature* of human behavior as such and might be considered an outcome of evolutionary processes that favor superstition and error (see Foster and Kokko, 2009). Certain social-psychological analyses of mass movements also propose that there is an unavoidable element of irrationality in all human conduct and therefore a natural, even mysterious limit to the range of behavior to which scientific knowledge, as the prime instance of rational conduct, can be expected to apply readily (cf. Moscovici, [1981] 1985: 35). The same logic applies to the thesis of a persistent and unavoidable presence of "ideological" thinking in social life (e.g. Wilensky, 1971: 191).

It is not the aim of the following sections, in which we will discuss the persistent social function of common sense knowledge in detail, to interpret the limits of science as an indicator of the irrationality that may govern social and political relations, as evidence for the lack of enlightenment of specific social groups[3] or even as the outcome of a deliberate campaign of science or powerful groups to leave certain segments of the public in the dark about scientific knowledge in an effort to foster their hold on power.[4]

Finally, it is not our intention to explore, in this context, the important question of the changing preconditions for the "principle of excusable ignorance." That is, "our ancestors were, relative to us, epistemically impoverished: there were few means of finding out much about non-local, non-immediate effects and problems, so they could plan and act with a clear conscience on the basis of a more limited, manageable stock of local knowledge. They were thus capable of living lives of virtue – of a virtue that depended on unavoidable ignorance" (Dennett, 1986: 144).

A first sensible theoretical suggestion, in this regard, has been advanced by Mary Douglas (e.g. 1986: 3). She notes that our inability to be "converted by reasoned argument [is due] to the hold that institutions have on our processes of classifying and recognizing." Similarly, Robert Merton ([1942] 1973b) has suggested that for most people everyday knowledge provides greater plausibility and more useful means of comprehension than scientific knowledge, as well as considerable substantive affinity to existing cultural prejudices, thereby constituting a potential source of *competition* for scientific knowledge claims. Merton's observations amount to a kind of middle-range theory of the limits of the societal power of scientific knowledge and go far beyond considerations about the conditions for the practicality of scientific knowledge primarily driven by epistemological concerns since his conception refers to systemic attributes of everyday knowledge missing from scientific knowledge forms.

A useful procedure to further delimit the issue at hand might be to refer to certain answers which, although superficially relevant to the question of the limits of scientific knowledge, should be set aside because they are affected by the dominant theoretical conception of the relation between science and culture in general and scientific knowledge and its consequences in particular. It might appear as if the issue of the limits of scientific knowledge has been extensively examined in studies concerned with the diffusion of or resistance to modern scientific-technological knowledge (or its objectifications) (see Nimkoff, 1957; Rogers, 1964; Dierkes, 1981), or as part of the analysis of anti-science movements (Merton, [1938] 1973a: 254–266; Moore, 1974). The attitude of the public toward science and technology is beyond our focus, as is the critique or fear of science and technology which has to varying degrees accompanied its entire development (see Stehr, 2003). Although the critique of science has been particularly vocal throughout history and is perhaps rather vocal at the present time, as our discussion on policing knowledge has shown, and possibly not without repercussions for the development of science (see Stehr and Grundmann, 2003), this fact itself does not alter the possibility that the power of scientific knowledge as such is limited.

6.2 The power of everyday knowledge

In addition to the ideas Mary Douglas and Robert Merton offered, there are a number of other theoretical positions worth examining that engage the issue of the possible limits of the power of scientific knowledge or, as it were, the peculiar features of everyday life that limit the societal influence of scientific knowledge and hence augment the usefulness of everyday knowledge and its unusual attributes. The answers to be discussed in this section include reference to the intellectual resistance toward scientific knowledge and technical artifacts in everyday life, the thesis of the compartmentalization of the lifeworld, the difference between mythological and scientific "truths," a reference to the distinction between traditional and "organized" knowledge, and the thesis of the link between laboratory knowledge and social practice. Whatever the specific objection to the assertion that the power of scientific knowledge knows or should know no boundaries (cf. Gieryn, 2008), all accounts mentioned share an emphasis on the existence of multiple forms of knowledge and therefore include, if only implicitly, a reference to the social constructivist position of multiple claims to knowledge.

Scientific knowledge has always had its opponents. Social strata and social institutions that have resisted scientific knowledge may therefore have developed a style of thought which has articulated opposition quite effectively and may have contributed to a slowing in the pace of the dissemination of scientific knowledge. As we have seen, Max Weber has argued that the capitalistic process of rationalization and the spread of rational conduct to many spheres of life go hand in hand with the development of modern science and technology, but this is true also for the critique of capitalism and the opposition to modern technology and a rationalist style of thought. The critique of the capitalist economic system is inaugurated by opposition voiced from the conservative position of the political spectrum (cf. Mannheim, [1925] 1986: 63–71). Some of the basic features of the emerging conservative style of thinking and experiencing, in response to the Enlightenment and the capitalist economy, include, following Karl Mannheim ([1925] 1986: 100):

> its experience of the qualitative, its concrete rather than abstract ways of experiencing, its experiencing on the grounds of what is and not what ought to be, its experience of imaginary spatial relationships in contrast with the linear experience of historical development, its substitution of landed property for the individual as the substratum of history, its preference for "organic" associations over "classes," and others.

Modern science strives to generate experiences that are generally demonstrable and universally valid. As Mannheim ([1925] 1986: 60) explicates further, science constitutes a project that strives for "socializable knowledge" in stark contrast to the kind of cognitive insights emphasized by conservative thinking which are possible and accessible only to particular, more circumscribed "experiential communities" (*Erfahrungsgemeinschaften*). Therefore, conservatives maintain that scientific knowing involves a systemic indifference toward all specific and concrete elements in the object or toward phenomena that can only be demonstrated to a particular experiential community. For the conservative, scientific knowledge eliminates, to its own detriment and that of all human beings, "all particular essential references to man, nature, and things in which every piece of knowledge comes embedded" (Mannheim, [1925] 1986: 61).

During the era of the Weimar Republic and the Nazi regime, a rapprochement can be observed in the work of influential conservative intellectuals, especially Hans Freyer, Werner Sombart, Ernst Jünger, Carl Schmitt and Oswald Spengler, between culture and technology. Jeffrey Herf (1984) has called the sympathetic connection between what used to be contradictory categories in conservative-romantic thought an expression of "reactionary modernity." The genesis of this rapprochement may be traced to the experiences made by this generation of intellectuals during World War I and the pragmatic political realization that certain national goals could only be reached in conjunction with an affirmative attitude toward modern technology. At the same time, intellectual resistance against the Enlightenment and its aims no longer required opposition to the manifestations of modern technology. The ideology of National Socialism in Germany represents the most radical manifestation of such a connection between *Innerlichkeit* ("inwardness") and technology. The rapprochement between conservative thinking and technology affirms that technical-industrial modernization does not need to go hand in hand with the modernization and rationalization of intellectual life.

The present-day critique of science and technology resembles, to some extent, the conservative assault on science in the 1920s, although conceptual similarities cannot disguise essential differences. Among the resemblances are the shared conviction about the potency of scientific knowledge and technical artifacts and the belief that scientific rationality may somehow be monopolized in the hands of a few, forming the basis for the exercise of power in social relations. How else is one to interpret the persistent warnings about an impending "imperialism of instrumental rationality" (Weizenbaum, 1976), the danger of an aggressive "colonialization of the lifeworld" (Habermas, 1981), or the unavoidable "Taylorization of the world of work" (Volpert, 1985)?

The compartmentalization of the lifeworld

Not only explicit resistance against a particular style of thought may limit the success or channel the dissemination of scientific knowledge. The differentiation or compartmentalization of the lifeworld into more or less separate spheres may also impede the process of the dominance of scientific knowledge. However, this does not imply that scientific and non-scientific convictions cannot be found simultaneously among the same individuals, groups and classes.

Like Max Weber, Karl Mannheim ([1925] 1986) has pointed out that the capitalist-rationalist process may have limits or be only partially capable of supplanting existing views and social processes. While the realm of public social relations is rationalized, the sphere of private relations and convictions might be more immune to transformation. Even strata, Mannheim ([1925] 1986: 64) suggests, that were at the forefront of the rationalizing process "did not entirely lose their original bearing towards life. It merely disappeared from what we may call the foreground of their public and official life. Their intimate relationships, insofar as they remained untouched by the capitalist process, proceeded in a non-calculating, non-rationalized manner. The relationship to life did not become abstract in these spheres." As Mannheim himself indicates, the spheres of life that retreat into inwardness are those left untouched by the process of rationalization. They do not remain unaffected, however; these intimate spheres evidently live a fragile and precarious existence.

Simmel's analyses of the limits of the "intellect" are more specific. He speaks about its averaging or leveling character and its close proximity to the principles of individualism and egoism. In particular, in the *Philosophy of Money*, Simmel ([1907] 1978: 437) asserts that the nature of the (objective) contents of the intellect can be communicated universally and that, assuming its validity, everyone with a sufficiently predisposed mind will be persuaded by them. In this respect, there is no analogous function in the sphere of the will and the emotions. The basic antagonism of (individual) reason and inner feelings becomes further evident by virtue of the fact that the "contents of the intellect […] do not possess the jealous exclusiveness that is common in the practical contents of life" (ibid.). The distinction between intellect and emotions finds its analogy in the dichotomy between means and ends; both fulfill distinct functions and cannot be substituted for one another.

Certain emotions, for example, involved in intimate personal relationships, would completely lose their significance and value if others were entitled to share them. It is also essential for certain objectives of the will that other people are excluded from both pursuing them as well as gaining them. It has been rightly suggested that theoretical notions, on the other hand, are like a torch whose light does not become dimmer by igniting innumerable others from it. In as much as their potentially boundless dissemination has no influence whatsoever upon their importance, they elude private ownership more than any other contents of life (Simmel, [1907] 1978: 437–438).

Mythological and scientific truths

In Emile Durkheim's lectures on "Pragmatism and Sociology" held shortly before World War I, a prominent place is reserved for considerations concerning the dichotomy of mythological and scientific knowledge. Mythological truths are accepted without further inquiry and testing while scientific truths are always subject to verification and proof. The persuasive character of mythological knowledge, its constraining and objective nature, is linked to the fact that such knowledge is collective knowledge, but mythological knowledge is by no means unconnected to reality. The reality represented by mythological truths is the reality of society. Mythological knowledge is erroneous with respect to things or objects but it is true with respect to the thinking subject (cf. Durkheim, [1955] 1983: 87).

Scientific knowledge is, for Durkheim, also a form of collective consciousness. However, scientific knowledge becomes possible only in a society that is differentiated. As such, mythological and scientific knowledge correspond in many ways to Durkheim's distinction between organic and mechanical solidarity. The function of scientific truth is therefore to mediate and strengthen the collective consciousness. The difference between mythological and scientific knowledge may be found, above all, in their respective relationship to collective beliefs and individual consciousness. In other words, scientific thought, just like mythological knowledge, can form the basis for social solidarity, but what are the preconditions for social communication? The answer is, according to Durkheim ([1955] 1983: 88):

> either by uniting to form a single collective mind, or by communicating in one object which is the same for all, with each however retaining his own personality; like Leibnitz's monads, each expressing the entirety of the universe while keeping its individuality. The first way is that of mythological thought, the second that of scientific thought.

Scientific knowledge represents and expresses societal formations and their state of development, in which individual differences and individualism are the foundation for collective solidarity rather than a threat to it. Durkheim ([1955] 1983: 92) therefore concludes that "intellectual individualism, far from making for anarchy, as might be expected during the period of the domination of mythological truth, becomes a necessary factor in the establishment of scientific truth, so that the diversity of intellectual temperaments can serve the case of impersonal truth."[5]

However, Durkheim is not as certain as, for example, Auguste Comte that scientific truths will displace mythological claims rapidly and completely. Durkheim suggests that it must be assumed that the power of scientific knowledge is, for the time being, limited to the world of physical objects. Sociology is faced with a most complex domain and is, therefore, at best able to produce frail and limited hypotheses. Moreover, these knowledge claims have not affected public consciousness to any great degree. Social action is subject to constraints, especially to the pressure to act, and cannot be postponed until a scientific solution of social issues is at hand. Society is forced to operate with certain images of itself. The relative backwardness of sociology and the uneven development of science assure the survival of mythological claims. Mythological knowledge does not fully lose its social relevance, even in societies in which natural scientific knowledge appears to dominate. Actors are constrained to orient themselves in specific ways, and the kinds of orientations provided by mythological truths are capable of serving as such orientations for action.

More generally, Durkheim ([1955] 1983: 91) insists that scientific truths cannot govern or dominate orientations by themselves because "there is, and there always will be, room in social life for a form of truth which will perhaps be expressed in a very secular way, but will nevertheless have a mythological and religious basis." What Durkheim has concretely in mind are ideas or taken-for-granted "dogmas" such as "democracy," "progress" and "the class struggle," which continue to contain, since they are rarely questioned, mythological components. Although Durkheim by no means suggests that the co-existence of scientific and mythological truth is inevitable, let alone a fate we must bear and cannot transcend, he does concede that the elimination of mythological claims will require a considerable period of time.

Organized knowledge and traditional knowledge

In contrast to these conceptions, there are accounts within sociological discourse about knowledge that imply, in the final analysis, that scientific knowledge is limited in its social effectiveness, although these limits are not fixed *a priori*. The most important perspective in this respect is derived from a linguistic rather than a sociological thesis.[6] A main example holds that the language of science, as differentiated from everyday language, cannot be fully formalized. This is related to the sociological thesis that scientific knowledge is ultimately based on other forms of knowledge, in particular everyday knowledge, and cannot entirely relinquish its ties to them, and that specialized scientific knowledge cannot replace everyday knowledge (Luckmann, 1981). Cicourel (1986) maintains, for example, that medical knowledge is dependent on everyday knowledge (declarative knowledge). The sociological variant of this argument points, therefore, to structural differences among forms of knowledge that perform different functions. A related thesis asserts that, under more or less stable social conditions, the demand for traditional knowledge does not decline decisively. Finally, the idea of competition among carriers of knowledge also belongs in this context. We would like to pursue, in greater detail, the notion of how structural features of knowledge depend on the conditions and the context of their production.

A critical analysis of the limits of the social power of scientific knowledge must incorporate some understanding of the special nature as well as the similarities of scientific and non-scientific knowledge and action. It can be shown that, from a sociological perspective, the dominant basis for the classification of scientific knowledge as a unique form of human knowledge is of limited use for the purposes at hand. That is, the dominant classification and attributes of scientific knowledge are too closely linked to now obsolete epistemological conceptions and ideals of scientificity such as universality, experience, rationality, necessity and practicality. Conceptions of scientific knowledge that are based on these attributes deny that scientific knowledge is socially based and a collective enterprise. They also ignore the fact that science is an historical enterprise.

However, Stephen Toulmin's (1972: 378) reference to scientific discourse as representing differentiated spheres of social action with special attributes, especially in the case of scientific laboratories, isolated from other social contexts, makes evident that the structure of knowledge produced under these circumstances affects its *reproduction* in other social contexts. The specific attributes assumed by scientific knowledge under these conditions may be thought of as "material" and cognitive attributes, but both sets of features impinge upon the conditions under which scientific knowledge may be reproduced.

First, we will consider what may be called the material attributes assumed by scientific knowledge as a result of the conditions of its production. Knowledge claims or knowledge effects produced under special conditions in scientific laboratories can undoubtedly be only reproduced outside the laboratory if the special conditions that allowed such outcomes are also reproduced outside the laboratory. That is, the special circumstances that allowed for the original observation of the effect must be extended to the context in which a successful transfer is to be made. Thus, the notion that scientific knowledge, unlike other forms of knowledge, is not bound or limited institutionally has to be questioned in light of the conditions necessary for the reproduction of scientific knowledge claims outside the circumstances of their initial discovery. It is by no means certain, in other words, that only the influence of conventional forms of knowledge contracts as the functional differentiation of society progresses and once powerful institutions such as religion, as well as institutionally based knowledge in general, diminish in importance.

Second, knowledge claims not only take on features derived from the material conditions of their production but also reflect institutionally bound cognitive attributes. These attributes include, importantly, a suspension of the pressure to act as constitutive of scientific discourse. Knowledge produced within the scientific community is released from the pressures or contingencies to which it must respond and the tasks it must perform outside science. One of the most salient attributes of everyday life situations is, in contrast, the *persistent constraint to act*, the pressure to reach a decision, to observe a specific rule, to follow a particular course of action by discarding alternative possibilities or to provide an account of a completed action *ex post facto*. [7]

The suspension of the constraint to act within scientific discourse may be described, on the one hand, as a virtue of intellectual activity taking place under privileged conditions which moderate the effect that the pressing interests, rapidly passing opportunities and ambiguous dependencies of everyday contexts can have on the production of scientific knowledge claims. On the other hand, the result of this suspension of the pressure to act (or to achieve closure) is that scientific knowledge takes on qualities of incompleteness, fragility, provisionality, fragmentation or expansiveness, which reduce its effectiveness as knowledge in circumstances in which action (and therefore closure) is the foremost requirement. As Durkheim ([1912] 1965: 479) puts it so succinctly: "Life cannot wait" (cf. also Gehlen, [1950] 1988: 296–297).

Incompleteness or the lack of any "impetus to action" is constitutive of scientific knowledge: "Faith is before all else an impetus to action, while science, no matter how far it may be pushed, always remains at a distance from this. Science is fragmentary and incomplete; it advances but slowly and is never finished" (Durkheim, [1912] 1965: 479). The probability that myths and half-truths are employed by large segments of the population in "advanced" societies may well be even more characteristic of crisis situations in which various dangers appear imminent, as Norbert Elias (1989: 500–501), for example, argues. In this respect, present-day societies do not differ from allegedly "primitive" societies in which similar responses are elicited by the dangers brought about by illness, drought, thunderstorms or floods. However, Elias is convinced that this state of affairs can be corrected in principle as adequate (scientific) knowledge is diffused more widely throughout society.

In most social contexts the need to act takes precedence over the need to know. Perhaps there is, as Simmel ([1890] 1989a: 1) surmises, a kind of anthropological constant in the form of a general and widespread preference among humans, namely to *do* something rather than to *know about* something, and knowing, in turn, may flow from or require prior doing.

In the aforementioned lectures on "Pragmatism and Sociology," Durkheim ([1955] 1983), discussing the scientific status of the discipline of sociology, refers to the same set of issues when he attempts to enumerate some of the reasons for the relative scientific backwardness of sociological knowledge. He underlines, for example, that the fragmentary and uncertain knowledge of sociology cannot but produce skepticism or doubt about the contingencies of practical action in the social world. This might be appropriate with respect to natural science knowledge, but we have to live in the social world, and to live means to act. "[S]ociety cannot wait for its problems to be solved scientifically. It has to make decisions about what action to take, and in order to make these decisions it has to have an idea of what it is" (Durkheim, [1955] 1983: 90). As a rule, scientific knowledge is, however, produced under conditions that consider "waiting," distancing, careful reflection, the elimination of time-bound constraints to reach a decision, or even the deliberate abstention from judgment until the "evidence" is in, to be distinct attributes of the validity and the virtue of such knowledge claims. Reducing, and at times even eliminating, urgency as a part of the production process of scientific knowledge, makes for results that, from the perspective of everyday life in which the urgency to act is often a constitutive characteristic, are inadequate for such conditions.

The site for the production of scientific knowledge does not differ much from the sites for the production of conventional or everyday knowledge. From this it follows that scientific rationality, once it appears outside the boundaries of the scientific community – for instance, in the form of expert knowledge in the determination of curricula, the allocation of public funds for research, or as expert witness or counsel – is often met with severe disappointment by the public because the scientific knowledge fails to display the expected reliability and consensus.

A final trait of scientific knowledge (especially of the natural sciences) that results from its laboratory origins needs to be considered here. It is to do with the differentiation of distinct spheres of action of the scientific discourse, which, in turn, strongly delimit the reproduction of such knowledge in different contexts. As already indicated, one cannot simply copy findings achieved in a laboratory setting into and onto contexts outside the lab. Only if it were possible to create almost the exact same conditions could one expect to recreate the original effects. In other words, "one must to a certain extent extend the laboratory context itself if this transfer is to be successful" (Rouse, 1987: 227). In addition to these considerations, following Pierre Bourdieu ([1980] 1987), for example, it is possible to assign to practical contexts a logic that is less stringent than the logic of logic. The social scientific analysis of everyday contexts reduces the urgency to act in such situations. The effect that is achieved might be called a depragmatization of everyday contexts, or the elevation of practical circumstances to the level of theoretical contingencies. At the same time, the depragmatization of everyday contexts through social scientific discourse makes visible features of the former and, thus, offers resistance against theoretical transformation. Among these features are aspects of a practical logic such as the ease of operation and control, subjective adequacy, economy, and its practical persuasiveness represented in the union of a totality of judgments and their ambivalence. This opposition of practical and theoretical logic prompts Bourdieu to draw the radical conclusion that any theoretical reconstruction of practical situations amounts necessarily to a distortion of the "truth" of praxis. The peculiar character of practical circumstances happens to be that they resist theoretical reconstruction because the truth of praxis resides in its blindness to its own truth. Scientific discourse and praxis have different purposes and attempt to realize different functions.

Science and ignorance

We have already indicated that the assumption of the irreversible and forceful progress of scientific knowledge and the concomitant demise of traditional forms of knowledge (which cannot measure up, in their practical efficacy, to knowledge produced by science) includes the assertion, at least implicitly, that only scientific knowledge advances. In contrast, non-scientific forms of knowledge seem to be void of any real formational capacity and dynamic. The same thesis of the inefficacy of conventional knowledge asserts, finally, that such knowledge is not really capable of defending itself. The conviction that traditional forms of knowledge are essentially helpless finds its parallel in the belief that scientific knowledge consistently reduces the volume of conventional knowledge rather than adding to it.

However, is the pool of conventional knowledge merely static knowledge? As a matter of fact, in an age of somewhat reduced enthusiasm for scientific knowledge, the idea that science might well be one of the important sources of the growth and the transformation of conventional knowledge becomes more plausible (cf. Brzezinski, 1970: xii). When Jerome Ravetz (1987: 100) suggests, for instance, "while our knowledge continues to increase exponentially, our relevant ignorance does so even more rapidly. And this is ignorance generated by science," he alerts us to the possibility that advances in scientific knowledge and their practical application are accompanied by a wide range of unsolved problems, often in the form of risks, and by unanticipated consequences.

From the point of view of scientific discourse, "scientific progress" produces immediately and incessantly ignorance (i.e. "certified ignorance," or a term Robert Merton [1987] advances, "specified ignorance," that awaits resolution by the scientific community; see also Abbott, 2010). In an indirect manner, therefore, the production of scientific knowledge and its realization – for example, in the responses of affected groups and individuals to unintended and unexplicated consequences, multiple risks and unattributable costs – contributes to the persistence and transformation, perhaps even expansion, of conventional knowledge. Of course, these patterns occur in response to developments in science and their dissemination to and translation into practical contexts, but as a result, paradoxically, science itself can be seen to represent a source for the perpetuation and the dynamics of traditional forms of knowledge in society.

One of the additional sets of limits of the power and authority of science knowledge in modern societies emerges according to a number of observers by virtue of the persistent influence of indigenous or traditional knowledge.

6.3 Indigenous or traditional knowledge

In recent years, interest in the topic of indigenous knowledge has been stimulated by a number of major socio-political and socio-economic developments, most prominently, of course, by the process of globalization and its impact on societies around the world. More to the point of the nature of indigenous knowledge, anthropologists in particular have carried out fieldwork in order to examine indigenous knowledge and its role in developing societies. Ben Orlove and his anthropological colleagues, in the context of their own fieldwork into climate knowledge among farmers in southern Uganda, have employed a useful, if restricted, definition of indigenous knowledge (Orlove et al., 2009). According to their working definition, indigenous knowledge is:

place-based knowledge that is rooted in local cultures and generally associated with long-settled communities which have strong ties to their natural environments. Such knowledge tends to be the result of cumulative experience and observation, tested in the context of everyday life, and devolved by oral communication and repetitive engagement rather than through formal instruction.

(Orlove et al., 2009: 244)

The United Nations Environment Programme (UNEP) employs a similar definition stressing the locality, historicity, experiential quality of this kind of knowledge, which "encompasses all forms of knowledge – technologies, know-how skills, practices and beliefs – that enable the community to achieve stable livelihoods in their environment."[8] The term "indigenous knowledge" is closely related to the concept of "local knowledge" and sometimes even used synonymously. The strong connection of such definitions to the notion of locality is obvious. Whereas scientific knowledge and its derivatives much in use in the northern hemisphere draw on their scientifically produced universality, indigenous knowledge is seen as a pragmatic if mythically underpinned entity, deeply rooted in the environment, the experience and the everyday life of indigenous people. It is thus seen to be: 1 bound to *a people* and their culture; 2 strongly tied to *everyday practices* and *rituals* and rooted in a sense of community; 3 based on experiential modes of trial and error; and 4 usually *transferred orally* in the form of tradition and folklore, thus serving the function of a shared memory.

The contextual boundedness of knowledge and knowledge claims becomes clearly visible in the instance of indigenous knowledge that conforms to its social functions rather than to universal claims to truth. Subsequently, it is usually of a rather specific nature and also serves as a repository for a common memory. As such, it plays a vital role in a people's history, as it has a crucial part in "defining the identity of the community. It has developed over the centuries of experimentation on how to adapt to local conditions. It therefore represents all the skills and innovations of a people and embodies the collective wisdom and resourcefulness of the community."[9]

Based on these traits, some theorists approach it in terms of *implicit* knowledge while others place it in line with ethnographic approaches to ethnic cultures. Implicit knowledge is sometimes used as a synonym for "traditional knowledge," thus emphasizing the historic aspects of its accumulation, or "local knowledge" stressing its contextual quality as regards the place of its inception and use. Typically, it is produced, passed on, and continues to grow outside a formal educational system and may thus be termed a cultural practice insofar as it is embedded in local cultures and unique to regions and peoples. It seems plausible to attribute indigenous knowledge to a group of people who, for generations, have adapted to their external conditions of existence (soil, climate, etc.) and, in turn, have shaped the natural environment by and to their subsistence. Indigenous knowledge carries with it a focus on the existential importance of forms of such knowledge: "Indigenous knowledge is the local knowledge that is unique to a given culture or society […] It is the basis for local-level decision-making in agriculture, health care, food preparation, education, natural resource management, and a host of other activities in rural communities" (Warren, 1991: 4).

As indigenous knowledge consists of a multitude of cultural practices taking shape in economic, agricultural and labor routines, it is not necessarily codified. In many traditional societies or groups, the prevalent mode of passing on knowledge is still oral, while written accounts of successful practices are not of great importance. Not only does this strengthen traditional modes of imparting knowledge, but it also makes it adaptive as indigenous cultures are neither static nor isolated. It is important for local communities to base their economy on a framework of knowledge that enables them to adjust to changes. Thus indigenous knowledge can be understood as "the information base for a society, which facilitates communication and decision-making. Indigenous information systems are dynamic, and are continually influenced by internal creativity and experimentation as well as by contact with external systems" (Flavier et al., 1995: 479). Contrary to widespread belief, indigenous knowledge tends to be holistic as well as dynamic, and adaptive rather than static and formalized.

In this respect indigenous knowledge – although based on *traditional* repositories of knowledge, and *local* in its spatial scope – comprises more than these other categories of knowing. One must be careful not to connote it as primitive knowledge as it draws on a rich experience and has proven successful; it also continues to develop. So, while indigenous knowledge often bears the connotation of traditional, ancient and local knowledge and meanings, it has become the object of recent endeavors to approach it from different angles. Folklore or non-formal knowledge is not solely the object of anthropological research, and does not necessarily have to bear the ethno-label. Driven by more pragmatic attempts that acknowledge the efficacy of seemingly simple solutions to practical problems, indigenous knowledge has been discovered as a source of furthering development in underdeveloped regions all over the world. Since the early 1990s it has played an important part in the struggle for new advances of development aid that stray from older approaches that were aiming at implementing new and substituting traditional knowledge.

Still, scientific knowledge and indigenous, local knowledge are not necessarily rivaling entities. This is particularly visible in the stark rise in attention such knowledge has received over the last two decades – often driven by commercial interests or in the development literature and policy represented, for example, by the World Development Report of 1998 from the World Bank (1999), entitled *Knowledge for Development*.

Local procedures, knowledge about the effects of alternative treatments, the use of local herbs and plants have attracted the attention not only of Western science but also of corporate actors searching for new medicines and technologies. As indigenous knowledge is based on the close ties between the people and their environment, it reflects intimate familiarity with the fauna and flora, the characteristics of plants and herbs. As local knowledge evolves as it is passed on, it can both be incorporated into modern forms of knowledge to develop new practices and techniques (such as in the case of the tractor developed with the help of the Honey Bee Network; see Gupta, 2006), as well as inform scientific progress. "The discourse on indigenous knowledge is also a discourse on politics of attribution and acknowledgement of learning from those who are supposedly good subjects of study but are seldom considered lead producers of knowledge" (Gupta, 2007: 2).

Indigenous knowledge can thus be understood as an important asset in an emerging global knowledge society and economy. It is the basis from which to introduce new modes of exchange, growth and learning. Indigenous knowledge not only provides the foundation of subsistence for developing countries or regions, but also holds valuable resources for the development process.[10] Recent attempts to collect and preserve indigenous practices regarding agriculture, animal husbandry, natural resource management and so forth aim at building a database for this important branch of global knowledge that could aid development by providing best practice examples. It also plays an important role for local measures of launching small businesses (with the help of the expanding micro-equity initiatives) and, as such, for alternative approaches to regional development outside the one-sided development programs of the past. As the sum total of the skills and experiences of indigenous peoples and communities, indigenous knowledge also represents a merit in itself. As such, it is part of human history and the rich tradition of humankind's struggle with nature, its own sociality and the progress of human knowledge.

Whether or not traditional knowledge can be legally protected is an essentially contested matter. The World Intellectual Property Association (WIPO) in Geneva, established in 1967 as a specialized agency of the United Nations, has been trying for decades without success to develop a legal frame of reference and standards for the protection of indigenous knowledge.[11]

6.4 Tacit knowledge

The concept of tacit knowledge has seen considerable attention in various disciplines such as philosophy (Ryle, [1949), sociology (Polanyi, 1969), and economics (Nonaka and Takeuchi, 1994; Cowan et al., 2000), albeit with various meanings and to various depths. Perhaps the term tacit knowledge is self-exemplifying and resists a definition in conscious cognitive terms. Usually the term tacit knowledge refers to what is taken for granted, unspoken or undeclared, and is often contrasted with "codified knowledge."

The idea of tacit knowledge is part of Edmund Husserl's phenomenology, takes center stage in Alfred Schütz's (1964) seminal text on knowing as socially situated, and features in one way or another in any kind of constructionist approach that tackles the question of how cognitively autonomous systems can achieve any kind of stable coordination about a shared reality. Thus, any discussion of knowledge, such as ours, might as well begin or end with the discourse that surrounds the ever so slightly mystical concept of tacit knowledge.

The theme of tacit knowledge is canonically traced back to the 1950s and the work of Michael Polanyi, and grows out of his critique of positivist philosophies of science. Polanyi is convinced that tacit knowledge is not merely another form of knowledge but is fundamental to the fabrication of scientific knowledge: "All knowledge is either tacit or rooted in tacit knowledge" (Polanyi, 1969: 144). The basic idea of tacit knowledge acquired further impetus in meta-theoretical analyses of science through the work of Thomas Kuhn (1962) and his distinction between normal and revolutionary science. In both instances of scientific activity, the notion of tacit knowing plays a critical role.

Implicit or tacit knowledge (in contrast to explicit or formal knowledge) refers, not always in the same manner in different intellectual contexts, to knowledge that is difficult to articulate and transfer to another person, is hard to access empirically for external observers, difficult to subject to rationalist analyses, has an ineliminable subjective dimension and, in economic discourse, for example, often becomes the label for the residual category of "intangible" information or knowledge (cf. Cowan et al., 2000: 212).[12]

Eric von Hippel's (1991, 1994: 430–432) term "sticky information" roughly describes the same notion. Implicit, difficult to acquire and transfer stocks of knowledge, cognitive skills and personal experience strongly reduce the mobility of knowledge, facilitate control over it and thus reduce the necessity of legally protecting such forms of knowledge. Antonelli (1999: 244) emphasizes structural and cultural processes and claims that *technical* knowledge in particular is highly dependent on context, arguing that it:

> tends to be localized in well-defined technical, institutional, regional and industrial situations. It is specific to each industry, region and firm and consequently costly to use elsewhere. The localized character of technical knowledge increases its appropriability but reduces its spontaneous circulation in the economic system.

The transfer of tacit knowledge often occurs by doing. Observing and doing a certain task such as cycling may convey the knowledge required to ride a bike, but the articulation of what it is that allows someone to ride a bike is very difficult to express except by doing it and, therefore, showing what it means to cycle. In management studies, especially in the work of Nonaka and Takeuchi (1994), tacit knowledge is defined as knowledge-not-yet-articulated. Such a definition assumes that such knowledge can be converted to the benefit of a firm into explicit knowledge – a position criticized, for instance, by Tsoukas (1996), who stresses that tacit knowledge is essentially ineffable. The very definition of tacit knowledge as a kind of hidden form of knowledge indicates that it is very difficult, if not impossible, to specify with any robustness how large the component of tacit knowledge may be in any given social context or, for that matter, different types of implicit knowledge.[13]

Georg Hans Neuweg (2001) identifies at least six semantically different uses of the concept: 1 tacit knowing (Ryle, [1949: 35); 2 implicit memory (submerged experience); 3 tacit knowledge in the narrower sense of knowing how to do things without knowing the rules for such actions; 4 non-verbalizability, which lies at the heart of Polanyi's famous quote that "we can know more than we can tell" (Polanyi, 1967: 4), but might even have deeper roots, as knowledge might be (5) impossible to formalize, which would also account for the fact that it is impossible for it to be fully put in words. It is worth noting that this also implies that not even external actors are in a position to lay out and structure that which they observe as someone else's knowledge in action. Taken to the extreme, this stance would ultimately lead to some kind of nomadic thesis of knowledge (see also Neuweg, 2001: 17). The last of Neuweg's synonyms is: 6 tacit knowledge as intimately tied up with (personal, first-hand) experience, in the sense of "untaught knowledge," i.e. knowledge that emanates from learning by doing or is incorporated in doing itself (ibid.: 19).

Tacit knowledge, then, refers to knowledge that is unstated due to its invisibility (involuntary) or due to neglect (acceptance of certain unquestioned rules as taken for granted), untaught, or even unteachable, remains in the background and/or is intimately tied up with corporeal experience (such as learning to ride a bike or to ski properly).

Drawing a line of demarcation between implicit and explicit knowledge is, then, at least as hard as arriving at a single definition. Again we encounter the notion that propositional, declarative knowledge ("to know that") which might be relayed and formalized is complemented by a dimension of knowledge that makes up our "know how," and that these dimensions might exist separately from each other. We can do things without having deeper insight into their rules and inner workings, we may know some skills in theory but remain unable to perform them, and we are aware of situations where we know how something works both theoretically and practically (or of its counterpart: not knowing how something works and not being able to do it). We might then heuristically separate substantive knowledge (know that) from methodical knowledge (know how) from knowledgeable doing, in which we may be – but do not necessarily *have* to be – aware of doing something in a specific, methodical way. We just do it.

That such discussions are not merely academic becomes obvious when we consider their practical impact, not only for scientific research (cf. Polanyi's implications of implicit knowledge for what is being researched), but also for doing business (see Nonaka and Takeuchi's work on a new kind of knowledge management in businesses) or for the general theory of education and pedagogy that is confronted with the question: "What can be taught and how?"

Tacit knowledge and the discussions that surround the concept – in whichever terminological guise – are in fact referring to an ancient philosophical problem: Where does knowledge reside and how might it be transferred? That such questions lie at the heart of any sociological inquiry into (tacit) knowledge is apparent, as they problematize any notion of both the self-sufficient rational individual and the question of how social exchange can be organized at all.

Whether it appears as *sticky* knowledge, *inert* knowledge or *hidden* knowledge, tacit knowledge denotes all those things we know but cannot express adequately. Even more to the point, tacit knowledge ultimately ushers in the question of what knowledge actually *is*. One of the insights that has long since become consensual with regard to this discussion is that any kind of knowledge might be divorced from some kind of personal experience and is thus intimately tied up with its bearer to begin with. Thus knowledge can never be conceived of as a kind of substance that might easily be conferred or kept inside the mind, to subsequently be employed stringently when needed. Some proponents suggest that any kind of knowing must at least partly exist before it can be perceived and conceived of in the form of explicit knowledge (see Neuweg, 2001: 5). The widely shared experience of not being fully able to verbally convey what we know, and the equally widespread problem that no matter how we try we might even confuse our audience more and more as we describe our insights are cases in point. What seems to be separating implicit from explicit knowledge is the act of comprehension (as a fundamentally individual, immanent act): It is the moment when something that made no sense to us beforehand, or was only grasped superficially, suddenly bursts into a new quality of understanding.

Notes

1 However, Steven Lukes (2007) has recently made an interesting effort to examine the problem of apparently irrational beliefs in everyday life.
2 Jean Lave (1988: 76–83) documents and criticizes such a categorization of everyday knowledge and the neglect of systematic research into its role in social action. She urges, therefore, the development of a social anthropology of cognitive activities as they occur in practical situations and describes the results of a number of empirical studies which benefited from such a theoretical program.
3 The public controversies that question scientific knowledge and subsequent public policy often revolve around this particular allegation (see Shils, 1974: 14). Take as an example the campaigns for and against water fluoridation in North America (Barnes, 1972: 281).
4 Compare, for example, Helmut Schelsky's (1975) notions about the massive authority of the so-called *Reflexionseliten* (elites that produce meaning and purpose) in modern societies and who consciously disguise their exceptional power in society (cf. Stehr, 1992: 131–143; Stehr and Adolf, 2009).
5 We have changed the translation slightly to capture the original meaning.
6 The linguistic conception about the limits to scientific knowledge is of particular importance because it tends to be taken seriously within science itself, especially among theoreticians of knowledge and science. Its attractiveness to epistemology could well be linked to the fact that it allows the invocation of logical or formal considerations (cf. Goedel's Theorem).
7 In their discussion of expertise and how expertise may be justified, Harry Collins and Robert Evans (2002: 241) advance similar observations about the essential difficulties encountered in the public domain if one had to wait for expert advice: "Decisions of public concern have to be made according

to a timetable established within the political sphere, not the scientific or technical sphere; the decisions have to be made before the scientific dust has settled, because the pace of politics is faster than the pace of scientific consensus formation."
8 See UNEP website, unep.org/IK/Pages.asp?id=About IK (accessed June 23, 2013).
9 Ibid.
10 For a constructive critique of the "neo-indigenismo," see Agrawal (1995). Reviewing the literature for a definition of indigenous (traditional) knowledge, he eventually identifies three dimensions that he summarizes as follows: "1) substantive – there are differences in the subject matter and characteristics of indigenous vs. western knowledge; 2) methodological and epistemological – the two forms of knowledge employ different methods to investigate reality, and possess different world-views; and 3) contextual-traditional and western knowledge differ because traditional knowledge is more deeply rooted in its context" (ibid.: 418). However, none of these dimensions, Agrawal suggests, survives thorough investigation. Ultimately, Agrawal (1995: 421f) warns against the superficial and dichotomous classification of "western, scientific" and "southern, indigenous" knowledge as distinct categories of knowledge, since such broad categorizations: 1 fail to acknowledge the internal heterogeneity of the knowledges thus separated; 2 because such a distinction fails to take into account the historical intercourse between local stocks of knowledge; and 3 since such a perspective overstresses the differences between "traditional" and "scientific" knowledge altogether: "A classification of knowledge into indigenous and western is bound to fail not just because of the heterogeneity among the elements – the knowledges filling the boxes marked indigenous or western. It also founders at another, possibly more fundamental level. It seeks to separate and fix in time and space (separate as independent, and fix as stationary and unchanging) systems that can never be thus separated or so fixed. Such an attempt at separation requires the two forms of knowledge to have totally divorced historical sequences of change – a condition which the evidence simply does not bear out" (ibid.: 421f).
11 In 1998 and 1999, WIPO conducted fact-finding missions in 28 countries to identify intellectual property needs and expectations of traditional knowledge holders. A report on the results of the missions was published in April 2001 (WIPO, 2001).
12 Tacit knowledge has much in common "with the knowledge of athletes, pianists, and circus performers. It resides in the body or those parts of their mind that activate the body and it must be communicated by example and action – words do not suffice" (Feyerabend, 2011: 105–106).
13 Harry Collins (2007) distinguishes, though these types of tacit knowledge are rarely differentiated, between "somatic-limit tacit knowledge" and "collective tacit knowledge." The former is the result of the limited capacities of the human brain and body while collective tacit knowledge has to do with the relations between individuals and society.

7
GLOBAL KNOWLEDGE[1]

This part of our study is concerned with the thesis of globally valid or globally present knowledge, or the hope for *global knowledge* as a special, if not outstanding, form of modern knowledge.[2] The premise here is that global knowledge is knowledge that, like human rights, is seemingly invariant with respect to social conventions, institutions, culture, religion or economic development. The thesis of global knowledge relates almost exclusively to the worldwide dissemination of scientific-technical knowledge. That is, more specifically, to scientific knowledge that has to date been primarily generated and assimilated in Western societies. Whether this dominance of science produced in Western societies will continue in the future may well be doubted. The rapid rise of science in countries such as Brazil, China or India suggests a potential geographical shift of focus in knowledge production. Since skepticism as to whether such a thing as "global knowledge" (in the singular) does or can exist at all seems advisable, we will in this chapter rather refer to "global" or "globalizing" *worlds* of knowledge. After all, as the anthropologist Clifford Geertz (1996: 262) laconically voices his doubts about the possibility of global knowledge: "No one lives in the world in general."

7.1 Basic reflections on global knowledge

Knowledge in general, and scientific knowledge in particular, are – as we have emphasized – not only a way of probing into the secrets of the world, but also the *coming into being* of a world, the preventing of its change. However, are general and scientific knowledge the coming into being of *one* world? In other words, given their power to control the very foundations of social action, are general and scientific knowledge helping to neutralize the multiple social, cultural and economic differences in this world? Is it worldwide circulating knowledge that is globalizing, or is it economic conditions, political power, cultural values or transnational institutions (cf. Agnew, 2015: 237)? Conversely, does globalization create the need for a new kind of globally circulating knowledge (see Giddens, 1990; Black, 2014)?

An amplification seems in order at this point: as indicated, we will use the term *worlds of knowledge*, or "global knowledge worlds," as a plural concept and, therefore, do not refer to *world knowledge* in the singular.[3] World knowledge in the singular not only suggests knowledge that aims to achieve indisputability and relies on, for instance, a naturalistic understanding of the world of man and of nature and how to access them, but is also oriented to a form of cognition that fundamentally conceives of itself as existing independently of social conditions and derives its distinction as (objective) knowledge (of the world) from this very fact. Our own observations of world knowledge, or "global knowledge worlds," are constrained by four basic assumptions.[4]

1. To justify speaking of global knowledge worlds, knowledge needs to *travel*.[5] This implies that the producers and the consumers of knowledge must not be identical. There is, therefore, no speaking of global knowledge worlds unless the groups of actors that represent the supply can be shown to be different from the groups of actors that constitute the demand.

This distinction also holds for such knowledge as is anchored in social constructions (such as organizational forms, or institutions), or technological artifacts (such as appliances or infrastructures) – that is, knowledge that circulates widely as an integral part of a product but whose content is *not directly* "consumed." Typical examples are knowledge that is incorporated in material substances such as pharmaceuticals (van der Geest et al., 1996) or foodstuffs (Arce and Marsden, 1993), in technological artifacts such as cars, but also in pictures or symbols (for instance, in advertising, see Leslie, 1995), or in popular culture and, more specifically, in the media (e.g. Crane, 2002).[6] Global knowledge worlds may, for example, refer to differences, one dimension of which we propose to highlight in this context, namely a "horizontal" rather than "vertical" division of knowledge (that is, a division of knowledge that is sectoral, for instance between corporations, rather than societal, by social class or stratum) (see also Stiglitz and Greenwald, 2014: 267).

2. We assume that we are dealing with forms of knowledge that are not from the start, and for whatever reasons, subject to specific regulatory regimes such as secrecy obligations, be it in the context of a reticence, driven by professionally and commercially motivated self-interest, towards an unrestrained circulation of ideas, or in the context of a distribution constrained or dictated by international conventions (TRIPS – (Trade-Related Aspects of Intellectual Property Rights),[7] or in the context, controversially discussed in recent times, of forms of knowledge that are prohibited from dissemination for so-called "national security" reasons (see Krige, 2014).

3. Our concern is also *not* – a point already made in passing above – with the worldwide dissemination of the *institution* of science (see Drori et al., 2003), or of specific scientific disciplines,[8] nor with the practices of *resistance* to the established scope and limits of the cognitive dominance of scientific knowledge (as, for instance, in the recurrent social conflicts over the theory of evolution). Nor do we address the structural convergence of scientific practices (Meyer et al., 1997; Boli and Thomas, 1997; Beerkens, 2009) or the methodological disciplining (standardization) of these practices as a prerequisite for knowledge to become globally mobile (Livingstone, 2002: 1771–1177). Last but not least, we are also not concerned with the global spread of the role of the scientist, or with the worldwide networking among scientists or among governmental and non-governmental scientific institutions (Schofer, 1999; Schott, 1998, 2001; Burgers and Touburg, 2013).

Furthermore, global knowledge worlds are nothing to do with the fact that educational systems, professions (Freidson, 2001), universities (as the production sites of "universal" knowledge; see Fuller, 2003; Bleikle, 2005), the Internet (Mattelart, [1996] 2000; Lessig, 2004) or, as the case may be, digital information systems relying on software-hardware integration (Ernst, 2005; Featherstone and Venn, 2006: 2) can today be found in almost *any* society; nor with the claim that the potentially worldwide interest in ritualized spectacles such as, for example, the Olympic Games is evidence of a "global culture" (Lechner and Boli, 2005); nor with certain globally implemented technological practices (Meyer et al., 1992; David, 1993; Marten, 2014). Institutional facilities like these and infrastructures that are increasingly going global, for instance in the form of technological platforms,[9] serve to hierarchically organize, circulate and regulate knowledge.

We will also not go into the highly intriguing question of who it is, in terms of social strata as well as individual proponents, that supports or rejects the thesis of global knowledge worlds: precisely who – in different societies – the social advocates are of the pursuit of "universal" knowledge, and who the groups and persons are that oppose this universalization of knowledge. These are open questions worth exploring, relating as they do to specific historical processes such as nationalism, globalization, rationalization, modernization, worldviews, religious systems, etc., to name but a few of the relevant processes and factors (cf., for instance, Huntington, 2004, on the denationalization of American elites).

Finally, it is in the present context impossible to discuss in any detail the complex issue of whether or not the current economic and social transformations that are commonly, and summarily, subsumed under the heading of globalization will indeed enhance and intensify the worldwide dissemination of knowledge, as compared to past historical epochs. After all, any more in-depth exploration of the coupling between globalization processes and knowledge dissemination cannot from the very start rely on a definition that conceives of "globalization as the integration, across borders, of markets for capital, goods, services, knowledge, and labor" (Ernst, 2005: 89). Any such definition would anticipate the answer as it precludes addressing the really interesting issue, i.e. the interplay between globalization processes and knowledge (or, in the best of cases, would only serve to highlight the mechanisms that are the drivers of globalization), with the frequent result that the only answer left to a question thus narrowed down is a reference to specific technological systems.

What can be said, however, is that there are widely disseminated *epistemic institutions* that, besides offering genuine first instances of global forms of discourse, actually respond to problems defined as "global" (such as, for instance, air pollution, climate change, health) and produce worldwide forms of *governance* (Mörth, 1998). Many of these institutional facilities of science indeed claim to be generating universal worlds of knowledge, but whether successful global cognitive cultural frames of reference actually exist (Meyer, 1999: 126–128), or should exist, and what these might be (see Harding, 2002), remains an open question. Institutional boundaries may well (co-)demarcate the very boundaries beyond which knowledge cannot spread.

4. As a last caveat for what is to follow, even if *all* individuals could be supposed to have a grasp of *all* knowledge, as certain economic models, for instance, will assume, albeit in a rather unrealistic fashion and for other, more limited action contexts, this cannot be taken as evidence for the existence of global knowledge. Quite a few economic market models start out from the assumption that all market players have a comprehensive understanding of the relevant conditions of their action. In his classical critique of this premise, Friedrich August von Hayek (1948a: 77) already pointed out that in practice, it is impossible for any single person to have mastery of this comprehensive and concentrated knowledge: "The peculiar character of the problem of a rational economic order is determined precisely by the fact that the knowledge of the circumstances of which we must make use never exists in concentrated or integrated form but solely as the dispersed bits of incomplete and frequently contradictory knowledge which all the separate individuals possess."[10] Therefore, this argument is an even less suitable basis for qualifying global knowledge worlds (or "global markets").

7.2 Global knowledge worlds[11]

"Knowledge is like light," the 1998/99 World Bank Development Report, *Knowledge for Development*, says. "Weightless and intangible, it can easily travel the world, enlightening the lives of people everywhere. Yet billions of people still live in the darkness of poverty – unnecessarily" (World Bank, 1999: 1). These observations imply that although knowledge seems to have next to no problem traveling around the world, on the one hand, its dissemination is subject to strong constraints, on the other. Ultimately, however, the report optimistically states, barriers and obstacles can be overcome. The project of global knowledge as seen by the World Bank is a goal worth striving for, if as yet unrealized. Regarding the reality of global knowledge, what can be diagnosed in this special case is the "non-contemporaneity of the contemporaneous" in societal phenomena (i.e. the coexistence of local and global knowledge).[12] An even more daunting task is that of analyzing whether the imbalance found in the spatial and temporal manifestation and distribution of social phenomena such as knowledge can be overcome in the future and whether something at least approaching a world society will, thus, be realized.

From this it follows that the concept of global knowledge does not refer to existing global knowledge worlds but to the social and intellectual processes that are required, and the obstacles that need to be overcome, for knowledge to become globally valid knowledge and, thus, to live up to the metaphor of the "demise of distance" in the modern world (see Brown and Duguid, [2000] 2002: 167–170; Beck, 1996: 291).[13]

However, one of the most definitive assertions about the global spread and control of knowledge may be found in a socio-economic perspective with a Marxian flavor that detects the emergence of *intellectual capitalism* out of monopoly capitalism or, at the same time, discounts the control of the state over knowledge (e.g. Carnoy and Castells, 2001: 9). Thus Ugo Pagano (2014: 1410), echoing assertions that can already be found in the *Manifesto of the Communist Party*, claims that since the mid-1990s a form of intellectual monopoly capitalism has become the dominant form of organization of big business. The core implication is the closed "global monopolisation of knowledge" (Pagano, 2014: 1409). We conclude that this is a slight overstatement based on the erroneous assumption that powerful actors and organizations find it easy to control knowledge for their purposes and interests.

From a cultural-scientific perspective, the question of whether there are global knowledge worlds in modern societies[14] implicates a largely uncharted and highly complex terrain. In the context of some discussions on globalization processes, the issue of globalizing knowledge worlds, ideas and political agendas is touched upon, albeit marginally (cf. Dobbin et al., 2007). Sometimes the thesis of global knowledge even turns up as a taken-for-granted assumption. As a rule, what comes to mind when referring to global knowledge is the global spread of scientific-technical knowledge, and it seems to be no less taken for granted that this means knowledge generated in the West, rather than any traditional or indigenous forms of knowledge and whatever global presence they may have (cf. section 5.3).

The terrain of the exploration of global knowledge comes with a number of basic, and complex, questions such as: Can knowledge in modern societies be at all equitably distributed? How easy is it for knowledge to be communicated? To what degree does the dissemination of knowledge depend on social structures (for instance, "global" job markets) or on the relevance of social or political "problems" (e.g. environmental, health care or security problems; cf. Krige and Barth, 2006; Krige, 2014) that are conducive to a global spread of pertinent forms of knowledge? Is knowledge a public good that must be put to equitable and, thus, worldwide use, for instance in a health care context (see Chen et al., 1999)? Why is new knowledge in demand, and does knowledge change in the process of being transferred (cf. Adams and Miranti, 2007)? Is knowledge the symbolic signature of an age of world-spanning knowledge societies? Inasmuch as knowledge is going global, what are the advantages and what are the possible drawbacks of this globalization, i.e. should knowledge go global at all, and are there incentives to the contrary?[15] However, given the wide range of fundamental questions concerning the likelihood of global knowledge, we can take up only some of those that we believe are important in the present context.

We will start our observations by referring to the current "global" context of the issue. There is, on the one hand, the social reassessment of "local" or "traditional" knowledge in the light of globalization processes. Opinions as to how important "local," or "traditional," knowledge is for the economy and the health care system are changing (Fernando, 2003; Fielding and Frieden, 2004; Martin and Vermeylen, 2005; Heinrich and Prieto, 2008). The World Bank (1998) initiative that encourages harnessing local knowledge for developmental processes is one side of this revaluation; the other side of this reassessment of local agrarian, technological or botanical knowledge are increasing endeavors to protect local knowledge (e.g. Agrawal, 2002; Leach and Fairhead, 2002; World Commission on the Social Dimensions of Globalization, 2004).

As for cultural science, sociology and the humanities, researchers have for quite a number of years acted as critical observers of and commentators on the globalization of culture and knowledge in the context of Western-centered cultural phenomena. For example, Mike Featherstone and Couze Venn's (2006) observations are based on the assumption that there is a novel form of instability of culture; they propose and expound a theoretical perspective that, rather than focusing on a worldwide cultural homogenization or on processes of linear temporality, emphasizes the contradictory global variability, global interrelatedness, and global means of communication of culture and knowledge.

In contrast, many observers stress – as well as deplore – the rapid advance, unstoppable dissemination and, thus, local as well as seemingly universal relevance of scientific-technical knowledge (e.g. Wright, 2005: 905). In our modern-day world, scientific knowledge is essentially produced by highly specialized experts in highly specialized contexts, such as laboratories, museums, botanical gardens or field stations, and yet this knowledge is supposed to have ubiquitous validity and usability (Livingstone, 2003) – if only in the networks of multinational corporations around the globe. The research interest is, then, centered on how to efficiently administrate this global dissemination of expert knowledge (e.g. Gupta and Govindarajan, 2000; Jensen and Szulanski, 2004; Hong and Nguyen, 2009).

The global relevance of these (Western) forms of knowledge is, in turn, reflected in transnational agreements on the protection of intellectual property, such as the so-called TRIPS agreement of the World Trade Organization (WTO).[16] If the deep divides with respect to the appropriation and implementation of knowledge both within and between societies cannot be evened out, new elites can be more or less expected to emerge, as argued by Ralf Dahrendorf in terms of his concept of a new emerging global class, wielding an economic power not to be underestimated (see Radhakrishnan, 2007; see also section 3.4).

Finally, knowledge about forms of knowledge that radically demarcate themselves from the unequal assessment, once taken for granted, of the relevance of different forms of knowledge also needs to be taken into account in the context of the issue of "global knowledge worlds" we propose to discuss. Thus, both science studies and the sociology of knowledge no longer insist on the strict distinction between, for instance, scientific and non-scientific knowledge. Nevertheless, and irrespective of the different intentions that may drive local or global efforts, the question of the conditions of possibility of global knowledge worlds remains largely unanswered.

Perhaps the question can be more precisely reformulated, in sociological terms, as follows: Is what may be called "unbounded knowledge" a function of the growing worldwide standardization of organizational forms (states, firms or the scientific community)? If so, are there forms of knowledge (and their carriers) that transcend the local/contextual conditionality of knowledge in increasingly globalizing job markets and, thus, promote the convergence of social contexts around the world (see Freeman, 2006)?[17]

7.3 Structures of global knowledge spaces

We propose to distinguish between different knowledge spaces and, thus, between the opportunities (or lack of opportunities) for knowledge worlds to become horizontally and vertically integrated across institutional, social and national boundaries.[18]

We assume that it is impossible for any distribution of knowledge to be absolutely even, homogeneous, and unaffected by societal differentiations of whatever kind (cf. Luckmann, [1982] 2002: 83). Societal knowledge spaces, therefore, are hardly ever homogeneous sites of knowledge even in traditional societies. Rather, typical knowledge spaces are marked by knowledge that is controversial and subject to more or less soft or rigid forms of a hierarchical and spatial *division of knowledge*.

Given that the societal differentiation of knowledge is not fixed once and for all, the question arises whether the modern world might actually be one of decreasing knowledge differentiation. Indicators that might help answer this question are the levels of horizontal and vertical knowledge integration within and across societies. The dimensions of *horizontal* and *vertical* knowledge integration thus relate to:

1. The worldwide level of concentration of the social bases of knowledge production and consumption (conceived of as incorporated into persons, objects, books, specialist journals, and laboratories). Increased *horizontal* convergence of the social bases of knowledge production may, for instance, mean that today, as compared to previous forms of the division of knowledge, scientists with similar levels of expertise are found all over the world, or that the ways and means of knowledge production are less concentrated in terms of space. Increased *vertical* knowledge integration may mean that (in contrast to the frequently found thesis that there is knowledge concentration as an instrument of power in the hands of the powerful) the boundaries between and the access to highly specialized, or expert, knowledge and the everyday knowledge of various social groups have become less rigid – as compared to previous civilizational epochs – and that, therefore, one may well speak of a knowledge-based increase of opportunities for the more vulnerable strata of a society (see also Elias, 1984).
2. Action agenda, i.e. the questions asked, or the problems for which advice and solutions are sought, are framed in transnational terms and concern the interests of all social groups of a society and of all nations (examples being, for instance, climate change or certain diseases).
3. The forms of (material) embeddedness of knowledge (forms of communication and access) and the demands put on knowledge, which tend to be increasingly similar regardless of political borders between or social differentiations within societies.[19]

While scientific-technical knowledge may well be assumed to have penetrated a substantial part of the world on the level we have described as horizontal, the same is not necessarily true for the vertical integration of knowledge within and across societies. At this point, the question of the persistent relevance of indigenous knowledge and the resistance it offers to a vertical integration of forms of knowledge gains in importance (see also Wright, 2005).

7.4 Forms of global knowledge worlds

The approach to, if not implementation of, global or globalizing knowledge worlds has to date been primarily realized in normative terms (cf. the discussion about the global imperative of sustainability, see Baptista, 2014: 364), by decree, by external imposition, as thought experiments, expert rationality[20] or business plans. We will discuss some of these visions in what follows.[21]

1. One of the first modern optimistic theorists and fervent proponents of global knowledge worlds was the Austrian social philosopher Otto Neurath (see Hartmann and Bauer, 2002; Sandner, 2014; Stehr, 2015a). Even when in exile, Neurath, advising on the redevelopment of the slums of an English industrial town in 1941, chose to call himself a *consulting sociologist of human happiness*. According to Neurath, the question of how to achieve the greatest happiness of all (Bentham) boils down to the question of conditions for democratizing knowledge: liberty is a daughter of knowledge. The democratic right to "global knowledge worlds" (to be established at least on the intra-societal level) is claimed as a due in almost all of Neurath's writings. The medium of this democratization is the "picture language" (Isotope), a science-based method designed by Neurath to enlighten the masses on their situation by visualizing relevant facts. For Neurath (1991: 645) there is "no field where a humanization of knowledge through the eye would not be possible." Thus, getting about does *not* require extended traveling, as is also shown by the example of Dr Schnitzler, another Viennese (see Gay, 2002).

Cybernetics, like many other burgeoning fields of new knowledge, initially conceived of itself as an imperial knowledge hub, as the umbrella science of global knowledge worlds in both theory and practice. More recently, it is the environmental sciences, for instance climate science, that assert to be generating global knowledge claims with implications for badly needed political action on the global level. The "rediscovered" field of social physics raises similar claims based on universally valid data sets (cf. Adolf and Stehr, 2015).

2. Knowledge *should* or must be a (global) public good (e.g. Stiglitz, 1999, 2007: 103–118; World Bank, 1998). From a perspective of economics, this implies that knowledge lacks the characteristics, otherwise

typical of economic goods, of rivalry and excludability,[22] but while this may be true for a society's everyday knowledge capital, it is not true for new incremental knowledge, which yields profits. Therefore, only such forms of knowledge as have been on the market for a certain time can be public goods, if at all. Even in the sciences, the phenomenon of privatization can be increasingly observed. Currently, only 1% of all scientific publications are publicly available, i.e. free to access. A new enterprise launched by scientists in the United States, the Public Library of Science (PLOS), is trying to counter this development.[23] Its aim is to publish scientific papers on the Internet rather than in journals that are controlled by commercial publishing houses or held in fee-based digital libraries. By their action, the founders want to ensure the existence of global scientific knowledge worlds or, at any rate, global access to new knowledge.[24]

Last but not least, the relevant literature offers reflections on what a successful future handling, on the socio-political level, of various global political challenges such as terrorism, nuclear warfare or current environmental problems could be like, culminating in the claim that solutions can only be found through collective and worldwide efforts in terms of educational systems, that is, efforts that will result in the emergence and prevalence of a so-called "global mindset" or "global intelligence" as the only conceivable solution to these globally relevant challenges (cf. Spariosu, 2005).

3. Global knowledge worlds can also be found in practice[25] as business plans or as part of thought experiments. On the largely globally accessible Internet, in particular, there is a multitude of companies or, rather, multinationals in whose business plans "global knowledge worlds" have already been realized and are up for sale. An example is a firm called "Global Knowledge" (slogan: "experts teaching experts"), owned by a New York investment bank, and with more than 1,300 employees worldwide. As its name suggests, this consultancy offers worldwide useable knowledge for boosting a company's profit situation.[26] Another example, launched at the beginning of the new millennium, is Google Print, later renamed Google Books, which appears to have been a key step toward realizing what Google's corporate website describes as the company's mission: "to organize the world's information" and make it "universally accessible and useful" (cf.

Lowood, 2008; a critique of Google's position may be found in Jeanneney, 2007)

Reflections based on similar premises are also found in the economic or management literature. Ideas on how to develop unbounded knowledge worlds are set forth not only in discussions about the emergence of a knowledge-based global economy (for instance, in terms of global production networks, see Chen, 2002), but also in studies in the field of so-called knowledge management, which increasingly relate to global knowledge agendas (e.g. Carillo, 2002; Desouza and Evaristo, 2003), to the institutionalization of global knowledge experts (Covaleski et al., 2003), and to global knowledge management strategies (Davenport et al., 1998; Desouza and Evaristo, 2003).

4. Moreover, there are empirically grounded observations that would seem to suggest a globalizing world at least on the level of scientific-technical knowledge. In a study on the national innovative capacities of the Organisation for Economic Co-operation and Development (OECD) countries (i.e. each country's capacity to develop and commercialize innovative technologies) Scott Stern, Michael Porter and Jeffrey Furman (2000: 31) come to the conclusion, among others, that there is a "*convergence* in measured innovative capacity among OECD countries over the past quarter century." Given the assumption that scientific and technological knowledge is increasingly accessible irrespective of locations and borders,[27] this result is not really surprising. On the other hand, a country's innovative capacity is definitely co-determined, as controversial discussions about the conditions for innovation processes show (Romer, 1990; Porter, 1990; Nelson, 1993), by a variety of location factors including the general micro- and macroeconomic as well as political, cultural and legal frameworks. Speaking of a global spread of innovative capacities seems, thus, hardly warranted as yet (cf. Adolf et al., 2013).

Furthermore, global knowledge exists in a number of thought experiments and, more particularly, economic models. The economists Stephen Parente and Edward Prescott (1994: 302), for instance, refer to the existence of "practical world knowledge" that (ideally) is disseminating, directly and unimpeded, all over the world and is open to shared use by all firms.[28] Parente and Prescott's epistemological interest is in the existence and likely causes of the massive differences between national incomes in our modern-day world (see also Piketty, [2013] 2014). Unable to explain income gaps between nations by different saving rates, Parente and Prescott go on to ask to what extent *knowledge available to all* might account for differential growth rates. The term of world knowledge is, here, taken to refer to the existence of a "stock of general and scientific knowledge in the world (i.e., blueprints, ideas, scientific principles, and so on)" (Parente and Prescott, 1994: 302; Parente and Prescott, 2000: 84). Constructing their model, they assume that all the firms of the world have equal access to these stocks of knowledge; i.e. that this knowledge "spills over the entire world equally" (Parente and Prescott, 1994: 302).

However, a theory of economic development that starts out from the observation of large differences in economic growth needs to be able to explain why some nations indeed manage to exploit this world knowledge efficiently while firms in other societies fail to benefit from it. Thus, Parente and Prescott's model draws attention to the fact that the observable differences in economic growth are likely to be due to differences in the capacity of firms to adapt to technological innovations and existing global knowledge. In a later enhancement of their model, national policies are identified as the cause of differential capacities, in the countries concerned, to assimilate world knowledge (Parente and Prescott, 2000).

Often, however, these normative visions, promising business plans and announcements of global knowledge worlds are eventually revealed to be Eurocentric prejudices. Therefore, visions like these are often criticized for denying, in the final analysis, non-Western actors the capacity to successfully govern themselves, create singular cultural artifacts or substantially contribute to rational discourse. Eye-opening socio-historical contextualizations like these highlight the controversial nature of claims to global relevance and the interpretative wariness that characterizes current reactions to "global" pronouncements that raise know-no-borders claims (e.g. Gough, 2002; Tomaselli, 2014). Nonetheless, there may well be attributes of knowledge itself as well as social attributes and processes that promote a globalization of knowledge in the modern world.

7.5 Attributes of knowledge that promote globalization

What structural or institutional attributes of knowledge can be relied on, on the other hand, to enhance the chances for global knowledge worlds? How and why is it possible – or, inversely, perhaps rather unlikely – for global knowledge worlds to emerge? As it is, the list of these attributes of knowledge is rather short. What we have particularly in mind in this context are two attributes of knowledge that do *not* at the same time imply an urgent need to regulate and monitor it or to control its dissemination. Thus, these attributes can also serve as an incentive to keep knowledge as a common property precisely because, from this perspective, there is no risk of it becoming a resource that will fall victim to the so-called "tragedy of the commons" (Hardin, 1968). Given that these two attributes have already been described in more detail elsewhere (cf. Chapter 5), we will here only briefly discuss them.

First, and understandably enough, many cultures are prejudiced against resources that are available in the commons. For, as indicated by the metaphor of the tragedy of the commons, unlimited access to resources in the commons will result in over-exploitation and, finally, depletion. However, not all resources are subject to this law since some are seemingly inexhaustible, or have different limits to growth. Knowledge, obviously, is one of the latter. The priority task would therefore be to promote the access to and diffusion of knowledge rather than protecting it against unsustainable use, at least as far as this implies capacities to act that are not implicated in "undesirable consequences" (see Stehr, 2005).

Second, it could be argued that knowledge, as has been discussed above, is self-realizing. There are two parallel lines of argumentation in this context, both of which amount to saying that the self-realization of knowledge is due to its intrinsic dynamic and, thus, largely independent of context. Regulating and restricting the realization of knowledge in whatever way is, thus, unnecessary, if not doomed to fail (cf. Stehr, 2003, 2004b).

One line of argumentation holds that the exploitation of knowledge is built into its very structure. The fabrication of knowledge necessarily implies that it will be realized and, thus, precludes controlling its use. A case in point is the conceptual definition, once much discussed, of the different (implicit) epistemological interests that guide scientific research (Habermas, 1964). In this context, the category of the technology-oriented epistemological interest, often undisclosed, accounts for the fact that knowledge (or objects) thus fabricated have an intrinsic drive toward realization or, to be more precise, are from the start associated with their own specific utility.[29] A less direct way for knowledge to be self-realizing, for instance in the case of modern genetics, refers to the understanding that any attempt to prevent the – meanwhile largely publicized – manipulation of the human genome is doomed to fail (cf. Brave, 2001: 3). Once revealed, knowledge will cut its way all by itself.[30] An implicit consequence of the argument that knowledge is self-realizing is the conclusion that due to this quality, knowledge can easily overcome national or cultural boundaries as well as the specific boundaries of functional systems.

A related assumption that can also be taken to indicate certain attributes of knowledge conducive to unimpeded dissemination relates to the difference between *codified* and *implicit* knowledge. Knowledge, it has often been claimed, moves from the implicit to the codified. Economic constraints, for instance, ensure that the development from implicit to codified knowledge is increasingly observed in modern societies (see Cowan and Forey, 1997).[31] For codified knowledge, in turn, it is much easier to overcome social and cultural boundaries than it is for implicit, context-sensitive knowledge.

7.6 Limits to the globalization of knowledge[32]

In the post-World War II era the hope, or fear, of living to see the emergence of a more or less homogeneous world society has given rise to comparative studies, from a great diversity of perspectives, of modern societies. The concept of *globalization* has been dominant for quite some time now in these comparative studies, filling the role that in previous theory-of-science models was that of concepts such as *mass society*, *rationalization* or *modernization*. In recent decades, most of these studies have observed, if not cautioned against, a potential adjustment among, or standardization of, global living conditions.

The broader thesis of the unstoppable homogenization of living conditions, of the emergence of a world without borders, can be reasonably assumed also to include or at least support the thesis of the emergence of global knowledge worlds. However, we feel that this thesis is questionable given that globalization processes may as well have the opposite effect and encourage an affirmation of national or regional social and cultural differences (cf. Yeung, 1998). We will, therefore, first offer some general observations on the issue of globalization, and then discuss some of the specific limits set to the possibility of globalizing knowledge.

Studies on *cultural* globalization[33] have a particularly close affinity to the discussions, meanwhile brought into discredit, about the theory of modern society as a mass society. In many countries worldwide there is a marked sensitivity, at least among intellectuals, toward any forms of cultural imperialism. Given the massive pressure from primarily American trivial culture, cultural imperialism is assumed to involve the risk for local, regional or national cultural frames to be submerged. The fact that there is growing economic and ecological interdependence but also an internationalization of knowledge and information is hardly called into question anymore in the rapidly accumulating literature.

The lines of argumentation followed by the opponents as well as the proponents of the dynamism and the unstoppable advance of globalization are contradictory only at first glance. Both sides, for example, tend to systematically overestimate (just as in previous analyses of the phenomenon of mass society or of modernization) the efficiency and the pace that mark the worldwide progress of the rationalization of the irrational, for instance the disappearance of traditional values and behaviors (cf. Chapter 2 of this book).

In economics, it is rarely assumed that all relevant economic changes will follow one and the same direction and will therefore converge. It is no doubt true that some of the classical causes of economic underdevelopment no longer apply today, in particular the slow spread of modern technologies and scientific knowledge that was still a salient feature in the 1950s and 1960s. Multinational corporations are almost ubiquitous. *Nevertheless*, these changes have not led to a convergence of economic conditions or an equal distribution of the production of knowledge-intensive goods and services. High-tech and knowledge-based production sites are still concentrated in a small number of regions and countries that can boast an outstanding knowledge and technology infrastructure (Patel and Pavitt, 1991; Storper, 1996).

Although, from a political perspective, it may seem ever more obvious that the production of technological knowledge is increasingly internationalizing, the fact that it remains concentrated in the home countries of the big corporations is due, along with other factors, to the very properties of the processes of technological invention themselves, as Pari Patel and Keith Pavitt (1991: 18) have pointed out, namely "the primacy of multidisciplinary and tacit knowledge inputs, and the commercial uncertainties surrounding outputs. Physical proximity facilitates integration of multidisciplinary knowledge that is tacit and therefore 'person-embodied' rather than 'information-embodied'. It also facilitates rapid decision-making needed to cope with uncertainty."

In a case study of one Japanese and one British high-technology firm, Alice Lam (1997: 993) shows how the social embeddedness of the organizations' knowledge and work systems "between firms in different societal settings can seriously inhibit the collaborative work and impede effective knowledge transfer across national boundaries."

Furthermore, the thesis, already promoted by Adam Smith, that economic *specialization* is important for economic growth, has by no means been invalidated by what is described as globalization. The ongoing process of significant macro-economic specialization may well be accompanied by an inter-societal *division of labor* in terms of *learning* that is very likely to make it harder for global knowledge worlds to emerge (cf. Stiglitz, 1987). There seems to be a very specific relation between the differential learning capacities of the society as a whole and its history and culture, and differential learning capacities of societies indicate differential futures.

Finally, the often singular fascination caused by the sudden appearance, unerring directness and obvious power of global processes tends to mislead us into underestimating the persistence of "national" and "local" realities and their potential for active resistance, as well as the persistence of traditional ways of acting,[34] and thus into assuming that global knowledge exists (cf. Mokyr, 1990: 186–190).

In what follows, we will focus on two specific forms of constraining the development of globalizing knowledge worlds, that is the capacity, varying among societies (e.g. due to their technological infrastructure or their pool of work-related skills), to exploit knowledge that has been produced in a particular location in the world (see Castellacci and Archibugi, 2008). These constraints are:

1. Intra- and inter-societal barriers, for instance a society's legal practices, inequality regimes (forms of the cognitive division of labor; incentives for asymmetries in the access to knowledge, e.g. in defense of market power), social divides, geographical distances (see Bahar et al., 2013; Keller and Yeaple, 2013) between social organizations (firms, laboratories), and trade barriers between societies.
2. Properties that can be directly attributed to certain dispositions of modern-day knowledge. One of the properties that characterizes modern scientific knowledge is its short "lifespan," which may act as a barrier to its global spread. Modern science not only assumes that knowledge is subject to systematic obsolescence but may even demand and encourage it, with the result that knowledge indeed ages rapidly. Along with the often non-negligible transaction costs of acquiring new knowledge this means that – despite the basic openness of science systems and economic functional systems – a global distribution of knowledge is nipped in the bud, so to speak.

Max Weber was primarily concerned, if such a generalization is at all permissible, with the *barriers* to the implementation of modern technologies and modern scientific thought outside the Western world. The reasons why technologies come to be implemented in Western societies, in the first place, for instance for the purpose of revolutionizing production routines, were of much less interest to him.

Weber does, however, call attention, in his *Protestant Ethic*, to the fact that the rise of technology in Western societies was due to a stratum of people committed to a certain way of life. Thus, a gap in Weber's comparative analysis can now be filled relying on Weber's own approach, namely by emphasizing the specific relevance of cultural practices for the development of a society and for the migration of knowledge: we know that the bearers of scientific-technical knowledge have played a decisive role in the societal implementation of modern technology and science.[35] For this to happen on a general level, however, the bearers of scientific-technical knowledge have to have some autonomy from the ruling strata of the society, enabling them to break with traditional forms of knowledge, as well as access to an organizational infrastructure that allows their knowledge to spread.

The historian of technology Ian Inkster (1991: 32–59) describes the results of these processes in terms of a transfer of "cultural capital." That this is a Weberian approach is made evident by the fact that Inkster stresses in his analysis the role both of the bearers of culture and of cultural barriers (for instance, the prevalence of magical practices or deeply entrenched cultural traditions),[36] thus attributing the rise of Western (rational) technologies to cultural preconditions (see Schroeder and Swedberg, 2002: 390).

In the post-World War II era, the general conditions of knowledge production in the United States (and subsequently also in other nations) twice underwent a radical change. The first revolution, launched about 70 years ago by Vannevar Bush (cf. O'Mara, 2005), consisted in the decoupling of knowledge production from military and political objectives. It initiated the rise of the great research universities in the United States and can be seen as the trigger for improving the conditions of possibility of global knowledge worlds. Knowledge could now circulate more easily. The beneficiaries of this development were not only US scientists and students, but also specifically selected foreign researchers and students (for instance, through the Fulbright Program).[37]

At the time, philosophers of science as different as Karl Popper, Michael Polanyi, John Bernal or Vannevar Bush were unanimous in stressing the autonomy of science as a prerequisite of "uncontaminated" knowledge generation, but also of knowledge that is effective in practice. As a consequence, the utility of knowledge is a daughter of the "truth" of knowledge, and truth, in turn, is the supreme goal of scientific work.

The second transformation that resulted, as has often been argued, in re-constraining the free circulation of knowledge and, thus, in increasing the chances for knowledge *not* to become a *global public good* (Stiglitz, 1999) was triggered in 1980 by the US Senate's passage of the Bayh-Dole Amendment to the Patent Act. The Bayh-Dole Amendment enabled researchers to have their findings patented even though they had been obtained with public funding. The result was a dramatic shift of research activities from the public to the private sector (see Kennedy, 2002).[38]

The subsequent changes in the dissemination of knowledge or its material substrates are today especially felt in biomedical research. In this field, it is not only the material substrates of research – such as cell lines or specific breeds of mice whose production is cost-intensive – that are no longer free for use by other research groups, but even the methods, data and research findings from commercial as well as academic production, which are no longer made available for reasons of competition.[39] In short, access to the conditions of production of new knowledge and to the results of this production is being increasingly *regulated* (Pottage, 1998).[40]

At the same time, the barriers between different social organizations, be it firms or laboratories, are not so porous and negligible as to justify speaking of a largely unimpeded circulation of knowledge, or of the need to adapt to local conditions (Hong and Nguyen, 2009), which facilitate this circulation. A study, conducted between 1995 and 1999 in the United States, of thousands of clinical trials of new drugs carried out by pharmaceutical companies has shown that knowledge-intensive clinical tests were primarily an internal affair, i.e. carried out in and by the companies themselves. In contrast, information-intensive clinical trials or the generation and/or reworking of symbols in view of producing data were often outsourced to external companies (Azoulay, 2003).[41]

In positive terms, trade with services and goods is an important *inter*societal vehicle for the diffusion of knowledge and the development of globalizing knowledge worlds.[42] Extending global trade, and in particular reducing trade barriers for developing economies, can thus lead to a non-intended worldwide diffusion of ideas and knowledge, as well as to a reduction of information and knowledge deficits around the world.

As Joseph Stiglitz (2001: 515) emphasizes, "one of the most important determinants of the pace of growth is, for developed countries, the investment in research, and for less developed countries, efforts at closing the knowledge gap between themselves and more developed countries." However, this should not be thought of in terms of a simple transfer of knowledge and artifacts but, rather, in terms of hybrid forms of knowledge being developed. The fact that knowledge is embedded in a specific knowledge infrastructure (in terms of, for instance, the capacity of learning to learn) and is, thus, neither circulating freely nor capable of being reconstituted regardless of contextual requirements could, after all, constitute the very basis of its self-protection (as discussed in more detail elsewhere, cf. section 5.2).[43]

Studies by Eric von Hippel ("sticky information," cf. von Hippel, 1991, 1994) and Christiano Antonelli (1999: 244) also rely on the assumption that (technological) knowledge is heavily dependent on persons and contexts. These arguments and findings, inasmuch as they are "universally applicable, suggest that there are barriers that are hard to overcome even for globalizing knowledge" (cf. also Polanyi, 1958, 1967; Cowan, et al., 2000: 6–7).

That the transfer of technological knowledge is far from being unimpeded is also shown by a number of empirical studies dealing with technology transfer. Their findings, for instance those of the classical study by George Hall and Richard Johnson (1970) on the transfer of aircraft technology from the United States to Japan, clearly show that far from being linear or mechanical, the transfer of technological knowledge needs to be "interactive and embedded in existing capabilities on both sides and in the social relationships between both sides of the transaction" (Grandori and Kohut, 2002: 224).

In his recent study on the worldwide development and diffusion of the information and computer industry in the decades after World War II, James W. Cortada portrays a very efficient transnational network for technological knowledge transfer across the Soviet Union, China and India, as well as across the United States and Western Europe.

The diffusion of technological knowledge was ensured by a kind of information ecosystem. These information exchange networks were interconnected but neither formalized nor organized as a unit, and characterized by "a combined near-simultaneous interaction of engineers, scientists, politicians, and business employees working in educational research centers, government agencies, user communities, publications and associations, and for vendors in scores of countries, sometimes independently, sometimes in collaboration" (Cortada, 2014: 72).

One implication of Cortada's study is that the international information technology network could have been the driver of the post-1970s onset of globalization. On the other hand, relevant questions are left unanswered in Cortada's study: To what extent do his findings for the transnational diffusion of computer technologies apply to other technologies and forms of knowledge, as well, and what were the barriers that the transnational diffusion of technological knowledge, not to mention the globalizing software and computer industries, had to overcome in the process?

7.7 The project of worldwide worlds of knowledge, and the doubts about its likelihood

Global knowledge, like the concept of globalization, is a term fraught with risk. At the level of politics, global knowledge stirs hopes for a less divided world but at the same time conjures up the danger of as yet independent lifeworlds and forms of knowledge disappearing.

Knowledge is often seen as the public good *par excellence*; thus, the ethos of science demands that knowledge should be accessible to all at least in principle. However, is it really "equal" knowledge for all? Do globalizing knowledge worlds require a (natural) global language (cf. De Swaan, 2001), if not globally valid social conditions? Is scientific knowledge that has been converted into technology still subject to the same normative rules? What are the costs accruing from knowledge transfer? Moreover, notwithstanding its good reputation, knowledge is almost always contestable and contested, but while these properties are seen as an advantage and a virtue in scientific theory, this fact is often ignored in practice. As a consequence, scientific knowledge is either seriously over- or systematically under-rated, and since knowledge is in seemingly unlimited supply without losing any of its relevance, it is only to a very limited degree associated with claims of private ownership (Simmel, [1907] 1989b: 438).

Modern communication technologies seem to ensure that access to knowledge and information becomes easier and that the constraints associated with formally existing reservations of proprietary rights are at least partly removed. The ease with which (codified) knowledge and information can be accessed gives rise to certain fears, for instance the fear of bioterrorism (see Lane and Fauci, 2001), but modern technologies also allow for knowledge and information to be concentrated in the hands of the few, a development that no doubt is a cause of misgivings for many observers (see Ginsberg, 1986: 127). At the same time, it is no less possible, or so we suppose, that the enhanced social relevance of knowledge will in the end undermine its exclusivity. However, for the time being, the contrary seems to be true, which again raises the issue of the persistence of conditions that allow for the power of knowledge to be concentrated in the hands of the societally powerful (cf. Chapter 3).

The disenchantment of *science* by science goes along with the call for a philosophy of *research*, given that scientific research can be what science must not be: research may generate disputes and may formulate contested knowledge claims. While science is expected to put an end to controversy and to keep aloof from society, research is allowed and even expected to interfere, as argued by Bruno Latour (1998). However, science, in a marked contrast to the beliefs of the classical functionalist theory of societal differentiation, is every so often precisely not able to provide cognitive certainty. Scientific discourse is de-pragmaticized; it is unable to propose definite, let alone true, statements (in terms of proven causal propositions) for practical purposes. All it can do is offer more or less plausible assumptions, scenarios or probability statements (cf. Stehr, 1991). Science, therefore, is both a provider of reliable knowledge *and* a source of uncertainty (Grundmann and Stehr, 2000).

Silvio Funtowicz and Jerome Ravetz (1990: 7), for instance, argue that modern science is confronted with historically novel problems and that this is what injects uncertainty into scientific work. They point out that:

> amidst all the great progress in scientific theory and in technological development, […] we are confronted by a new class of environmental challenges and threats. Among these are hazardous wastes, greenhouse effect and ozone depletion. These give rise to problems of a different sort from those of traditional science, either in laboratory, classroom, or industry. Science was previously understood as achieving ever greater certainty on our knowledge

and control of the natural world; now it is seen as coping with
increasing uncertainties in these urgent environmental issues.

(Funtowicz and Ravetz, 1990: 7)

This uncertainty is not a sign of ignorance or of a (temporary) knowledge deficit (cf. Chapter 3). It is a constitutive property of both knowledge and the context in which knowledge must work.[44] In contrast to what rational theory-of-science reflections suggest, these problems cannot be brought under control, let alone solved, by distinguishing between "good" and "bad" (or pseudoscientific and adequate) science. Under conditions of uncertainty, how is this supposed to be possible at all?

Finally, it can be concluded that there can be no such thing as a globally equal distribution of knowledge, in the first place, and in spite of societal processes that would seem to point in this direction (or are construed as homogenizing and globalizing factors). There can be no globally equal horizontal and vertical distribution of knowledge in societies with a highly developed division of labor, as well as due to the demographical fact that there is a continuous flow of incoming and outgoing members of society (see also Luhmann, 2002: 83–87). As a consequence, a conclusive answer to the questions raised here about the present existence or future likelihood of globalizing knowledge can only be given by saying that while specific forms of knowledge, and in particular those embedded in projects or objects (see Woolgar, 2002: 265; Orlikowski, 2006: 466; Sarewitz and Nelson, 2008), may indeed acquire global characteristics, most forms of knowledge will find it difficult to attain the level of universality.

In the next chapter, we turn to the question of how knowledge may be diffused, or even created, through processes of communication. Typically for modern societies, communication comes to rely on media, a transformation that has consequences not only for society itself, but also for the communication process. The mediation of communication, as we will see, detaches information and knowledge from some contexts while at the same time introducing new parameters and frameworks into the process. The advent of digital media, and the changes they imply, is but the latest stage of this historical development.

Notes

1 Translated from German by Hella Beister. The following discussion of the possibilities of a worldwide spread of knowledge and its power that, therefore, can be characterized by its ability to overcome any form of social, political and cultural particularity benefits from previous work dedicated to a critical analysis of the barriers to and opportunities for knowledge dissemination. For first systematic reflections on the concept of global knowledge, see Nico Stehr and Ulrich Ufer (2009) in a special edition of the *International Social Science Journal*.
2 The search for the German term of "globales Wissen" ("global knowledge") on the Internet resulted in 951,000 Google hits in diverse documents (accessed December 15, 2015; one year before, the number of hits was 849,000, and on May 13, 2008 it was still as low as 25,000); in contrast, the English term of "global knowledge" resulted in 403,000,000 Google hits (accessed January 15, 2014; on May 13, 2008 the number was 1,050,000). This difference can be taken as primarily documenting the fact that the number of documents available on the Internet has multiplied in the few years between the searches.
3 Anssi Paasi (2015: 509–510) laments the globalization and the geopolitics of scientific knowledge pushed along by forms of academic capitalism but at the same time strongly endorses patterns of asymmetries of knowledge production, the uneven publication, circulation and consumption of knowledge, and the heterogeneity of knowledge spaces around the world, which appears to deny the possibility of global knowledge as long as the world remains stratified.
4 This first definition should make it clear that we will *not* deal with what is called "world knowledge" in *linguistics*. In linguistics, world knowledge, or "background knowledge," is a term used to explain meanings that are "not explicitly denoted by signs" (Plümacher, 2006: 247). This also holds for a premise, reluctantly shared by anthropologists in the heroic times of anthropology, "that science, ideology, art, religion, or philosophy, or at least the impulses they serve, are not the common property of all mankind" (Geertz, 1975: 6). "Thus," Geertz (ibid.) goes on to specify, "Durkheim found elementary forms of religious life among the Australian aborigines, Boas a spontaneous sense of design on the Northwest Coast, Levi-Strauss a 'concrete' science in the Amazon, Griaule a symbolic ontology in a West African tribe, and Gluckman an implicit *jus commune* in an East African one."
5 In this sense, global knowledge as the result of a societal process begins as both "external" knowledge hitherto located in other social contexts and as knowledge that does not discriminate against any potential recipient, is "free of cost," and is voluntarily disclosed (cf. Pénin, 2007: 326).
6 Another relevant constraint for our topic relates to a more in-depth discussion of the widespread thesis that due to the very fact of its being open

to *unlimited* use, *scientific knowledge* represents global knowledge worlds (e.g. Drori et al., 2003: 8–9).
7 Inasmuch as legal norms, as pointed out by Sarah Wright (2005: 906), increasingly define what can be patented in line with the Europe-based *International Union for the Protection of New Varieties of Plants* (UPOV), "they become a universally valid norm, a spatially unlimited framework for knowledge."
8 The case of the worldwide dissemination of the scientific field and the technological practices of modern meteorology is discussed in Edwards (2006), among others.
9 In an interview with *The New York Times* (Thomas L. Friedman, "It's a flat world, after all," 3 April, 2005), Nandan Nilekani, the then chairman of the Indian multinational corporation InfoSys Technologies in Bangalore, describes the consequences of the worldwide dissemination of these technological platforms by saying that technological platforms enable "intellectual work, intellectual capital, [to] be delivered from anywhere. It could be disaggregated, delivered, distributed, produced and put back together again – and this gave a whole new degree of freedom to the way we do work, especially work of an intellectual nature. And what you are seeing in Bangalore today is really the culmination of all these things coming together."
10 Which implies that the problem of how to put to use knowledge that nobody masters in its totality becomes the real problem of the analysis of economic processes, but also of economic policy (see also Sowell, 1980).
11 An early reference to an inescapable global dissemination (also) of "intellectual creations," at least under conditions of the modern capitalist economic order, can be found in the 1848 *Manifesto of the Communist Party* by Karl Marx and Friedrich Engels: "In place of the old local and national seclusion and self-sufficiency, we have intercourse in every direction, universal inter-dependence of nations. And as in material, so also in intellectual production. The intellectual creations of individual nations become common property. National one-sidedness and narrow-mindedness become more and more impossible, and from the numerous national and local literatures, there arises a world literature" (Marx and Engels, [1848] 1969).
12 As far as we can see, the metaphor was first introduced into sociology by Karl Mannheim ([1928] 1993: 358), who used it to describe existing social phenomena, particularly in the context of his by now classical essay on the social phenomenon of generations. In his analysis of the non-contemporaneity of contemporaneous phenomena, Mannheim drew on an idea that was first developed by art historian Wilhelm Pinder (1926). Another relevant example is Ernst Bloch's ([1918] 2000) theory of the simultaneity of non-simultaneous art forms as elaborated in his work *Geist der Utopie*, as well as William F. Ogburns's ([1922] 1950) thesis of the cultural retardation of social phenomena, and Arnold Gehlen's ([1957] 2004: 35) "law of differential development." The observation of the simultaneity of distinct social processes – e.g. within global society – shows that the simultaneous

presence of global interdependencies and discrepancies is not necessarily contradictory; on the contrary, divergent processes like these are mutually interdependent (cf. Luhmann, 1988: 170).

13 There are even robust empirical findings to the contrary, albeit as yet restricted to a certain number of professions: "The transmission of knowledge diminishes with physical distance" (Johnson et al., 2006: 19; Keller, 2002). Economists have relied on these empirical findings to explain the spatial concentration of clusters of innovation and industry (e.g. Anselin et al., 1997). The distances that knowledge is able to overcome are not *a priori* limited, at least not among individuals engaged in *collaborative* work in research projects, and can currently be reduced by means of new social arrangements and new technological devices (see Johnson et al., 2006).

14 Our question concerning the existence of global knowledge worlds needs to be narrowed down to *modern* societies, especially as there is quasi-unanimity in the literature that the emergence of *shared knowledge worlds* is a *modern* phenomenon. Thus, in his Fifteenth Lecture on pragmatism Émile Durkheim ([1955] 1983: 76; cf. also Gehlen, [1950] 1988: 320) emphasizes: "It is in the very earliest ages that men, in every social group, all think in the same way. It is then that uniformity of thought can be found. The great differences only begin to appear with the very first Greek philosophers. The Middle Ages once again achieved the very type of the intellectual consensus. Then came the Reformation, and with it came heresies and schisms which were to continue to multiply until we eventually came to realize that everyone has the right to think as he wishes." On the other hand, our question becomes immaterial if it is taken for granted, as the proponents of a scientistic perspective do, that "the insights of science and technology [...] are valid and can be tapped into all over the world – therefore they ought to be more effective in bringing people together than any other discipline of human thought" (Gustav Born, "Zum Nachdenken zwingen. Die Wissenskluft wächst gefährlich," *Frankfurter Allgemeine Zeitung*, June 23, 2004, S. N2).

15 As far as we can see, the uncommon question of what the *point* is of global knowledge, which we cannot discuss in more detail in the present context, has in recent times been increasingly building on certain beliefs: if, for instance, the assumption is that "Western science" is only one of several possible ways of gaining knowledge, which, moreover, result in different but equally valid findings, then the question of what the point is of global knowledge is also a question of the possible dominance of one of several forms of knowledge. If, on the other hand, the assumption, perhaps based on economic considerations, is that globally accessible and usable knowledge eliminates comparative advantages that go hand in hand with regional, national or corporation-based knowledge monopolies, then global knowledge is an undesirable development (cf. Freeman, 2006; see also Paul Feyerabend's [1993] doubts as to the virtue of a dominant knowledge culture).

16 See the relevant WTO website: www.wto.org/english/tratop_e/trips_e/trips_e.htm (accessed April 3, 2015). The specific norms (precisely what is

patentable?) of the contractual arrangement for the protection of intellectual property are, of course, the product of a specific socio-economic milieu and an unmistakable geographical knowledge space.

17 See also Thomas L. Friedman, "It's a flat world, after all," *The New York Times*, April 3, 2005: "When the world is flat, you can innovate without having to emigrate." In a similar vein, James N. Rosenau (2005: 73) for the first time refers to the age of the transnational "networked individual" that has meanwhile become a global presence and has succeeded in bringing the history of empires to an end.

18 An appropriate assumption would be that the horizontal transfer of knowledge is not only the vastly more frequent but also the vastly more rapid process of knowledge dissemination. Also, related concepts and perspectives such as the "lateral diffusion" (e.g. in the context of innovations; cf. Rogers, 1964) of knowledge and technological artifacts, or the "transfer" of models, metaphors, analogies and methods from one discourse community to another (cf. Gissis, 2009) are essentially descriptions of horizontal knowledge dissemination.

19 The cost issue associated with the options for accessing knowledge is not necessarily the most important form of restricted access. Mancur Olson (1996: 7), for instance, argues that "[p]erhaps most advances in basic science can be of use to a poor country only after they have been combined with or embodied in some product or process that must be purchased from firms in the rich countries." However, a case study on economic growth in South Korea between 1973 and 1979 (Koo, 1982) that attempts to quantify the costs of making available relevant knowledge from other countries has shown that "the world's productive knowledge is, as for the most part, available to poor countries, and even at relatively modest cost" (Olson, 1996: 8). The costs of acquiring knowledge (in the broadest sense of the term) from other countries were less than 1.5% of the increase in Korea's gross domestic product (GDP) over the period discussed.

20 Anthony Giddens (1996) conceptualizes expert rationality in terms of a globally circulating medium that, in the form of knowledge, co-determines the foundations of and change in social action and moves largely without hindrance.

21 A conception of global knowledge modeled on the differentiation of societal institutions would, for instance, have to account for political, scientific, technological and economic visions of global knowledge worlds. The economic and the scientific visions will be discussed below. The generally accepted *technological* vision today assumes that the Internet, that is the World Wide Web, allows for global knowledge to be realized as the Internet transforms local knowledge into global knowledge. The currently prevalent *political* vision, as manifest in the resolutions of the United Nations (such as the Geneva 2003 UN World Summit on the Information Society), calls for existing boundaries of various kinds to be overcome and sustainably removed to pave the way for a global knowledge world. According to this vision, global knowledge will be possible as soon as the so-called "digital divide" within and between societies has been overcome.

22 The economist Paul A. Samuelson (1954) was the first to outline a *formal* concept of collective goods that are suited for "nonrivalrous consumption." The economist Fritz Machlup (1979b: 408), who was deeply engaged in working towards a quantification of knowledge in the 1950s and 1960s (e.g. Machlup, 1962), calls attention to the difference between "stocks of knowledge" and "flows of knowledge," noting that "while the flow [of knowledge] never reduces the stocks of knowledge possessed by the transmitters, it does not always increase the recipients' stocks." Machlup invokes a number of reasons why this asymmetry may come about, one of which being that knowledge cannot be conserved; also, knowledge may rapidly become irrelevant or obsolete.

23 www.plos.org. See also "New premise in science: Get the word out quickly, online," *The New York Times*, December 17, 2002.

24 The European Commission, the US House of Representatives and the British House of Commons have recently addressed the issue of restricted access to research findings. Their investigations will no doubt result in support given to efforts to facilitate this access (see also the "Berlin Declaration," www.zim.mpg.de/openaccess-berlin/berlindeclaration.html, by scientific organizations from Germany, Switzerland and Austria, as well as the article "Access all areas," *The Economist*, August 5, 2004, www.economist.com/science/displayStory.cfm?story_id=3061258).

25 An example would be the so-called "born globals," i.e. small technology outfits that have been operating on international markets from the very start (Knight and Cavusgil, 1996: 11).

26 www.globalknowledge.com (accessed December 20, 2015).

27 In these models, a country's participation in the growing international competition and the creation of conditions for action that enable participation in competition, in the first place, are identified as the drivers of knowledge diffusion, along with improved opportunities to access stocks of knowledge and learning opportunities (Grossman and Helpman, 1991: 238–242).

28 These theses are not least based on the classical intuitive assumption – found, for instance, in epistemology or in economics (Bates, 1988) – that knowledge, once communicated, is rather easily (and at low cost) available to the potential "consumer," i.e. without comprehensive transaction costs. Compared to the costs of generating knowledge, dissemination costs are low. Steve Fuller (1992: 168) critically observes that "the 'hard work' of invention or discovery comes with the original development of an idea, and that the subsequent work of transmitting the idea to others is negligible by comparison […] all the information is seen as packed into the initial conception, with transmission regarded as mere reproduction, whereby the initial conception is either preserved or lost, depending on the receptiveness of the targeted customers." However, this classical thesis underestimates the importance (as well as the high costs and lengthy process) of acquiring the intellectual competences that are needed for a person to be able to consume knowledge generated by others: there is quite a difference

between making an engineer understand a new invention and doing the same for a layperson.
29 In this context, cf. the thesis, set out above, by Pinch and Bijker (1984: 419–424) that technological developments are, from the start, characterized by being "hardwired" in terms of their practical fate. This means that it is unlikely, if not outright impossible, for technologies to come with ambivalent or alternative forms of development and, thus, have "interpretative flexibility."
30 John Kay (1999: 12) notes that forms of knowledge (information) such as they are typically generated in the natural sciences and relate to a specific technical skill (for instance, how to write an email or make a video player), are extremely easy to transmit and, as a consequence, hard to protect effectively, if at all: "Scientific knowledge knows no corporate or national boundaries and is easily transmissible."
31 Cowan and Forey (1997: 596) define the codification of knowledge as "the process of conversion of knowledge into messages which can be processed as information." Dissemination, the authors assume, is much easier, or at least bound up with lower marginal costs, for information than for non-codified knowledge.
32 A discussion about the boundaries of global knowledge would need to take into account the variously motivated attempts, discussed in greater detail in Chapter 10, deliberately to limit the spread of knowledge by means of patents, copyright regulations and other provisions. It would further need to take into account nation-state bans on specific technological options or artifacts, or opportunities for action (possible examples being the European regulations concerning genetically modified seeds or the use of fracking technologies for the production of fossil fuels, which are more restrictive than global trends would suggest). The success or non-success, however, of such efforts made on the grounds of economic or security reasons is another highly controversial issue (cf. Martin, 2014).
33 Laura Adams (2008: 614) reminds us that the vast literature on the globalization of *culture* is Western-based and primarily focuses on the impact the patterns of Western cultural production have on cultural production in the non-Western world.
34 Moreover, the well "guarded" disciplinary as well as theory-based boundaries in the social sciences help to obscure the importance of the *mutual* influence between cultural, political and economic forces, making it harder for them to be measured.
35 By way of analogy, this also holds for the diffusion, brought about by the "work" of local "intellectual entrepreneurs," of *ideas* from one of the world's regions or societies to another region or society, as Xiaoying Qi (2013), for instance, has shown, taking China as an example.
36 Deborah Davis (2004), for instance, shows that in contemporary China deeply entrenched cultural traditions can be relied on to help mobilize considerable resistance to globalization in terms of real estate privatization.

37 In 2011, Chinese students alone numbered 195,000 at American universities (Krige, 2014: 50).
38 Daniel Kevles (2001) explores the US history of patenting *living* entities. Pharmaceutical products seem to be the primary beneficiaries of patenting, all the more so as some minimal change in a drug's composition may warrant a new patent. If the definition of knowledge is extended to include the so-called "branding" or the reputation of a product (such as, for instance, Coca-Cola, Nike, Mercedes), then the diffusion – in terms of "imitation" – of this form of knowledge is severely constrained by the successful branding, or the reputation of a product or service (cf. Kay, 1999: 13).
39 Kennedy (2002: 125) calls attention to the following case: the journal *Proceedings of the National Academy of Sciences* "has, within the past three years, published two papers in which data essential to confirming the claimed result were available to commercial researchers only for a price, and another in which sequence data were not available at all."
40 Conventional utilitarian economic theories emphasize that while the protection of intellectual property by patents, copyright laws and similar state-sanctioned norms indeed yields short-term monopolistic profits, it at the same time provides incentives to innovation that in the long run will serve the common good (for the first time in Smith, [1776] 1976: 277–278; Bentham, 1839: 71; Pigou, 1924: 151; Arrow, 1962a: 616–617). More recently, however, Boldrin and Levine (2002) have argued that the (competitive) market is very well able to offer rewards for entrepreneurial research and development (R&D) investments, which implies that patent laws are not only unnecessary but have a negative effect, for instance on the pricing of new products (see also Plant, 1934a, 1934b; Hirshleifer, 1971).
41 Azoulay's (2003) empirically grounded observations of the typical behavior of a whole industry regarding the commissioning of knowledge- or information-intensive studies does little to elucidate the question of precisely why firms – apart from economic incentives – behave in this way. However, an interpretation of the findings of Azoulay's study suggests that experiences to the effect that the "journey" of knowledge is impeded by system-inherent structures and processes may well have an impact on decision making.
42 See the study by Park (1995) which, however, is confined to the international diffusion of knowledge generated by R&D activities in OECD countries.
43 Furthermore, specific forms of organizing knowledge may help protect it, as Edmund Kitch (1980: 712), for instance, points out: "Managers can avoid increasing the ease with which information can be transmitted by resisting the temptation to assemble the information in organized written form."
44 To cite but one example from climate science: hardly anybody still doubts, as we have already emphasized, that the globally averaged Earth temperature has risen in the course of the previous century. As for the causes and for further climatic change, however, there is great uncertainty, and in spite of intensified research efforts, this uncertainty is not diminishing at all but

even seems to increase. This is true not only for potential future climatic changes and associated impacts on a global level but even, and particularly so, for regional ecological and social transformations induced by and depending on the climate. A study published by Chris E. Forest and a number of other authors (Forest et al., 2002) was unable to offer an answer to the decisive question of climate sensitivity (i.e., for instance, of how the climate might respond to a doubling of the carbon dioxide content of the atmosphere). The authors suggest a rise of 1.4° to 7.7° C while the Intergovernmental Panel on Climate Change (IPCC), by something like a compromise, assumes 1.5° to 4.5° C. Also, the authors of the study assume a probability of more than 30% for sensitivity to exceed the figures set by the IPCC. In other words, uncertainty about the decisive measure for climate projections is still great, if not greater than before.

8

DIGITAL WORLDS AND KNOWLEDGE/INFORMATION[1]

With the arrival of the Internet and its web-based services many commentators were convinced that a new age had begun: the era of the Information Society. The advent of the digital revolution, for most observers synonymous with the rapid diffusion of the Internet as a means of business and household usage from the mid-1990s, was accompanied by both high hopes and deep fears concerning the ramifications of these new technologies for modern society. The Internet and its new ways of interaction established a decentralized, real-time communication infrastructure which immensely increased the ease and speed with which data could travel, potentially around the world. It also exploded the amount of information circulating around the globe and drastically diminished its half-life. In this chapter we will track discussions about the consequences that the "new" media of communication – in the following information and communication technologies (ICTs) and *digital media* – which have emerged during the last two decades will have for the societal organization of knowledge and power as well as the general attendant debate about their rise, at least allegedly, to epochal relevance.

8.1 Information, communication and technology

We propose to start with a general overview of the technological innovations whose intimate connection to information, communication and thus knowledge is already reflected by the name they were widely given: ICTs. While traditional media of mass communication (i.e. the media of dissemination or "mass media"; Luhmann, [1996] 2000) gave rise to what has been termed the era of the "broadcast-paradigm" (Simonson, 2010) typical of the structure of societal communication in early modernity, the Internet brought with it a new form of the social organization of communication between people, organizations and institutions within and across societies.

These changes were – and to some extent still are – captured in a narrative of disruption. While the "old media" streamlined the flow of information and channeled what was deemed of interest by a chosen few to "the masses," the digital media exhibit a quite different architecture. Whereas radio and television, the broadcast media of the twentieth century, were "gatekeepers" (White, 1950), the new media of the Internet era rang loud with the promise of a democratization of communication, untainted by partisan politics or commercial interests.

In order to appreciate the widespread and often overly optimistic hopes attached to ICTs, we need to remember the pivotal role that the media of communication play in the context of (not only, but especially *democratic*) politics. The public sphere of modern, democratic society is necessarily a mediated public sphere – only the media can bridge the spatial and temporal expanse, the topical and ideological diversity, as well as the moral plurality of modernity. Thus, it is by no means an exaggeration to assert the centrality of the media for the flow of information and as the locus of public debate in societies. While traditional media organizations have come under pressure, not least due to the transformational force of technological and business innovation, the so-called new (digital) media have often been hailed as agencies of a democratic renewal and as the decentralized means of a new freedom of expression and dissemination of new, "marginal" knowledge.

8.2 Societal communication and shared knowledge

A social-theoretical appraisal of the role of the media as a means of communication, and of their role in a discussion of knowledge, emphasizes another set of properties and functions. If knowledge, in the sociological sense discussed here, is knowledge *for* the world, what kind of knowledge is created and transmitted in and through the media? From the vantage point of social theory it has been suggested that the most crucial property of (mediated) communication lies with its important role in the *construction of social reality* itself. While this line of reasoning may be detected in many traditional media theories, for example in critical accounts that refer back to the Frankfurt School's powerful media critique (Horkheimer and Adorno, [1944] 1972), it is certainly most explicit in system theoretical and explicitly constructivist models of communication as well as in approaches that have their roots in the sociology of knowledge (Berger and Luckmann, 1969).

Another and more recent account that affords communication a central place within its theory of society is Niklas Luhmann's "The Reality of the Mass Media" ([1996] 2000), in which he assesses in great detail the modern role of the media and elevates the media to a central functional subsystem within modern society. From such a theory-of-society perspective, the anthropological significance of communication – as the process by which sociality is created – is replenished with the role of *mediated* communication in the emergence of modern social formations.

Thus the expanding resources of mediated communication were – and are – not only a means of establishing, negotiating and defining social situations on the micro-scale, but became increasingly important in providing the themes and topics (the "agenda") of social exchange and debate in modern societies. The development of what was quickly called the *mass* media was not only constitutive for the emergence of social conventions and cultural techniques (such as the standardization of language, or the rise of literacy, cf. Thompson, 1995), but became increasingly central for orienting people in a functionally differentiated and increasingly complex society. This becomes apparent, for example, in the observation of Niklas Luhmann that "it would be hard to imagine how a society of communicative operations that extends far beyond individual horizons of experience could function if this indispensable condition were not secured through the communication process itself" (Luhmann, [1996] 2000: 100).

As the authority of the large social institutions waned toward the end of the twentieth century (cf. Stehr, 2001), the role of the media lay with compensating these declining agencies of social integration by providing a common horizon, the social imaginary of increasingly heterogeneous societies.

In conclusion, all these approaches, whether they focus on social interaction, social solidarity, social legitimacy or public discourse, posit mediated communication as central for the coherence of modern communities. Public communication becomes vital both for the functioning of the various societal spheres (politics, commerce, culture, etc.) and for the constitution of society in general. The shared knowledge that makes us part of a community or social structure that can no longer be ascertained individually, is communicatively created, disseminated and debated; made possible and viable only by the expanding uses of technological media. While James Cooley certainly did not have the Internet in mind, he already stated more than a century ago: "[When] we come to the modern era, especially, we can understand nothing rightly unless we perceive the manner in which the revolution in communication has made a new world for us" (Cooley, 1909: 65).

8.3 Analyzing the ubiquity of media: mediatization

Today, the proliferation of media technologies and the multiplication of content as well as the growing reliance on all forms of media for contemporary society has led media and communication scholars to speak of a process of increased *mediatization* – an historical process akin to more common concepts such as globalization, individualization or rationalization (see Krotz's [2007] notion of "meta-processes"; also Lundby, 2009, 2014). These concepts have been used to describe social and cultural developments of long duration, summarizing numerous changes in the socio-structural and socio-cultural makeup of a society. In analogy, *mediatization* helps to account for the significance and the mechanisms by which the media, especially ICTs, (re)shape social processes such as everyday interaction, communication patterns, education, social conflicts, the political landscape and social organization, but also the economy of modern societies.

Mediatization research tries to model the interdependence of media development and social, economic and cultural change, and thus departs in many ways from traditional *media effects* research. It widens the scope to include media as evolutionary forces of societal development. Rather than focusing on particular media or specific media texts, the media system is studied as a social and cultural force *in toto*. As modern society is increasingly dependent on media for its communication and patterns of social change, and since the technological as well as institutional properties of the media are never *neutral* with regard to the communication they enable, influence or prevent, a change in the material makeup of the media system also affects society as a whole (see Adolf, 2012a).

One may distinguish two distinct approaches to studying mediatization. The first perspective of mediatization research emphasizes the ubiquity of the media and the way they infiltrate individual lifeworlds. Everyday communication is increasingly carried out by means of media technology, impacting on the way we relate to others and, ultimately, comes to play an increasing role in the social construction of social reality. Special attention is paid to the digital media of "mass self-communication" (Castells, 2009), and how their novel *affordances* (Hutchby, 2001) alter established and introduce new patterns of social interaction.

An "institutional" perspective (Hjarvard, 2008) strives to identify the specific rationality and forms of the organization of public communication and aims at explaining how, as Winfried Schulz (2013: 55) describes it, a "certain worldview [becomes] accepted" by society: if it is not in the media, it did not happen. That in turn leads to the adoption of a *media logic* (Altheide and Snow, 1979) by social institutions and actors in order to pass the threshold of attention and selection. So while the media have hugely increased the volume and capacity to communicate, escalating the flow of information and knowledge, they have also affected both the organization and the form of communication. As the media become complex technological infrastructures based on specific forms of societal organization, and develop their own professions and economy, that which passes through such social institutions – the message or content – is changed.

Despite their differences, both strands of mediatization research capture the contemporary role of the media in a broader cultural context and situate the media as one of the main drivers of societal development. Whether the media's growing power for and within modern society is attributed to the *anticipated possibility of becoming the subject of its attention* or to the media's role in *building and maintaining social relations*, both approaches shed light on the interrelation between processes and modalities of communication and knowledge: the media become robust dimensions of the creation, dissemination and reception of information and knowledge within and across societies.

So while the media have become the main drivers of flows of information and knowledge in modern society, and while they produce and circulate knowledge, their role in disseminating these resources, topics and narratives is never neutral, as the mediation of communication always affects the meaning of what is communicated (cf. Innis, [1950] 2007; McLuhan, 1962). Against the backdrop of these findings, we will in the next sections take a look at how the digital media's *manner of operation* impacts on communication processes and their social consequences.

8.4 New media, old media and the hybrid media system

While new media technologies in their early stages often mimic existing media, they eventually develop their own forms and traits, properties which in turn impact on the communication they process. The website "Facebook" may initially have been a digital, interactive version of a college yearbook but has since been developed to become a distinct and novel phenomenon, a "social networking site," and a very popular one.[2] Hence, the digital media that sweep across modern life are not merely variations or more efficient extensions of traditional modes of communication.

The novel "architecture" of digitized mediated information reorganizes mediated interaction and the way other members of the network are encountered. While most of the time social media extend "real world" relationships into the virtual realm, they do facilitate encounters with loose acquaintances and even strangers, previously unknown sources of information, and new ways of getting in touch with knowledge. Such profiles allow referring to and referencing information in a manifest and visible way. Indeed, their significance may rest with how they modify patterns of interaction, since they alter prior forms of sociability in view of new modalities of communicative integration. These changed interactional patterns consist of a permanent process of addressing and referencing information/knowledge. From countless contingent possibilities information is shared with others, creating reference networks that provide individualized users with allusion potential, and while this process is far from new, as it is typical of interpersonal communication, its new relevance lies with the institutionalization of this kind of interaction on a global scale – a process that has been termed "networked integration" (Adolf and Deicke, 2015).

However, instead of singling out digital media as the sole focus of contemporary changes in the communication structure, the new media complement existing mass media (Schrape, 2011: 423). "Old" and "new" media together form what Andrew Chadwick (2013) calls a "hybrid media system."

8.5 ICTs, surveillance and knowledge

In addition to a discussion of the knowledge the media provide, and the knowledge in which all forms of communication are necessarily embedded, we need to turn our attention to another important phenomenon that connects the (digital) media to knowledge: the knowledge/ information they produce *about the individual*. We refer to the increased awareness of the consequences of the rampant mediatization of societal relations *and* of individual communicative action in the wake of recent revelations about the collection of data facilitated by digitization and networked information technology. We will discuss this aspect of the development of the mediatization of social conduct by introducing the term *involuntary mediatization* (cf. also Adolf, 2014).

As we have noted, the ongoing expansion of networked ICTs does not simply amount to a *quantitative* increase in the prevalence of media technology. Today's affordances of ICTs prompt a *qualitative* change in our relations to and mediation by media technologies which needs to be included in an examination of the way media change and social change are intertwined. As digital media become increasingly "smart" and mobile, they develop into an inescapable component of human environments and, so it seems, literally a part of the body of the individual. There is hardly any portable media device manufactured today that is not equipped with versatile sensor technology, ranging from cameras and microphones to GPS modules, and many more. The technical development helps transform individuals into *objects* of knowledge.

At this point in our discussion of the impact of ICTs it is helpful to distinguish between two dimensions of the change process in question (Adolf, 2014). The first dimension captures *material* and *structural* changes on an ecological level, namely the *digitization* of our media infrastructure. The second dimension describes the corresponding *informationalization* of modern life as situated on social and cultural levels (cf. also Webster's [2014] notion of an "informatization of relationships"). *Digitization* refers to the material foundations of our information and communication infrastructure based on the new, computer-based, digital and interconnected form. Digital media exhibit a number of properties that have fundamental consequences for the various acts of communication they support. At least three attributes of digital media should be considered (see Seemann, 2014).

First, the *non-discriminatory nature of sensors*, which, together with their ubiquity, amounts to a new visibility of human life. There is a multitude of measuring devices that see, hear and follow us through our days, being all the time connected to servers around the world and creating an endless flow of data. Some of these ICTs we consciously wear (e.g. fitness trackers). Others we carry around with us without paying them much heed (such as smartphones). Yet others, such as CCTV cameras or license plate readers, are installed in our environment whether or not we know of them.

Second, *digital data are universal*, i.e. may convey any kind of information that is readable by virtually any computer in the world. Digital information is boundless, a trait exacerbated by the fact that digital data are not so much "transported," i.e. *moved* from A to B, but rather multiplied, *copied*, with every transaction.

Third, the continued increase in calculation power, network capacities (*bandwidth*) and storage space makes it feasible to gather *all* data by default. An originally discrete set of variables might be correlated with another formerly confined set of information and result in new information that was not previously available (the so-called *option value* of data; see Mayer-Schönberger and Cukier, 2013: 122).

The concept of *informationalization* represents the social dimension of these processes. It denotes the propensity of businesses and administrations to extract, collect and correlate the informational value of any human activity. In a world awash with miniaturized, mobile and connected devices, the media are not only an indispensable means of information and communication, but track our personal behavior and our communicative interactions. Smart TVs measure our viewing activity, mobile devices track our location, newspaper apps record our reading habits, and social networking sites mine our information and communication behavior. Informationalization thus refers to the *cultural conceptions* that frame and the *institutional purposes* that motivate the use of the new media, as well as the *social uses* to which the new media and the "big data" they invariably produce are put.

An appraisal of the process of mediatization would be incomplete without considering these more problematic aspects of digital media technology. Thus, if mediated communication impacts on "our knowledge, our social relationships, our identities, our culture and society, on politics – in short our reality" (Krotz, 2012: 45), then it does so also by accruing vast amounts of information about users and citizens. ICTs allow for hitherto unknown or unfeasible possibilities of observing and learning about our natural and social environment, but they do so irrespective of traditional norms and conventions.

This development may amount to an epistemological shift in society's relation to knowledge and information. The changes in the makeup of the media system and its core technologies impact on the way we generate *knowledge* about the world, on how we apply our capacity to act, of how we *engage* with others, as well as on social conventions, norms and values and ultimately political and regulatory power. Vast troves of data, increased computing capacity and proprietary algorithms (and the powerful interests behind them), for example, may lead to practices such as *predictive policing*, based on the identification of "hot spots" (areas) and "hot dots" (suspects) of crime. As digitization and informationalization inform public policies, business strategies and everyday behavior, they transcend the immediate usage of ICTs and must be understood as a part of the larger mediatization dynamic.

Ultimately, the boundaries between voluntary visibility and involuntary surveillance are dissolving. Visibility becomes the default mode, since in a digitized ecosystem, opting out is not possible, as it would amount to curtailing one's social contacts and freedom of movement, and indeed one's participation in social life. Purely individual strategies of avoiding surveillance or being careful with personal information are of diminishing value. We are dealing with a societal development that is beyond individual adaptation, and thus tantamount to a structural change. With the advent of digital media-based big data collection the default setting of personal information has changed, and the right of "informational self-determination" (Federal Constitutional Court of Germany) is challenged. If privacy was once understood as an individual's personal sphere that could only be encroached by lawful measures that served the common good, this relation is now inverted: we have to accept that, by default, all that is not proactively defended as a private sphere may be known. Again, it must be stressed that this is not merely a technological development, but that the effects of digitization are accompanied and transformed in conjunction with ideational currents and moral sentiments, such as, for example, the high valuation of transparency.

Crucially, such information tends to accrue asymmetrically, resulting in new *power differentials*. Individual actors do not possess the know-how or the opportunity to access server protocols, CCTV archives and credit card records which would enable them to regain sovereignty over such data. The individual finds him- or herself in a structurally weaker position than that of the government agencies and private companies that collect, pass on and even trade in personalized usage data. Since such data are potentially retroactive this entails the possibility for them to become informative only in the future, depending on new technological possibilities, new scientific insights or changed political regimes. While the logics behind such processes of "de-anonymization" and "re-identification" are not easily explained, neither are the potential consequences they hold for unconcerned citizens. Big data analyses and *probabilistic predictions* based thereupon concern, statistically speaking, the basic population, the universe, and are thus comprehensive in nature. They reveal something about everyone concerned, if only through the *absence* of certain behaviors and practices. The process of the mediatization of society attains a new, *involuntary* quality. Surely, the opportunities created by the unprecedented processing of large troves of data hold immense possibilities for human learning and new knowledge. At the same time they amount to a pivotal change in the epistemological foundations of human sociality: in a digital world there will be new rules to what we know, how we know, how we validate and assess what we know, and how we make use of what we know.

8.6 Communication, media and knowledge

In our discussion of the social nature of knowledge we have tried to elaborate that the term media stands for both the *technological and material* structure and the historically specific social *organizational forms* of communication. The media's central role in providing the *symbolic horizon* of a social formation is as important as the *concrete messages* and their forms (texts, programs, memes, etc.). All these components need to be considered in a discussion of the way knowledge is (re)produced by and applied through the media.

As such, the media of communication have long since become a central factor for the development of modern societies. As we have shown, the historical process by which the media came to play this role is still evolving, and the media, old *and* new, continue to organize the flow of communication throughout the complex structure that underpins modern society. The media play an active part in the production, diffusion and storage of information and knowledge; they are means of individual learning as well as of collective debate, and crucial for the organization of social actions. To this end, we have identified at least three distinct dimensions of how communication, its media, and information and knowledge are intertwined.

First, from a *(media-)cultural* perspective, knowledge features prominently as the contextual foundation for shared meanings and codes. We require knowledge, acquired in processes of socialization and enculturation, to be able to communicate in a meaningful way, and thus to become a part of social relationships. Culture and communication are mutually constitutive and provide the prerequisite for all forms of human interaction and intersubjective exchange. In a cultural environment that is suffused with communication and permeated by media, both as technologies as well as institutions, the media have moved to the center of social and cultural analysis.

Second, from a *functional* perspective mediated communication could be described as a lubricant that allows the various parts of a highly diversified social whole to interact with each other. Moreover, the media also connect different lifeworlds, everyday realities of people near or far which would otherwise be inaccessible to us. The media have become the specialized social subsystem that connects social institutions and their idiosyncratic stocks of knowledge to each other. Complex modern social formations only ever achieve their identity as imagined constructs disseminated in mediated communication. They are of an ideational character that is only manifest in the narrations and depictions provided by the media system, whose most fundamental function is to provide a society with its own totalistic, however fleeting, reflection: we only *know of* the society we live in from a mirror image of that society. Our knowledge of the world is largely mediated knowledge, and in conveying such knowledge, for example in the form of ideas or narratives, we are again dependent on communication.

Third, a sociological perspective of knowledge refers to situated knowledge, its subjects and objects, the organizations that produce it, the way it is disseminated and employed. In this context the media enter our analytical scope as specific sources of information and (potential) knowledge, as means of individual and collective learning (appropriation of ideas), expression (dissemination of ideas), and organization (application of ideas). It is on this foundation that our analysis of the social role of knowledge is based, as for example the emancipatory power of education, the role of universities and research and development (R&D) departments for the production of specialized theoretical knowledge, and the professional groups to which it gives rise, or the resilient traits of traditional knowledge for navigating everyday life. The media in their technological (i.e. "means" of communication) as well as institutional ("sources" of information as well as "arenas" of discourse) roles take on particular functions with regard to the ways they come to be used. Importantly, such an understanding of the social role of the media must incorporate the specific characteristics media represent for creating/shaping, codifying/storing and sending/receiving information/knowledge and communication.

Notes

1 As indicated, information and knowledge are easily confounded. The narratives discussed in the chapter at times are equally prone to such conflation, influenced not least by a discourse on the digital worlds that regularly fails to make such a distinction.
2 By early 2016 Facebook reports the staggering number of 1.04 billion daily active users and 1.59 billion monthly active users, effectively becoming a "web within the web." One in four people in Germany has a Facebook account, while for the UK and the United States it is roughly one in two (Facebook Statistics 2015/16, see newsroom.fb.com/company-info).

9
FUNCTIONS OF KNOWLEDGE

It is far from evident that knowledge can be or has been successful in performing the demanding task of enhancing the liberty of the human race, or that knowledge may offer the key to our survival in dignified conditions in light of the massive challenges that lie ahead, such as the consequences of environmental degradation. Aside from the historically and politically important function of knowledge as enlightenment, although in this general ambivalent sense of enlightenment, knowledge also performs a range of "lesser" social functions.

The extent to which the growing volume of knowledge held by groups of social actors and social institutions represents a further enlargement of the already existing power and authority of the powerful – including the owners of the means of production – is a contentious matter. Indeed, some observers – in agreement with the general thesis that knowledge and science are immensely productive forces that are replacing the traditional forces of production (capital, labor and land) – not only argue that the growing importance of knowledge already represents, or perhaps allows us to expect, a reversal of the dominant role of capital in general, but also hold that we are at the beginning of the realization of the promise of radical changes in the world of work – in the sense of greater autonomy from constraints imposed by work itself and by the authority of management and the owners of the means of production. Knowledge, for those observers, may also serve as the catalyst for democratization and the chances for sustainable forms of democracy around the world.

As a matter of fact, the views of scholars are rather divided. The economic and political functions of knowledge are either seen as emancipatory forces or as developments that will only cement the iron grip of the already powerful forces and interests in modern societies.

It is in one of the mutually exclusive senses that Aronowitz and DiFazio (1994: 339), for example, portray the social consequences of the ascendancy of knowledge in a somewhat bleak fashion: rather than fostering "full individual development, production and reproduction penetrate all corners of the lifeworld, transforming it into a commodity world not merely as consumption but also in the most intimate processes of human interaction." The invasion of knowledge into the lifeworld in the form of its economic derivatives is without any discernible benefits to those colonized by scientific and technological knowledge in particular. The so-called stratum of "knowledge workers" continues to be the handmaiden of the powerful, and knowledge is still subordinate to the imperatives of technical innovation for profitability and hegemony. Such disparaging comments about the social role of knowledge are not new.

In a small, unsigned note published in 1832 in the *Satirist or, the Censor of the Times*, the author refers to the famous metaphor "Knowledge is Power" and adds "but with those already powerful, it operates with tenfold force." What makes this note remarkable is the fact that the statement is a call to arms for the "people" to appropriate and utilize knowledge for their own benefit which in turn proves their sovereignty against the ruling "oligarchy." The statement displays a considerable confidence in the very possibility of the benefits derived from a general diffusion of knowledge and, therefore, the inherently democratic potential of knowledge. In the sections that follow, we will turn to a discussion of how these functions, especially the linkage between power and knowledge, have been viewed and are discussed by major thinkers.

9.1 Knowledge as power and authority

Two contentious notions almost always compete for pre-eminence in discussions about the power of knowledge and ideas: On the one hand, there is the difference to which Max Horkheimer points in a 1932 essay in the inaugural issue of the *Zeitschrift für Sozialforschung*, where he favors a clear separation between the *utility* and the *truth* of knowledge. On the other hand, there is the widely held notion that "knowledge is power," which of course dates back to Francis Bacon's *Novum Organum Scientiarum* (1620).

Horkheimer ([1932] 1972: 3) stresses that "the fact that science contributes to the social life-process as a productive power and a means of production in no way legitimates a pragmatist theory of knowledge." This distinction is one of the traditional cleavages in philosophical reflections about the attributes of knowledge that may make ideas powerful in practice. The year 1932 is, of course, a sensitive one, and Horkheimer's insistence that it is not for economic and political interests to determine what is true or not echoes and renews societal and political struggles about the role of science in society. Science and the ideas that emerge from the scientific community should not be the handmaidens of power. In defending the autonomy of science, Horkheimer ([1932] 1972: 4) also insists that this position does not lead to a separation between theory and action. The commitment of scientists to the truth and the conformity of any knowledge with reality necessarily imply that the scientific community must be autonomous in society. The emphasis on the autonomy of science – as the precondition for the production of "uncontaminated" knowledge claims and for knowledge that is, in fact, in the final analysis, efficacious in practice – is shared by a wide range of philosophers of science, among them Karl Popper, Michael Polanyi, John Desmond Bernal or Vannevar Bush. It follows that the utility of knowledge is the daughter of the truth of such knowledge and that the truth is the highest goal scientists are aiming for in their scientific work. As Max Weber ([1904] 1922a: 213) emphatically stresses, "we have nothing to offer a person to whom this truth is of no value – and belief in the value of scientific truth is the product of certain cultures, and is not given to us by nature."

In the following section, we will inquire with greater detail into the possible reasons for the power of knowledge, especially social scientific knowledge. We may be able to best illustrate the significant interrelations between theory and action, and therefore the power of ideas, by referring to social scientific treatises with immense influence and, in at least one case, of great practical consequence. We are referring to John Maynard Keynes's *General Theory* which appeared in 1936, only a few years after Max Horkheimer's essay, and to Max Weber's influential theory of modern bureaucracy.

9.2 The power of ideas

The work of Max Weber, in this case his theory of bureaucracy, is one of the most famous analyses of the power of (instrumental) knowledge and technical expertise. Weber's work and John Maynard Keynes's *General Theory* represent alternative answers to the question of the bases for the power and authority of knowledge. The alternative ways that are seen to ensure that knowledge is powerful may be based: 1 on attributes of knowledge itself (e.g. its truthfulness or object adequacy); 2 more interestingly, on features of the social action or institutions in which knowledge becomes knowledge-in-use; or 3 in contrast, on a "convergence" of attributes of knowledge-in-use and characteristics of the social action or institutions in which knowledge is applied. Weber's theory of bureaucracy represents, as far as we can see, the case for the importance of institutions or the context of social action. Keynes's revolutionary *General Theory* makes the case for a convergence of knowledge attributes and characteristics of social institutions as the foundation for the influence of knowledge. We will first refer to Keynes's theory, an academic effort that deeply changed economic theorizing and economic policymaking.

Keynes's (1936: 383–384) monograph *The General Theory* closes with the following, now almost classic, observations:

> The ideas of economists and political philosophers, both when they are right and when they are wrong, are more powerful than is commonly understood. Indeed the world is ruled by little else. Practical men, who believe themselves to be quite exempt from

any intellectual influences, are usually the slaves of some defunct economist. Madmen in authority, who hear voices in the air, are distilling their frenzy from some academic scribbler of a few years back. I am sure that the power of vested interests is vastly exaggerated compared with the gradual encroachment of ideas. Not, indeed, immediately, but after a certain interval; for in the field of economic and political philosophy there are not many who are influenced by new theories after they are twenty-five or thirty years of age, so that the ideas which civil servants and politicians and even agitators apply to current events are not likely to be the newest. But, soon or later, it is ideas, not vested interests, which are dangerous for good or evil.

Hidden in these sentences is not only a prophetic anticipation of the practical political fate of the ideas of his *General Theory*, but also a biting rhetorical attack on classical economic theory. Moreover, Keynes argues that the potential *practical influence* of social science knowledge is propelled by the "ideas" produced by social science. The ambivalent term "ideas" (meaning) was probably chosen quite deliberately by Keynes and seems to signify, among other things, that the practical consequences (or, for that matter, the lack of practical relevance) of ideas generated in the social sciences depends less on their contribution to the discussion and the informed reflection about the *means* (that is, the instruments) of social action. Is Keynes correct in emphasizing the political and practical influence of economic *ideas*, including his own?[1]

Opposing Keynes's conviction of the importance of economic ideas, theories and worldviews in society is a broad alliance of theoretical perspectives in a number of social science disciplines that emphasize, for example, the decisive influence of vested and organized interests or the influence of self-interest on the course of many societies, or simply the derivative (and perhaps even subservient) role of ideas in economic and political struggles.

Although Keynes signals in the title of his *General Theory* that he aspires to formulate a general theory of employment, interest and money, his approach does not really constitute a general theoretical model, especially when judged against the widely supported and rather demanding methodological ideals about object-adequate social science knowledge. With respect to those widely accepted criteria, Keynes fails to refer and examine, as explanatory factors, the *broad range* of attributes and complex processes of economic and other variables, any and all of which may affect the rate of employment, the value of money and the interest rate.

Such a conclusion is strengthened by two observations. One observation is that of Collingridge and Reeve, who point out that there is in fact the distinct possibility that access to impressive amounts of information and knowledge-claims can be quite "dysfunctional" in practical decision-making processes. Their comment is also intended to combat the prevailing view of certain qualities of rationality: in particular, the thesis that the rationality of political decisions somehow improves, and in an almost linear manner, with the quantity of information available to the actors. Collingridge and Reeve (1986: 5) therefore state: "It is simply not the case that a good decision can only be made once the uncertainties surrounding it have been reduced by gathering as much relevant information as possible. On the contrary, policy decisions may be made quite happily with the very scantiest information."

The second relevant observation can be found in the work of Karl Mannheim. "If we seek a science of that which is in the process of becoming, of practice and for practice," Mannheim ([1929] 1936: 152–153) stipulates in *Ideology and Utopia*, that is, in an essay concerned with the foundations of political knowledge or a science of politics, "we can realize it only by discovering a new framework in which this kind of knowledge can find adequate expression." As we have already shown in discussing the notion of practical knowledge, a theory of the pragmatic transformation of social science knowledge as a capacity for action should be governed by the elementary insight that all social action is bound to specific situations and affected by local constraints. The transformation of knowledge for action into knowledge-in-use (practical knowledge) demands that theoretical knowledge take on features that constitute the conditions for practical knowledge as a special type of knowledge. This means that theoretical knowledge has to be re-attached to the social context; that is, its relations to situational interests, purposes and worldviews, from which it had been detached for the purposes of theoretical reflection, have to be re-established.

Despite the fact that only a few pertinent attributes of the totality of economic action are examined by Keynes in his *General Theory*, vigorous voices could be heard almost immediately after its publication – and certainly a chorus of voices in later years – praising Keynes's theory and insisting that it may well have very important practical implications and benefits for the economic affairs of a nation. The practical success of Keynes's ideas is the result of his ability to successfully couple his theoretical notions to conditions of action that could be influenced and changed in directions desired by the actors of the day. In short, what we encounter in the case of the practical success of Keynes's reflections – after all, he has been credited with saving capitalism from itself – is a convergence of the practical contingencies of action, for example the broad-base sovereignty of the nation-states and the ideas championed by his theory.

Max Weber's ([1922] 1964: 339) theory of bureaucracy stresses first and foremost:

> the exercise of control on the basis of knowledge (*Herrschaft kraft Wissen*). This is the feature of [bureaucracy] which makes it specifically rational. This consists on the one hand in technical knowledge which, by itself, is sufficient to ensure its position of extraordinary power. But in addition to this, bureaucratic organizations, or the holders of power who make use of them, have the tendency to increase their power still further out of experience in the service. For they acquire through the conduct of office a special knowledge of facts and have available a store of documentary material peculiar to themselves.

In short, bureaucracy constitutes a form of "domination based on knowledge." It is capable of attaining levels of efficiency, reliability, precision or modes of rational control, however, only as the administrative apparatus of the state that no other form of authority is able to attain. However, the authority of the administrative apparatus derives, in the final analysis, from impersonal legal norms[2] and continuous procedurally correct work carried out by officials in offices with clearly circumscribed spheres of competence, and this authority is based on technical knowledge. Thus, there is a convergence or even symbiosis of legal norms, sanctions, and knowledge; the effective application of general, standardized legal norms requires the use of general, abstract knowledge. Domination by legal norms routinizes and strengthens domination by technical knowledge. In its classical nineteenth-century vision, the primary object of knowledge within the state bureaucratic organization in particular "was the legal system, particularly those parts of it establishing the governmental and administrative apparatus, controlling its activities, and regulating its relations to private individuals. Law was seen as the speech itself of the state" (Poggi, 1982: 356).

It is therefore decisive for Weber ([1922] 1968: 979) that, despite the realm of relatively unregulated conduct even in highly rational settings (for example, in the legal system), "in principle a system of rationally debatable 'reasons' stands behind every act of bureaucratic administration, namely, either subsumption under norms, or a weighing of ends and means." It is, as Weber describes it, the institutional shell of modern bureaucracy that provides for the power of knowledge. Of course, Weber's *ideal type* of bureaucracy has been subject to many critiques; as a matter of fact, in *Economy and Society* Weber delineates "legal authority with a bureaucratic apparatus" or the superiority of technical knowledge, but elsewhere in his own political writings he explores the "dysfunctions" and imperfections of bureaucracies, the limits of bureaucratic conduct and its institutional linkages, for example those to social class, and its aspirations in specific historical contexts. Legal authority becomes subject to routinization, "trained incapacities" and antinomies, conflicts can arise (Merton, 1939: 560–568), and the costs of subordination as well as inertia can mount. Bureaucracies not only accumulate knowledge, but attempt to protect this knowledge from access by "outsiders" (cf. Weber, [1922] 1968: 990–993), and strive almost completely to avoid public discussion of its techniques while political leaders are increasingly "dilettantes." The experts can only be controlled and kept at bay by other experts (Weber, [1922] 1968: 994).

Who controls the administrative apparatus? According to Weber ([1922] 1964: 338), for the non-specialist such control is possible only to a certain degree; in general, the "trained permanent official is more likely to get his way in the long run than his nominal superior, the Cabinet minister, who is not a specialist." However modern bureaucracies are strained by societal development and less and less resemble, if they ever did, the ideal type of bureaucracy Weber described, the lesson of his theory of bureaucracy remains that powerful institutions can monopolize and deploy knowledge for their singular purpose and benefit because of the degree of control they manage to exercise over the conditions of social action within and without their boundaries.

In one of his influential treatises on the relation between knowledge and power, Michel Foucault echoes – at least to some extent – the fears that are so unsettling in Weber's classic account. In his much-discussed *The Archaeology of Knowledge* (1969), Foucault depicts knowledge as an anonymous discourse that exercises control over a powerless individual. Whereas Foucault (1979: 100–102) later allows for the possibility of human agency manifest in discursive resistance, his analysis of this conflict, its basis and its potential and productive force, is not convincing (cf. also Giddens, 1984: 157). While he acknowledges that "[d]iscourse transmits and produces power; it reinforces it, but it also undermines it, renders it fragile and makes it possible to thwart it," agency remains strangely invisible in his theory. More importantly, he underestimates the malleability of knowledge, the uncertainties associated with it, and the extent to which knowledge is contested (cf. the extensive discussion of the ideas of power and knowledge in Nola, 1998). His approach forgoes the capacity of individuals and groups such as civil society organizations to mobilize knowledge in order to evade, disrupt, oppose and restrain the oppression or the power that may be exercised by major social institutions. Ultimately, the conviction of the inescapable affinity between knowledge and power produces an aporetic dilemma, such as in the related thesis that an increase in collective human capital, though it "raises the people's ability to resist oppression," also "raises the ruler's benefits from subjugating them" (Barro, 1999: 159). In such a view, knowledge, then, is not only useless; its acquisition paradoxically contains the seed of its own defeat (cf. section 3.3).

9.3 Knowledge and the economy

We are still without an economic theory of knowledge. Economists have treated knowledge, as have many of their fellow social scientists, in a taken-for-granted manner and often introduced it as an exogenous or external factor or, to put it simply but not inaccurately, as a black box. In discussing the function of knowledge in the economic system, we concentrate our attention on a couple of ways in which knowledge acquires both "constructive" and controversial functions. Since we have already touched upon the role of knowledge for and within economic questions repeatedly and in various contexts, we here need to confine our remarks to two manifestations of knowledge that are of great economic significance: On the one hand, there is the emergence of (scientific) knowledge as an immediately productive force, as a source of economic growth. On the other hand, and subject to greater dispute, there is the question of how knowledge fits the categories of a property or a commodity, which we will discuss in the subsequent section.

Science and technology began as a marginal enterprise of amateurs in the seventeenth century. However, modern science, especially after World War II, has received a large proportion of the public budget and constitutes a major source of investment for private capital. Individuals trained as scientists or engineers are a growing part of the labor force in modern society. The growth in the system of modern higher education is both the result and the motor of the increased importance of science and technology, especially but not only for the modern economic system. Institutions that produce, distribute or reproduce knowledge are now comparable in size to the industrial complex.

The changes in and for science occur in three steps. First, up to the end of the eighteenth century, the scientific community had the function of *enlightenment*, that is, it was a producer of *meaning*. Second, in the following century, science became a *productive* force. Third, since the middle of the last century, science has increasingly been seen as an *immediate productive* or "performative" force. "Immediacy" means that science now may, contrary to the relationship between production and science in the nineteenth century, be relevant for production without being mediated by living, corporeal labor. Hence one might be able to speak about the possible abolition of manual labor, especially of factory labor that requires strength and physical dexterity, and the exteriorization of human labor from production into the preparation and organization of production. What does science actually produce as an immediately productive force?

The answer must be that science increasingly produces action (practical) knowledge, that is, knowledge in the form of data and theories or, rather, data and programs. For example, the results of public opinion research claim to be the immediately applicable, technical foundation for government action in the sense that such findings offer a steering mode for public opinion (cf. Rose, 1991; Noelle-Neumann, 1995). Hence, science can be called an immediately productive force only in cases where data and programs *as such* become components or even constitutive elements of society, a society in which the production of knowledge is immediate social production. Indeed, this is often the case today.

A considerable part of the total work within advanced societies already takes place on the meta-level; it is second-level production. Production, to a large extent, is not metabolism with nature any longer, that is, the material appropriation typical of industrial society. Part of production presupposes that nature is already materially appropriated; it consists in rearranging appropriated nature according to certain programs. The "laws" that govern the appropriation of appropriated nature, or secondary production, are not the laws of nature but the rules of social constructs. At the level of social practice we *potentially* meet an analogous situation. Some fields of the social sciences whose subject is society in the state of being appropriated include, for instance, operations research, cybernetics, theory of planning, decision theory and rational choice theory.

However, social sciences of this kind presuppose, in order to be successful and able to produce action knowledge as well, that society is bureaucratically conditioned and prepared for data processing. It is questionable if this precondition is met in today's society. Our analysis suggests that, paradoxically, the appropriation of society by the social sciences produces the opposite effect, namely fragility rather than successful planning and regulatory opportunities.

The outcome of these developments is also that scientific knowledge, in the sense of an immediate productive force, becomes a societal resource with functions comparable to that of labor in the productive process, but unlike labor under capitalism, the owners of the resource "knowledge" in a knowledge society acquire power and influence because owners of capital cannot, as was still the case for corporeal labor, reduce its share in production by the substitution of capital for knowledge. At best, knowledge can be substituted by other knowledge. Notwithstanding the mechanization of brain work, there always remains an irreducible amount of "personal knowledge," which can be converted into and valued as "intellectual" or "cultural" capital.

9.4 Knowledge as property and public good

The discussion of whether knowledge in general, or specific forms of knowledge, can take on the qualities that allow it to be treated as an isolated commodity that can be bought and sold for money, or as a fixed property, is complicated by shifting points of reference, disagreements about the role of knowledge in different social contexts, and contested claims about the transfer of knowledge attributes across the boundaries of differentiated social systems.

We have already cautioned against the unqualified, context-insensitive notion that knowledge can be treated in close analogy to commodities. The assertion that knowledge in some ways possesses characteristics of commodities contradicts the more commonly encountered observation that it is impossible to establish ownership rights over knowledge because of its non-rival attributes – for example, as the result of the possibility of its almost unlimited and unhindered reproducibility.

Nonetheless, it would appear to be almost self-evident that in a society in which knowledge becomes the dominant productive force, at least certain types of knowledge acquire such prominence that knowledge turns into a commodity and can be appropriated, recognized and treated as property. For this reason, one might conjecture that the capitalist economies of knowledge societies are unlikely to lose their identity as capitalist entities. However, since the answer to the question of the private appropriation of knowledge is not all that clear-cut, the nature of capitalism could well be transformed in fundamental ways allowing for the question, as asked by Thurow (1996: 279), "What does capitalism become when it cannot own the strategic sources of its own competitive advantage?"

Jean-François Lyotard (1984 [1979: 4]) is convinced that societal changes have contributed to changes in the social role of knowledge that propel it much closer to commodities. Especially as the result of technological transformations in conjunction with the proliferation of information-processing machines, a radical "exteriorization" of knowledge with respect to the "knower" has taken place. The outcome is that the relationship of the "suppliers and users of knowledge to the knowledge they supply and use [...] will increasingly tend to assume the form already taken by the relationship of commodity producers and consumers to the commodities they produce and consume – that is, the form of value. Knowledge is and will be produced in order to be sold, it is and will be consumed in order to be valorized in a new production: in both cases the goal is exchange." What therefore counts, according to Lyotard, is the exchange value and not so much the use value of knowledge.

The precondition for the possibility that something is transformed into a commodity is the institution of (private) property. Indeed, for the most part, the actual possession and *legal definition* of property is exclusive: "A thing over which I exercise the right of property is a thing which serves myself alone" (Durkheim, [1950] 1992: 141). However, the exclusive legal command and personal possession of knowledge or the practical isolation of knowledge as an object is much more difficult to realize, if at all possible. As Evenson and Putnam (1987: 34) emphasize, "material property has the feature that use by its owners excludes use by anyone else. Ideas, being nonmaterial, are non-excludable. Thus, in the absence of government sanction, ideas have the character of public goods."

The legal system, however, has provisions, and presumably may evolve more and different ones in the future, that assign an apparently exclusive status to non-material goods (including certain forms of knowledge). The most relevant extension of the concept of property rights in this context is, of course, the creation of the notion of "intellectual property." The spectrum of legal protections, depending on the jurisdiction, now extends to a wide variety of human creations including trademarks, the good will of firms and the exclusive rights to products of biotechnology. Whether it is possible really to enforce such rights is another matter, as is the question of whether incremental knowledge that draws on a common stock of knowledge can be unambiguously identified and assigned to a specific individual or organization.

Nonetheless, pressures to regulate and "police" the use of knowledge in modern society will increase considerably – as we have already pointed out. One might want to speculate that in knowledge societies efforts designed to extend social control to the utilization and even prevention of the use of knowledge just discovered (or anticipated to be discovered) will become one of the foremost political issues, if not the most significant. Equally important in this context is that the (meta-)capacity to generate new increments of knowledge – which are most likely to confer comparative economic advantages – is not a collective property. Therefore, it is not contradictory to argue that knowledge is neither strictly comparable to property or commodities nor without attributes that elevate it, under certain conditions, nearer to property and commodities.

Charles Derber and his colleagues (cf. Derber et al., 1990: 16–18) arrive at a somewhat different conclusion in their analysis of the societal authority and influence of professional occupations in the United States. On the basis of the assumption that there is an enormous historical variability to what passes for and is accepted as knowledge, and therefore the suspicion that almost anything may be sold as "knowledge" – as long as a certain group or occupation is successful in persuading clients that they have a use and a need for the knowledge controlled by this certain group or occupation and that this knowledge is superior to everyday knowledge – "professional" knowledge takes on the typical attributes of the construct of "property." Knowledge becomes a commodity because the peculiar nature of the demand (as well as the needs it serves) and the strategies to meet the demand are fully controlled by those who offer the knowledge in question. One crucial strategy is the privatization of knowledge. The prohibition barring lay practice is one of the most powerful strategies to "privatize" knowledge. In a kind of self-created enclosure and self-policed circle, knowledge becomes a commodity.

Even if one assumes that in practice it is relatively easy to legitimize and monopolize knowledge, Derber and his colleagues overestimate the passivity of the consumer and the solidarity of the professional fraternities. The assumption that the professions are capable of creating the demand for their services and are able to fully control the supply of knowledge – in this day and age of greater knowledgeability of clients and of easier access to relevant knowledge bases – is likely a rather fragile assumption. A more significant drawback of their positions is the fact that they once again discard any concrete analysis of the knowledge base of the professionals and rest their case with the fairly formal attributes of the knowledge of professionals. The status of the attributes Derber and colleagues invoke appears to be applicable to any knowledge claim, and the case boils down to a question of the power that enables professionals to set and control cognitive agendas. It is not clear, for example, why scientific knowledge claims have displaced magic since both are functional equivalents as a source of control for the powerful. However, knowledge types are different.

Moving to the arena of economic discourse, i.e. to reflections that focus on the role of commodities in society, it appears that, more often than not, knowledge is treated in a peculiar and often even less than plausible fashion. Theories range from assuming "perfect" knowledge of market participants to treating knowledge merely as an exogenous dimension. Efforts may also be made to argue that knowledge can be treated in a reductionist manner, that is, as a conventional economic category to which orthodox concepts, such as utility or fixed and variable costs, apply with benefit and without restriction.

It would seem that economists tend to prefer a conception of the value of knowledge that closely resembles their conception of value in the case of any other commodity, namely, value that derives from the utility of the "product" knowledge (use value), but there remains a considerable range of indeterminacy when it comes to the expected value of knowledge. In an effort to arrive at ways of determining the value of information as an economic good, Bates (1988: 80) argues that there is an inherent imbalance in the fixed and variable cost components of producing (and reproducing) information. The production of information has an exceptionally high component of fixed and a very low, even non-existent, component of variable costs, i.e. the costs associated with the replication of the information. This is due to the fact that information is infinitely reproducible and consumes all other resources. Such a treatment of "information" is only plausible as long as one is convinced that reproduction is virtually unproblematic (e.g. transcends the initial conditions of production including the costs associated with it) and can be repeated at will because production is definitive and does not require any intermediaries or subsequent interpretation.

It is true that knowledge has always had its "price" and was never available in an unlimited supply. Knowledge has been, not unlike other commodities, scarce, and in order to utilize it, it sometimes had to be purchased. Still, what exactly determines the value of knowledge is by no means self-evident. The value of knowledge depends not merely on the utility it may represent to some individual or firm, but is linked to the ability or inability of other actors (e.g. competitors) to utilize and exploit it to their advantage. Whether the purchaser can in fact exploit the knowledge bought is very difficult to establish until it has been acquired and the buyer begins to comprehend what has been bought and whether the capacity for action can actually be put to use.

For a significant part, the service sector of society lives off the selling of knowledge. The educational system employs millions of individuals who make a living by reconstructing and disseminating socially necessary knowledge. Limiting access to the social and cognitive pre-conditions for its acquisition but also, in a legal way, by assigning property rights to it, hampers the free circulation of knowledge.[3] One only has to refer to patent and copyright laws. In many countries, patent and copyright laws are no longer confined to technical artifacts and processes but include intellectual ownership of art, music, literature and, increasingly, the commercialization of inventions in the scientific community.

We have already noted that in economic settings *incremental* knowledge has particular importance as a source of added value and possible sustainable rather than ephemeral and precarious growth. We are, thus, able to conclude that if knowledge may be seen in analogy to commodities, this is most likely the result of control over incremental or additional knowledge. In other words, the strategic importance of incremental knowledge in economic contexts derives from the ability of private firms to temporarily appropriate the marginal additions to knowledge and, therefore, the economic advantages that may accrue from the control over such knowledge. In a societal context in which the tempo with which knowledge is added grows exponentially, incremental knowledge has, in addition, the peculiar and disconcerting trait that it rapidly appears *and* disappears as additional knowledge.

However, the forms of knowledge that may be utilized to achieve such advantages are not confined to scientific-technical knowledge. Such a conclusion already follows from the theorem that knowledge is a kind of anthropological constant, but it also arises from a conception of knowledge as a capacity for action because knowledge then becomes, as Lyotard (1984 [1979: 18) stresses, "a question of competence that goes beyond the simple determination and application of truth, extending to the determination and application of criteria of efficiency (technical qualification), of justice and/or happiness (ethical wisdom), of beauty of a sound or color (auditory and visual sensibility), etc."

Social scientists and especially economists see knowledge as a collective commodity or *public good* par excellence.[4] For example, the ethos of science demands that knowledge be made available to all, at least in principle (see Merton, [1942] 1973b). The ethos of science at least as formulated by Robert K. Merton, includes, as is well known, the norm of collective ownership of knowledge in the scientific community, which signals that the notion of knowledge as a public good is largely a normative matter. Whether scientists actually conform to the norm of "communism" in their conduct and do not, for example, keep research results hidden is a contentious issue.

By reducing knowledge to information, economists assimilate the qualities of knowledge more easily to those of a circulating and exchangeable (material) thing that has a certain use value to the person obtaining it. However, these and other stipulations about the "nature" of knowledge are highly contentious. For example, is it the "same" knowledge that is allegedly available to all? Is scientific knowledge, when transformed into technology, still subject to the same normative conventions?[5] What are the costs of the transmission of knowledge? These and a range of other pertinent, basic questions about the social role of knowledge in general and its economic functions in particular have to be clarified. Knowledge is not homogeneous. In any case, knowledge is far less homogeneous than those "physical" property assets that play such a central role in industrial society and are used to statistically represent the economic performance of this form of society.

Even the general, mundane stock of knowledge is hardly ever completely excludable or without rivalry, whether its use by others is prevented by either legal norms or by some other apparatus within which it may be inscribed. Moreover, there is no "essential" feature of scientific knowledge that prevents it from being transformed into a commodity.

However, incremental, additional or new knowledge is much more likely to be rival and excludable knowledge. Otherwise, it would be very difficult to account for research and development in industry and/or for the interest of corporations to privatize knowledge as well as the organizations in which it happens to be generated. To put it simply, and looking at the relation from the side of the producer rather than that of the consumer who is interested in *buying* information or knowledge, a person may repeatedly buy the same product from a supermarket while each purchase of information or knowledge has to be a purchase that differs from other "pieces" of knowledge or information already acquired; otherwise, it is not *novel* knowledge since the buyer is already in possession of that information.[6] In many instances, the production of incremental knowledge is by no means an inexpensive undertaking. One must consider the investments in symbolic, human and physical capital that must be made and the chains of infrastructure or networks outside the direct control of an organization (educational institutions, libraries, publishing houses, media, etc.) that have to be maintained and supported by corporations. Incremental knowledge is, in turn, produced and inscribed in human and physical capital. Its transfer, application and reconfiguration can also involve both considerable cost and a significant infrastructure.

A transaction involving incremental knowledge could therefore include a transfer of property rights. Inasmuch as conventional economic goods are seen to have the property of rivalry and excludability, incremental knowledge is likely to resemble a conventional economic good, but since marginal additions to knowledge are often generated in contexts that explicitly champion non-ownership, there is no iron-clad guarantee that incremental knowledge – particularly if generated in the scientific community – will always behave like a conventional economic good. Moreover, and contrary to neo-classical assumptions, the unit price for knowledge-intensive commodities and services decreases with the increase of production, reflecting "progress down the learning curve."

Notes

1 Especially in the last half of the twentieth and the early years of the current century, and under peaceful circumstances, *the most powerful idea* is that of economic growth, a vision shared by most nation-states and their citizens (cf. McNeill, 2000: 36; Mann, 2013: 365).
2 The "belief in the 'legality' of patterns of normative rules and the right of those elevated to authority under such rules to issue commands" constitutes the foundation of legal authority (Weber, [1922] 1964: 328).
3 See also the notion of an "ecology of knowledge" (e.g. Rosenberg, 1997; Akera, 2007).
4 Karl Marx ([1885] 1976: 508), for example, notes: "Science, generally speaking, costs the capitalist nothing, a fact that by no means prevents him from exploiting it." Compare the enumeration of attributes of knowledge (and its economic consequences) that make it basically a public good according to Geroski (1995: 92–93; also Callon, 1994).
5 The answer one economist provides, for example, is that technology must be considered, in contrast to the convictions concerning scientific knowledge in the scientific community, a "private capital good." In the case of technology, disclosure is not the rule and rents, which can be privately appropriated for its use, can be earned by its producers (cf. Dasgupta, 1987: 10).
6 It follows, as Joseph Stiglitz (2000b: 1449) points out, that "markets for information are inherently characterized by imperfections of information concerning what is being purchased; and mechanisms like *reputation* – which played no role at all in traditional competitive theory – are central."

10
THE PRICE OF KNOWLEDGE

The economist Herbert Simon (1999: 24) emphatically stresses that all aspects of knowledge "can be (and have been) analyzed with the tools of economics. Knowledge has a price and a cost of production; there are markets for knowledge, with their supply and demand curves, and marginal rates of substitution between one form of knowledge and another." However, Simon (1999: 24) at least partly retracts his strong statement about the rigor with which the tools of economics can be applied by pointing out that knowledge "is simply one among the many commodities in which our economy trades, albeit one of large and rapidly growing importance. It requires special treatment only because of its special properties."

Our examination of the mainly economics literature[1] that proclaims to deal with the value or price of knowledge as an asset and the monetary return to knowledge exemplifies, first, our general contention that the terms of knowledge and information are not only liberally conflated (e.g. Hess and Ostrom, 2003),[2] but that, second, efforts by economists that remain and are genuinely concerned with the value of knowledge, for example in the sense of knowledge assets as "intangibles," display for the most part a strongly ambivalent idea of the value of knowledge and indicate strong doubts about the possibility of arriving at a price of knowledge.

The very definition of intangibles as "unseen wealth" (Blair and Wallman, 2001; Leadbeater, 1999; Teece, 1998),[3] although it is seen as critically important for firms in the contemporary competitive economic environment, already indicates the difficulties of devising ways of measuring the monetary value of copyrights, patents, trade secrets, brand loyalty, organizational capabilities – let alone knowledge skills (see Fulmer and Ployhart, 2014).[4] Such ambivalence or lack of precision (how profitable is private investment in research and development?) perhaps exemplifies and satisfies the numerous critics who are convinced that knowledge does not or should not carry a price tag and be part of the "public domain" (cf. Boyle, 2003) or is particularly ill suited for conversion to private property and market pricing.[5] To begin with, therefore, we are able to assert that there is – as is the case for the social phenomenon of power – no standardized or objective approach to quantify the value of knowledge (or information).

Even assuming that one is able to specify a price, the value of knowledge will not be a constant but will presumably increase or decay (become obsolete), depending on circumstances such as the time that has passed since the initial discovery of a product, the difficulty of keeping it from other agents (cf. the case of generic drugs) or the assets that have to be mobilized to transmit it (cf. Pakes and Schankerman, 1979). In our attempt to reconstruct various perspectives that aim to gain insight into the value of knowledge we will cover three cases that suggest that the value of knowledge is at issue in these discussions, decisions or valuations of the benefit to be derived from knowledge.

The accounts that are of interest to us either attempt to gain insight into the value of knowledge by treating knowledge as a form of *input*, for example in the production process, and as one of the factors of production such as human capital. Another notable approach takes the opposite perspective. In this case, knowledge becomes relevant and hence subject to attempts to value it by being treated as a form of *output*, for example in the sense of patents, copyright restrictions and the like.

Many of the studies and discussions that can be found in the literature that claims to deal with the price of knowledge actually are about the price of *information* (e.g. Rosewall, 2005). This is most notable in consumer behavior research, which examines the impact of consumers' knowledge of the price of a product/commodity on the decisions made by them in supermarkets (e.g. Olavarrieta et al., 2012; Dickson and Sawyer, 1990), the effect the product price has on consumer satisfaction (e.g. Homburg et al., 2012), or the impact of the price of tertiary education on university students (e.g. Junor and Usher, 2004/05).

Most other efforts that aim to discuss the price of knowledge can be subsumed under some form of a critique of the commodification of knowledge; these efforts are mainly critical since scientific and economic activities are embedded in distinct functional subsystems of society. The point of departure here tends to be the observation that a growing volume of scientific activity, especially in the fields of genetics and biochemistry, is no longer curiosity-driven but carried out in the laboratories of private corporations; as a result, knowledge increasingly takes on the characteristics of a *commodity*. The economization of science is criticized (e.g. Balzer, 2003), for example, in the case of efforts to patent genes (see Matthijs, 2004; Resnik, 2004).

Both of these approaches affirm the sensitivity of claims that knowledge comes with a price tag. Knowledge is simply a much too "valuable," "special" and unique human or "largely unobservable"[6] resource for it to be measured in any strictly monetary sense. After all, knowledge in many ways resembles wisdom, insight and good judgment that are not at home in the market place. Hence the often-repeated assertion that what cannot be counted or quantified is not necessarily without value. We will return to this observation in our discussion of patents.

According to some of the most influential international organizations, the World Bank (e.g. 2011) and the United Nations (e.g. UNU-IHDP and UNEP, 2014), human capital is the most significant component of human wealth for most countries in the modern world. Economic growth requires capable workers. In other words, there is widespread agreement among social scientists that knowledge is the core determinant of economic growth in modern societies. For example, Claudia Goldin and Lawrence Katz (2008) show how human capital has been the defining factor for the economic identity of the industrialized world of the twentieth century (also Acemoglu and Autor, 2012). However, there also is a widespread disagreement about the terms of analysis. The terms "human capital," "skills," "information," "capacities and "knowledge" applicable to all occupations, jobs, tasks and sectors of the economy are widely conflated in many of the studies. Since human capital is seen to be virtually identical to the acquired knowledge individuals command, it would appear to be self-evident that the value human capital offers should constitute a road to an assessment of the value of knowledge. However, this is not the case, as we will show in the next section.

10.1 Human capital[7]

Among the theoretical approaches and concepts that might be regarded as a proxy for the price of knowledge, *cultural capital* and *human capital* theories stand out. For example, efforts are made by economists to estimate the value of the "most valuable asset most people own [which] is their human capital" (Haggett and Kaplan, 2015: 1). The struggle between the relative weights for the share of collective income generated in the economy by different forms of capital has significant repercussions for the inequality formation in a society. Thomas Piketty ([2013] 2014: 21), for example, notes "the progress of technological rationality is supposed to lead automatically to the triumph of human capital over financial capital and real estate, capable managers over fat stockholders, and skill over nepotism." He adds the cautionary remark, "inequalities would thus become more meritocratic and less static (though not necessarily smaller): economic rationality would then in some sense automatically give rise to democratic rationality" (ibid.: 21).

The notion of human capital has been developed and deployed primarily within *economic* discourse (Schultz, 1961; Becker, 1964; Tan, 2014).[8] It is within the context of human capital theory that the *value* of knowledge, skills and capabilities of active economic agents and its *costs* become a relevant consideration.

Just as physical capital is created by changes in the means of production by generating instruments and artifacts that facilitate production, human capital rests on the transformation of *individual* persons who impart skills and capacities[9] allowing them to contribute to productive processes.[10] Human capital is related to the worker's earning capacity in the labor market. In its most simplified variety, human capital theory – with its strong influence on neo-liberal economic theory – expects that *income differences* are a strict reflection of acquired skill differentials of occupations. You earn what you deserve, as David Ricardo had already argued. The evaluation of human capital proceeds by analogy with the valuation of fixed capital.

The acquisition of skills is a form of durable investment rather than consumption. The acquisition of human capital is fostered by the desire of the individual agent to maximize utilities, a future-oriented perspective, constant rational conduct and stable preferences. The choices of the individual are constrained by market forces, time, income and available opportunities (Becker, 1993).

Skills can be acquired by attending school and job training. In research on human capital, the number of years of schooling and job training typically are a proxy for differential skills. Existing estimates of the rate of return rely almost exclusively on school attainment as a substitute for various skills relevant to occupational achievement (focusing characteristically on early career workers) rather than any *direct* measures of cognitive skills and capacities over the full occupational history of workers such as ongoing learning (see Hanushek et al., 2015). These estimates indirectly indicate the price of knowledge in the form of skills that make the employee more productive. Louis Garicano and Esteban Rossi-Hansberg (2015: 5) make the point that it is not merely an estimate of the value of educational achievement that allows one to calculate the value of human capital: "Perhaps the best measure of the marketable knowledge and skills of an agent is his or her wage." In the end, the close correlation between wages and education assures that an analysis of human capital value arrives at the same conclusion independent of its point of departure. Educational attainment as such is of course not irrelevant to occupational success and, as internationally comparative studies have indicated, both the quality and quantity of education contribute to country differences in income and economic growth (e.g. Schoellman, 2012).

The initial reduction in consumption or the abandonment of other investment opportunities of *rationally* acting and motivated actors should pay off at a later time in the form of higher levels of income. Indeed, it is one of the governing assumptions in economic discourse on human capital that differential earnings in fact are related to the individual (atomistic) capital at hand in an unambiguous fashion and based on motives that are constant across time and space (for a competing, sociological perspective see Fevre et al., 1999; Hilmer and Hilmer, 2012).

On the basis of these assumptions, estimates about the price of skills (Mincer, 1974) and the rate of return on investments in human capital are calculated (e.g. Blaug, [1965] 1968). What proportions of the return to skill will be appropriated by the individual who has invested in these skills is indeed a contentious matter. The corporation expects benefits (e.g. Barney, 1991; Becker and Gerhart, 1996) and may even *appropriate* most of the return to the skills of the individual worker.

As long as the labor market competition is free especially from extraneous constraints, and competition therefore approaches perfect competition, human capital theory assumes that income differentials among individuals amount immediately to the different investments in acquiring relevant skills. Human capital theory then amounts to a theoretical perspective that explains equality rather than inequality. Only competitive distortions generate "unearned income" (see Atkinson, 1983: 104; Berger, 2004: 367–368). From a macro-perspective an increasing supply of human capital to the economy will reduce – assuming a demand for human capital that is lower than the supply – the skill premium or the value commanded by human capital (cf. Acemoglu and Autor, 2012: 427).

Human capital is not homogeneous; for example, it is possible to distinguish between general human capital that is mobile, and context-sensitive specific human capital that is not mobile across boundaries. As the result of changes in technology, it is often argued that the kinds of skills in demand on the labor market change. Only the individual who made the investment in the first place can, under most circumstances, appropriate returns on human capital. Human capital is embodied capital. It cannot be separated from the individual, but the value of the investment depends also on the judgments of other agents (see van Doorn, 2014) or on the network of social relations the individual is able to mobilize. The stock of human capital cannot be directly traded and transferred unless one trades and transfers the individual person. Human capital theory is silent on the influence of collective factors, for example the societal reputation of the educational degree, that affect the successful acquisition of human capital or, correspondingly, the failure to do so. It is equally opaque on the question of the depreciation of human capital and therefore on how the earning streams may decline or, for that matter, continue to grow over time.[11] Unlike the impact on capital invested in the plants and the equipment of a corporation, the impact of recessionary economic times, for example, on the value of human capital (does it depreciate or even increase in value?) is an unresearched question (see Stiglitz, 2015: 6–10).

By the same token, human capital theory tends to be quiet on the impact of socio-structural features of society and the nature of the economic system that may enhance or reduce payoffs in return for the investments made by the individual. Finally, human capital theory is silent "on what factors determine the skills that are demanded [...] empirical analysis of the return to education is not directly informative about what skills workers use on the job, why these skills are required, and how these skill requirements have changed over time" (Autor and Handel, 2009).

Human capital theories as well as efforts to apply them empirically remain hamstringed by the superficial notion of how human capital manifests itself in social reality. The empirical representation of human capital is for the most part seen, as we have pointed out, to reflect the numbers of years of schooling; schooling being taken to represent a homogenous variable and a valid indication for differential skills and knowledge of the individual. The Becker-Tomes (1986) model of the intergenerational transmission of human capital recognizes the impact of previous generations on the individual's acquisition of human capital. Specifically, the Becker-Tomes model proposes that the level of human capital and the abilities of parents matter for the human capital of their children if credit constraints limit the parents' ability to invest in the human capital formation of their offspring. Whether or not the rational understanding of economic constraints or opportunities by parents, let alone their educational attainment, plays a role in the intergenerational transmission of human capital is a contested issue. A similar open question is the influence of grandparents on the transmission of human capital (see Lindahl et al., 2014). In the final analysis, however, human capital theory tends to treat the complex dimension of cognitive capacities and skills and the intergenerational transmission of these abilities as a black box.

Eric Hanushek and his colleagues (2015) have tried to partly fill this gap by providing information about the returns to *cognitive skills* across the entire labor force, using data from the Programme for the International Assessment of Adult Competencies (PIAAC) for 23 countries. How do earnings (expressed in pre-tax and pre-transfer wages) of full-time workers between 35 and 54 years of age differ depending on a direct measure of cognitive skills?[12] The results obtained in this analysis of the PIAAC data focus on the numeracy skills, that is, the "ability to access, use, interpret, and communicate mathematical information and ideas in order to engage in and manage the mathematical demands of a range of situations in adult life," which the authors of the study considered comparable across countries.

The results "consistently indicate that better skills are significantly related to higher labor-market earnings, […] a one-standard-deviation increase in numeracy skills is associated with an average increase in hourly wages of 17.8 percent across the 23 countries" (Hanushek et al., 2015: 108). The returns to skills, measured across numeracy, literacy and problem-solving domains, however, vary significantly from country to country. Returns to skills are twice as high in the United States than in the Scandinavian countries.

10.2 Symbolic and knowledge capital

In contrast and in addition, the theory of cultural, symbolic and social capital mainly explicated by Pierre Bourdieu within *sociological* discourse and the idea of knowledge capital proposed by André Gorz ([2003] 2010: 1–2) begin to open up the black box of symbolic capital and alert us to the existence of immaterial forms of capital and the complex ways of its context-sensitive acquisition. Pierre Bourdieu ([1983] 1986: 241; see also Michels, [1908] 1987: 140–141) clarifies his insights into the role of immaterial capital that can be translated into economic capital (that is "immediately and directly convertible into money") with the economic perspective, particularly a Marxist approach, very much in mind.

Bourdieu ([1983] 1986: 243) first encountered the usefulness of the notion "cultural capital" in social inequality research. The origins of Bourdieu's theory of the reproduction of privilege have a considerable impact on the ways in which the notion of cultural capital designed to enlarge the orthodox concept of class is strategically deployed in discourse. Bourdieu's research was designed to explain the unequal scholastic achievement of children from different social classes in France; unequal academic success, or the "specific profits" (failures) students are able to acquire in the academic market are related to the existing stratified distribution of cultural capital among social classes and the unequal chances of acquiring such capital domestically (cf. Bourdieu and Passeron, [1964] 1979). Cultural capital is added to existing cultural capital stocks, thereby reproducing the structure of the distribution of cultural capital between social classes (cf. Bourdieu, [1971] 1973: 73). It is possible therefore to argue that the benefits that derive from the unequal distribution of cultural capital represent a form of *unearned income*. Given its intellectual origins, Bourdieu's theory of cultural capital is fundamentally about societal power and domination. Bourdieu's main concern is, as a result, with the role such capital plays in the reproduction of social hierarchies.

Although the educational system is of course not the only social site where cultural capital may be acquired, education not only fulfills a role in converting academic into social hierarchies but plays a function also in the legitimation and perpetuation of the social *status quo*. The pretensions of "merit," "gifts," skills, equality of opportunity and democratic selection that appear to put the chances of acquiring cultural capital in the educational systems onto an equal footing are weakened by virtue of the fact that "the ruling classes have at their disposal (to begin with) a much larger cultural capital than the other classes" (Bourdieu, [1971] 1973: 85). The modern educational system canonizes privilege by ignoring it.

Bourdieu distinguishes between different forms of cultural capital: its embodied or symbolic form as internalized culture, its objectified form in material objects and media, and its institutionalized form (for example, as academic certificates).[13] These distinctions signal the ways in which cultural capital is stored and passed on by way of becoming an integral habitus of the individual. Bourdieu identifies two additional forms of capital, economic capital and social capital. Social capital refers to the gains individuals may derive from their network of social relations (also Coleman, 1988).[14] The various forms of capital correlate highly with each other and form what could be called capital "repertoires." One form of capital "comes to be added, in most cases" to other forms of capital – for example, cultural to economic capital (Bourdieu, [1971] 1973: 99).

We will focus on Bourdieu's concept of cultural capital (or informational capital) since it resonates, at least on the surface, more closely with the concept of knowledge as used in this study. In Bourdieu's sense, cultural capital as a form of *symbolic capital* is much broader but also less tangible than the concept of human capital as favored in economic discourse.[15] In contrast, the idea of knowledge capital developed by André Gorz[16] is a form of knowledge that is not acquired in settings of formal education but in everyday life and belongs to everyday culture. As a matter of fact, the notion of knowledge capital resonates closely with the concepts of *knowledge skills* that we have explicated elsewhere (Stehr, 2016).

As we have seen, modern economic human capital theory relates deliberate and measurable educational investments (and achievements) in the acquisition of useful skills and knowledge to the *monetary* gains or losses they generate, and therefore to the value of knowledge. As one of the originators of the idea of human capital, Theodore W. Schultz (1961), contends skills and knowledge have grown in Western societies at a much faster rate than nonhuman capital. Schultz suggests that investment in human capital embodied in human beings has driven much of the growth in real wages of income-earning persons in recent decades as well as economic growth generally (cf. Benhabib and Spiegel, 1994).[17]

In strong contrast, cultural capital theory does not proceed from the assumption of a kind of *tabula rasa* that allows all individuals to enter and participate in the competitive market where human capital is allocated and where success or failure is most affected by unequal natural aptitudes. Cultural capital theory acknowledges not only preexisting unequal access to the distributional channels for its accumulation, but also the different ways in which the "market" favors the chances of particular players from the very beginning. In a largely undifferentiated society or community, of course, culture does not function as a vehicle for the emergence of differential cultural capital. As the societal division of labor increases, one notices that the social conditions of the transmission of cultural capital tend to be much more disguised than those that govern the transmission of economic capital. The portion of individual lives that can be afforded for the acquisition of cultural capital is highly significant. Cultural capital yields benefits of distinction for its owner.

Even though the analysis of the acquisition and transmission of cultural capital is situated within what Bourdieu calls "social fields" (see Wacquant, 1989: 39), one of the most evident drawbacks of Bourdieu's explication of cultural capital theory is, first, its strong individualistic bias, that is, the extent to which he stresses the fusion of cultural capital and the personality of the individual owner. Cultural capital is not a homogenous phenomenon. Not all cultural capital is equal. Cultural capital is fragile. Fashion and the demand for novelty change the value of specific forms of cultural capital.

The emphasis in Bourdieu remains for the most part on cultural capital as an inherent attribute of the individual carrier. Cultural capital in the form of educational credentials, for example, declines and dies with its carrier since it has the same biological limits as its carrier. Bourdieu's individualistic conception of cultural capital appears to be linked to his determination not to dispossess cultural capital theory of the ability to calculate and attribute investment gains that derive from cultural capital, and such returns of investment are seen to accrue primarily to the investor. In this sense, cultural capital theory continues to resonate with human capital theory. It contains crucial residues of economic discourse.[18] Frequent references to the marketplace, to supply and demand, to costs, investments and profits would be examples of such a conflation of perspectives. It is important to recognize that cultural capital is embodied in collective processes and structures; hence the benefits typically do not accrue only to those who have invested resources, which raises the free-rider issue. The production as well as consumption of such capital is not charged to the individual. It is borne by the collectivity. At one extreme, such capital can even be seen to be entirely free, in that its use by certain individuals does not diminish its utility for or availability to others. Cultural capital is human-made capital and as such subject to limits and dynamics applicable to all human products and creations, especially in modern societies.

Second, and as we have emphasized already, Bourdieu discovers and utilizes the concept of cultural capital in the context of social inequality research. The concept derives much of its coherence and its critical tone from this context, a context in which the persistence of distinction, of processes of inclusion and exclusion, domination and subordination play a decisive role. Bourdieu thereby retains a strong reference for the objective, inescapable presence and constraint of the social, economic and political presence of social class in modern society.[19] Cultural capital, in the end, is merely derivative and closely mirrors the objective realities of class. As John R. Hall (1992: 257) therefore observes, "the dazzling variety and endless differences of culture obtain surprising coherence when we look at them through the lens of social stratification."

Cultural capital becomes a peculiar entity that apparently is acquired and transmitted (*reproduced*) almost mechanically, though in a selective fashion, with great ease, considerable precision and success. The risks of failure appear to be at a minimum while the possibility of a perpetuation of the cultural and socio-structural patterns is at a maximum. Whether such a description conforms to reality is questionable, as is the idea that there is a close correspondence between particular manifestations of culture and class membership (see Halle, 1992: 134–135). Culture is much more fluid and leaves "much opportunity for choice and variation" (DiMaggio, 1997: 265).

Access today, at least, is much more open than suggested by a theory of cultural capital that stresses the stratification of power and domination in society. Pierre Bourdieu's distinction and the openness accorded to the capacities of individuals and groups for change, resistance and innovation are limited (cf. Garnham and Williams, 1986: 129), but cultural frames and meaning production as well as reproduction, in an immense and creative variety of ways, are the hallmark of the work that cultural capital conceived of in a less mechanical fashion may well accomplish for individuals and collectivities. It must also be asked if the relevance of class divisions is not undermined or even eliminated by virtue of the transformation of economic realities. In such a society, distinctions and advantages that are linked to cultural processes are not merely derivative and subordinate but foundational (Stehr, 2002). The extent to which the educational system in modern societies actually fails to reproduce faithfully the existing system of social inequality (Boudon, 1974) is testimony not only to the dynamic character of modern society but also to profound changes in inequality regimes in which knowledge and knowledge skills play a more significant and independent role (see Stehr, 1999, 2015a).

Third, although the notion of human cultural capital is not employed in a fully ahistoric manner, it is for the most part devoid of historical specificity, lacks linkage to different major societal formations such as industrial society, the state or science, and at times is also utilized in close proximity to the notion of years of education in human capital theory (e.g. Bourdieu, [1984] 1988: 230–232). Bourdieu does not explore the socio-historical conditions under which different strategies and regimes of inequality formation become possible. In principle it seems that one should be able to apply the idea of different forms of capital everywhere although the extent and ease of convertibility – for example the extent to which parental labor at home can be translated into status attainment for their children – varies within historical contexts (see Calhoun, 1995: 139–141).

New "structures of consciousness" (to use a term coined by Benjamin Nelson, 1973) cannot be captured by Bourdieu's theory of cultural capital. In many ways, the structure of consciousness of knowledge societies is of course not novel. It resonates with the consciousness of modernity that dates – although this too is a highly contested question – at least from the more immediate socio-historical origins of the French Revolution. In other respects, the *conscience collective* in knowledge societies is at variance with the belief systems and mental sets that are usually identified as uniquely modern and therefore warrants the designation of a new structure of consciousness. In any event, the notion of cultural capital is not well designed, it seems, to capture such transformations. Given its close reliance on the assertion that cultural capital is about power and domination, it is unable to capture the opposite phenomenon, namely the extent to which knowledge is strategically deployed to soften and undermine authority, power and domination.

10.3 Patents[20]

Patents represent a legal grant (a category in law) by (typically) a state or bundle of states such as the European Patent Office (EPO). A simple definition of a patent would be that the inventor is granted property rights for a specified time (17 years in the United States) and space in analogy to the general legal rules governing property in general. The owner of the invention acquires a legal title that prevents others from making, using or selling the invention but thereby grant the owner the right to sell her "intangible" asset for a prize. A patent – often acquired in a lengthy administrative process involving highly specialized experts – allows the owner the right to practice the invention described in the patent. Thus, patents convert knowledge into private property[21] and knowledge becomes scarce in a legal sense.

Since the 1980s policies with regard to the legal protection of intellectual property (patents, trademarks, copyrights) have changed radically and litigation about patent infringements have risen (for example, the patent struggle between Apple and Samsung about the design of the smartphone).[22] With the World Trade Organization's (WTO) Agreement on Trade-Related Aspects of Intellectual Property Rights (TRIPS), stringent and unprecedented obligations have been enacted for all members of WTO with respect to their national intellectual property policies. In order to take part in international trade and access markets abroad, every member country has to adopt legal frames that conform to patent laws in the economically dominant countries of the world. Moreover, the transnational integration of the major patent offices in the United States, Europe and Japan has created a global network of knowledge governance that leads a "concealed" harmonization of patent laws (Drahos, 2010).[23]

However, patent protection is not just a technical or economic matter. Patent laws have social, political as well as economic implications. Intellectual property rights (IPRs) are intended to offer incentives to stimulate innovation (Stiglitz and Greenwald, 2014: 429–456).[24] The counterpart to IRPs is the public domain. William Landes and Richard Posner (2003: 14–15) note that even the strongest defenders of property rights "acknowledge the economic value of preserving public domains – that is, of areas in which property is available for common use rather than owned – even in regard to physical property and a *fortiori* in regard to intellectual property."

A debate surrounding IPRs that is just starting (cf. Li et al., 2015), is getting more intense and concerns the extent to which scientific texts, for example, are freely made available by companies (such as Google, Academia or ResearchGate) or libraries, to the dismay of publishers and authors.[25] Opponents of *free access* see in these developments a one-sided privilege favoring the "consumer" of texts and neglecting the rights of the "producers" of the same intellectual accomplishments. Supported by law and court decisions, for example, in Germany libraries are permitted to scan textbooks and make them available on sticks to students – who of course can pass them on without restrictions.[26]

Critical issues surrounding patents involve the question of whether patents actually stimulate innovation, the extent to which patents add to the price the consumer has to pay (for example, for pharmaceuticals), the meaning of fencing in knowledge in the first place, which we have discussed, or the scope and the degree of novelty demanded for granting a parent. Answers to these issues are highly contestable. Every invention that is granted legal protection for a limited period of time relies, of course, on previously accumulated knowledge (cf. Stiglitz, 1999: 314–316; Stiglitz, 2012: 78). "Because patent lawyers are masters of obfuscation," as *The Economist* ("Time to fix patents," August 8, 2015) argues, patents in fact tend to slow innovation by slowing the dissemination of knowledge; patents tend to lock in the advantages of the patent holders. Hence the conclusion that follows from critical questions about the role of patents would be that the patent system should not be enhanced but reduced in its impact or even abolished (see Boldrin and Levine, 2013).[27]

Private IPRs now widely employed by law makers at international (cf. Fink and Maskus, 2005), national and regional levels are not restricted to patents but extend also to copyrights (in contrast to patents, almost instantly acquired upon creation), databases (David, 2000), trademarks, designs, software (see Harison, 2008; Bonaccorsi et al., 2011), plant varieties, and trade secrets (in the sense of information and knowledge held by a business that is kept out of the public domain through agreements with employees or other firms).[28]

It is not surprising, therefore, to observe that there are many types of IPRs and many types of institutions that deal with their administration. The variety of IPRs and how they interrelate to law, markets, corporations and individuals makes it most difficult, if not impossible, to gain a robust general insight into the value of (distinctive) ideas, inventions, knowledge and copyrights. The propensity to attempt to patent an invention or make ideas freely available depends on the social context in which new knowledge is discovered. For example, "using data collected by the National Research Council within the U.S. National Academies from their survey of firm's [sic] that received National Institutes of Health Phase II Small Business Innovation Research awards between 1992 and 2001 [Link and Ruhm, 2009] find that entrepreneurs with academic backgrounds are more likely to publish their intellectual capital compared to entrepreneurs with business backgrounds, who are more likely to patent their intellectual capital" (Link and Ruhm, 2009: 1).

The benefits that accrue to intellectual property may arrive in many ways, depending on the nature of the invention (such as a license granted or the signal a patent sends to others; see Long, 2002). At best, we will be able to arrive at an indirect and ambivalent assessment, especially in terms of quantity, of the value and costs associated with intellectual proper rights.[29]

In the strict sense of the term, knowledge tends to be embedded only in patents and not in trademarks. Trademarks are names affixed by a company to their products or similar attributes; hence, based on our definition of information, trademarks convey information. From an economic perspective, a patent – if well enforced – represents a monopoly that offers a rent to the owner. In the context of examining the value of knowledge, we are interested in the rent patents may generate.[30]

As Margaret Blair and Steven Wallman (2001: 73) point out in their report on "unseen wealth," "once an intangible [such as a copyright] has been defined by law as a piece of property, and the rights associated with that property have been delimited, it becomes easier to estimate a value associated with those property rights and to sell, or transfer, or enter into other transactions involving that piece of property." Assigning property rights to an invention, a text, to a musical score or to software as such does not immediately allow one to arrive at a value for intellectual property. In fact, the value of intellectual property could be zero or even negative if the investment in generating the invention is never returned. Presumably not all patents are successful. The value will be a function of the many additional features related to the activity of the owner, for example, the willingness to invest in activities protecting the monopoly or, last but not least, the nature of the intellectual property itself.

From an economic perspective, a patent enshrined in law represents a capacity to act and a solution to the "appropriability problem" (a protective function for new knowledge), or is seen to offer an answer to the free-rider issue since knowledge is viewed as "non-excludable." Patent protection translates non-rival goods into excludable goods. Only the patent holder is legitimized to appropriate the benefits of the invention. Others are excluded from enjoying the profits of the knowledge in question. In addition, from an economic point of view patents are seen to serve as an incentive to produce socially and economically desirable innovations.

Patent laws are powerfully influenced by assumptions about knowledge and innovation from neo-classical economics (see Dempsey, 1999), but a comprehensive theory of the economic effects of patents must also take into account that legal intellectual property protections can restrain rather than encourage innovation, the growth of knowledge and socio-economic development. If knowledge is defined as a *public good* (Stiglitz, 1995; cf. Zhou, 2015), that is, as non-rival and non-excludable, the ideas associated with knowledge claims "may even stimulate others to have an idea with large commercial value" (Stiglitz, 1999: 309).[31] André Gorz ([2003] 2010)[32] defends the desirability of treating knowledge as a common good on the basis of a couple of considerations: 1 knowledge does not have the attributes of commodities, which escape the owner's control upon being sold or losing legal control; and 2 the societal utility of knowledge would be restricted by privatization.

However, as Charlotte Hess and Elinor Ostrom (2007: 5) warn, a common good leads to conduct "such as competition for use, free riding and over-harvesting," and "[t]ypical threats to knowledge commons are commodification or enclosure, pollution and degradation, and nonsustainability."

In a "well-functioning" economy the monetary value of an individual good should be represented by its price. Many efforts have been made to accomplish precisely this. Most often efforts to establish the value of intellectual property are based on the use of *proxies*.[33] For example, the value of IPRs are inferred from the value of the prices of shares of a company listed on the stock exchange whereby IPRs are part of the "unseen wealth" of a corporation. Intangibles "can be related to brand names, process or product innovations, advertising, managerial skill, human capital in the workforce, and other aspects of the firm" (Greenhalgh and Rogers, 2007: 551). Such arithmetic indicates that highly contentious figures could result from such an effort. It is virtually impossible to arrive at a robust conclusion regarding whether such accounting under- or overestimates the value of the intellectual property of a firm. In short, "the eventual returns to individual patents or trade marks can vary enormously: most returns are very small, but a few generate huge returns."

What is possible, however, is to revert to broad collective income and expenditures of royalty and license fees received and paid by entire nations. The World Bank (2015) offers such statistics for a wide range of nations, and as recent data (see Table 10.1) from the "2014 World Development Indicators" show, the "Balance of Technology Trade" is heavily tilted in favor of a few countries whose expenditures on research and development (R&D) as a percentage of the gross national product (GNP) have been high (also Ganguli, 2000).

Large expenditures on R&D in a country appear to ensure that the balance of royalty and license fees received is positive (e.g. in the case of Finland, Germany, Japan, Sweden, the United Kingdom and the United States), while comparatively low expenditures on R&D correlate with a negative balance (e.g. in the case of Brazil, Canada, Ireland, Portugal and Russia). However, there are cases where this correlation does not hold, in the case of Austria, for example, with high expenditures on R&D but a negative balance of royalty and license fees both in 2007 and 2014. In many instances of nations with a significant balance of inter-nation technology trade, the gap has increased in recent years (e.g. Canada, Austria, India, Italy and the Republic of Korea).

The statistic of the inter-nation technology trade balances does not allow for a precise inference regarding many relevant data about the value and costs of IPRs. They provide only a very broad indication that such rights are translated into national monetary advantages, that both payments and receipts of royalty and license fee tend to increase in

TABLE 10.1 Inter-nation technology trade

Name of country	Expenditure for R&D in % of GNP 2010–12	High-technology exports $ millions 2013	High-technology exports % of manufactured exports 2013	Royalty and license fees Receipts ($ millions) 2007	Royalty and license fees Receipts ($ millions) 2014	Royalty and license fees Payments ($ millions) 2007	Royalty and license fees Payments ($ millions) 2014	Balance ($ millions) 2007	Balance ($ millions) 2014	Patent applications filed Residents 2014	Patent applications filed Non-residents 2014
Australia	2.4	4,565	12.9	714	814	2,809	3,983	−2,096	−3,170	3,061	26,656
Austria	2.8	18,412	13.7	945	1,070	1,801	1,970	−856	−900	2,162	244
Brazil	1.2	8,392	9.6	319	597	2,259	3,669	−1,940	−3,071	4,959	25,925
Canada	1.7	29,137	14.1	3,835	4,066	8,162	10,871	−4,327	−6,805	4,567	30,174
China	2.0	560,058	27.0	343	887	8,192	21,033	−7,849	−20,146	704,936	120,200
Finland	3.5	3,725	7.2	1,281	3,715	1,441	1,834	−159	1,882	1,596	141
France	2.3	113,000	25.8	13,469	11,556	7,674	10,150	5,795	1,406	14,690	2,196
Germany	2.9	193,088	16.1	6,309	13,114	7,501	8,425	−1,191	4,689	47,353	15,814
India	0.8	16,693	8.1	163	446	1,160	3,904	−997	−3,458	10,669	32,362
Ireland	1.7	21,915	22.4	1,185	5,287	24,017	46,407	−22,832	−41,120	333	57
Israel	3.9	9,635	15.6	786	1,007	913	985	−127	22	1,201	4,984
Italy	1.3	29,752	7.3	1,050	3,707	1,680	5,381	−630	−1,674	8,307	905
Japan	3.4	105,076	16.8	23,229	31,587	16,678	17,831	6,551	13,756	27,1731	56,705
Korea, Rep. of	4.0	130,460	27.1	1,827	4,328	5,334	9,837	−3,508	−5,509	15,9978	44,611
Netherlands	2.2	69,040	20.4	4,322	6,317	3,662	4,495	660	1,822	2,315	449
Portugal	1.5	1,942	4.3	85	39	450	440	−366	−401	647	22
Russia	1.1	8,656	10.0	352	738	2,704	8,371	−2,352	−7,633	28,765	16,149
Spain	1.3	16,346	7.7	537	968	3,620	2,096	−3,083	−1,128	3,026	218
Sweden	3.4	17,025	14.0	4,733	7,455	1,805	2,722	2,927	4,733	2,332	163

Name of country	Expenditure for R&D in % of GNP	High-technology exports		Royalty and license fees						Patent applications filed	
	2010–12	$ millions 2013	% of manufactured exports 2013	Receipts ($ millions) 2007	2014	Payments ($ millions) 2007	2014	Balance ($ millions) 2007	2014	Residents 2014	Non-residents 2014
United Kingdom	1.7	24,216	7.6	17,828	17,103	9,181	10,529	8,647	6,574	14,972	7,966
United States	2.8	147,833	17.8	97,802	129,178	26,479	39,016	71,323	90,162	287,831	283,781

(databank.worldbank.org/data//reports.aspx?source=2&Topic=14)

more recent years, that disadvantages and benefits are unequally distributed across the globe, and about the size of the receipts and payments. The economic role of IPRs, one is able to conclude, increases measurably and signifies the transformation of national economies into what are at times designated as knowledge-based economies.

10.4 Taxation[34]

It is not only the professional but also the common-sense view that citizens of democratic societies should be knowledgeable and well informed. Being knowledgeable and well informed comes at a price. One avenue that is open to social scientists interested in the question of the price of knowledge is to examine specific contested cases in which the question of the price of knowledge does play a role, if only indirectly. We will describe such a conflict about the resources that should be mobilized by the state to ensure that its citizens acquire the desirable level of knowledge and information for a democratic society.[35]

During the last century the relation between education and democracy had become almost conventional wisdom. John Dewey ([1916] 2005), for example, views broad and even high levels of educational attainment as a precondition for democracy, while Seymour Martin Lipset (1959: 80), in the postwar era, concludes a cross-national empirical study with the observation that "high" levels of educational achievement are a necessary condition for the existence and stability of democratic society. Even more recent empirical work tends to support the same conclusion (e.g. Barro, 1999; and Przeworski et al., 2000). An examination of the role and experience of science advising and the formation of science policy in the United States in the late 1950s (last but not least in the wake of the launching of the first manmade satellite, Sputnik, by the Soviets in the fall of 1957) emphatically concludes that "a democratic nation can only cope with the scientific revolution if thoughtful citizens know what it truly entails" (Dupré and Lakoff, 1962: 181).

However, it is also John Dewey ([1916] 2005: 108–110) who warns against treating education as a *black box*. An authoritarian personality, an elevated deference to the state and a high level of formal education are – as the case of Germany demonstrates – compatible. Dewey

([1916] 2005: 57) notes that in the case of the German educational system, "the educational process was taken to be one of disciplinary training rather than of personal development [...] only in and through an absorption of the aims and meaning of the organized institutions does [the individual] attain true personality." In other words, the philosophy of education and the aims of the educational system "required subordination of individuals to the superior interests of the state." The realization of the subservient personality as the primary goal of the educational policy, not only in imperial Germany but for decades to come, demanded the "thoroughgoing 'disciplinary' subordination to existing institutions." Dewey's observations are a useful reminder that a high formal level of education in a society does not necessarily lead to support for democratic values and conduct. The association between formal educational achievement and democracy is a complex relationship that requires careful attention to the nature of the actual education system.

This raises the question of how much knowledge and information the citizen of a modern society needs to acquire, and the related issue of the volume of resources the state has to invest to accomplish such an outcome. There can be little doubt that these questions are highly complex and contentious, as the long-lasting conflict between the State of New York and the City of New York over educational finances readily demonstrates.[36]

For over a decade, the State of New York and the City of New York were entangled in a legal battle over the question of whether the State of New York provided fair and sufficient financial means for the gigantic public school system of the City of New York.[37] The legal dispute ran its course parallel to the so-called "educational standards movement," which has been fighting for the continual improvement of the expectations and standards attached to a high school diploma. In a number of American states, for example Kentucky, courts have indeed prescribed much higher, clearly defined standards.

At first glance, this is apparently one of those everyday rhetorical disputes between different political jurisdictions over contested questions of revenue sharing between various political levels – a familiar occurrence in any democratic society. The State of New York provides approximately half of the school budget for the City of New York.

One of the most recent judgments in this legal action, however, has made reference to a fundamental philosophical or constitutional problem: Which skills, information and proficiencies should the modern state be *minimally* obligated to communicate successfully to students in its schools, and how expensive must an education system be that guarantees standards of this type? The developments in the New York dispute make it evident that this conflict over how to answer the question under debate is ultimately based on a problem that must be decided within the political system.

The constitution of the State of New York stipulates that the state is obligated to guarantee "the maintenance and support of a system of free common schools wherein all the children of this state may be educated." The interpretation of this constitutional norm as an obligation for the state to make possible a "sound, basic" education is concretized by the Court of Appeals of the State of New York, in a judgment of 1995. This court further ruled that the public school system must be in a position to guarantee that students "function productively as civic participants capable of voting and serving on a jury." In a later judgment of 2001, a judge of the Constitutional Court of the State of New York ruled that as jurors, citizens are required to answer complex questions: Jurors "must determine questions of fact concerning DNA evidence, statistical analysis and convoluted financial fraud, to name only three topics." The state successfully appealed this judgment.

In June 2002, however, the Appellate Division of the State Supreme Court of New York defined a restrictive interpretation of this constitutional norm: On the basis of relevant constitutional standards, the state is not obliged to finance more than a *minimal* education. More concretely, after eight or nine years, students should be able to read political parties' campaign literature, serve the courts as jurors and fulfill the requirements of an employment that makes minor demands on them. The high school diploma should only ensure that the student had acquired the ability "to get a job, and support oneself, and thereby not be a charge on the public fiscus."

The court's decision was variously received. In some quarters, this minimal educational requirement was understood as a kind of capitulation on the part of the state. In others, the judges were praised for their wise decision, since (more) money was not necessarily an adequate solution to the educational dilemma – other factors also influenced students' opportunities of acquiring cultural capital. The court emphasized that its task had been only to determine the citizen's minimum rights to education as laid out in the constitution; indeed, the schools of the City of New York guarantee this minimum demand. A claim for compensatory education, for instance, is therefore untenable. To the extent that the citizens disagree with these minimum goals, they will have to replace the responsible politicians by electoral means. The plaintiff, the Campaign for Fiscal Equity, filed an appeal.

Could this ruling by one of the highest courts of the State of New York be an arbitral verdict that reflects the spirit of the industrial, and not that of the knowledge society, namely that what matters is that its citizens are able to find their way to the voting booth and function as a juror? Indeed, as the court formulated in its opinion of 2001, jurors must nowadays be well acquainted with complex statistical analyses, DNA-based evidence or convoluted financial transactions.

The legal dispute finally ended (with no possibility of appeal) on November 20, 2006, with a verdict by the highest court of the State of New York, the Court of Appeals, in which the State of New York was ordered to provide an additional US$1.93 billion annually for the city school system. This sum is considerably less than the $4.7 billion that a lower court had ruled appropriate. The final judgment was based on the recommendation of a commission appointed by New York State Governor George Pataki in 2004. In a dissenting opinion from that of the majority of the court, one of the two judges in the minority states "a sound basic education will cost approximately $5 billion in additional annual expenditure. I remain hopeful that, despite the court's ruling today, the policymakers will continue to strive to make schools not merely adequate, but excellent, and to implement a statewide solution." The four judges responsible for the majority judgment of the court were all appointees of then New York Governor Pataki (1995–2006).

Notes

1 Samuli Leppälä (2015) summarizes the intellectual origins and the defining characteristics of the economic analysis of knowledge; he employs the

"standard epistemological definition" of knowledge as "justified belief." It is also noteworthy that Leppälä does not raise the issue of the price or value of knowledge in his survey of the diverse economics literature that attends to the *economic* role of knowledge.

2 Gary Becker (1994: 53) notes, for example, that increased *knowledge* raises the real income of individuals, and specifies his hypothesis, "*information* about the prices charged by different sellers would enable a person to buy from the cheapest, thereby raising his command over resources; information about the wages offered by different firms would enable him to work for the firm paying the highest" (our emphasis). On the other hand, Olivier Gossner (2010: 95) defines matter-of-factly that "'knowledge' refers to the information possessed by the agent."

3 In his discussion of "the nature of capital" more than a century ago, Thorstein Veblen ([1908] 1919: 325–326) refers to part of the capital of a community as "immaterial equipment" or "intangible assets" mainly consisting of knowledge and information that "in the early days at least, […] is far and away the most important and consequential category of the community's assets or equipment."

4 Moreover, at least in the United States, the widely accepted accounting principles (GAAP) that govern the reporting of financial information to external sources prohibit companies from recording the value of human capital resources as assets. Instead, human capital expenses are recorded as expenditures (cf. Tan, 2014). Since the expenditures for and the values of human capital might not correspond, the actual price of human capital assets remains a mystery.

5 After all, the doubt expressed toward efforts to monetarize knowledge at times even refers to Socrates teaching his students without demanding any monetary compensation. Socrates expressed nothing but malice for teachers who claimed to be able to generate a lofty income from their wealthy students, but what was the reason for Socrates to refuse to take money in return for knowledge? If he charged for his teaching, Socrates maintained, he would be forced to teach students he did not appreciate; in other words, he wanted to protect his liberty (see Bertram Schefold, "Die Ökonomisierung der Wissenskultur," *Frankfurter Allgemeine Zeitung*, April 12, 2010).

6 Dominique Forey (2006: 9), for example, emphasizes that "knowledge is largely unobservable" and "most phenomena relating to knowledge are largely unmeasurable."

7 The section on human capital draws on and substantially extends a discussion of "forms of capital" that can be found in Stehr (2001: 48–53). For a history of the concept of human capital, see Kiker (1966), and for a discussion of Gary Becker's early work on human capital theory, see Teixeira (2014).

8 An early critique of treating persons as human capital that constituted individuals not based on moral or ethical actors but on the logic of economic discourse may be found in Shaffer (1961). Harry Shaffer objects that the term "investment" is not really applicable to the issue of human capital;

"investment" in individual employees should not be used as a basis for policy formation.
9 An exceptional, deviant definition of human capital that extends to so-called *innate abilities* of individual agents can only rarely be found in economic discourse; but see Laroche and Mérette (1999: 88) for such a conception.
10 Human capital theory resonates strongly with postwar mainstream sociological theory of social stratification – for example, Talcott Parsons's ([1949] 1954: 327) theory of social stratification: "the status of the individual must be determined on grounds essentially peculiar to himself, notably his own personal qualities, technical competence, and his own decisions about his occupational career and with respect to which he is identified with any solidary group […] it is fundamental that status and role allocation and the processes of mobility from status to status are in terms of the individual as a unit and not in solidary groups, like kinship groups, castes village communities etc."
11 It is on the basis of such considerations that Michel Feher ([2007] 2009: 27) argues that "an investor in his or her human capital is concerned less with maximizing the returns on his or her investments – whether monetary or psychic – than with appreciating, that is, increasing the stock value of, the capital to which he or she is identified. In other words, insofar as our condition is that of human capital in a neoliberal environment, our main purpose is not so much to profit from our accumulated potential as to constantly value or appreciate ourselves – or at least prevent our own depreciation."
12 PIAAC attempted to measure cognitive and workplace skills necessary to advance both on the job and in society. In 23 countries, a representative sample of adults was interviewed. Information about three fields of cognitive skills were collected: literacy, numeracy and problem solving in a high-technology environment. Literacy, for example, was defined as "ability to understand, evaluate, use and engage with written texts to participate in society, to achieve one's goals, and to develop one's knowledge and potential" (Hanushek et al., 2015: 108).
13 It might be pointed out that Bourdieu's discussion of cultural capital resonates strongly with Georg Simmel's ([1907] 1978: 439–440) observations in *The Philosophy of Money* about the role of the "intellect" in modern society. Simmel notes "the apparent equality with which educational materials are available to everyone interested in them is, in reality, a sheer mockery. The same is true for other freedoms accorded by liberal doctrines which, though they certainly do not hamper the individual from gaining goods of any kind, do however disregard the fact that only those already privileged in some way or another have the possibility of acquiring them. For just as the substance of education – in spite of, or because of its general availability – can ultimately be acquired only through individual activity, so it gives rise to the most intangible and thus the most unassailable aristocracy, to a distinction between high and low which can be abolished neither (as can socio-economic differences) by a decree or a revolution, nor by the good

will of those concerned [...] There is no advantage that appears to those in inferior positions to be so despised, and before which they feel so deprived and helpless, as the advantage of education."

14 For James Coleman (1988: 100–101) social capital "comes about through changes in the relations among persons that facilitate action [...] Just as physical capital and human capital facilitate productive activity, social capital does as well. For example, a group within which there is extensive trustworthiness and extensive trust is able to accomplish much more than a comparable group without that trustworthiness and trust." Coleman's definition of social capital indicates that it is impossible to quantify the value of individual social capital.

15 More specifically, symbolic capital represents a social process and accomplishment; symbolic capital refers to intellectual or cognitive capacities; symbolic capital "is made [...] by those who are submitted to it but if, and only if, the objective structure of its distribution is at the basis of the cognitive structures that they bring into play in order to produce it – as, for example, with such structuring oppositions as masculine/feminine, young/old, noble/common, rich/poor, white/black, etc." (Bourdieu, 1999: 336).

16 André Gorz's ([2003] 2004: 9) notion of knowledge capital or, rather, the knowledge that counts in the modern knowledge economy can be found in his introduction to the German edition of his book on *The Immaterial. Knowledge, Value and Capital* (Gorz, [2003] 2010). However, Gorz's idea is closely linked to economics; it is knowledge that is requisite in all branches of the economy and due to the growing "informatization," knowledge not in the forms that are acquired in formal education institutions but, rather, "non-formalized forms of knowledge [...] What is required is empirical knowledge, judgment, coordination, self-organization and communication ability, i.e. forms of living knowledge that can be acquired in everyday social dealings and is part of popular culture." It is only on the basis of his specification of relevant knowledge forms that a proximity to the concept of knowledge capability becomes visible.

17 Mara Squicciarini and Nico Vogtlaender (2014) demonstrate that human capital (in the sense of worker skills) is a strong predictor for economic development not only today but was so already at the beginning of the Industrial Revolution (also Mokyr, 2005).

18 In Bourdieu's defense one has to recognize that the actual acquisition, however strongly the quantity of capital acquired may depend, for example, on the stock of capital already accumulated in the family of an individual, is – as Simmel ([1907] 1989b: 439) already observed – ultimately an individual activity. Moreover, Bourdieu (Wacquant, 1989: 41–42) defends himself against the charge of a narrow "economism"; his choice of the term "capital," for example, does not signal that he also adopts the narrow, economic conception of interests manifest in a single universal interest.

19 Sympathetic critics of Bourdieu's capital theory have pointed to other attributes of his approach as problematic; for example, reference is made to the holistic presupposition as a general theoretical assumption. Bourdieu

tends to postulate cultural capital as a generalized medium of accumulation and distinction that is unsuitable for the analysis of a society with multiple cleavages and divisions (see Lamont and Lareau, 1988; Halle, 1992).

20 An informative discussion and description of intellectual property concepts and procedures including a brief reference to patent law systems may be found in Knight (2013: 1–48). A history of the idea of intellectual property rights may be found in Long (1991) and Hesse (2002).

21 On the sociological definition of private property rights and its implicit utilization ban, see Popitz, 1986: 111–112.

22 As the *Guardian* (February 12, 2013) reported, "the agricultural giant Monsanto has sued hundreds of small farmers in the United States in recent years in attempts to protect its patent rights on genetically engineered seeds that it produces and sells." A report by the Center for Food Safety and the Save Our Seeds campaigning groups "has outlined what it says is a concerted effort by the multinational to dominate the seeds industry in the US and prevent farmers from replanting crops they have produced from Monsanto seeds."

23 The resistance by nongovernmental organizations to TRIPS-inspired legislation is chronicled in Matthews (2011).

24 Economic or innovation-centric perspectives have indeed dominated the discussion surrounding patents. More recently, a broader view relies on a "rights-based" perspective. Stephen Hilgartner (2002: 945) has argued that "decisions about intellectual property are about much more than simply finding ways to stimulate and reward innovation; they are also about accountability, control, and governance," leading to a politics of patents conception.

25 Consider the following recent example: "During the past few years, as the cost of TV rights for sporting events has escalated apparently without limit, so has the ease by which conventional broadcast methods can be circumvented. Despite the best efforts of global authorities, including the City of London Police's Intellectual Property Crime Unit (PIPCU), the proliferation, accessibility and reliability of sport streaming sites have only increased. 'Historically, most arrests and attempted prosecutions are made under the provision of the Copyright, Designs and Patents Act 1988, which prohibits the broadcast of material without the license of the copyright owner. However, in February 2012, during a case between the Premier League and a pub landlady from Portsmouth named Karen Murphy, the European Court ruled that live sporting events could not be regarded as 'intellectual creations.' They were instead 'subject to rules of the game, leaving no room for creative freedom.' The court decided that 'accordingly, those events cannot be protected under copyright'" (see www.theguardian.com/football/2015/aug/01/faster-easier-free-illegal-football-streams, accessed August 1, 2015, and www.theguardian.com/media/2012/feb/24/pub-landlady-karen-murphy-premier-league, accessed August 1, 2015).

26 See Roland Reiss, "Eine Kriegserklärung an das Buch" [A declaration of war on books], *Frankfurter Allgemeine Zeitung*, October 13, 2015.

27 Michele Boldrin and David Levine (2013: 3) sum up their case against the economic efficacy of patents as follows: "There is no empirical evidence that [patents] serve to increase innovation and productivity, unless productivity is identified with the number of patents awarded – which, as evidence shows, has no correlation with measured productivity."
28 We have to recognize – although this attribute of the concept of intellectual property is not part of our analysis of the value of knowledge – that the notion of intellectual property is an essentially contested concept across different cultures – for example, in cultures that mainly rely on oral or written transmission (cf. Garmon, 2002) or in societies that recognize hybrid ownership between strictly individual or collective (public domain) ownership (e.g. Strathern, 2005; Ghosh and Soete, 2006; for the case of software, see Ghosh, 2005).
29 With 157 US universities responding to a 2011 survey of the Association of University Technology Managers they reported an earned income of "more than $1.8-billion from commercializing their academic research in the 2011 fiscal year, collecting royalties from new breeds of wheat, from a new drug for the treatment of HIV, and from longstanding arrangements over enduring products like Gatorade." See "Universities Report $1.8-Billion in Earnings on Inventions in 2011," *Chronicle of Higher Education*, August 28, 2012.
30 Whether or not monopolies are a burden on value-adding activities, even encourage desirable innovations or lead to overpricing and undersupply is not at issue in our examination of patents (but see Nordhaus, 1969; Boldrin and Levine, 2005; Crampes and Langinier, 2009).
31 As a matter of practical considerations, the strength, the design and the range of intellectual property rights has a strong influence on the "extent to which innovation adds or subtracts from the pool of ideas that are available to be commercially exploited, i.e. to technological opportunities" (Stiglitz, 2014: 1; Stiglitz, 2010).
32 Interview with André Gorz, "Entsinnlichung des Wissens," *Die Tageszeitung*, August 8, 2003.
33 There are, of course, legal remedies to enforce the rights inherent in a patent, trademark and copyright. The recognition of the considerable economic value, perhaps also economic power and prestige, has led to an increase in litigation activity surrounding IPRs (cf. Hoti and McAleer, 2006).
34 An initial discussion of the taxation regime on the price of knowledge can be found in Stehr, 2015a.
35 The discussion in the scientific literature of the "direct" taxation of knowledge or intangible resources is in its infancy. The only discussion of the practice of taxation, in the United States in this case, we could find is a brief article by Luscombe (1996).
36 A comparable and equally drawn-out legal dispute between the State of New Jersey and plaintiffs who argued that the state provided inadequate funding to some school districts in order to ensure the "provision of

educational services sufficient to enable pupils to master the Core Curriculum Content Standards" was settled by the Supreme Court of New Jersey on May 24, 2011 in favor of the plaintiffs. The court enjoined the State of New Jersey to increase state education aid by US$500 million in the coming school year, distributed among 31 school districts in historically poor cities. The court concluded that the state failed to meet its constitutional burden to make sure that a "thorough and efficient education" was provided. The New Jersey constitution indeed charges the state with the fundamental responsibility to educate schoolchildren: "The Legislature shall provide for the maintenance and support of a thorough and efficient system of free public schools for the instruction of all the children in the State between the ages of five and eighteen years" (N.J. Const. art. VIII, § 4, 1). The fundamental right to an adequate education extends to all children in the state. The court relied in its decision on Special Master's Opinion/Recommendations to the Supreme Court, submitted by Judge Peter E. Doyne (source www.judiciary.state.nj.us/opinions/index.htm, and Winnie Hu and Richard Pérez-Peña, "Court orders New Jersey to increase aid to schools," *The New York Times*, May 25, 2011).

37 We rely on the accounts of the conflict between the State of New York and the City of New York found in *The New York Times*, especially the article dated June 30, 2002 ("Johnny can read, not well enough to vote?"); and subsequent coverage in the same newspaper, especially "School financing case argued before State's highest court," *The New York Times*, October 11, 2006 (also Scherer, 2004–05).

11
THE BENEFITS OF KNOWLEDGE

We have concentrated to this point on outlining and examining the complex nature of knowledge. We have been virtually silent about the benefits or, for that matter, and given the thrust of much of the critical discourse about modern science, the possible dysfunctions and "destructive consequences" of knowledge.

Let us start examining the benefits of knowledge with an observation by the philosopher John Stuart Mill published in *The Spirit of the Age* (1831) after his return to England from France, where he had encountered and taken in the philosophy of history in the political thinking of the Saint-Simonians and of the young Auguste Comte. Mill affirms his conviction that progress is possible in society as the result of the intellectual accomplishments of his own age. However, progress and the improvement of social conditions, Mill ([1831] 1942: 13) argues, are not the outcome of an "increase in wisdom" or of the collective accomplishments of science, but are rather linked to the general diffusion of knowledge throughout society:

> Men may not reason better, concerning the great questions in which human nature is interested, but they reason more. Large subjects are discussed more, and longer, and by more minds.

Discussion has penetrated deeper into society; and if greater numbers than before have attained the higher degree of intelligence, fewer grovel in the state of stupidity, which can only co-exist with utter apathy and sluggishness.

In recent years, almost taken-for-granted political, economic and social benefits of knowledge in general and scientific knowledge in particular have given way to a much more skeptical assessment of the social role of knowledge. Rapidly growing capacities for action have led to a reassessment of knowledge. Gernot Böhme (1992: 51) sums up the dramatic shift as follows: "The 'scientification' of the lifeworld is connected with the loss of people's ability to help themselves; they become dependent on experts. 'Verwissenschaftlichung' is connected with bureaucratic centralization, with increased governmental power, with loss of regional differences and personal knowledge."

Today, the idea that advances of knowledge invariably equal progress is no longer taken for granted. Praising the benefits of knowledge was not widely practiced until the age of the philosopher Francis Bacon. Bacon did much to expedite the acceptance and promotion of knowledge. He is, of course, the author of the famous metaphor "knowledge is power." In much of antiquity the idea of progress was completely absent, and in the Middle Ages human progress was not expected to arrive with, or derive from, the secular sciences. If one wants to point to a date or an historical event that represents the beginnings of modern *knowledge politics* – that is, to efforts by society to regulate knowledge – one has to refer to what is called the nuclear age. This era begins with the deployment of the atom bomb in 1945, in particular, but also with the development of (and resistance to) nuclear power generation in the 1950s.

The political discussion about the "moral" status of nuclear science prompted John Dewey ([1927] 1954: 231) to point out, in his afterword written in July 1946 to his *The Public and its Problems*, that although:

aspects of the *moral* problem of the status of physical science have been with us for a long time […] the consequences of the physical sciences […] failed to obtain the kind of observation that would bring the conduct and state of science into a specifically *political* field. The use of these sciences to increase the destructiveness of war was brought to such a sensationally obvious focus with the splitting of the atom that the political issue is now with us.

In recent years, against the backdrop of ever faster and ever more consequential scientific progress, efforts to police and control knowledge continue to gain legitimacy in many societies (cf. Stehr, 2005).

Historically speaking, the idea of a "natural" progression, of a relentless, exponential development of scientific knowledge and its technical application as a key to unlocking the mysteries of the world, as a release from pain and freedom from suffering, as the basis for a better and just society and as a means for greater prosperity, or the idea that more knowledge simply represents the master key to an emancipation from all kinds of troubling ills and harsh constraints, was short-lived. The straightforward assumption that specialized knowledge ought to command respect, in general, and that any increase in knowledge automatically brings with it an increase in benefits to humankind, in particular, is becoming porous and vulnerable.

Not surprisingly, the idea that the "uselessness" of science is a virtue and that the uses that humans "have drawn from science have contributed to their misery" (Chargaff, 1975: 21) is no longer a marginal voice, rarely heard. The optimistic faith, nurtured in a period of unprecedented economic growth in the 1950s and early 1960s, that a constant expansion of scientific knowledge might even prompt a displacement of politics and ideology (e.g. Bell, [1965] 1988) has also been thoroughly demystified.

If one no longer regards the fabrication and use of additional scientific knowledge as a humanitarian project, "as an unquestioned ultimate good, one is willing to consider its disciplined direction" (Sinsheimer, 1978: 23). This is what lies at the heart of the notion of knowledge politics. The fear that we may know too much and that we are about to assume the role of God or to commence a "self-transformation of the species" (Habermas, [1998] 2001: 42) increasingly replaces the concern that we do not know enough and that we are to a large degree poorly informed. Apprehension and skepticism replace the rhetoric of hope that until recently dominated the societal discourse about new developments in science and technology in modern societies.

The concern that we may know too much is no longer — as was the case in the 1970s for example — based on the assumption that we are amassing, at a high price, a large store of trivial and practically irrelevant knowledge that does not promise any useful or even moral gains. It is now based on concerns about the accumulation of novel knowledge that appears to have questionable social consequences — for example, in the fields of medical, biological, agricultural or psychological knowledge. In that sense at least, current concerns directed toward science represent a return to the conflicts science experienced in the past. In past disputes, when discussions about the consequences of science were not driven by complaints about its deficient social, moral and economic utility in tackling the social *problems of the day*, disputes were directed at a possible surplus of the practical effects of science and technology, especially with respect to traditional worldviews, established lifeworlds, and the limits to what can be manipulated by humans in nature and society.

11.1 The distribution of knowledge

A different, but not unrelated concern refers to the nature of the distribution of knowledge including the concept of knowledge (e.g. Hornidge, 2007) within and among modern societies. Is it possible to describe the history of the distribution of knowledge — in the sense of access to knowledge — as the growing democratization of knowledge? Does the wide dissemination of knowledge culminate in an almost equal contact with knowledge throughout societies and around the world? More specifically, does the pending digitization of the major libraries of the world[1] represent "the ultimate stage in the democratization of knowledge set in motion by the invention of writing, the codex, moveable type, and the Internet" (Darnton, 2008)?

Nelson (2000: 118) describes the complexity of the societal distribution of knowledge as follows:

> Various parts of the relevant know-how are located in different kinds of places, and stored in different forms. Some is related to how to do it, some with why doing it that way works. Some is possessed by individuals, some by organisations; some is in

networks or communities. Some is held in trained fingers, some in trained minds, some in texts, and some in materials and machines.

The problems resulting from the unequal distribution of knowledge have troubled social thinkers for a long time. Over a century ago, Georg Simmel – in his *Philosophy of Money* – inquired into a most invidious and insidious form of social inequality in modern society. Though it remains widely invisible, at least to the professional eye, its importance may well have increased manifold since the early twentieth century. Simmel's ([1907] 1978: 439–440) referent is formal education:

> For just as the substance of education – in spite of, or because of its general availability – can ultimately be acquired only through individual activity, so it gives rise to the most intangible and thus the most unassailable aristocracy, to a distinction between high and low which can be abolished neither (as can socio-economic differences) by a decree or a revolution, nor by the good will of those concerned.

In modern societies, the distribution of knowledge, the growing specialization of knowledge claims and the patterns of inequality in educational achievement evidently create novel problems. The division of knowledge, for example, leads to the fact that *knowledge about* the division of knowledge or *knowledge about* knowledge becomes crucial. The segregation of knowledge implies that the control over certain stocks of knowledge may turn into struggles over power, or that particular professions, especially experts, consultants and advisors who enable us as their clients to gain access to specialized knowledge, increase in both number and importance. Hence, the so-called *knowledge divide*, not necessarily unknown in past societies, and its acceleration develop into a significant social and political issue in contemporary societies.

Discussions about what has been termed the *knowledge divide* that separates different social strata in modern society primarily concern the distance of many segments of the population from highly specialized scientific knowledge. For example, in an essay in the *New York Review of Books* (November 18, 2004: 38), the molecular biologist Richard Lewontin maintains that "the knowledge required for political rationality, once available to the masses, is now in the possession of a specially educated elite, a situation that creates a series of tensions and contradictions in the operation of representative democracy." By the same token, English chemistry Nobel Laureate Harry Kroto in an opinion piece in *The Guardian* (May 22, 2007, Education 1–2) denounces the UK government for wrecking British science and science education. This is in the face of the "need for a general population with a satisfactory understanding of science and technology [that] never has been greater." Kroto adds that "we live in a world economically, socially, and culturally dependent on science not only functioning well, but being wisely applied." Moreover, in light of the growing specialization of the production of scientific knowledge, an eminent social scientist observes that all but a few individuals are deprived of the "capacity for individual rational judgment either about the quality of the evidence proffered or about the tightness of the theoretical reasoning applied to the analysis of the data. The 'harder' the science, the truer this is" (Wallerstein, 2004b: 8).

The historian James Harvey Robinson had already identified the claim that underpins these statements nearly 100 years ago. In a treatise entitled *The Humanizing of Knowledge* – that is, ensuring that the "scientific frame of mind" and specialized scientific knowledge are not esoteric enterprises confined to a small number of members of the scientific community – he stresses that the "divisions of knowledge form [...] the most effective barriers to the cultivation of a really scientific frame of mind in the young and the public at large." The solution therefore lies, according to Robinson (1923: 76), in "re-synthesizing" and "re-humanizing" knowledge.

This quote shows that the distance of science from common sense knowledge is not a new phenomenon. Still, it is widely assumed that the gradient of the separation between the command of specialized scientific knowledge and the command of everyday knowledge has increased in modern societies and, hence,[2] on the political plane a growing authority and power are assumed by "elite public policy specialists" (Dahl, 1989: 337) who are no longer intellectually and politically accountable to large segments of the public. Dwight D. Eisenhower's warning in his famous "military-industrial complex" farewell speech of 1961 comes to mind, in which he cautioned that "in holding scientific research and discovery in respect, as we should, we must also be alert to the equal and opposite danger that public policy could itself become the captive of a scientific-technological elite."

Recently, a US survey (by the Pew Research Center, 2009) for The People & the Press and the American Association for the Advancement of Science (AAAS), which involved about 2,000 members of the public and 2,500 scientists (including teachers, administrators and others involved in science as well as researchers), found that 85% of the scientists see the public's lack of scientific knowledge as a critical issue. Almost one half of all the scientists questioned fault the public for unrealistic expectations about the speed of scientific advancements.

Paradoxically, the sum of these observations coincides with what other observers of the relation between modern science and society have described as the need for or the possibility of "public participation" in science. Hence, the once "widespread feeling that scientists alone should have domain over the scientific enterprise is being replaced by a philosophy that calls for public involvement in science, irrespective of the fact that many of the elders of science find the idea abhorrent" (Culliton, 1978: 147). Whether this drive toward increased public participation in science will democratize scientific work and ensure that the public regains confidence in science and science policymaking is a contested matter (cf. Whatmore, 2009: 589; see also Nowotny et al., 2001) and will have to await future developments.

Richard Lewontin, Harry Kroto and Immanuel Wallerstein are representative of a far greater number of voices and reflections in the *science community* that skeptically comment on the increasing usage of contemporary, especially natural scientific, knowledge not only by governments but also as a tool of politics (cf. Pielke, 2007) and, hence, on the massive increase – paralleling the swollen gradient between rich and poor in many developed societies[3] – in the inability of large segments of citizens to take part in democratic decision making. Given these assumptions and the premise that democratic governance rests on the participation of the populace, "ordinary" citizens (as well as citizen representatives) apparently are also robbed of the ability to enter rationally into a discourse about modern science and technology and its social consequences such as climate change, biotechnology, nanotechnology, nuclear power or genetic modification of foodstuff, to mention but a small number of important issues.

The predominant assumption among prominent scientists in, for example, the field of climate science, is that scientific knowledge ought to be the (only) foundation for policy decisions and, with these, the ways we collectively organize our lifeworld and cope with its problems. The same observers appear to agree that science has indeed the capacity to be a robust foundation of politics and that scientific knowledge is a beneficial source of public wisdom and good government. What also logically follows from this argument is that a growing "scientific illiteracy" disenfranchises citizens and threatens to undermine the foundation that makes for democratic governance. Among the empirical indicators that might speak to these issues is the decline in citizen engagement and formal participation in the democratic processes of Western societies, or the erosion of public confidence in, and perhaps even a sense of profound popular disaffection with, not only politics but also modern science and technology (cf. Wynne, 2001; Stehr, 2005).

As Mancur Olson (1982: 26), for example, notes, referring to the economic consequences of the knowledge divide, "individuals in a few special vocations can receive considerable rewards in private goods if they acquire exceptional knowledge of public goods […] Withal, the typical citizen will find that his or her income and life chances will not be improved by zealous study of public affairs, or even of any single collective good." Olson's observations also raise the question of the *incentive* for ordinary citizens to learn about complex public issues that need to be decided in different contexts in everyday life. If the acquisition of relevant specialized knowledge claims entails costs and if the possible consequences of the decision making or participation are obscure, citizens presumably have little incentive to obtain relevant knowledge, at least according to the claim put forward by Anthony Downs (1957) in his *Economic Theory of Democracy*.[4]

We therefore arrive at the fundamental question of the relationship between knowledge and democratic governance. The widespread, and rather superficial, assumption that scientific or technological knowledge always is of utmost advantage, as well as the position that sees political governance best confined to an elite that commands specialized knowledge, is not only undemocratic but underestimates the power of the knowledge of the "weak" (cf. Stehr, 2013a). Since democracy may be succinctly characterized as the "the rule of the layperson," will mounting knowledge differentials undermine democracy? Do two of the pillars and motors of modern society – the productive force of advancing (technological) knowledge *and* democratic politics – stand in irreconcilable opposition?

The history of the theory of democracy is full of discussions of these and related basic questions about knowing and participating in democratic decision making. In the digital age, we continue to have controversial debates regarding, for example, the status of whistleblowers who claim to uphold the promise of public transparency of the political process by leaking clandestine information and knowledge on warfare and intelligence agencies (e.g. WikiLeaks' Julian Assange, Bradley Manning, or Edward Snowden, to name just a few of the most recent).

11.2 Knowledge, power and participation

It is a signature trait of differentiated and highly complex modern societies that access to and command of knowledge is stratified. To some extent, this is the price to be paid for increasing specialization and the greater biographical freedom of the modern individual. As we have indicated, the growing role of scientific knowledge as capacity for action in politics and everyday life has increasingly become – often to its detriment – the (alleged) source of emerging problems for democratic politics. Prominent examples are global degradation, the demise of biodiversity, climate change or the extended possibilities of medical expertise that may interfere with the very foundations of the biological and environmental conditions of life.

The perceived risks of the societal role of scientific knowledge are overlooked by observers who are convinced, for example, that scientific knowledge is capable of overcoming conflicts, competing interests and disputes. In order realistically to assess the relationship between scientific (and political) expertise and civil society, the specific context needs to be taken into account (see Bohman, 1999: 190). We need to think of the interaction between civil society and the carriers of scientific expertise as mediated by cultural identities and changing conceptions of the social benefits of science and technology on both sides of the alleged divide. The resourcefulness with which civil society organizations reconstruct science and technology is affected by contingent political, economic and moral circumstances, and, not least, by the workings of the media and their focus of attention.

In the age of knowledge politics, marked as we have seen by efforts to regulate and police new knowledge and technical artifacts, it no longer makes sense to view the public as naively resistant to new capacities to act and showing an elementary inability to take such knowledge on board. Instead, the public as represented by civil society and its organizations should be seen as cautious, uncertain, and curious about the possible consequences of new knowledge and information, reflecting their worldviews, values and beliefs. Rather than proclaiming the increasing domination of technocratic expertise, there are numerous indicators that, within the context of knowledge, politics and public discourse about authorizing innovative capacities to act, the balance of power between science and civil society may be shifting toward civil society organizations such as nongovernmental organizations and/or single issue groups fighting against or promoting specific goals and interests, be it in the field of environmental issues, human rights or economic concerns.

One of the founding fathers of the social sciences, the French Enlightenment philosopher Marquis de Condorcet, gives an early testimony of this classic problem of democratic decision making. Writing in 1785, he was convinced that "the argument that the citizen could not take part in the whole discussion and that each individual's argument could not be heard by everyone can have no force" (Condorcet, 1994: 194). For Condorcet, the issue was not one of competence with respect to the matter at hand but one of good rules and settings within which individuals would be able to access relevant information and deliberate jointly: "In order to decide in full knowledge of the case, it is not necessary to have read or heard all the arguments which have been put forward on each subject by the men required to make the decision [...] The important thing is to have had constant and free access to all means of instruction available. It is up to each individual to choose his preferred method of learning, and to adapt his studies to his enlightenment and intelligence" (ibid.). In a democracy, it is the right of ordinary citizens to be heard on policy matters, no matter how much specialized knowledge they command about the issue. It is one of the virtues of liberal democracies that citizens are to be involved in political decisions. Such participation, whatever formal basis it may assume, does not hinge, as a prerequisite, on the degree of technical or intellectual competence citizens may command. In short, the boundaries between expertise and everyday knowledge are much less fixed and more robust than it has often been surmised, especially in those observations cited that lament the growing distance between expert knowledge and the public's knowledge. The evolution of modern societies as knowledge societies leads to the democratization of knowledge claims that are increasingly open for negotiation. Rather than toward a rule by technocrats, we are slowly moving toward a much broader, shared form of knowledge-claims governance (cf. Leighninger, 2006), for in a knowledge society it is not only the exponential growth of specialized knowledge that continues to drive social change due to its inherently enabling nature and incremental advances. Against the background of societies that have never been more affluent and knowledgeable, it is the unprecedented ability of individuals and social groups to get engaged in political matters by employing their knowledgeability which is not so much premised on detailed, in-depth knowledge; rather, this pivotal competence is the product of the general development of modern society. As for the social sciences and the humanities, they continue to play an important role, in the sense of enhancing our capacities to act.

11.3 Knowledge societies[5]

In light of what we have depicted as the central role of knowledge for contemporary social, economic and political life, one may justifiably term contemporary modern societies "knowledge societies." In our concluding section, we will use this denomination to sum up the many ways that knowledge has come to define not only our way of life in highly developed, Western societies, but also how knowledge – as knowledge for the world – shapes up to create our future.

Early notions of the knowledge society

The term knowledge society first appears, as far as we can see, as part of the names of "benevolent" societies in England in the nineteenth century. The purpose of one of these societies, the *Provident Knowledge*

Society "under the patronage of Lord Derby, Lord Shaftesbury, and other distinguished men," is:

> to make regular weekly saving a national habit, and so to increase the facilities for saving that it shall be as easy for a man to put by a small sum as it is now for him to spend that sum in beer or spirits. The Society has published a series of tracts upon *Penny Banks, Pensions, Insuring One's Life*, and other subjects, which are intended to promote thrift and forethought among the working classes; and of these tracts many thousands have been circulated.
> (The British Medical Journal, *1875: 283; also* The Scottish Historical Review, *1920)*

Inasmuch as the benevolent knowledge societies in England saw their mission to enlighten the uninformed public, especially members of the working class, there is at least some resemblance to features of the modern-day knowledge societies that also rest on the broad dissemination of knowledge, information and knowledgeability throughout society.

Social scientific conceptions of the knowledge society

In its contemporary, social scientific version, the term knowledge society and the idea that modern societies are knowledge societies are much more recent. The usage and development of the idea that *modern society* is a knowledge society dates to the early 1970s and more prominently to the 1980s and later.

One of the first social scientists to employ the term "knowledgeable society" is Robert E. Lane (1966: 650). He justifies the use of this concept by pointing to the growing societal relevance of *scientific knowledge*, and defines a knowledgeable society, in a "first approximation":

> Just as the "democratic" society has a foundation in governmental and interpersonal relations, and the "affluent society" a foundation in economics, so the knowledgeable society has its roots in epistemology and the logic of inquiry.

Lane's conception of a knowledgeable society is coupled rather closely to the promise of a particular theory of science and reflects, also, the great optimism or fear, as the case may be, of the early 1960s which suggested that science would somehow allow for the possibility of a society in which common sense would be replaced by scientific reasoning. That is, as Lane stresses in his definition, members of the knowledgeable society are guided in their conduct, if only subconsciously, by the standards of "veridical truth."

The very promise Lane attached to scientific knowledge as the motor that would transform modern society into a knowledgeable society is the reason for other social scientists to reflect on the emergence of a "*technical state.*" One prominent social scientist who warned about the possibility of a technical state is Helmut Schelsky. Schelsky was one of the most eminent social scientists of the postwar era in Germany. His influence reached well beyond the narrow boundaries of academic social science. It was based on the distinctive understanding of the evolution of modern society and the terms he coined to capture core cultural and socio-structural developments. The theories he offered were distinctly middle-range and not of a grand design. Lane and Schelsky share in the conviction that scientific knowledge will assume dominance throughout society and in the case of the political system reduce decision to technical matters. A brief quote from Schelsky ([1961] 1965: 459) transports the essence of the meaning of the notion of the technical state: "The 'technical state or government' deprives [...] democracy of its substance. Technical and scientific decisions cannot be subject to democratic decision-making, for in this manner they only become ineffective." Helmut Schelsky adds what is perhaps obvious – namely, that once political decisions are executed based on scientific knowledge alone, the basic premise of democratic participation is eliminated: that is, the assumption that reason and reasoned judgments are equitably distributed throughout society.

In *The Age of Discontinuity*, Peter Drucker (1968) explicitly and consistently employs the term *knowledge society*.[6] The general thesis places knowledge "as central to our society and as the foundation of economy and social action" (Drucker, [1968] 1972: 349). In this most general sense, Drucker's concept of a knowledge society resonates closely with the idea of modern society as a knowledge society, as explicated in subsequent decades. Although Drucker's emphasis on knowledge is, in many ways, pioneering, it is not evident, however, whether he attributes to the knowledge principle, in the late 1960s at least, the same centrality for society as does Daniel Bell, for example, at about the same time. Nor is there any direct evidence of cross-fertilization between Drucker and Bell. Nonetheless, both theorists contributed their reflections about the rise in the significance of knowledge as an economic resource displacing leading observations about the existence of a *managerial capitalism* immediately after World War II (cf. Chandler, 1977; Burnham, 1941).

Peter Drucker goes to considerable and informative lengths to describe some of the novel features and functions of contemporary knowledge. His definition of what counts as knowledge in a knowledge society is not restricted, as is the case for Lane's knowledgeable society, to scientific knowledge. Drucker's account of the emergence of knowledge societies and the knowledge-based economy must be counted among his original contributions to the theory of the knowledge society. The popular response to the questions about the origins of the knowledge society and the knowledge-based economy typically refers (see Drucker, [1968] 1972: 279) to the more technically demanding and more complex tasks of jobs. Drucker rejects the "demand"-induced transformation of industrial society and instead points out that "the direct cause of the upgrading of the jobs is […] the upgrading of the educational level of the entrant into the labor force." Moreover, Drucker suggests that the stimulus for the increasing demand for knowledge-based work has to do less with changing technological regimes, the growing complexity and specialization of the economy or enhanced functional steering and coordination needs, and more to do with the substantial extension in the working lifespan of individuals and the enhanced knowledge with which they come to the labor market in the first place. If we follow Drucker, it is not so much the *demand* for labor and particular skills as the result of more complex and exacting jobs, but a societal transformation that results in the *supply* of highly skilled labor which in turn underlies the transformation of the world of work.

Among the surprising and even startling properties of the transformation of the labor market is that the American economy at least was able to:

satisfy the expectations of all these people with long years of schooling [...] As a result of the change in supply, we now have to create genuine knowledge jobs, whether the work itself demands it or not. For a true knowledge job is the only way to make highly schooled people productive [...] That the knowledge worker [Drucker first proposed the term knowledge worker in 1959 in his *Landmarks of Tomorrow*] came first and knowledge work second – that indeed knowledge work is still largely to come – is a historical accident. From now on, we can expect increasing emphasis on work based on knowledge, and especially skills based on knowledge.

(Drucker, [1968] 1972: 285–286; also Drucker, 1992: 91)[7]

Daniel Bell also employs the term "knowledge society" in the context of his discussion of the emergence of *post-industrial society*, a designation he ultimately prefers. Bell at times uses the concept of knowledge society interchangeably with the notion of "post-industrial society." For example, he exclaims at one point in his discussion that "the post-industrial society, it is clear, is a knowledge society" (Bell, 1973: 212). The basic justification for such an equivalence is, of course, that "knowledge is a fundamental resource" of post-industrial society. As a matter of fact, Bell (1973: 37) indicates that he could have substituted "knowledge society" for "post-industrial society" because either term, and others, for example "intellectual society" (Bell, 1964: 49), might be just as apt in describing at least some salient aspects of the emerging structure of society that he proposes to examine in his study of the structure and culture of modern society.

Radovan Richta et al.'s (1969) theory of the scientific-technical revolution constitutes the socialist counterpart to Bell's theory of society. Bell (1973: 212) argues that post-industrial society is a knowledge society for two major reasons: 1 "the sources of innovation are increasingly derivative from research and development (and more directly, there is a new relation between science and technology because of the centrality of theoretical knowledge)"; and 2 "the weight of the society – measured by a larger proportion of Gross National Product and a larger share of employment – is increasingly in the knowledge field." The pace and scale of the translation of knowledge into technology provides the basis for the possibility of modernity.

Thus, if there is a "radical gap between the present and the past, it lies in the nature of technology and the ways it has transformed social relations and our ways of looking at the world" (Bell, 1968: 174).

What is evident in both Peter Drucker's and Daniel Bell's designation of modern societies as knowledge societies is their common assumption that the significant transformations that bring about new constitutive principles of social relations and hence a new societal configuration are changes within the economic system which then radiate throughout society and affirm the dominance of the economy. As a result, the emergence of knowledge or post-industrial societies out of industrial societies has not undermined in the eyes of Drucker and Bell the preeminence of the economy. In the course of further reflections about knowledge societies, hypotheses about a reversal of the equation of sub- (that is, the material foundations) to superstructure (the cultural or cognitive foundations) become a primary research agenda.

Contemporary theories of the knowledge society

From the late 1970s onward, the analysis of modern societies as knowledge societies became more sophisticated, looking both backward to the existence of past knowledge societies as well as forward in time to major social transformations of contemporary society (Böhme and Stehr, 1986). The theory of the knowledge society was developed alongside and in competition with theories of modern society such as the *information society*, the *risk society* or the *network society*.

In general we can say that the transformation of modern societies into knowledge societies continues to be based – as was the case for industrial society – on changes in the structure of the economies of advanced societies. Economic capital – or, more precisely, the source of economic growth and value-adding activities – increasingly relies on knowledge. The transformation of the structures of the modern economy by knowledge as a productive force constitutes the "material" basis and the core justification for designating advanced modern society as a knowledge society.

The significance of knowledge grows in all spheres of life and in all social institutions of modern society. The historical emergence of knowledge societies does not represent a revolutionary development, but rather a gradual process during which the defining characteristics of society change and new traits emerge. While, until recently, modern society was primarily conceived of in terms of property and labor, today "knowledge" has been added as a new principle. This development has been challenging our understanding of property and labor as the constitutive mechanisms of modern society for quite some time now. Even outside the economic system, the transformation of modern societies into knowledge societies has had, and continues to have, profound consequences, as we have tried to show. One of the more noteworthy consequences is the extent to which modern societies become fragile.

The Fragility of Modern Societies (Stehr, 2001) is a unique condition. Modern societies tend to be fragile from the viewpoint of those large and once-dominant social institutions (e.g. the state, the economy or science) which find it increasingly difficult to impose their will on all of society. Societies are fragile because individuals and small groups are capable, within certain established rules, to assert their own interests by opposing or resisting the (not too long ago) almost unassailable monopoly of truth of major societal institutions. That is to say, legitimate cultural practices based on the enlargement and diffusion of knowledge enable a much larger segment of society to effectively oppose power configurations that turned out or are apprehended to be tenuous and brittle. Hence we are returned to our understanding of knowledge as a capacity to act. Adopting a phrase by Adam Ferguson, one might say that knowledge societies are the result of human action – but often not of deliberate human design. Knowledge societies emerge as they adapt to persistent but evolving needs and changing circumstances of human conduct.

We have also come to realize that despite our striving for safety and security, modern societies are increasingly *vulnerable* entities. Large-scale natural catastrophes, human-made natural degradation and the global impact of terrorism have characterized much of the first decades of the new millennium. Our modern economy, our communication and traffic systems are vulnerable to malfunctions of self-imposed practices typically designed to avoid breakdowns. Modern infrastructures and technological regimes are subject to accidents including large-scale disasters as the result of fortuitous, unanticipated human action, to non-marginal or extreme natural events that may dramatically undermine the taken-for-granted routines of everyday life in modern societies, or to deliberate sabotage. The attacks on the World Trade Center on September 11, 2001, the catastrophic meltdown of the Fukushima nuclear power facility, or the challenges posed by climate change are just prominent examples.

However, contemporary social systems may be seen to be fragile and vulnerable in yet another sense. We refer to the fragility that results from conduct as well as the deployment of artifacts originally designed to stabilize, routinize and delimit social action. In the process of even more deeply embedding computers into the social fabric of society, that is, redesigning and reengineering large-scale social and socio-technical systems in order to manage the complexities of modern society, novel risks and vulnerabilities are created, as has become evident in the complex management of power grids or the irregular breakdown of high-frequency financial trading routines.

Among the major but widely invisible social innovations in modern society is the immense growth of the "civil society" sector. This sector provides an organized basis through which citizens can exercise individual initiative in the private pursuit of public purposes. The considerable enlargement of the informal economy – but also corruption and the growth of wealth in modern society as well as increasing but often unsuccessful efforts to police these spheres – can therefore be interpreted as evidence of the expanded capacity of individuals, households and small groups to take advantage of and benefit from contexts in which the degree of social control exercised by larger (legitimate) social institutions has diminished. Contemporary knowledge society also sports an unprecedented communication infrastructure that not only spans the globe but has advanced into virtually all spheres of everyday life. Digital media and global information networks have given rise to new practices of communication and sociation, as well as inaugurated new forms of information, public speech and political participation.

By discussing the many facets of the concept of knowledge and by firmly establishing it as a social concept, we hope to have shown the many ways knowledge plays a decisive role for the past and future development of modern society. To conceive of contemporary modern society as a knowledge society is, of course, only one way of approaching the complexity of social life in the new millennium. Still, we hold this approach to be particularly helpful as it highlights the way in which knowledge – as a capacity for action – is knowledge *for* the world, as much as it is knowledge *of* the world. In this sense, knowledge is becoming. The future of modern society no longer mimics the past to the extent to which this has been the case until recently. History will increasingly be full of unanticipated incertitude, peculiar reversals, proliferating surprises, and we will have to cope with the ever greater speed of significantly compressed events. The changing agendas of social, political and economic life as the result of our growing capacity to make history will also place inordinate demands on our mental capacities and social resources.

Notes

1 For example, in the form of Google Books, the Digital Public Library of America (DPLA) or Europeana.eu.
2 A related yet not identical observation concerns apparently inevitable (maybe even non-linear) increases in the volume of "non-knowledge" as the result of the growth of knowledge in modern societies (e.g. Ravetz, 1986: 423; Luhmann, 1997: 1106; Wehling, 2008: 31), including an emergence of the so-called "knowledge-ignorance paradox" that refers to how the growth of *specialized knowledge* implies a concurrent increase in widespread ignorance in society (see Bauer, 1996; Ungar, 2008). For a skeptical examination of the alleged phenomenon of non-knowledge, see Chapter 4 (also Stehr, 2013a).
3 The nature of inequality, in turn, is associated with the observation that societies that do best for their citizens, for example in the quality of life or life expectancy, are those with the narrowest income differential. The most unequal – the United States as a whole, the United Kingdom and Portugal – do worst (cf. Wilkinson and Pickett, 2009).
4 It would, however, be shortsighted to limit the possible incentives to acquire knowledge to mere economic considerations. Furthermore, aside from the *ability* to enter a field of discourse, there is also the question of the *desire* to enter a field of discourse in an active manner. On a psychological plane, ability and desire are likely to interact, and desire and ability do vary from person to person as well as from issue to issue (see Mulder, 1971).
5 We draw on the following essay: Stehr, 2015b.
6 Drucker's ([1949] 1962: xi) earlier monograph about the *New Society* first published in 1949 therefore represents his reflections about the nature of *industrial society* as a "new and distinct society of the twentieth century, world-wide rather that 'Western' or 'Capitalist' […] This new society has a specific social institution: the industrial enterprise with its management, its

plant community and its Siamese twin, the labor union" (see also Aron, 1962, 1990: 265–285).
7 For a contrast and comparison between Peter Drucker's notion of the knowledge society and self-organizing knowledge labor as cognitive capitalism (cf. Boutang, [2007] 2011) and the more recent Italian Marxist-inspired analysis of capitalism's cognitive phase (Hardt and Negri, 2000), see Peters and Reveley, 2012.

BIBLIOGRAPHY

Abbott, Andrew (2010) "Varieties of ignorance," *American Sociologist* 41: 174–189.
Abel, Günter (2008) "Forms of knowledge problems, projects, perspective," pp. 11–34 in Peter Meusburger, Michael Welker and Edgar Wunder (eds), *Clashes of Knowledge, Orthodoxies and Heterodoxies in Science and Religion.* Heidelberg: Springer.
Acemoglu, Daron and David Autor (2012) "What does human capital do? A review of Goldin and Katz's The Race Between Education and Technology," *Journal of Economic Literature* 50: 426–463.
Adams, Laura L. (2008) "Globalization, universalism, and cultural form," *Comparative Studies in Society and History* 50: 614–640.
Adams, Stephen and Paul J. Miranti (2007) "Global knowledge transfer and telecommunication: The Bell system in Japan, 1945–1952," *Enterprise and Society* 9: 96–124.
Adolf, Marian (2011) "Clarifying mediatization. Sorting through a current debate," *Empedocles. European Journal of the Philosophy of Communication* 3(2): 153–175.
Adolf, Marian (2012a) "Media society," in George Ritzer (ed.), *Encyclopedia of Globalization.* Blackwell. DOI: 10.1002/9780470670590.wbeog375.
Adolf, Marian (2012b) "Media culture," in George Ritzer (ed.), *Encyclopedia of Globalization.* Blackwell. DOI: 10.1002/9780470670590.wbeog375.

Adolf, Marian (2014) "Involuntaristische Mediatisierung. Big Data als Herausforderung einer informationalisierten Gesellschaft," pp. 19–37 in Heike Ortner, Daniel Pfurtscheller, Michaela Rizzoli and Andreas Wiesinge (eds), *Datenflut und Informationskanäle*. Innsbruck: Innsbruck University Press.

Adolf, Marian and Dennis Deicke (2015) "New modes of integration: Individuality and sociality in digital networks," *First Monday*, 20(1–5) January. dx.doi.org/10.5210/fm.v20i1.5495.

Adolf, Marian and Nico Stehr (2014) *Knowledge*. London: Routledge.

Adolf, Marian and Nico Stehr (2015) "The return of social physics?" Presentation at the conference The Technology of Information, Communication and Administration – An Entwined History, Swiss Federal Archives, Bern, 26–27 March 2015.

Adolf, Marian, Nico Stehr and Jason Mast (2013) "Culture and cognition: The foundations of innovation in modern society," pp. 25–39 in Frane Adam and Hans Westlund (eds), *Innovation in Socio-Cultural Context*. London: Routledge.

Agnew, John (2015) "The geopolitics of knowledge about world politics: A case study in U.S. hegemony," pp. 235–246 in Peter Meusburger and Derek Gregory, *Geographies of Knowledge and Power*. Dordrecht: Springer.

Agrawal, Arun (1995) "Dismantling the divide between indigenous and scientific knowledge," *Development and Change* 26: 413–439.

Agrawal, Arun (2002) "Indigenous knowledge and the politics of classification," *International Social Science Journal* 59: 287–297.

Akera, Atsushi (2007) "Constructing representation for an ecology of knowledge," *Social Studies of Science* 37: 413–441.

Akerlof, George A. (1970) "The market for 'lemons': Quality, uncertainty, and the market mechanism," *The Quarterly Journal of Economics* 84: 488–500.

Alford, Robert (1985) *Powers of Theory*. Cambridge: Cambridge University Press.

Allern, Elin and Karina Pedersen (2007) "The impact of party organizational changes on democracy," *West European Politics* 30: 68–92.

Allport, Gordon W. (1958) *The Nature of Prejudice*. New York: Doubleday.

Almquist, Alan J. and John E. Cronin (1988) "Fact, fancy, and myth on human evolution," *Current Anthropology* 27: 520–522.

Altheide, David L. (2006) *Terrorism and the Politics of Fear*. Lanham, MD: AltaMira Press.

Altheide, David and Robert Snow (1979) *Media Logic*. Beverly Hills, CA: Sage.

Ancori, Bernard, Antoine Bureth and Patrick Cohendet (2000) "The economics of knowledge: The debate about codification and tacit knowledge," *Industrial and Corporate Change* 9: 255–287.

Anderson, Benedict ([1983] 1991) *Imagined Communities. Reflections on the Origin and Spread of Nationalism*. London: Verso.

Anselin, Luc, Attila Varga and Zoltan Acs (1997) "Local geographic spillovers between university research and high technology innovations," *Journal of Urban Economics* 42: 422–448.

Antonelli, Christiano (1999) "The evolution of the industrial organisation of the production of knowledge," *Cambridge Journal of Political Economics* 23: 243–260.

Appadurai, Arjun (1990) "Disjuncture and difference in the global cultural economy," *Public Culture* 2: 1–24.

Appleyard, Bryan (1998) *Brave New Worlds. Staying Human in the Genetic Future.* New York: Viking.

Arce, Alberto and Terry K. Marsden (1993) "The social construction of international food: A new research agenda," *Environment and Development* 69: 293–311.

Aron, Raymond (1962) *Eighteen Lectures on Industrial Society.* New York: Free Press

Aron, Raymond ([1983] 1990) *Memoirs. Fifty Years of Political Reflection.* New York: Holmes & Meier.

Aronowitz, Stanley and William DiFazio (1994) *The Jobless Future: Sci-Tech and the Dogma of Work.* Minneapolis: University of Minnesota Press.

Arrow, Kenneth (1962a) "Economic welfare and the allocation of resources of invention," pp. 609–625 in Richard R. Nelson (ed.), *The Rate and Direction of Inventive Activity, Economic and Social Factors. A Report of the National Bureau of Economic Research.* Princeton, NJ: Princeton University Press.

Arrow, Kenneth (1962b) "The economic implications of learning by doing," *Review of Economic Studies* 29: 155–173.

Atir, Stav, Emily Rosenzweig and David Dunning (2015) "When knowledge knows no bounds self-perceived expertise predicts claims of impossible knowledge," *Psychological Science.* DOI: 10.1177/0956797615588195.

Atkinson, Anthony B. (1983) *The Economics of Inequality.* Second Edition. Oxford: Clarendon Press.

Attewell, Paul (1992) "Technology diffusion and organizational learning: The case of business computing," *Organization Science* 3: 1–19.

Austin, John L. (1962) *How to Do Things with Words.* London: Oxford University Press.

Autor, David H. (2014) "Skills, education, and the rise of earnings inequality among the 'other 99 percent'," *Science* 344: 843–851.

Autor, David H. and Michael J. Handel (2009) "Putting tasks to the test: Human capital, job tasks and wages," NBER Working Paper No. 15116. www.nber.org/papers/w15116.

Azoulay, Pierre (2003) "Acquiring knowledge within and across firm boundaries: Evidence from clinical development," Working Paper 10083. National Bureau of Economic Research. www.nber.org/papers/w10083.

Baetjer, Howard (2000) "Capital as embodied knowledge: Some implications for the theory of economic growth," *Review of Austrian Economics* 13: 147–174.

Bahar, Dany, Ricardo Hausmann and Cesar A. Hidalgo (2013) "Neighbors and the evolution of comparative advantage of nations: Evidence of international knowledge diffusion," *Journal of International Economics* 92: 111–123.

Bakshy, Eytan, Solomon Messing and Lada Adamic (2015) "Exposure to ideologically diverse news and opinion on Facebook," *Science* 7, May. DOI: 10.1126/science.aaa1160.

Balzer, Wolfgang (2003) "Wissen und Wissenschaft als Waren," *Erkenntnis* 58: 87–110.

Baptista, João Afonso (2014) "The ideology of sustainability and the globalization of a future," *Time & Society* 23: 358–379.

Barnes, Barry (1972) "On the reception of scientific beliefs," pp. 269–291 in Barry Barnes (ed.), *Sociology of Science*. Harmondsworth: Penguin.

Barnes, Barry (1985) *About Science*. Oxford: Blackwell.

Barnes, Barry (1988) *The Nature of Power*. Urbana, IL: University of Illinois Press.

Barnes, Barry (1995) *The Elements of Social Theory*. Princeton, NJ: Princeton University Press.

Barney, Jay B. (1991) "Firm resources and sustained competitive advantage," *Journal of Management* 17: 99–120.

Barro, Robert (1999) "The determinants of democracy," *Journal of Political Economy* 107: S158–S183.

Bataille, Georges (2001) *The Unfinished System of Nonknowledge*. Minneapolis, Minnesota: University of Minnesota Press.

Bates, Benjamin (1988) "Information as an economic good," pp. 76–94 in Vincent Mosco and Jane Wasko (eds), *The Political Economy of Information*. Madison, WI: University of Wisconsin Press.

Bateson, Gregory (1972) *Steps to an Ecology of Mind*. New York: Ballantine.

Bauer, Martin (1996) "Socio-demographic correlates of DK-responses in knowledge surveys: Self-attributed ignorance of science," *Social Science Information* 35: 39–68.

Bauerlein, Mark (2008) *The Dumbest Generation: How the Digital Age Stupefies Young Americans and Jeopardizes Our Future (or, Don't Trust Anyone Under 30)*. New York: Tarcher Jeremy.

Bechmann, Gotthard and Nico Stehr (2002) "The legacy of Niklas Luhmann," *Society* 39: 67–75.

Beck, Ulrich (1994) "Self-dissolution and self-endangerment of industrial society: What does this mean?," pp. 174–183 in Ulrich Beck, Anthony Giddens and Scott Lash (eds), *Reflexive Modernization. Politics, Tradition and Aesthetics in the Modern Social Order*. Cambridge: Polity.

Beck, Ulrich (1996) "Wissen oder Nicht-Wissen? Zwei Perspektiven reflexiver Modernisierung," pp. 289–315 in Ulrich Beck, Anthony Giddens and Scott Lash, *Reflexive Modernisierung. Eine Kontroverse*. Frankfurt am Main: Suhrkamp.

Beck, Ulrich ([1996] 1999) "Knowledge and unawareness? Two perspectives on 'reflexive modernization'," pp. 109–132 in Ulrich Beck, *World Risk Society*. Oxford: Polity.

Beck, Ulrich and Peter Wehling (2012) "The politics of non-knowing: An emerging area of social and political conflict in reflexive modernity," pp. 33–57 in Fernando Domínguez Rubio and Patrick Baert (eds), *The Politics of Knowledge*. London: Routledge.

Becker, Gary (1964) *Human Capital*. New York: National Bureau of Economic Research.

Becker, Gary (1993) "The economic way of looking at behavior," *Journal of Political Economy* 101: 385–409.

Becker, Gary (1994) *Human Capital: A Theoretical and Empirical Analysis, with Special Reference to Education*. Third Edition. New York: National Bureau of Economic Research.

Becker, Gary and Barry Gerhart (1996) "The impact of human resources management on organizational performance: Progress and prospect," *Academy of Management Journal* 39: 779–801.

Becker, Gary and Kevin M. Murphy (1992) "The division of labor, coordination costs, and knowledge," *Quarterly Journal of Economics* 107: 1137–1160.

Becker, Gary S. and Nigel Tomes (1986) "Human capital and the rise and fall of families," *Journal of Labor Economics* 4: S1–S39.

Beerkens, Eric (2009) "Centres of excellence and relevance: The contextualization of global models," *Science, Technology & Society* 14: 153–175.

Bell, Daniel (1964) "The post-industrial society," pp. 44–59 in Eli Ginzberg (ed.), *Technology and Social Change*. New York: Columbia University Press.

Bell, Daniel (1968) "The measurement of knowledge and technology," pp. 145–246 in Eleanor B. Sheldon and Wilbert E. Moore (eds), *Indicators of Social Change: Concepts and Measurements*. Hartford, CT: Russell Sage Foundation.

Bell, Daniel (1969) "Die nachindustrielle Gesellschaft," pp. 351–363 in Claus Grossner et al. (ed.), *Das 198. Jahrzehnt. Eine Team-Prognose für 1970 bis 1980*. Hamburg: Christian Wegner Verlag.

Bell, Daniel (1973) *The Coming of Post-Industrial Society. A Venture in Social Forecasting*. New York, New York: Basic Books.

Bell, Daniel (1976) *The Cultural Contradictions of Capitalism*. New York: Basic Books.

Bell, Daniel (1979) "The social framework of the information society," pp. 163–211 in Michael L. Dertouzos and Joel Moses (eds), *The Computer Age: A Twenty-Year View*. Cambridge, MA: MIT Press.

Bell, Daniel ([1965] 1988) *The End of Ideology*, with a new Afterword by the author. Cambridge, MA: Harvard University Press.

Benavot, Aaron, Yun-Lyung Cha, David Kamens, John W. Meyer and Suk-Ying Wong (1991) "Knowledge for the masses: World models and national curricula, 1920–1986," *American Sociological Review* 56: 85–100.

Ben-David, Josef (1971) *The Scientist's Role in Society: A Comparative Study*. Englewood Cliffs, NJ: Prentice-Hall.

Benhabib, Jess and Mark M. Spiegel (1994) "The role of human capital in economic development. Evidence from aggregate cross-country data," *Journal of Monetary Economics* 34: 143–173.

Bentham, Jeremy (1839) *A Manual of Political Economy*. New York: G.P. Putnam.

Berger, Johannes (2004) "Über den Ursprung der Ungleichheit unter den Menschen," *Zeitschrift für Soziologie* 33: 354–374.

Berger, Peter and Thomas Luckmann (1969) *Die gesellschaftliche Konstruktion der Wirklichkeit: eine Theorie der Wissenssoziologie*. Frankfurt am Main: Fischer.

Berrill, Kenneth (ed.) (1964) *Economic Development with Special Reference to East Asia*. New York: St Martin's Press.

Black, Jeremy (2014) *The Power of Knowledge. How Information and Technology Made the Modern World*. New Haven, CT: Yale University Press.

Blair, Margaret M. and Steven H.M. Wallman (2001) *Unseen Wealth. Report of the Brookings Task Force on Intangibles*. Washington, DC: Brookings Institution.

Blaug, Mark ([1965] 1968) "The rate of return on investment in education," pp. 215–259 in Mark Blaug (ed.), *Economics of Education 1*. Harmondsworth: Penguin.

Bleikle, Ivar (2005) "Organizing higher education in a knowledge society," *Higher Education* 49: 31–49.

Bloch, Ernst ([1918] 2000) *The Spirit of Utopia*. Stanford, CA: Stanford University Press.

Bloor, David (2004) "Sociology of scientific knowledge," pp. 919–962 in I. Niiniluoto, M. Sintonen and J. Wolenski (eds), *Handbook of Epistemology*. Dordrecht: Springer.

Blumenberg, Hans ([1973] 1983) *The Legitimacy of the Modern Age*. Cambridge, MA: MIT Press.

Bohman, James (1999) "Citizenship and norms of publicity. Wide public reason in cosmopolitan societies," *Political Theory* 27: 176–202.

Böhme, Gernot (1992) *Coping with Science*. Boulder, CO: Westview Press.

Böhme, Gernot and Nico Stehr (eds) (1986) *Knowledge Society*. Dordrecht: D. Reidel Publishing.

Boldrin, Michele and David K. Levine (2002) "Perfectly competitive innovation," in Federal Reserve Bank of Minneapolis, *Research Department Staff Report 303*. www.dklevine.com/papers/pci23.pdf.

Boldrin, Michele and David K. Levine (2005) "The economics of ideas and intellectual property," *PNAS* 102: 1252–1256.

Boldrin, Michele and David K. Levine (2013) "The case against patents," *Journal of Economic Perspectives* 27: 3–22.

Boli, John and George M. Thomas (1997) "World culture in the world polity: A century of international non-governmental organization," *American Sociological Review* 62: 171–190.

Bonaccorsi, Andrea, Jane Calvert and Pierre-Benoit Joly (2011) "From protecting texts to protecting objects in biotechnology and software: A tale of changes of ontological assumptions in intellectual property protection," *Economy and Society* 40: 611–639.

Borgmann, Albert (1999a) "Society in the postmodern era," *The Washington Quarterly* 23: 189–200.

Borgmann, Albert (1999b) *Holding on to Reality: The Nature of Information at the Turn of the Millennium.* Chicago, IL: University of Chicago Press.

Boudon, Raymond (1974) *Education, Opportunity and Social Inequality.* New York: Wiley.

Boulding, Kenneth (1955) "Notes on the information concept," *Explorations* 6: 103–122.

Boulding, Kenneth E. (1966) "The economics of knowledge and the knowledge of economics," *The American Economic Review* 56: 1–13.

Bourdieu, Pierre ([1971] 1973) "Cultural reproduction and social reproduction," pp. 71–112 in Richard Brown (ed.), *Knowledge, Education, and Cultural Change.* London: Tavistock.

Bourdieu, Pierre ([1972] 1977) *Outline of a Theory of Practice.* Cambridge: Cambridge University Press.

Bourdieu, Pierre ([1983] 1986) "The forms of capital," pp. 241–258 in John G. Richardson (ed.), *Handbook of Theory and Research for the Sociology of Education.* New York: Greenwood.

Bourdieu, Pierre ([1980] 1987) *Sozialer Sinn. Kritik der theoretischen Vernunft.* Frankfurt am Main: Suhrkamp.

Bourdieu, Pierre ([1984] 1988) *Homo Academicus.* Oxford: Polity Press.

Bourdieu, Pierre (1999) "Scattered remarks," *European Journal of Social Theory* 2: 334–340.

Bourdieu, Pierre and Jean Claude Passeron ([1964] 1979) *French Students and their Relation to Culture.* Chicago, IL: University of Chicago Press.

Boutang, Moulier Yann ([2007] 2011) *Cognitive Capitalism.* Cambridge: Polity.

Boyd, Danah and Nicole Ellison (2008) "Social network sites: Definition, history and scholarship," *Journal of Computer-Mediated Communication* 13: 210–230.

Boyle, James (2003) "The second enclosure movement and the construction of the public domain," *Law and Contemporary Problems* 66: 33–74.

Braudel, Fernand ([1949] 1995) *The Mediterranean and the Mediterranean World in the Age of Philip II*. Berkeley: University of California Press.

Brave, Ralph (2001) "Governing the genome," *The Nation*, December 10.

Brimnes, Niels (2004) "Variolation, vaccination and popular resistance in early colonial South India," *Medical History* 48: 199–288.

Brown, John Seeley and Paul Duguid ([2000] 2002) *The Social Life of Information*. Cambridge, MA: Harvard Business School Press.

Bruner, Jerome (1990) *Acts of Meaning*. Cambridge, MA: Harvard University Press.

Bruns, Axel (2010) "From reader to writer: Citizen journalism as news produsage," *International Handbook of Internet Research*: 119.

Brzezinski, Zbigniew (1970) "America in the technetronic age. New questions of our time," *Encounter* 30: 16–26.

Burgers, Jack and Giorgio Touburg (2013) "International mobility of professional knowledge from the global south: Indian IT workers in the Netherlands," *Global Networks* 13: 517–534.

Burke, Peter (2000) *A Social History of Knowledge. From Gutenberg to Diderot*. Oxford: Polity Press.

Burnham, James (1941) *The Managerial Revolution. What is Happening in the World*. New York: John Day.

Burton-Jones, Alan (1999) *Knowledge Capitalism: Business, Work, and Learning in the New Economy*. Oxford: Oxford University Press.

Bush, Vannevar (1945) "As we may think," *Atlantic Monthly* (July): 101–108.

Calhoun, Craig (1995) *Critical Social Theory. Culture, History, and the Challenge of Difference*. Oxford: Blackwell.

Callon, Michel (1992) "The dynamics of techno-economic networks," pp. 132–161 in Rod Coombs, Paolo Saviotti and Vivien Walsh (eds), *Technological Change and Company Strategies*. London: Academic Press.

Callon, Michel (1994) "Is science a public good?," *Science, Technology, & Human Values* 19: 395–424.

Campante, Filipe R. and Davin Chor (2011) "'The people want the fall of the regime': Schooling, political protest, and the economy," Working Papers 03-2011. Singapore Management University, School of Economics.

Campbell, Colin (2007) *The Easternization of the West*. Boulder, CO: Paradigm Publishers.

Canguilhem, Georges (1978) *On the Normal and the Pathological*. Dordrecht: D. Reidel.

Carillo, Francisco J. (2002) "Capital systems: Implications for a global knowledge agenda," *Journal of Knowledge Management* 6: 379–399.

Carley, Kathleen (1986) "Knowledge acquisition as a social phenomenon," *Instructional Science* 14: 381–438.

Carlsson, Bo, Zoltan J. Acs, David B. Audretsch and Pontus Braunerhjelm (2009) "Knowledge creation, entrepreneurship, and economic growth: A historical review," *Industrial and Corporate Change*, advance access published October 13: 1–37.

Carnoy, Martin and Manuel Castells (2001) "Globalization, the knowledge society, and the network state: Poulantzas at the millennium," *Global Networks* 1: 1–18.

Carolan, Michael S. (2008) "Making patents and intellectual property work. The asymmetrical 'harmonization' of TRIPS," *Organization & Environment* 21: 295–310.

Castellacci, Fulvio and Daniele Archibugi (2008) "The technology clubs: The distribution of knowledge across nations," *Research Policy* 37: 1659–1673.

Castells, Manuel ([1996] 2000a) *The Information Age. Economy, Society and Culture. Volume 1: The Rise of the Network Society*. Second Edition. Oxford: Blackwell.

Castells, Manuel (2000b) "Materials for an exploratory theory of the network society," *British Journal of Sociology* 51: 5–24.

Castells, Manuel (2009) *Communication Power*. Oxford, New York: Oxford University Press.

Cerny, Philip G. (1999) "Reconstructing the political in a globalising world: States, institutions, actors and governance," pp. 89–137 in Frans Buelens (ed.), *Globalisation and the Nation-State*. Cheltenham: Edward Elgar.

Chadwick, Andrew (2013) *The Hybrid Media System: Politics and Power*. Oxford: Oxford University Press.

Chambers, John, Nicholas Epley, Kenneth Savitsky and Paul D. Wendschitl (2008) "Knowing too much. Using private knowledge to predict how one is viewed by others," *Psychological Science* 19: 542–548.

Chandler, Alfred D. (1977) *The Visible Hand. The Managerial Revolution in American Business*. Cambridge, MA: Harvard University Press.

Chargaff, Erwin (1975) "Profitable wonders: A few thoughts on nucleic acid research," *The Sciences* 17: 21–26.

Chen, Lincoln C., Tim G. Evans and Richard A. Cash (1999) "Health as a global public good," pp. 284–304 in Inge Kaul, Isabelle Grunberg and Marc A. Stern (ed.), *Global Public Goods*. Oxford: Oxford University Press.

Chen, Shin-Horng (2002) "Global production networks and information technology: The case of Taiwan," *Industry and Innovation* 9: 249–265.

Chinco, Alex and Christopher Mayer (2014) "Misinformed speculators and mispricing in the housing market," NBER Working Paper 19817. www.nber.org/papers/w19817.

Cicourel, Aaron (1986) "The reproduction of objective knowledge: The common sense reasoning in medical decision-making," pp. 87–122 in

Gernot Böhme and Nico Stehr (eds), *The Knowledge Society*. Dordrecht: D. Reidel.

Coleman, James S. (1988) "Social capital in the creation of human capital," *American Journal of Sociology* 94 (Supplement): 95–120.

Collingridge, David and Colin Reeve (1986) *Science Speaks to Power. The Role of Experts in Policymaking*. London: Frances Pinter.

Collins, Harry (2007) "Bicycling on the moon: Collective tacit knowledge and somatic-limit knowledge," *Organization Studies* 28: 257–262.

Collins, Harry M. and Robert Evans (2002) "The third wave of science studies: Studies of expertise and experience," *Social Studies of Science* 32: 235–296.

Collinson, David (1994) "Strategies of resistance: Power, knowledge and subjectivity in the workplace," pp. 25–68 in John M. Jermier, David Knights and Walter R. Nord (eds), *Resistance and Power in Organizations*. London: Routledge.

Condorcet, Jean-Antoine-Nicolas de Caritat, Marquis de (1994) *Condorcet: Foundations of Social Choice and Political Theory*. Translated and edited by Iain McLean and Fiona Hewitt. Cheltenham: Edward Elgar Publishing.

Cook, Philip J. (1971) "Robert Michels' political parties in perspective," *The Journal of Politics* 33: 773–796.

Cooley, Charles Horton (1909) *Social Organization*. New York: Charles Scribner's Sons.

Cortada, James W. (2014) "When knowledge goes global: How people and organizations learned about information technology, 1945–1970," *Enterprise & Society* 15: 68–102.

Covaleski, Mark A., Mark W. Dirsmith and Larry Rittenberg (2003) "Jurisdictional disputes over professional work: The institutionalization of the global knowledge expert," *Accounting, Organizations and Society* 28: 323–355.

Cowan, Robin, Paul A. David and Dominique Forey (2000) "The explicit economics of knowledge certification and tacitness," paper prepared for the 3rd TIPIK workshop, Strasbourg, France, April.

Cowan, Robin and Dominique Forey (1997) "The economics of codification and the diffusion of knowledge," *Industrial and Corporate Change* 6: 595–622.

Crampes, Claude and Corinne Langinier (2009) "Are intellectual property rights detrimental to innovation?," *International Journal of the Economics of Business* 16: 249–268.

Crane, Diana (2002) "Culture and globalization: Theoretical models and emerging trends," pp. 1–25 in Diana Crane, Nobuko Kawashima and Kenichi Kawasaki (eds), *Global Culture. Media, Arts, Policy, and Globalization*. New York, New York: Routledge.

Crick, Malcolm R. (1982) "Anthropology of knowledge," *Annual Review of Anthropology* 11: 287–313.

Crozier, Michel ([1963] 1964) *The Bureaucratic Phenomenon*. Chicago, IL: University of Chicago Press.

Crozier, Michel ([1979] 1982) *Strategies for Change: The Future of French Society*. Cambridge, MA: MIT Press.

Culliton, Barbara J. (1978) "Science's restive public," *Daedalus* 107: 147–156.

Dahl, Robert A. (1989) *Democracy and its Critics*. New Haven, CT: Yale University Press.

Dahrendorf, Ralf (2000) "Die globale Klasse und die neue Ungleichheit," *Merkur* 54: 1057–1068.

Darnton, Robert (2008) "The library in the new age," *New York Review of Books* 55 (June 12).

Dasgupta, Partha (1987) "The economic theory of technology policy," pp. 7–23 in Partha Dasgupta and Paul Stoneman (eds), *Economic Policy and Technological Performance*. Cambridge: Cambridge University Press.

Dasgupta, Partha S. and Paul A. David (1994) "Toward a new economics of science," *Research Policy* 23: 487–521.

Davenport, Thomas H., David H. de Long and Michael C. Beers (1998) "Successful knowledge management projects," *Sloan Management Review* 39: 43–57.

David, Paul (1993) "Intellectual property institutions and the panda's thumb: Patents, copyright, and trade secrets in economic theory and history," pp. 19–57 in Mitchell B. Wallerstein, Mary Ellen Mogee and Roberta A. Schoen (eds), *Global Dimensions of Intellectual Property Rights in Science and Technology*. Washington, DC: National Academy Press.

David, Paul A. (2000) "The digital technology boomerang: new intellectual property rights threaten global 'open science'," World Bank Conference Paper.

Davis, Deborah S. (2004) "Talking about property in the new Chinese domestic property regime," pp. 288–307 in Frank Dobbin (ed.), *The Sociology of the Economy*. New York: Russell Sage Foundation.

Dawkins, Richard (2001) "The word made flesh," *The Guardian*, December 27.

Dean, Mitchell (2001) "Michel Foucault: 'a man in danger'," pp. 324–338 in George Ritzer and Barry Smart (eds), *Handbook of Social Theory*. London: Sage.

Del Vicario, Michela, Alessandro Bessi, Fabiana Zollo, Fabio Petroni, Antonio Scala, Guido Caldarellia, H. Eugene Stanley and Walter Quattrociocchi (2016) "The spreading of misinformation online," *PNAS* 113(3): 554–559.

Dempsey, Gillian (1999) "Revisiting Intellectual Property Policy: Information Economics for the Information Age," *Prometheus* 17: 33–40.

Dennett, Daniel C. (1986) "Information, technology, and the virtues of ignorance," *Daedalus* 115: 135–153.

Derber, Charles, William A. Schwartz and Yale Magrass (1990) *Power in the Highest Degree. Professionals and the Rise of a New Mandarin Order.* New York: Oxford University Press.

Desouza, Kevin and Roberto Evaristo (2003) "Global knowledge management strategies," *European Management Journal* 21: 62–67.

De Swaan, Abram (2001) *Words of the World. The Global Language System.* Oxford: Polity Press.

Dewey, John (1948) "Common sense and science: their respective frames of reference," *Journal of Philosophy* 45: 197–208.

Dewey, John ([1927] 1954) *The Public and its Problems.* Athens: Ohio University Press.

Dewey, John ([1916] 2005) *Democracy and Education.* Stilwell, KS: Dirireads.com.

Dickson, Peter R. and Alan G. Sawyer (1990) "The price knowledge and search of supermarket shoppers," *Journal of Marketing* 54: 42–53.

Dierkes, Meinolf (1981) "Perzeption und Akzeptanz technologischer Risiken und die Entwicklung neuer Konsensstrategien," pp. 125–141 in Jürgen von Kruedener and Klaus von Schubert (eds), *Technikfolgen und sozialer Wandel. Zur politischen Steuerbarkeit der Technik.* Köln: Wissenschaft und Politik.

Dilley, Roy (2010) "Reflections on knowledge practices and the problem of ignorance," *Journal of the Royal Anthropological Institute* 16 (Supplement 1): 176–192.

DiMaggio, Paul (1997) "Culture and cognition," *Annual Review of Sociology* 23: 263–287.

Dobbin, Frank, Beth Simmons and Geoffrey Garrett (2007) "The global diffusion of public policy policies: Social construction, coercion, competition, or learning?," *Annual Review of Sociology* 33: 449–472.

Donald, Merlin (1991) *Origins of the Modern Mind. Three Stages in the Evolution of Culture and Cognition.* Cambridge, MA: Harvard University Press.

Donaldson, Lex (2001) "Reflections on knowledge and knowledge-intensive firms," *Human Relations* 54: 955–963.

Dosi, Giovanni (1996) "The contribution of economic theory to the understanding of a knowledge-based economy," pp. 81–92 in Organisation for Economic Co-operation and Development, *Employment and Growth in the Knowledge-Based Economy.* Paris: OECD.

Dosi, Giovanni and Marco Grazzi (2009) "On the nature of technologies: Knowledge, procedures, artifacts and production inputs," *Cambridge Journal of Economics* 34: 173–184.

Douglas, Mary (1986) *How Institutions Think.* Syracuse: Syracuse University Press. New York: Oxford University Press.

Dove, Michael R., Daniel S. Smith, Marina T. Campos, Andrew S. Mathews, Anne Rademacher, Steve Rhee and Laura M. Yoder (2007) "Globalisation and the construction of Western and non-Western knowledge," pp. 129–154 in Paul Sillitoe (ed.), *Local Science vs. Global Science. Approaches to Indigenous Knowledge in International Development*. Oxford: Berghahn Books.

Downer, John (2011) "'737-cabriolet': The limits of knowledge and the sociology of inevitable failure," *American Journal of Sociology* 117: 725–762.

Downs, Anthony (1957) *An Economic Theory of Democracy*. New York: Harper.

Drahos, Peter (2010) *The Global Governance of Knowledge: Patent Offices and their Clients*. Cambridge: Cambridge University Press.

Dretske, Fred I. (1983) *Knowledge and the Flow of Information*. Cambridge, Massachusetts: MIT Press.

Drori, Gili S., John W. Meyer, Francisco O. Ramirez and Evan Schofer (2003) *Science in the Modern World Polity. Institutionalization and Globalization*. Stanford, CA: Stanford University Press.

Drucker, Peter ([1949] 1962) *The New Society. The Anatomy of Industrial Order*. New York, New York: Harper.

Drucker, Peter F. ([1968] 1972) *The Age of Discontinuity. Guidelines to our Changing Society*. New York: Harper & Row.

Drucker, Peter F. (1986) "The changed world economy," *Foreign Affairs* 64: 768–791.

Drucker, Peter F. (1992) "The post-capitalist world," *The Public Interest* 109: 89–100.

Drucker, Peter (1993a) *Post-Capitalist Society*. New York, New York: Harper Business.

Drucker, Peter F. (1993b) "The rise of the knowledge society," *Wilson Quarterly* 17: 52–71.

du Bois-Reymond, Emil Heinrich ([1872] 1974) "Über die Grenzen des Naturerkennens," pp. 54–77 in Emil du Bois-Reymond, *Vorträge über Philosophie und Gesellschaft*. Hamburg: Meiner.

Dulleck, Uwe and Rudolf Kerschbamer (2006) "On doctors, mechanics and computer specialists: The economics of credence goods," *Journal of Economic Literature* 44: 5–42.

Dunkmann, Karl (1926) "Die Bedeutung der Kategorien Gemeinschaft und Gesellschaft für die Geisteswissenschaften," *Kölner Vierteljahrshefte für Soziologie* 5: 35–50.

Dupré, J. Stefan and Sanford Lakoff (1962) *Science and the Nation. Policy and Politics*. Englewood Cliffs, NJ: Prentice-Hall.

Durkheim, Emile ([1912] 1965) *The Elementary Forms of Religious Life*. New York: Free Press.

Durkheim, Emile ([1955] 1983) *Pragmatism and Sociology*. Cambridge: Cambridge University Press.

Durkheim, Emile ([1950] 1992) *Professional Ethics and Civic Morals*. London: Routledge.

Earl, Peter F. (2009) "Information technology and the economics of storing, spreading and generating knowledge," *Prometheus* 27: 389–401.

Easterbrook, Frank H. (1982) "Insider trading, secret agents, evidentiary privileges, and the production of information," *The Supreme Court Review* 11: 309–365.

Easton, David (1991) "The division, integration, and transfer of knowledge," pp. 7–36 in David Easton and Corinne S. Schelling (eds), *Divided Knowledge: Across Disciplines, Across Cultures*. Newbury Park, CA: Sage.

Easton, David (1997) "The future of the postbehavioral phase in political science," pp. 13–46 in Kirsten Renwick Monroe (ed.), *Contemporary Empirical Political Theory*. Berkeley, CA: University of California Press.

Edwards, Paul N. (2006) "Meteorology as infrastructural globalism," *OSIRIS* 21: 229–250.

Edwards, Paul N., Lisa Gitelman, Gabrielle Hecht, Adrian Jones, Brian Larkin and Neil Safier (2011) "AHR conversation: Historical perspectives on the circulation of information," *American Historical Review* 116: 1393–1435.

Eggertsson, Thráinn (2009) "Knowledge and the theory of institutional change," *Journal of Institutional Economics* 5: 137–150.

Elias, Norbert (1978) *Über den Prozess der Zivilisation*. Frankfurt am Main: Suhrkamp.

Elias, Norbert (1982) "Scientific establishments," pp. 3–69 in Norbert Elias, Herminio Martins and Richard Whitley (eds), *Scientific Establishments and Hierarchies. Sociology of the Sciences Yearbook 1982*. Dordrecht: Reidel.

Elias, Norbert (1984) "Knowledge and power," pp. 252–292 in Nico Stehr and Volker Meja (eds), *Society and Knowledge. Contemporary Perspectives on the Sociology of Knowledge*. New Brunswick, NJ: Transaction Books.

Elias, Norbert (1989) *Studien über die Deutschen: Machtkämpfe und Habitusentwicklung im 19. und 20. Jahrhundert*. Frankfurt am Main: Suhrkamp.

Elias, Norbert ([1987] 2006a) "Über den Rückzug der Soziologen auf die Gegenwart," pp. 297–333 in Norbert Elias, *Gesammelte Schriften. Volume 16: Aufsätze und andere Schriften III*. Frankfurt am Main: Suhrkamp.

Elias, Norbert ([1984] 2006b) "Das Credo eines Metaphysikers. Kommentare zu Poppers 'Logik der Forschung'," pp. 7–59 in Norbert Elias, *Gesammelte Schriften. Volume 16: Aufsätze und andere Schriften III*. Frankfurt am Main: Suhrkamp.

Ernst, Dieter (2005) "The new mobility of knowledge: Digital information systems and global flagship networks," pp. 89–114 in Robert Latham and Saskia Sassen (eds), *Digital Formations. IT and New Architectures in the Global Realm*. Princeton, NJ: Princeton University Press.

Evenson, Robert and Jonathan Putnam (1987) "Institutional changes in intellectual property rights," *American Journal of Agricultural Economics* 69: 403–409.

Ezrahi, Yaron (2004) "Science and the political imagination in contemporary democracies," pp. 254–273 in Sheila Jasanoff (ed.), *States of Knowledge. The Co-production of Science and the Social Order*. London: Routledge.

Farkas, George (1996) *Human Capital or Cultural Capital. Ethnicity and Poverty in an Urban School District*. New York: Aldine de Gruyter.

Faulkner, Wendy (1994) "Conceptualizing knowledge used in innovation: A second look at the science-technology distinction and industrial innovation," *Science, Technology & Human Values* 19: 425–458.

Featherstone, Mike and Couze Venn (2006) "Problematizing global knowledge and the New Encyclopedia Project: An introduction," *Theory, Culture and Society* 23: 1–20.

Feher, Michel ([2007] 2009) "Self-appreciation; or, the aspirations of human capital," *Public Culture* 21: 21–41.

Fernando, Jude L. (2003) "NGOs and the production of indigenous knowledge under the condition of postmodernity," *Annals of the American Academy of Political and Social Science* 590: 54–72.

Fevre, Ralph, Gareth Rees and Stephen Gorard (1999) "Some sociological alternatives to human capital theory and their implications for research on postcompulsory education and training," *Journal of Education and Work* 12: 117–140.

Feyerabend, Paul (1993) *Against Method*. London: NLB.

Feyerabend, Paul (2011) *The Tyranny of Science*. Cambridge: Polity.

Fielding, Jonathan E. and Thomas R. Frieden (2004) "Local knowledge to enable local action," *American Journal of Preventive Medicine* 27: 146–152.

Fink, Carsten and Keith E. Maskus (2005) "Why we study intellectual property rights and what we have learned," pp. 1–15 in Carsten Fink and Keith E. Maskus, *Intellectual Property and Development. Lessons from Recent Economic Research*. Washington, DC: The World Bank.

Flavier, Juan M., De Jesus, A. and Navarro, C.S. (1995) "Why is indigenous knowledge important?," pp. 479–487 in D. Michael Warren, Jan Slikkerveer and David Brokensha (eds), *The Cultural Dimension of Development: Indigenous Knowledge Systems*. New Brunswick, NJ: Transaction Books.

Fleck, Ludwik ([1935] 1979) *Genesis and Development of a Scientific Fact*. Chicago, IL: University of Chicago Press.

Fleck, Ludwik ([1935] 1980) *Entstehung und Entwicklung einer wissenschaftlichen Tatsache. Einführung in die Lehre vom Denkstil und Denkkollektiv. Mit einer Einleitung von Lothar Schäfer und Thomas Schnelle*. Frankfurt am Main: Suhrkamp.

Forest, Chris H., Peter H. Stone, Andrei P. Sokolov, Myles R. Allen and Mort D. Webster (2002) "Quantifying uncertainties in climate system properties with the use of recent climate observations," *Science* 295: 113–117.

Forey, Dominique (2006) *The Economics of Knowledge*. Boston, MA: MIT Press.

Foster, Kevin R. and Hanna Kokko (2009) "The evolution of superstitious and superstition-like behaviour," *Proceedings of the Royal Society of London, Series B* 276: 31–37.

Foucault, Michel ([1969] 1972) *The Archaeology of Knowledge*. London: Routledge.

Foucault, Michel ([1975] 1977a) *Discipline and Punish: The Birth of the Prison*. New York: Random House.

Foucault, Michel (1977b) "Prison talk: An interview," *Radical Philosophy* 16: 10–15.

Foucault, Michel (1979) *The History of Sexuality. Volume 1: An Introduction*. London: Allen Lane.

Foucault, Michel (1980) *Power/Knowledge: Selected Interviews and Other Writings 1972–1977*, edited by Colin Gordon. New York: Pantheon Books.

Foucault, Michel (1981) "Omnes et Singulatim," in Sterling M. McMurrin (ed.), *The Tanner Lectures on Human Values. Volume 2*. Cambridge: Cambridge University Press.

Foucault, Michel (1982) "The subject and power," pp. 208–226 in Hubert L. Dreyfus and Paul Rabinow (eds), *Michel Foucault: Beyond Structuralism and Hermeneutics*. Chicago, IL: University of Chicago Press.

Foucault, Michel (1984) "What is Enlightenment?" pp. 32–50 in Paul Rabinow (ed.), *The Foucault Reader*. New York: Pantheon Books.

Foucault, Michel ([1984] 1987) "The ethic of care for the self as a practice of freedom," an interview with Michel Foucault by Raúl Fornet-Betancourt, Helmut Becker, Alfredo Gomez-Müller and J.D. Gauthier (January 20, 1984). *Philosophy & Social Criticism* 12: 112–131.

Foucault, Michel ([1994] 1998) "Polemics, Politics and Problematizations," in Paul Rabinow (ed.), *Essential Works of Foucault. Volume 1: Ethics*. New York: The New Press.

Foucault, Michel (2007) *Ästhetik der Existenz. Schriften zur Lebenskunst*. Frankfurt am Main: Suhrkamp.

Frank, David John (1997) "Science, nature, and the globalization of the environment, 1870–1990," *Social Forces* 76: 409–437.

Frank, David John, Ann Hironaka, John W. Meyer, Evan Schofer and Nancy Brandon Tuma (1999) "The rationalization and organization of nature in world culture," pp. 81–99 in John Boli and George M. Thomas (eds), *Constructing World Culture: International Non-governmental Organizations since 1875*. Stanford, CA: Stanford University Press.

Frank, David John, Ann Hironaka and Evan Schofer (2000) "The nation-state and the natural environment over the twentieth century," *American Sociological Review* 65: 96–116.

Fraumeni, Barbara M. (2015) "Choosing a human capital measure: Educational attainment gaps and rankings," NBER Working Paper 21283. www.nber.org/papers/w21283.

Freeman, Chris (1991) "Networks of innovators: A synthesis of research issues," *Research Policy* 20: 499–514.

Freeman, Richard (2006) "Does globalization of the scientific/engineering workforce threaten US economic leadership?," in *Innovation Policy and the Economy*. Cambridge, MA: MIT Press.

Freidson, Eliot (2001) *Professionalism. The Third Logic*. Chicago, IL: University of Chicago Press.

Freud, Sigmund ([1917] 1920) *A General Introduction to Psychoanalysis*. New York: Horace Liveright Publisher. www.gutenberg.org/ebooks/38219.

Fukuyama, Francis (1992) *The End of History and the Last Man*. New York: Free Press.

Fuller, Steve (1992) "Knowledge as product and property," pp. 157–190 in Nico Stehr and Richard V. Ericson (eds), *The Culture and Power of Knowledge. Inquiries into Contemporary Societies*. Berlin: de Gruyter.

Fuller, Steve (2003) "The university: A social technology for producing universal knowledge," *Technology in Society* 25: 217–234.

Fulmer, Ingrid Smithey and Robert E. Ployhart (2014) "'Our most important asset': A multidisciplinary/multilevel review of human capital valuation for research and practice," *Journal of Management* 40: 161–192.

Funtowicz, Silvio O. and Jerome R. Ravetz (1990) *Uncertainty and Quality in Science Policy*. Dordrecht: Kluwer.

Galbraith, John K. ([1967] 1971) *The New Industrial State*. Boston, MA: Houghton Mifflin.

Galison, Peter (2004) "Removing knowledge," *Critical Inquiry* 31: 229–243.

Gallie, Walter B. (1955–56) "Essentially contested concepts," *Proceedings of the Aristotelian Society New Series* 56: 167–198.

Ganguli, Prabuddha (2000) "Intellectual property rights. Imperatives for the knowledge industry," *World Patent Information* 22: 167–175.

Garicano, Luis and Esteban Rossi-Hansberg (2015) "Knowledge-based hierarchies: Using organizations to understand the economy," *Annual Review of Economics* 7: 1–30.

Garmon, Cecile W. (2002) "Intellectual property rights," *American Behavioral Scientist* 45: 1145–1158.

Garnham, Nicholas and Raymond Williams (1986) "Pierre Bourdieu and the sociology of culture: An introduction," in Richard Collins et al. (eds), *Media, Culture and Society*. London: Sage.

Gates, Bill, Nathan Myhrvold and Peter Rinearson (1995) *The Road Ahead*. New York: Viking Penguin.

Gay, Peter (2002) *Das Zeitalter des Doktor Arthur Schnitzler. Innenansichten des 19. Jahrhundert*. Frankfurt am Main: S. Fischer.

Geanakoplos, John (1992) "Common knowledge," *Journal of Economic Perspectives* 6: 53–82.

Geertz, Clifford (1975) "Common sense as a cultural system," *Antioch Review* 33: 5–26.

Geertz, Clifford (1996) "Afterword," pp. 259–262 in S. Feld and K.H. Basso (eds), *Sense of Place*. Santa Fe, NM: School of American Research.

Gehlen, Arnold ([1950] 1988) *Man: His Nature and Place in the World*. New York: Columbia University Press.

Gehlen, Arnold ([1957] 2004) "Die Seele im technischen Zeitalter," in Arnold Gehlen, *Die Seele im technischen Zeitalter und andere soziologische Schriften und Kulturanalysen. Gesamtausgabe Band 6.* Frankfurt am Main: Vittorio Klostermann.

Geiger, Roger (1986) *To Advance Knowledge. The Growth of American Research Universities, 1900–1940*. Oxford: Oxford University Press.

Geroski, Paul (1995) "Markets for technology: Knowledge, innovation and appropriability," pp. 90–131 in Paul Stoneman (ed.), *Handbook of the Economics of Innovation and Technological Change*. Oxford: Blackwell.

Ghosh, Rishab A. (ed.) (2005) *CODE. Collaborative Ownership and the Digital Economy*. Cambridge, MA: MIT Press.

Ghosh, Rishab A. and Luc Soete (2006) "Information and intellectual property: The global challenges," *Industrial and Corporate Change* 15: 919–935.

Giddens, Anthony (1984) *The Constitution of Society. Outline of the Theory of Structuration*. Cambridge: Polity Press.

Giddens, Anthony (1990) *The Consequences of Modernity*. Cambridge: Polity.

Giddens, Anthony (1996) "Leben in einer posttraditionalen Gesellschaft," in Ulrich Beck, Anthony Giddens and Scott Lash (eds), *Reflexive Modernisierung. Eine Kontroverse*. Frankfurt am Main: Suhrkamp.

Gieryn, Thomas F. (2008) "Cultural boundaries: Settled and unsettled," pp. 91–99 in Peter Meusburger, Michael Welker and Edgar Wunder (eds), *Clashes of Knowledge. Orthodoxies and Heterodoxies in Science and Religion*. Heidelberg: Springer.

Ginsberg, Theo (1986) "Wissen ohne Gewissen ist Macht ohne Verantwortung. Gedanken zum technischen Fortschritt," pp. 125–141 in Otto Neumaier (ed.), *Wissen und Gewissen: Arbeiten zur Verantwortungsproblematik*. Vienna: VWGÖ.

Ginzburg, Carlo (1976) "High and low: The theme of forbidden knowledge in the sixteenth and seventeenth centuries," *Past and Present* 73: 28–24.

Gissis, Snait (2009) "Interactions between social and biological thinking: The case of Lamarck," *Perspectives on Science* 17: 237–306.

Glaeser, Edward L., David Laibson, Jose A. Scheibkman and Christine L. Soutter (1999) "What is social capital? The determinants of trust and trustworthiness," NBER Working Paper No. 7216. www.nber.org/papers/w7216.

Glass, Bently (1971) "Science: Endless horizons or golden age?," *Science* 171 (January 8): 23–29.

Goldin, Claudia and Lawrence F. Katz (2008) *The Race between Education and Technology*. Cambridge, MA: Harvard University Press.

Goldman, Alvin I. (1999) *Knowledge in a Social World*. Oxford: Clarendon Press.

Goldstone, Jack A. (2006) "A historical, not comparative, method: Breakthroughs and limitations in the theory and methodology of Michael Mann's analysis of power," pp. 263–282 in John A. Hall and Ralph Schroeder (eds), *An Anatomy of Power. The Social Theory of Michael Mann*. Cambridge: Cambridge University Press.

Gorz, André ([2003] 2004) *Wissen, Wert und Kapital, Zur Kritik der Wissensökonomie*. Berlin: Rotpunktverlag.

Gorz, André ([2003] 2010) *The Immaterial. Knowledge, Value and Capital*. Chicago, IL: University of Chicago Press.

Gossner, Olivier (2010) "Ability and knowledge," *Games and Economic Behavior* 69: 95–106.

Gough, Noel (2002) "Thinking/acting locally/globally: Western science and environmental education in a global knowledge economy," *International Journal of Science Education* 24: 1217–1237.

Gouldner, Alvin W. (1976) *The Dialectic of Ideology and Technology: The Origins, Grammar and Future of Ideology*. New York: Seabury Press.

Graber, Doris A. (1988) *Processing the News: How People Tame the Information Tide*. Second edition. New York: Longman.

Grandori, Anna and Bruce Kohut (2002) "Dialogue on organization and knowledge," *Organization Science* 13: 224–232.

Greenhalgh, Christine and Mark Rogers (2007) "The value of intellectual property rights to firms and society," *Oxford Review of Economic Policy* 23: 541–567.

Griliches, Zvi (1990) "Patent statistics as economic indicators: A survey," NBER Working Paper W 3301. National Bureau of Economic Research.

Grossman, Gene and Elhanan Helpman (1991) *Innovation and Growth in the Global Economy*. Cambridge, MA: MIT Press.

Grundmann, Reiner and Nico Stehr (2000) "Social science and the absence of nature," *Social Science Information* 39: 155–179.

Grundmann, Reiner and Nico Stehr (2011) *Experts: The Knowledge and Power of Expertise*. London: Routledge.

Grundmann, Reiner and Nico Stehr (2012) *The Power of Scientific Knowledge. From Research to Public Policy*. Cambridge: Cambridge University Press.

Gunter, Barrie (1987) *Poor Reception: Misunderstanding and Forgetting Broadcast News*. Hillsdale, NJ: Lawrence Erlbaum.

Gupta, Anil K. (2006) "From sink to source. The Honey Bee Network documents indigenous knowledge and innovations in India," *Innovations*, Summer. mitpress.mit.edu/innovations.

Gupta, Anil K. (2007) *Indigenous Knowledge: Ways of Knowing, Feeling and Doing*. www.sristi.org/cms/publications (accessed July 2, 2010).

Gupta, A.K. and V. Govindarajan (2000) "Knowledge flows with multinational corporations," *Strategic Management Journal* 21: 473–496.

Habermas, Jürgen (1964) "Dogmatismus, Vernunft und Entscheidung – Zur Theorie und Praxis in der wissenschaftlichen Zivilisation," pp. 231–257 in Jürgen Habermas, *Theorie und Praxis*. Neuwied: Luchterhand.

Habermas, Jürgen ([1968] 1970) "Technology and science as 'ideology'," pp. 81–122 in Jeremy J. Shapiro, *Toward a Rational Society*. Boston, MA: Beacon Press.

Habermas, Jürgen ([1965] 1971) "Knowledge and human interest: A general perspective," in Jürgen Habermas, *Knowledge and Human Interest*. Boston, MA: Beacon.

Habermas, Jürgen (1981) *Theorie des kommunikativen Handelns. Band 1: Handlungsrationalität und gesellschaftliche Rationalisierung*. Frankfurt am Main: Suhrkamp.

Habermas, Jürgen ([1962] 1989) *The Structural Transformation of the Public Sphere: An Inquiry into a Category of Bourgeois Society*. Cambridge: Polity Press.

Habermas, Jürgen ([1998] 2001) "An argument against human cloning. Three replies," in Jürgen Habermas, *The Postnational Constellation. Political Essays*. Oxford: Polity Press.

Haggett, Mark and Greg Kaplan (2015) "How large is the stock component of human capital," NBER Working Paper No. 21238. www.nber.org/papers/w21238.

Hall, George R. and Richard E. Johnson (1970) "Transfers of United States aerospace technology to Japan," pp. 303–364 in Raymond Vernon (ed.), *The Technology Factor in International Trade*. Boston, MA: UMI.

Hall, John R. (1992) "The capital(s) of cultures: A nonholistic approach to status situations, class, gender, and ethnicity," pp. 257–285 in Michèle Lamont and Marcel Fournier (eds), *Cultivating Differences. Symbolic Boundaries and the Making of Inequality*. Chicago, IL: University of Chicago Press.

Halle, David (1992) "The audience for abstract art: Class, culture and power," pp. 131–181 in Michèle Lamont and Marcel Fournier (eds), *Cultivating Differences. Symbolic Boundaries and the Making of Inequality*. Chicago, IL: University of Chicago Press.

Hanushek, Eric A., Guido Schwerdt and Simon Wiederhold (2015) "Returns to skill around the world: Evidence from PIAAC," *European Economic Review* 73: 103–130.

Hardin, Garrett (1968) "The tragedy of the commons," *Science* 162: 1243–1248.

Hardin, Russell J. (2002) "Street-level epistemology and democratic participation," *The Journal of Political Philosophy* 10: 212–229.

Harding, Sandra (2002) "Must the advance of science advance global inequality?," *International Studies Review* 4: 87–105.

Hardt, M. and Antonio Negri (2000) *Empire*. Cambridge, MA: Harvard University Press.

Harison, Elad (2008) "Intellectual property rights in knowledge-based economy: A new frame-of-analysis," *Economic Innovation New Technology* 17: 377–400.

Hartmann, Frank and Erwin K. Bauer (2002) *Bildersprache. Otto Neurath Visialisierungen*. Wien: WUV.

Hayek, Friedrich A. (1937) "Economics and knowledge," *Economica* 4: 33–54.

Hayek, Friedrich A. ([1945] 1948a) "The use of knowledge in society," pp. 77–91 in Friedrich A. Hayek, *Individualism and Economic Order*. Chicago, IL: University of Chicago Press.

Hayek, Friedrich A. (1948b) *Individualism and Economic Order*. Chicago, IL: The University of Chicago Press.

Hayek, Friedrich A. (1960) *The Constitution of Liberty*. London: Routledge.

Hayek, Friedrich A. ([1960] 1978) "The creative powers of a free civilization," in Friedrich A. Hayek, *The Constitution of Liberty*. Chicago, IL: The University of Chicago Press.

Hayek, Friedrich A. ([1960] 2005) *Die Verfassung der Freiheit. Gesammelte Schriften in deutscher Sprache Band 3. 4. Auflage*. Tübingen: Mohr Siebeck.

Heinrich, Michael and José Prieto (2008) "Diet and healthy ageing 2100: Will we globalize local knowledge systems," *Ageing Research Reviews* 7: 249–274.

Hellwig, Christian and Laura Veldkamp (2009) "Knowing what other know: Coordination motives in information acquisition," *The Review of Economic Studies* 76: 223–251.

Helmstädter, Ernst (2000a) "Arbeitsteilung und Wissensteilung. Zur Institutionenökonomik der Wissensgesellschaft," pp. 118–141 in Hans G. Nutzinge and Martin Held (eds), *Geteilte Arbeit und ganzer Mensch. Perspektiveder Arbeitsgesellschaft*. Frankfurt am Main: Campus Verlag.

Helmstädter, Ernst (2000b) "Wissensteilung," in *Thünen-Vorlesung bei der Jahrestagung 2000 des Vereins für Sozialpolitik*. Gelsenkirchen: Institut Arbeit und Technik.

Herf, Jeffrey (1984) *Reactionary Modernism. Technology, Culture, and Politics in Weimar and the Third Reich*. Cambridge: Cambridge University Press.

Hess, Charlotte and Elinor Ostrom (2003) "Ideas, artifacts and facilities information as a common-pool resource," *Law and Contemporary Problems* 66: 111–148.

Hess, Charlotte and Elinor Ostrom (2007) *Understanding Knowledge as a Commons: From Theory to Practice*. Cambridge: MIT Press.

Hesse, Carla (2002) "The rise of intellectual property, 700 B.C.–A.D. 2000: An idea in the balance," *Daedalus* 131(2): 26–45.

Hilgartner, Stephen (2002) "Acceptable intellectual property," *Journal of Molecular Biology* 319: 943–946.

Hilmer, Michael J. and Christiana E. Hilmer (2012) "On the relationship between student tastes and motivations, higher education decisions, and annual earnings," *Economics of Education Review* 31: 66–75.

Hirsch, Fred (1977) *Social Limits to Growth*. London: Routledge & Kegan Paul.

Hirshleifer, Jack (1971) "The private and social value of information and the reward to innovative activity," *American Economic Review, Papers and Proceedings* 63: 31–39.

Hirschman, Albert O. (1994) "Social conflicts as pillars of democratic market society," *Political Theory* 22: 203–218.

Hjarvard, Stig (2008) "The mediatization of society: A theory of the media as agents of social and cultural change." *Nordicom Review* 29(2): 105–134.

Hobart, Mark (1993) "Introduction: The growth of ignorance?," pp. 1–30 in Mark Hobart (ed.), *An Anthropological Critique of Development*. London: Routledge.

Hobsbawm, Eric ([1994] 1996) *The Age of Extremes. A History of the World, 1914–1991*. New York: Vintage Books.

Hobsbawm, Eric (2007) *Globalisation, Democracy and Terrorism*. London: Little, Brown.

Homburg, Christian, Nicole Koschate-Fischer and Christian M. Wiegner (2012) "Customer satisfaction and elapsed time since purchase as drivers of price knowledge," *Psychology and Marketing* 29: 76–86.

Hong, Jacky F.L. and Thang V. Nguyen (2009) "Knowledge embeddedness and the transfer mechanism in multinational corporations," *Journal of World Business* 44: 347–356.

Hongling, Liang (2015) "The 'Chinese Century' and the dynamics of knowledge in a longue durée," *Cultural Dynamics* 27: 227–239.

Horgan, John (1996) *The End of Science. Facing the Limits of Knowledge in the Twilight of the Scientific Age*. New York: Addison Wesley.

Horkheimer, Max ([1932] 1972) "Notes on science and the crisis," pp. 3–9 in Max Horkheimer, *Critical Theory: Selected Essays*. New York: Continuum.

Horkheimer, Max and Theodor W. Adorno ([1944] 1972) *Dialectic of Enlightenment*. New York: Herder and Herder.

Hornidge, Anna-Katharina (2007) "Re-inventing society: State concepts of knowledge in Germany and Singapore," *Sojourns Journal of Social Issues in Southeast Asia* 22: 202–229.

Hoti, Suhejla and Michael McAleer (2006) "Intellectual property litigation activity in the USA," *Journal of Economic Surveys* 20: 715–729.

Howe, Henry and John Lyne (1992) "Gene talk in sociobiology," *Social Epistemology* 6: 109–163.

Hsiang, Solomon M., Kyle C. Meng and Mark A. Cane (2011) "Civil conflicts are associated with the global climate," *Nature* 476: 438–441.

Huber, George P. (1991) "Organizational learning: The contributing process and the literatures," *Organization Science* 2: 88–115.

Hunter, Ian (1996) "Assembling the school," in Andrew Barry, Thomas Osborne and Nikolas Rose (eds), *Foucault and Political Reason: Liberalism, Neo-liberalism, and Rationalities*. Chicago, IL: University of Chicago Press.

Huntington, Samuel P. (2004) "Dead souls: The denationalization of the American elite," *National Interest* 75: 5–18.

Hutchby, Ian (2001) "Technologies, texts and affordances," *Sociology* 35(2): 441–456.

Inkster, Ian (1991) *Science and Technology in History: An Approach to Industrial Development*. Basingstoke: Macmillan.

Innis, Harold ([1950] 2007) *Empire and Communications*. Toronto: Dundurn Press.

Jacoby, Susan (2008) *The Age of American Unreason*. New York: Pantheon Books.

James, William F. (1890) *The Principles of Psychology, Volume One*. New York: Dover Publications.

Jandhyaia, Sriviya and Anupama Phene (2015) "The role of intergovernmental organizations in cross-border knowledge transfer and innovation," *Administrative Science Quarterly*: 1–32.

Janich, Peter and Michael Weingarten (2002) "Verantwortung ohne Verständnis? Wie die Ethikdebatte zur Gentechnik von deren Wissenschaftstheorie abhängt," *Journal for General Philosophy of Science* 33: 85–120.

Japp, Klaus P. (2000) "Distinguishing non-knowledge," *Canadian Journal of Sociology* 25: 225–238.

Jasanoff, Sheila (2012) "The politics of public reason," in Fernando Domínguez Rubio and Patrick Baert (eds), *The Politics of Knowledge*. London: Routledge.

Jeanneney, Jean-Noel (2007) *Google and the Myth of Universal Knowledge*. Chicago: University of Chicago Press.

Jensen, Robert and Gabriel Szulanski (2004) "Stickiness and adaptation of organizational practices in cross-border knowledge transfer," *Journal of International Business Studies* 35: 508–523.

Jermier, John M., David Knights and Walter R. Nord (eds) (1994) *Resistance and Power in Organizations*. London: Routledge.

Jessoe, Katrina and David Rapson (2014) "Knowledge is (less) power: Experimental evidence from residential energy use," *American Economic Review* 104: 1417–1438.

Jischa, Michael F. (2008) "Management trotz Nichtwissens. Steuerung und Eigendynamik von komplexen Systemen," pp. 272–283 in Armin von Gleich and Stefan Grüling-Reisemann (eds), *Industrial Ecology*. Wiesbaden: Vieweg + Teubner.

Johnson, Daniel K.N., Nalyn Siripong and Amy S. Brown (2006) "The demise of distance? The declining role of physical proximity for knowledge transmission," *Growth and Change* 37: 19–33.

Jonas, Hans (1974) *Philosophical Essays: From Ancient Creed to Technological Man*. Englewood Cliffs, NJ: Prentice Hall.

Jonas, Hans ([1976] 1979) "Freedom of scientific inquiry and the public interest," pp. 33–39 in Keith M. Wulff (ed.), *Regulation of Scientific Inquiry. Societal Concerns with Research*. Boulder, CO: Westview Press.

Jones, Benjamin F. (2009) "The burden of knowledge and the 'death of the renaissance man': Is innovation getting harder?," *The Review of Economic Studies* 76: 283–317.

Junor, Sean and Alex Usher (2004/05) "The price of knowledge," *Policy Options*: 61–66.

Kaiser, Mario (2015) *Über Folgen. Technische Zukunft und politische Gegenwart*. Weilerswist: Velbrück Wissenschaft.

Kant, Immanuel ([1781] 1998) *Critique of Pure Reason*. Trans. and ed. by Paul Guyer and Allen W. Wood. Cambridge: Cambridge University Press.

Kanter, Rosabeth Moss (1991) "The future of bureaucracy and hierarchy inorganizational theory: A report from the field," pp. 63–87 in Pierre Bourdieu and James S. Coleman (eds), *Social Theory for a Changing Society*. Boulder, CO: Westview Press.

Katz, Richard S. and Peter Muir (1995) "Changing models of party organizations and party democracy: The emergence of the cartel party," *Party Politics* 1: 5–28.

Kay, John (1999) "Money from knowledge," *Science & Public Affairs* (April): 12–13.

Kay, Lily E. (2000) *Who Wrote the Book of Life? A History of the Genetic Code*. Stanford, CA: Stanford University Press.

Keller, Evelyn Fox (1992) "Nature, nurture, and the human genome project," pp. 281–299 in Daniel J. Kevles and Leroy Hood (eds), *The Code of Codes. Scientific and Social Issues in the Human Genome Project*. Cambridge, Massachusetts: Harvard University Press.

Keller, Wolfgang (2002) "Geographic localization of international technology transfers," *American Economic Review* 92: 120–142.

Keller, Wolfgang and Stephen Ross Yeaple (2013) "The gravity of knowledge," *American Economic Review* 103: 1414–1444.

Kennedy, Donald (2002) "On science at the crossroads," *Daedalus* 131: 122–126.

Kennedy, Donald (2005) "Bayh-Dole: Almost 25," *Science* 307: 1375.

Kennedy, Paul (2007) "Global transformations but local, 'bubble' lives: Taking a reality check on some globalizations concepts," *Globalizations* 4: 267–282.

Kepplinger, Hans Mathias (2008) "Was unterscheidet die Mediatisierungsforschung von der Medienwirkungsforschung?" *Publizistik* 53(3): 326–338.

Kerr, Clark (1963) *The Uses of the University*. Cambridge, MA: Harvard University Press.

Kettler, David, Volker Meja and Nico Stehr (1990) "Rationalizing the irrational: Karl Mannheim and the besetting sin of German intellectuals," *American Journal of Sociology* 95: 1141–1173.

Kevles, Daniel J. (2001) "Patenting life: A historical overview of law, interests, and ethics," Paper presented to the Legal Theory Workshop, Yale University, December 20, 2001.

Keynes, John Maynard (1936) *The General Theory of Employment, Interest and Money*. London: Macmillan.

Keynes, John M. (1937) "The general theory of employment," *Quarterly Journal of Economics* 51: 209–223.

Kiker, Billy F. (1966) "The historical roots of the concept of human capital," *Journal of Political Economy* 74: 481–499.

Kitch, Edmund W. (1980) "The law and the economics of rights in valuable information," *Journal of Legal Studies* 9: 683–723.

Kitcher, Philip (2010) "Two forms of blindness: On the need for both cultures," *Technology in Society* 32: 40–48.

Knight, G.A. and S.T. Cavusgil (1996) "The born global firm: A challenge to traditional internationalization theory," *Advances International Marketing* 8: 11–26.

Knight, H. Jackson (ed.) (2013) *Patent Strategy for Researchers and Research Managers*. Third Edition. New York: John Wiley.

Knoblauch, Hubert (2009) "Kommunikationsgemeinschaften. Überlegungen zur kommunikativen Konstruktion einer Gesellschaftsform," pp. 73–88 in R. Hitzler, Roland A. Honer and M. Pfadenhauer (eds), *Posttraditionale Gemeinschaften. Theoretische und ethnographische Erkundungen*. Wiesbaden: VS Verlag für Sozialwissenschaften.

Knorr-Cetina, Karin (2005) "Culture in global knowledge societies: Knowledge cultures and epistemic cultures," pp. 65–79 in Mark D. Jacobs and Nancy Weiss Hanrahan (eds), *The Blackwell Companion to the Sociology of Culture*. Oxford: Blackwell.

Koo, Bohn-Young (1982) "New forms of foreign direct investment in Korea," Korean Development Institute, Working Paper No. 82-02.

Krawarz, Teresa and Bessma Monmani (2013) "The World Bank as knowledge bank analyzing the limits of a legitimate global knowledge actor," *Review of Policy Research* 30: 409–431.

Krige, John (2014) "National security and academia: Regulating the international circulation of knowledge," *Bulletin of the Atomic Scientists* 70: 42–52.

Krige, John and Kai-Henrik Barth (2006) "Introduction: Science, technology, and international affairs," *OSIRIS* 21: 1–21.

Kritzman, Lawrence D. (ed.) (1988) *Michel Foucault: Politics, Philosophy, Culture: Interviews and Other Writings 1977–1984*. London: Routledge.

Krohn, Wolfgang (1981) "'Wissen ist Macht': Zur Soziogenese eines neuzeitlichen wissenschaftliches Geltungsanspruchs," pp. 29–57 in K. Bayertz (ed.), *Wissenschaftsgeschichte und wissenschaftliche Revolution*. Köln: Pahl-Rugenstein.

Krohn, Wolfgang (1988) *Francis Bacon*. München: C.H. Beck.

Krohn, Wolfgang and Johannes Weyer (1989) "Gesellschaft als Labor. Die Erzeugung sozialer Risiken durch experimentelle Forschung," *Soziale Welt* 40: 349–373.

Kroto, Harry (2007) "The wrecking of British science," *Guardian*, May 22, Education 1–2.

Krotz, Friedrich (2001) *Die Mediatisierung kommunikativen Handelns: Der Wandel von Alltag und sozialen Beziehungen, Kultur und Gesellschaft durch die Medien*. Wiesbaden: Westdeutscher Verlag.

Krotz, Friedrich (2007) *Mediatisierung: Fallstudien zum Wandel von Kommunikation*. Wiesbaden: SpringerVS.

Krotz, Friedrich (2012) "Von der Entdeckung der Zentralperspektive zur Augmented Reality. Wie Mediatisierung funktioniert," pp. 27–56 in Friedrich Krotz and Andreas Hepp (eds), *Mediatisierte Welten: Forschungsfelder und Beschreibungsansätze*. Wiesbaden: SpringerVS.

Kuhn, Thomas S. (1962) *The Structure of Scientific Revolution*. Chicago, IL: University of Chicago Press.

Kurlat, Pablo and Johannes Stroebel (2014) "Testing for information asymmetries in real estate markets," NBER Working Paper 19875. www.nber.org/papers/w19875.

Kusch, Martin (1991) *Foucault's Strata and Fields: An Investigation into Archaeological and Genealogical Science Studies*. Dordrecht: Kluwer Academic Publishers.

Lam, Alice (1997) "Embedded firms, embedded knowledge: Problem of collaboration and knowledge transfer in global cooperative ventures," *Organization Studies* 18: 973–996.

Lamont, Michèle and Annette Lareau (1988) "Cultural capital: Allusions, gaps and glissandos in recent theoretical developments," *Sociological Theory* 6: 153–168.

Landes, David (1980) "The creation of knowledge and technique: Today's task and yesterday's experience," *Daedalus* 109: 111–119.

Landes, William M. and Richard A. Posner (2003) *The Economic Structure of Intellectual Property Law*. Cambridge, MA: Harvard University Press.

Lane, H. Clifford and Anthony S. Fauci (2001) "Bioterrorism on the home front: A new challenge for American medicine," *Journal of the American Medical Association* 286: 2595–2597.

Lane, Robert E. (1966) "The decline of politics and ideology in a knowledgeable society," *American Sociological Review* 31: 649–662.

Laroche, Mireille and Marcel Mérette (1999) "On the concept and dimensions of human capital in a knowledge-based economy context," *Canadian Public Policy* 25: 87–100.

Lasch, Christopher (1992) "Toward a theory of post-industrial society," pp. 36–50 in M. Donald Hancock and Gideon Sjoberg (eds), *Politics in the Post-welfare State. Responses to the New Individualism*. New York: Columbia University Press.

Latour, Bruno (1998) "From the world of science to the world of research?," *Science* 280: 208–209.

Lave, Jean (1988) *Cognition in Practice. Mind, Mathematics and Culture in Everyday Life*. Cambridge: Cambridge University Press.

Lazarsfeld, Paul F. (1948) "Communication research and the social psychologist," pp. 218–273 in Wayne Dennis (eds), *Current Trends in Social Psychology*. Pittsburgh, PA: University of Pittsburgh Press.

Leach, Melissa and James Fairhead (2002) "Manners of contestation: 'Citizen science' and 'indigenous knowledge' in West Africa and the Caribbean," *International Social Science Journal* 59: 299–311.

Leadbeater, Charles (1999) "New measures for the new economy," in *International Symposium on Measuring and Reporting Intellectual Capital: Experience, Issues and Prospects*. Amsterdam: OECD, June.

Lechner, Frank J. and John Boli (2005) *World Culture. Origins and Consequences*. Oxford: Blackwell.

Leighninger, Matt (2006) *The Next Form of Democracy. How Expert Rule is Giving Way to Shared Governance and Why Politics will Never be the Same*. Nashville, TN: Vanderbilt University Press.

Lemert, Charles C. and Garth Gillan (1982) *Michel Foucault: Social Theory as Transgression*. New York: Columbia University Press.

Leppälä, Samuli (2015) "Economic analysis of knowledge: The history of thought and the central themes," *Journal of Economic Surveys* 29: 263–286.

Leslie, D.A. (1995) "Global scan: The globalization of advertising agencies, concepts, and campaigns," *Economic Geography* 71: 402–426.

Lessig, Lawrence (2004) "The information commons," in Nico Stehr (ed.), *The Governance of Knowledge*. New Brunswick, NJ: Transaction Books.

Lewontin, Richards (2004) "Dishonesty in science," *New York Review of Books*, November 18: 38.

Li, Xing, Megan MacGarvie and Petra Moser (2015) "Dead poet's property: How does copyright influence price?," NBER Working Paper 21522. www.nber.org/papers/w21522.

Liebknecht, Wilhelm ([1872] 1891) *Wissen ist Macht – Macht ist Wissen; Festrede gehalten zum Stiftungsfest des Dresdener Bildungsvereins am 5. Februar 1872. Neue Auflage.* Berlin: Verlag der Expedition des Vorwaerts.

Limoges, Camille (1993) "Expert knowledge and decision-making in controversy contexts," *Public Understanding of Science* 2: 417–426.

Lindahl, Mikael, Mårten Palme, Sofia Sandgren-Massih and Anna Sjögren (2014) "A test of the Becker-Tomes model of human capital transmission using microdata on four generations," *Journal of Human Capital* 8: 80–96.

Lindblom, Charles E. (1995) "Market and democracy – obliquely," *PS: Political Science & Politics* 28: 684–688.

Link, Albert and Christopher Ruhm (2009) "Public knowledge, private knowledge: The intellectual capital of entrepreneurs," NBER Working Paper 14797. www.nber.org/papers/w14797.

Lipset, Seymour Martin (1959) "Some social requisites of democracy: Economic development and political legitimacy," *American Political Science Review* 53: 69–105.

Lipset, Seymour Martin, Martin Trow and James S. Coleman ([1956] 1962) *Union Democracy: The Internal Politics of the International Typographical Union.* New York: Doubleday & Company.

Livingstone, David N. (2002) *Science, Space and Hermeneutics.* Fachbereich Geographie. Universität Heidelberg.

Livingstone, David N. (2003) *Putting Science in its Place. Geographies of Scientific Knowledge.* Chicago, IL: University of Chicago Press.

Livingstone, Sonia (2009) "On the mediatization of everything," *Journal of Communication* 59(1): 1–18.

Livio, Mario (2013) *Brilliant Blunders. From Darwin to Einstein – Colossal Mistakes by Great Scientists that Changed Our Understanding of Life and the Universe.* New York: Simon and Schuster.

Long, Clarisa (2002) "Patent signals," *University of Chicago Law Review* 69: 625–679.

Long, Pamela O. (1991) "Invention, authorship, 'intellectual property,' and the origin of patents: Notes toward a conceptual history," *Technology and Culture* 32: 846–884.

Lowe, Adolph (1971) "Is present-day higher education learning 'relevant'," *Social Research* 38: 563–580.

Lowood, Henry (2008) "Review of Jeanneney, Jean-Noel, Google and the Myth of Universal Knowledge," *Technology and Culture* 49: 298–300.

Loxbo, Karl (2013) "The fare of intra-party democracy: Leadership autonomy and activist influence in the mass party and cartel party," *Party Politics* 19: 537–554.

Luckmann, Thomas (1981) "Vorüberlegungen zum Verhältnis von Alltagswissen und Wissenschaft," pp. 39–51 in Peter Janich (ed.), *Wissenschaftstheorie und Wissenschaftsforschung.* München: C.H. Beck.

Luckmann, Thomas (1982) "Individual action and social knowledge," pp. 247–266 in Mario von Cranach and Rom Harré (eds), *The Analysis of Action. Recent Theoretical and Empirical Advances*. Cambridge: Cambridge University Press.

Luckmann, Thomas ([1982] 2002) "Individuelles Handeln und gesellschaftliches Wissen," pp. 69–89 in Thomas Luckmann, *Wissen und Gesellschaft. Ausgewählte Aufsätze 1981–2002*. Konstanz: UVK.

Luhmann, Niklas ([1981] 1987) "Gesellschaftsstrukturelle Bedingungen und Folgeprobleme des naturwissenschaftlich-technischen Fortschritts," pp. 47–63 in Niklas Luhmann, *Soziologische Aufklärung 4*. Opladen: Westdeutscher Verlag.

Luhmann, Niklas (1988) *Die Wirtschaft der Gesellschaft*. Frankfurt am Main: Suhrkamp.

Luhmann, Niklas ([1986] 1989) *Ecological Communication*. Chicago, IL: University of Chicago Press.

Luhmann, Niklas (1990) *Die Wissenschaft der Gesellschaft*. Frankfurt am Main: Suhrkamp.

Luhmann, Niklas (1992) *Beobachtungen der Moderne*. Opladen: Westdeutscher Verlag.

Luhmann, Niklas ([1984] 1995a) *Social Systems*. Stanford: Stanford University Press.

Luhmann, Niklas (1995b) "Die Soziologie des Wissens. Probleme ihrer theoretischen Konstruktion," pp. 189–201 in Niklas Luhmann, *Gesellschaftsstruktur und Semantik. Studien zur Wissenssoziologie der modernen Gesellschaft*. Volume 4. Frankfurt am Main: Suhrkamp.

Luhmann, Niklas (1997) *Die Gesellschaft der Gesellschaft*. Frankfurt am Main: Suhrkamp.

Luhmann, Niklas ([1996] 2000) *The Reality of the Mass Media*. Cambridge: Polity Press.

Luhmann, Niklas (2002) *Das Erziehungssystem der Gesellschaft*. Frankfurt am Main: Suhrkamp.

Luhmann, Niklas ([1989] 2008) "Ethik als Reflektionstheorie der Moral," pp. 270–347 in Niklas Luhmann, *Die Moral der Gesellschaft*. Frankfurt am Main: Suhrkamp.

Lukasiewicz, Julius (1993) *The Ignorance Explosion. Understanding Industrial Civilization*. Ottawa, Ontario: Carleton University Press.

Lukes, Steven (2007) "The problem of apparently irrational beliefs," pp. 591–606 in Stephen P. Turner and Mark W. Risjord (eds), *Philosophy of Anthropology and Sociology. Handbook of the Philos Sci*. Amsterdam: Elsevier.

Lundby, Knut (2009) *Mediatization – Concept, Changes, Consequences*. New York: Peter Lang.

Lundby, Knut (ed.) (2014) *Mediatization of Communication*. Berlin: Walter de Gruyter.

Luscombe, Mark A. (1996) "Taxation of knowledge," *Taxes* 74: 183.

Lynd, Robert S. (1939) *Knowledge for What?* Princeton, NJ: Princeton University Press.

Lyotard, Jean-Francois ([1979] 1984) *The Postmodern Condition: A Report on Knowledge*. Manchester: Manchester University Press.

Machlup, Fritz (1962) *The Production and Distribution of Knowledge in the United States*. Princeton, NJ: Princeton University Press.

Machlup, Fritz (1979a) "Use, value, and benefits of knowledge," *Knowledge* 1: 62–81.

Machlup, Fritz (1979b) "Stocks and flows of knowledge," *Kyklos* 32: 400–411.

Machlup, Fritz (1981) *Knowledge and Knowledge Production*. Princeton, NJ: Princeton University Press.

Machlup, Fritz (1983) "Semantic quirks in studies of information," in Fritz Machlup and Una Mansfield (eds), *The Study of Information*. New York: Wiley.

Machlup, Fritz (1984) *The Economics of Information and Human Capital*. Princeton, NJ: Princeton University Press.

Malik, Suheil (2005) "Information and knowledge," *Theory, Culture & Society* 22: 29–49.

Malinowski, Bronislaw (1955) *Magic, Science and Religion*. Garden City, NY: Doubleday Anchor.

Mann, Michael (2013) *The Sources of Social Power. Volume 4: Globalizations, 1945–2011*. Cambridge: Cambridge University Press.

Mannheim, Karl ([1929] 1936) *Ideology and Utopia*. London: Routledge.

Mannheim, Karl (1971) "The ideological and sociological interpretation of intellectual phenomena," in Kurt H. Wolff (ed.), *From Karl Mannheim*. New York: Oxford University Press.

Mannheim, Karl ([1925] 1986) *Conservatism. A Contribution to the Sociology of Knowledge*. Edited and introduced by David Kettler, Volker Meja and Nico Stehr. London: Routledge and Kegan Paul.

Mannheim, Karl ([1928] 1993) "The problem of generation," pp. 518–522 in *From Karl Mannheim*. New Brunswick, NJ: Transaction Publishers.

Marten, Lauren Jade (2014) "The world's not ready for this: Globalizing selective technologies," *Science, Technology & Society* 39: 432–445.

Martin, George and Saskia Vermeylen (2005) "Intellectual property, indigenous knowledge, and biodiversity," *Capitalism, Nature and Socialism* 16: 27–48.

Martin, Lauren Jade (2014) "The world's not ready for this: Globalizing selective technologies," *Science, Technology & Human Values* 39: 432–455.

Marx, Karl ([1885] 1976) *Capital*, Vol. 1. Harmondsworth: Penguin.

Marx, Karl and Friedrich Engels ([1848] 1969) "Manifesto of the Communist Party," pp. 98–137 in Marx/Engels, *Selected Works*, Vol. 1. Moscow: Progress Publishers.

Mattelart, Armand ([1996] 2000) *Networking the World, 1794–2000*. Minneapolis: University of Minnesota Press.

Matthews, Duncan (2011) *Intellectual Property, Human Rights and Development: The Role of NGOs and Social Movements*. Cheltenham: Edward Elgar.

Matthijs, Gert (2004) "Patenting genes: May slow down innovation, and delay availability of cheaper genetic tests," *British Medical Journal* 329: 1358.

Mauss, Marcel (1966) *The Gift: Forms and Functions of Exchange in Archaic Societies*. London: Cohen & West.

Mayer-Schönberger, Viktor and Kenneth J. Cukier (2013) *Big Data. A Revolution that will Transform How We Live, Work and Think*. London: John Murray.

Mazur, Allan (1973) "Disputes between experts," *Minerva* 11: 243–262.

McGoey, Linsey (2012) "Strategic unknowns: Towards a sociology of ignorance," *Economy and Society* 41(1): 1–16.

McLuhan, Marshall (1962) *The Gutenberg Galaxy: The Making of Typographic Man*. Toronto: University of Toronto Press.

McNeill, John (2000) *Something New Under the Sun. An Environmental History of the 20th Century*. New York: W.W. Norton.

Megill, Allan (1985) *Prophets of Extremity: Nietzsche, Heidegger, Foucault, Derrida*. Berkeley, CA: University of California Press.

Meja, Volker and Nico Stehr (2005) *Society and Knowledge. Contemporary Perspectives on the Sociology of Knowledge and Science*. Second Edition. New Brunswick, NJ: Transaction Publishers.

Merton, Robert K. (1939) "Bureaucratic structure and personality," *Social Forces* 18: 560–568.

Merton, Robert K. ([1957] 1965) *Social Theory and Social Structure*. Revised and enlarged edition. New York, New York: The Free Press.

Merton, Robert K. (1968) "The Matthew effect in science," *Science* 1959: 56–63.

Merton, Robert K. (1971) "The precarious foundations of detachment in sociology," pp. 188–199 in Edward A. Tiryakian (ed.), *The Phenomenon of Sociology*. New York: Appleton-Century-Crofts.

Merton, Robert K. ([1938] 1973a) "Science and the social order," pp. 254–266 in Robert K. Merton, *The Sociology of Science. Theoretical and Empirical Investigations*. Chicago, IL: University of Chicago Press.

Merton, Robert K. ([1942] 1973b) "The normative structure of science," pp. 267–278 in Robert K. Merton, *The Sociology of Science. Theoretical and Empirical Investigations*. Chicago, IL: University of Chicago Press.

Merton, Robert K. (1981) "Remarks on theoretical pluralism," pp. i–vii in Peter M. Blau and Robert K. Merton (eds), *Continuities in Structural Inquiry*. London: Sage.

Merton, Robert K. (1987) "Three fragments from a sociologist's notebook: Establishing the phenomenon, specified ignorance, and strategic research materials," *Annual Review of Sociology* 13: 1–28.

Meusburger, Peter, Michael Welker and Edgar Wunder (eds) (2008) *Clashes of Knowledge, Orthodoxies and Heterodoxies in Science and Religion.* Heidelberg: Springer, pp. 11–34.

Meyer, John W. (1999) "The changing cultural content of the nation state: A world society perspective," pp. 123–143 in George Steinmetz (ed.), *State/Culture. State-Formation after the Cultural Turn.* Ithaca, NY: Cornell University Press.

Meyer, John W., John Boli, George M. Thomas and Francisco O. Ramirez (1997) "World society and the nation-state," *American Journal of Sociology* 103: 144–181.

Meyer, John W., D. Kamens and Aaron Benavot (1992) *School Knowledge for the Masses.* Washington, DC: Falmer.

Michels, Robert ([1911] 1949) *Political Parties. A Sociological Study of the Oligarchical Tendencies of Modern Democracy.* Glencoe, IL: The Free Press.

Michels, Robert ([1915] 1970) *Zur Soziologie des Parteiwesens in der modernen Demokratie: Untersuchungen über die oligarchischen Tendenzen des Gruppenlebens.* Stuttgart: Alfred Kröner Verlag.

Michels, Robert ([1908] 1987) "Die oligarchischen Tendenzen der Gesellschaft. Ein Beitrag zum Problem der Demokratie," in Robert Michels, *Masse, Führer, Intellektuelle.* Frankfurt am Main: Campus.

Mill, John Stuart ([1831] 1942) *The Spirit of the Age.* Chicago, IL: University of Chicago Press.

Miller, Clark A. (2007) "Democratization, international knowledge institutions, and global governance," *Governance* 20: 325–357.

Miller, Jon D. (1983) *The American People and Science Policy.* New York: Pergamon.

Mincer, Jacob (1974) *Schooling, Experience, and Earnings.* New York: NBER Press.

Mokyr, Joel (1990) *The Lever of Riches. Technological Creativity and Economic Progress.* Oxford: Oxford University Press.

Mokyr, Joel (2005) "The intellectual origins of modern economic growth," *Journal of Economic History* 65: 285–351.

Moore, John A. (1974) "Creationism in California," *Daedalus* 103: 173–189.

Moore, Wilbert E. and Melvin M. Tumin (1949) "Some social functions of ignorance," *American Sociological Review* 14: 787–796.

Mörth, Ulrika (1998) "Policy diffusion in research and technological development: No government is an island," *Cooperation and Conflict* 33: 35–58.

Moscovici, Serge ([1981] 1985) *The Age of the Crowd. A Historical Treatise on Mass Psychology.* Cambridge: Cambridge University Press.

Moser, Petra, Joerg Ohmstedt and Paul W. Rohde (2015) "Patent citations and the size of the inventive step – evidence from hybrid corn," NBER Working Paper 21443. www.nber.org/papers/w21473.

Mulder, Mauk (1971) "Power equalization through participation," *Administrative Science Quarterly* 16: 31–39.

Myrdal, Gunnar (1944) *An American Dilemma. The Negro Problem and Modern Democracy*. With the assistance of Richard Sterner and Arnold Rose. New York: Harper & Brothers.

Narayanaswamy, Lata (2013) "Problematizing 'knowledge-for-development'," *Development and Change* 44: 1065–1086.

Negroponte, Nicholas (1995) *Being Digital*. New York: Knopf.

Nelkin, Dorothy (1975) "The political impact of technical expertise," *Social Studies of Science* 5: 35–54.

Nelson, Benjamin (1973) "Civilizational complexes and intercivilizational encounters," *Sociological Analysis* 34: 79–105.

Nelson, Richard (ed.) (1993) *National Innovation Systems: A Comparative Analysis*. New York: Oxford University Press.

Nelson, Richard R. (2000) "Knowledge and innovation systems," pp. 115–124 in OECD, *Knowledge Management in the Learning Society*. Paris: OECD.

Nelson, Richard R. (2003) "On the uneven evolution of human know-how," *Research Policy* 32: 909–922.

Nelson, Richard R. (2008) "What enables rapid economic progress: What are the needed institutions?," *Research Policy* 37: 1–11.

Neumann, Michael (2009) "Degrees of property," *Think* 22: 75–91.

Neurath, Otto (1991) *Schriften. Band 3: Gesammelte bildpädagogische Schriften*. Wien: Hölder-Pichler-Tempsky.

Neuweg, Hans Georg (2001) "Über die Explizierbarkeit flexibler Muster," pp. 91–108 in Manfred Moldaschl (ed.), *Neue Arbeit – Neue Wissenschaft der Arbeit?* Heidelberg: Kröning Asanger.

Nimkoff, Meyer F. (1957) "Obstacles to innovation," pp. 56–71 in Frances R. Allen et al. (eds), *Technology and Social Change*. New York: Appleton Century-Crofts.

Noelle-Neumann, Elizabeth (1995) "Public opinion and rationality," pp. 33–54 in Theodore L. Glasser and Charles T. Salmon (eds), *Public Opinion and the Communication of Consent*. Introductions by Elihu Katz. New York: Guilford Press.

Nola, Robert (1998) "Knowledge, discourse, power and genealogy in Foucault," *Critical Review of International Social and Political Philosophy* 1: 109–154.

Nonaka, Ikujiro (1994) "A dynamic theory of organizational knowledge creation," *Organization Science* 5: 14–37.

Nonaka, Ikujiro and Takeuchi, Hirotaka (1994) "A dynamic theory of organizational knowledge creation," *Organization Science* 51: 14–37.

Nordhaus, Wilhelm D. (1969) *Invention, Growth and Welfare. A Theoretical Treatment of Technological Change*. Cambridge, MA: MIT Press.

Norris, Pippa (2001) *Digital Divide: Civic Engagement, Information Poverty and the Internet World-wide*. Cambridge, MA: Cambridge University Press.

Nowotny, Helga, Peter Scott and Michael Gibbons (2001) *Rethinking Science. Knowledge and the Public in an Age of Uncertainty*. Oxford: Polity.

Ogburn, William F. ([1922] 1950) *Social Change. With Respect to Culture and Original Nature*. New 1950 edition with supplementary chapter. New York: Viking Press.

Olavarrieta, Sergio, Pedro Hidalgo, Enrique Manzur and Pablo Farias (2012) "Determinants of in-store price knowledge for packaged products: An empirical study in a Chilean hypermarket," *Journal of Business Research* 65: 1759–1766

Olson, Mancur (1982) *The Rise and Decline of Nations. Economic Growth, Stagflation, and Social Relations*. New Haven, CT: Yale University Press.

Olson, Mancur Jr. (1996) "Big bills left on the sidewalk: Why some nations are rich, and others are poor," *The Journal of Economic Perspectives* 10: 3–24.

O'Mara, Margaret Pugh (2005) *Cities of Knowledge. Cold War Science and the Search for the Next Silicon Valley*. Princeton, NJ: Princeton University Press.

Ong, Walter ([1982] 2002) *Orality and Literacy: The Technologizing of the Word*. New York: Routledge.

Orlikowski, Wanda (2006) "Material knowing: The scaffolding of human knowledgeability," *European Journal of Information Systems* 15: 460–466.

Orlove, Ben, Carla Roncali, Merit Kabugo and Abushen Majugu (2009) "Indigenous climate knowledge in southern Uganda: The multiple components of a dynamic regional system," *Climatic Change*. DOI 10.1007/s10584-10009-9586-9582.

Osborne, Thomas and Nikolas Rose (1999) "Do the social sciences create phenomena?: The example of public opinion research," *British Journal of Sociology* 50: 367–396.

Ostrom, Vincent and Elinor Ostrom (1977) "Public goods and public choices," in Emanuel S. Savas (ed.), *Alternatives for Delivering Services. Toward Improved Performance*. Boulder, CO: Westview Press.

Oyama, Susan (2000) *Evolution's Eye. A Systems View of the Biology–Culture Divide*. Durham, NC: Duke University Press.

Paasi, Anssi (2015) "Academic capitalism and the geopolitics of knowledge," pp. 510–523 in John Agnew, Virginia Mamadough, Anna J. Scott and Joanne Sharp (eds), *The Wiley Blackwell Companion to Political Geography*.

Pagano, Ugo (2014) "The crisis of intellectual monopoly capitalism," *Cambridge Journal of Economics* 38: 1409–1429.

Pakes, Ariel and Mark Schankerman (1979) "The rate of obsolescence of knowledge, research gestation lags, and the private rate of return to the research resources," NBER Working Paper No. 346.

Paras, Eric (2006) *Foucault 2.0: Beyond Power and Knowledge*. New York: The Other Press.

Parente, Stephen, L. and Edward C. Prescott (1994) "Barriers to technology adoption and development," *Journal of Political Economy* 102: 298–321.

Parente, Stephen, L. and Edward C. Prescott (2000) *Barriers to Riches*. London: MIT Press.

Park, Robert E. (1940) "News as a form of knowledge: A chapter in the sociology of knowledge," *American Journal of Sociology* 45: 669–686.

Park, Walter G. (1995) "International R&D spillovers and OECD economic growth," *Economic Inquiry* 33: 571–591.

Parker, Elisabeth S., Larry Cahill and James L. McHaugh (2006) "A case of unusual autobiographical remembering," *Neurocase: The Neural Basis of Cognition* 12: 35–49.

Parsons, Talcott (1937) *The Structure of Social Action*. New York: McGraw-Hill.

Parsons, Talcott (1938) "The role of ideas in social action," *American Sociological Review* 3: 652–664.

Parsons, Talcott (1951) "Illness and the role of the physician: A sociological perspective," *American Journal of Orthopsychiatry* 21: 452–460.

Parsons, Talcott ([1949] 1954) "Social classes and class conflict in the light of recent sociological theory," pp. 323–335 in Talcott Parsons, *Essays in Sociological Theory*. New York: Free Press.

Parsons, Talcott (1975) "The sick role and role of the physician reconsidered," *The Milbank Memorial Fund Quarterly* 53: 257–278.

Patel, Pari and Keith Pavitt (1991) "Large firms in the production of the world's technology: An important case of 'non-globalisation'," *Journal of International Business Studies* 22: 1–21.

Pénin, Julien (2007) "Open knowledge disclosure: An overview of the evidence and economic motivations," *Journal of Economic Surveys* 21: 326–348.

Peters, Michael A. and James Reveley (2012) "Retrofitting Drucker: Knowledge work under cognitive capitalism," *Culture and Organization*. DOI: 10.1080/14759551.2012.692591.

Petersen, Thomas and Malte Faber (2004) "Verantwortung, Kuppelproduktion, Wissen und die Bedeutung von Nichtwissen," pp. 173–200 in Martin Held, Gisela Kubon-Gilke and Richard Sturn (eds), *Normative und institutionelle Grundfragen der Ökonomik. Jahrbuch 3: Ökonomik des Wissens*. Marburg: Metropolis.

Pew Research Center for The People & the Press (2009) *Public Praises Science; Scientists Fault Public, Media. Scientific Achievements Less Prominent than a Decade Ago*. Washington, DC. www.people-press.org/files/legacy-pdf/528.pdf.

Phelps, Edmund (2013) *Mass Flourishing. How Grassroots Innovation Created Jobs, Challenge, and Change*. Princeton, NJ: Princeton University Press.

Philip, Scranton (1997) *Endless Novelty: Specialty Production and American Industrialization, 1865–1925*. Princeton, NJ: Princeton University Press.

Pickering, Andrew (ed.) (1995) The *Mangle of Practice, Time, Agency and Science*. Chicago, IL: University of Chicago Press.

Pielke, Roger A. Jr. (2007) *The Honest Broker. Making Sense of Science in Policy and Politics*. Cambridge: Cambridge University Press.

Pigou, Arthur C. (1924) *The Economics of Welfare*. London: Macmillan.

Piketty, Thomas ([2013] 2014) *Capital in the Twentieth-First Century*. Cambridge, MA: Harvard University Press.

Pilnick, Alison (1998) "Why didn't you say just that? Dealing with issues of asymmetry, knowledge and competence in the pharmacist client/encounter," *Sociology of Health & Illness* 20: 29–51.

Pinch, Trevor and Wiebe Bijker (1984) "The social construction of facts and artifacts: Or how the sociology of science and the sociology of technology might benefit each other," *Social Studies of Science* 14: 399–441.

Pinder, Wilhelm (1926) *Das Problem der Generationen in der Kunstgeschichte Europas*. Berlin: Frankfurter Verlagsanstalt.

Plant, Arnold (1934a) "The economic theory concerning patents for inventions," *Economica* 1: 30–51.

Plant, Arnold (1934b) "The economic aspects of copyright in books," *Economica* 1: 167–195.

Plotnitsky, Arkady (2002) *Knowledge and the Unknowable. Modern Science, Nonclassical Thought, and the "Two Cultures."* Ann Arbor, MI: University of Michigan Press.

Plümacher, Martina (2006) "'Weltwissen'. Ein sprachwissenschaftlicher Terminus phänomenologisch betrachtet," pp. 247–261 in Dieter Lohmar and Dirk Fontana (eds), *Interdisziplinäre Perspektiven der Phänomenologie*. Amsterdam: Springer Netherlands.

Poggi, Gianfranco (1982) "The modern state and the idea of progress," pp. 337–369 in Gabriel A. Almond, Marvin Chodorow and Roy Harvey Pearce (eds), *Progress and its Discontents*. Berkeley: University of California Press.

Polanyi, Michael (1958) *Personal Knowledge. Towards a Post-Critical Philosophy*. London: Routledge & Kegan Paul.

Polanyi, Michael (1967) *The Tacit Dimension*. New York: Doubleday.

Polanyi, Michael (1969) *Knowing and Being*. Chicago, IL: University of Chicago Press.

Popitz, Heinrich (1968) *Über die Präventivwirkung des Nichtwissens. Dunkelziffer, Norm und Strafe*. Tübingen: J.C.B. Mohr (Paul Siebeck).

Popitz, Heinrich (1986) *Phänomene der Macht. Autorität – Herrschaft – Gewalt – Technik*. Tübingen: J.C.B. Mohr (Paul Siebeck).

Popper, Karl ([1960] 1962) "On the sources of knowledge and ignorance," pp. 3–30 in Karl Popper, *Conjectures and Refutations. The Growth of Scientific Knowledge*. London: Routledge & Kegan Paul.

Popper, Karl ([1979] 1984) "Über Wissen und Nichtwissen," pp. 41–54 in Karl Popper, *Auf der Suche nach einer besseren Welt. Vorträge und Aufsätze aus dreißig Jahren*. München: Piper.

Porat, Marc (1977) *The Information Economy. Definition and Measurement*. Washington, DC: US Department of Commerce, Office of Telecommunications.

Porter, Michael E. (1990) *The Competitive Advantage of Nations*. New York: Free Press.

Poser, Hans (2011) "Knowledge of ignorance: On the problem of the development and the assessment of technology," *Rethinking Epistemology* 1: 369–391.

Pottage, Alain (1998) "The inscription of life in law: Genes, patents, and bio-politics," *The Modern Law Review* 61: 740–765.

Proctor, Robert N. and Londa Schiebinger (eds) (2008) *Agnotology. The Making & Unmaking of Ignorance*. Stanford, CA: Stanford University Press.

Prusak, Lawrence (ed.) (1997) *Knowledge in Organizations (Knowledge Reader)*. Boston, MA: Butterworth-Heinemann.

Przeworski, Adam, Michael Alvarez, José A. Cheibub and Fernando Limongi (2000) *Democracy and Development. Political Institutions and Material Well-being in the World, 1950–1990*. New York: Cambridge University Press.

Qi, Xiaoying (2013) "Intellectual entrepreneurs and the diffusion of ideas: Two historical cases of knowledge flow," *American Journal of Cultural Sociology* 1: 346–372.

Radder, Hans (1986) "Experiment, technology and the intrinsic connection between knowledge and power," *Social Studies of Science* 16: 663–683.

Radhakrishnan, Smitha (2007) "Rethinking knowledge for development: Transnational knowledge professionals and the 'new' India," *Theory and Society* 36: 141–159.

Ravetz, Jerome R. (1986) "Useable knowledge, useable ignorance," pp. 415–432 in William C. Clark and R.E. Munn (eds), *Sustainable Development of the Biosphere*. Cambridge: Cambridge University Press.

Ravetz, Jerome R. (1987) "Usable knowledge, usable ignorance." *Knowledge* 9: 87–116.

Ravetz, Jerome R. (1993) "The sin of science," *Knowledge: Creation, Diffusion, Utilization* 15: 157–165.

Rayner, Steve (2012) "Uncomfortable knowledge: The social construction of ignorance in science and environmental policy discourses," *Economy and Society* 41: 107–125.

Rescher, Nicholas (1978) *Scientific Progress*. Oxford: Blackwell.

Resnik, David B. (2004) *Owning the Genome: A Moral Analysis of DNA Patenting*. Albany, New York: State University Press of New York.

Richey, Lisa Ann (2008) "Global knowledge/local bodies: Family planning service providers' interpretations of contraceptive knowledge(s)," *Demographic Research* 18: 469–498.

Richta, Radovan et al. (1969) *Civilization at the Crossroads: Social and Human Implications of the Scientific and Technological Revolution*. White Plains, New York: International Arts and Sciences Press.

Ritter, Gerhard A. (1978) "Workers' culture in imperial Germany: Problems and points of departure," *Journal of Contemporary History* 13: 165–189.

Roberts, Joanne and John Armitage (2008) "The ignorance economy," *Prometheus* 26: 335–354.

Robinson, James Harvey (1923) *The Humanizing of Knowledge*. New York, New York: George H. Doran.

Rogers, Everett M. (1964) *The Diffusion of Innovation*. Glencoe, Ill.: Free Press.

Romer, Paul (1990) "Endogenous technological change," *Journal of Political Economy* 98: S71–S102.

Rose, Nikolas (1991) "Governing by numbers: Figuring out democracy," *Accounting, Organizations and Society* 16: 673–692.

Rose, Nikolas and Peter Miller (1992) "Political power beyond the state: Problematics of government," *British Journal of Sociology* 43: 173–205.

Rosenau, James N. (2005) "Illusions of power and empire," *History and Theory* 44: 73–87.

Rosenberg, Charles (1997) "Toward an ecology of knowledge: On discipline, context, and history," pp. 225–239 in Charles Rosenberg, *No Other Gods: On Science and American Thought*. Revised and expanded edition. Baltimore, MD: Johns Hopkins University Press.

Rosewall, Bridget (2005) "The knowledge of price and the price of knowledge," *Futures* 37: 699–710.

Rouse, Joseph (1987) *Knowledge and Power. Toward a Political Philos Sci*. Ithaca, NY: Cornell University Press; Princeton, NJ: Princeton University Press.

Rousseau, Jean-Jacques ([1762] 1979) *Emile, or On Education*, translation Allan Bloom. New York: Basic Books.

Ryle, Gilbert ([1949] 2000) *The Concept of Mind*. New York: Penguin Books.

Samuelson, Paul A. (1954) "The pure theory of public expenditures," *Review of Economics and Statistics* 36: 387–389.

Sandler, Todd (2001) *Economic Concepts for the Social Sciences*. Cambridge: Cambridge University Press.

Sandner, Günther (2014) *Otto Neurath. Eine politische Biographie*. Wien: Zsolnay Verlag.

Sarewitz, Daniel and Richard P. Nelson (2008) "Progress in know-how. Its origins and limits," *Innovations* 3: 101–117.

Sartori, Giovanni (1968) "Democracy," pp. 112–121 in Davis Sills (ed.), *International Encyclopedia of the Social Sciences*. Volume 4. New York: Macmillan and Free Press.

Saxer, Ulrich (1978) "Medienverhalten und Wissensstand – zur Hypothese der wachsenden Wissenskluft," pp. 35–70 in Deutsche Lesegesellschaft (ed.), *Buch und Lesen*. Gütersloh: Bertelsmann.

Scaff, Lawrence A. (1981) "Max Weber and Robert Michels," *American Journal of Sociology* 86: 1269–1286.

Scheler, Max ([1925] 1960) "The forms of knowledge and culture," pp. 13–49 in Max Scheler, *Philosophical Perspectives*. Boston, MA: Beacon Press.

Schelsky, Helmut ([1961] 1965) "Der Mensch in der wissenschaftlichen Zivilisation," pp. 439–480 in Helmut Schelsky, *Auf der Suche nach der Wirklichkeit. Gesammelte Aufsätze*. Düsseldorf: Diederichs.

Schelsky, Helmut (1975) *Die Arbeit tun die anderen. Klassenkampf und Priesterherrschaft der Intellektuellen*. Zweite Auflage, Opladen: Westdeutscher Verlag.

Scherer, Bonnie A. (2004–05) "Footing the bill for a sound education in New York City: The implementation of campaign for fiscal equity v. state," *Fordham Urban Law Journal* 32: 901–935.

Schiebinger, Londa (2008) "West Indian abortifacients and the making of ignorance," pp. 149–162 in Robert N. Proctor and Londa Schiebinge (ed.), *Agnotology. The Making & Unmaking of Ignorance*. Stanford, CA: Stanford University Press.

Schiller, Herbert I. (1996) *Informational Inequality. The Deepening Social Crisis in America*. New York: Routledge.

Schoellman, Tod (2012) "Education quality and development accounting," *Review of Economic Studies* 79: 388–417.

Schofer, Evan (1999) "The rationalization of science and scientization of society: International science organizations, 1870–1990," pp. 246–266 in John Boli and George M. Thomas (eds), *Constructing World Culture. International Nongovernmental Organizations since 1875*. Stanford, CA: Stanford University Press.

Schönbach, Klaus (2007) "'The own in the foreign': Reliable surprise – an important function of the media?" *Media Culture & Society* 29(2): 344–353.

Schott, Thomas (1988) "International influence in science: Beyond center and periphery," *Social Science Research* 17: 219–238.

Schott, Thomas (1993) "World science: Globalization of institutions and participation," *Science, Technology & Human Values* 18: 196–208.

Schott, Thomas (1998) "Ties between centers and periphery in the scientific world-system," *Journal of World-Systems Research* 4: 112–144. csf.colorado.edu/jwsr/archive/vol4/v4n2a3.htm (accessed 28. 12. 15).

Schott, Thomas (2001) "Global webs of knowledge," *American Behavioral Scientist* 44: 1740–1751.

Schrape, Jan-Felix (2011) "Social Media, Massenmedien und gesellschaftliche Wirklichkeitskonstruktion," *Berliner Journal für Soziologie* 21: 407–429.

Schroeder, Ralph and Richard Swedberg (2002) "Weberian perspectives on science, technology and the economy," *British Journal of Sociology* 53: 383–401.

Schultz, Theodore W. (1961) "Investment in human capital," *American Economic Review* 51: 1–17.

Schulz, Winfried (2013) "Medialisierung – Was war noch gleich die Frage?" pp. 49–66 in Jackob, Nikolaus et al. (eds), *Realismus als Beruf. Beiträge zum Verhältnis von Medien und Wirklichkeit*. Wiesbaden: SpringerVS.

Schumann, Jochen (2003) "Human capital, knowledge and knowledge sharing: A view from the history of economic thoughts," pp. 121–128 in Ernst Helmstädter (ed.), *The Economics of Knowledge Sharing: A New Institutional Approach*. Cheltenham: Edward Elgar.

Schumpeter, Joseph ([1912] 1934) *The Theory of Economic Development*. Cambridge, MA: Harvard University Press.

Schütz, Alfred (1946) "The well-informed citizen. An essay on the social distribution of knowledge," *Social Research* 13: 463–478.

Schütz, Alfred (1959) "Tiresias oder unser Wissen von zukünfigen Ereignissen," pp. 259–278 in Alfred Schütz, *Gesammelte Werke. Aufsätze II. Studien zur soziologische Theorie*. The Hague: Nijhoff.

Schütz, Alfred (1964) *Collected Papers*. Volume II. The Hague: Nijhoff.

Schütz, Alfred ([1964] 2003) *Theorie der Lebenswelt 2 – Die kommunikative Ordnung der Lebenswelt*. Konstanz: UVK.

Schwartz, Jacob T. (1992) "America's economic-technological agenda for the 1990s," *Daedalus* 121: 139–165.

Seemann, Michael (2014) *Das neue Spiel. Strategien für die Welt nach dem digitalen Kontrollverlust*. Berlin: Orange-Press.

Sen, Amartya (1981) "Ingredients of famine analysis: Availability and entitlements," *Quarterly Journal of Economics* 96: 433–464.

Shaffer, Harry G. (1961) "Investment in human capital: Comment," *American Economic Review* 52: 1026–1035.

Shannon, Claude ([1948] 1949) *The Mathematical Theory of Communication*. Urbana, IL: University of Illinois Press.

Shapin, Steven (1995) "Here and everywhere: Sociology of scientific knowledge," *Annual Review of Sociology* 21: 289–321.

Shapin, Steven (2001) "Proverbial economies: How an understanding of some linguistic and social features of common sense can throw light on more prestigious bodies of knowledge, science for example," *Social Studies of Science* 31: 731–769.

Shattuck, Roger (1996) *Forbidden Knowledge. From Prometheus to Pornography*. San Diego, CA: Harcourt Brace & Company.

Shils, Edward (1974) "Faith, utility, and the legitimacy of science," *Daedalus* 3(103): 1–15.

Shils, Edward (1982) "Knowledge and the sociology of knowledge," *Science Communication* 4: 7–32.
Shiva, Vandana (2001) "Biopiracy: The theft of knowledge and resources," pp. 283–289 in Brian Tokar (ed.), *Redesigning Life. The Worldwide Challenge to Genetic Engineering*. Montreal: McGill-Queen's University Press.
Sibley, Mulford Q. (1973) "Utopian thought and technology," *American Journal of Political Science* 17: 255–281.
Sillitoe, Paul (2007) "Local science vs. global science: An overview," pp. 1–22 in Paul Sillitoe (ed.), *Local Science vs. Global Science. Approaches to Indigenous Knowledge in International Development*. Oxford: Berghahn Books.
Simmel, Georg (1906) "The sociology of secrecy and of secret societies," *American Journal of Sociology* 11: 441–498.
Simmel, Georg ([1900] 1907) *Philosophie des Geldes. 2. vermehrte Auflage*. Leipzig: Dunker & Humblot.
Simmel, Georg ([1911/12] 1968) "On the concept and the tragedy of culture," pp. 27–46 in Georg Simmel, *The Conflict in Modern Culture and Other Essays*. New York: Teachers College Press.
Simmel, Georg ([1907] 1978) *The Philosophy of Money*. London: Routledge and Kegan Paul.
Simmel, Georg ([1890] 1989a) "Über sociale Differenzierung," pp.109–295 in Georg Simmel, *Aufsätze 1987–1980. Über sociale Differenzierung. Die Probleme der Geschichtsphilosophie. Gesamtausgabe 2*. Frankfurt am Main: Suhrkamp.
Simmel, Georg ([1907] 1989b) *Philosophie des Geldes. Gesamtausgabe Band 6*. Frankfurt am Main: Suhrkamp.
Simmel, Georg ([1908] 1992a) "Das Geheimnis und die geheime Gesellschaft," pp. 383–455 in Georg Simmel, *Soziologie. Gesamtausgabe Band 11*. Frankfurt am Main: Suhrkamp.
Simmel, Georg ([1908] 1992b) *Soziologie. Über die Formen der Vergesellschaftung*. Frankfurt: Suhrkamp.
Simmel, Georg ([1922] 2009) "The secret and the secret society," pp. 307–362 in Georg Simmel, *Sociology: Inquiries into the Construction of Social Forms*. Leiden and Boston: Brill.
Simon, Herbert (1999) "The many shapes of knowledge," *Revue d'Economie Industrielle* 88: 23–39.
Simonson, Peter (2010) *Refiguring Mass Communication: A History*. Chicago, IL: University of Illinois Press.
Sinsheimer, Robert L. (1978) "The presumptions of science," *Daedalus* 107: 23–35.
Smith, Adam ([1776] 1976) *The Wealth of Nations*. Oxford: Oxford University Press.
Smithson, Michael J. (1985) "Toward a social theory of ignorance," *Journal for the Theory of Social Behavior* 15: 151–172.

Sokol, D. Daniel and Kyle W. Stiegert (2009) "Exporting knowledge through technical assistance and capacity building," *Journal of Competition Law & Economics*: 1–19.

Sowell, Thomas (1980) *Knowledge and its Decisions*. New York: Basic Books.

Spariosu, Mihai I. (2005) *Global Intelligence and Human Development. Toward an Ecology of Global Learning*. Cambridge, MA: MIT Press.

Squicciarini, Mara P. and Nico Vogtlaender (2014) "Human capital and industrialization: Evidence from the age of enlightenment," NBER Working Paper No. 20219. www.nber.org/papers/w20219.

Stalder, Felix (2012) "Between democracy and spectacle: The front-end and back-end of the social web," pp. 242–256 in Michael Mandiberg (eds), *The Social Media Reader*. New York: NYU-Press.

Starbuck, William H. (1992) "Learning by knowledge-intensive firms," *Journal of Management Studies* 29: 713–740.

Stehr, Nico (1991) *Praktische Erkenntnis*. Frankfurt am Main: Suhrkamp.

Stehr, Nico (1992) *Practical Knowledge. Applying the Social Sciences*. London: Sage.

Stehr, Nico (1994) *Knowledge Societies*. London: Sage.

Stehr, Nico (1999) "The future of inequality," *Society* 36: 54–59.

Stehr, Nico (2000) *Die Zerbrechlichkeit moderner Gesellschaften. Die Stagnation der Macht und die Chancen des Individuums*. Weilerswist: Velbrück.

Stehr, Nico (2000a) *Knowledge and Economic Conduct: The Foundations of the Modern Economy*. Toronto: University of Toronto Press.

Stehr, Nico (2000b) "Deciphering information technologies: Modern societies as networks," *European Journal of Social Theory* 3: 84–93.

Stehr, Nico (2001) *The Fragility of Modern Societies. Knowledge and Risk in the Information Age*. London: Sage.

Stehr, Nico (2002) *Knowledge and Economic Conduct: The Social Foundations of the Modern Economy*. Toronto: University of Toronto Press.

Stehr, Nico (2003) *Wissenspolitik. Die Überwachung des Wissens*. Suhrkamp: Frankfurt am Main.

Stehr, Nico (2004a) "The social role of knowledge," pp. 84–113 in Nikolai Genov (ed.), *Advances in Sociological Knowledge*. Paris: International Social Science Council.

Stehr, Nico (ed.) (2004b) *The Governance of Knowledge*. New Brunswick, NJ: Transaction Books.

Stehr, Nico (2005) *Knowledge Politics. Governing the Consequences of Science and Technology*. Boulder, CO: Paradigm Press.

Stehr, Nico (2009) "Nothing has been decided: The chances and risks of feasible globalization," pp. 334–355 in Samir Dasgupta and Jan Nederveen Pieterse (eds), *Politics of Globalization*. London: Sage.

Stehr, Nico (2013a) "Knowledge and non-knowledge," *Science, Technology & Innovation Studies* 8: 3–13.

Stehr, Nico (2013b) "Mut zur Lücke. Zur Emanzipation des Nichtwissens in der modernen Gesellschaft," *Kursbuch* 173: 164–178.

Stehr, Nico (2015a) *Die Freiheit ist eine Tochter des Wissens*. Wiesbaden: Springer VS.

Stehr, Nico (2015b) "Knowledge society, history of," pp. 105–110 in James D. Wright (ed.-in-chief), *International Encyclopedia of the Social & Behavioral Sciences*. Second edition, Volume 13. Oxford: Elsevier.

Stehr, Nico (2016) *Information, Power, and Democracy. Liberty is a Daughter of Knowledge*. Cambridge: Cambridge University Press.

Stehr, Nico and Marian Adolf (2009) "Die neue Macht der Kreativität: Wissensklassen in modernen Gesellschaften," pp. 185–206 in Stephan A. Jansen, Eckhard Schröter and Nico Stehr (eds), *Rationalität der Kreativität? Multidisziplinäre Beiträge zur Analyse der Produktion, Organisation und Bildung von Kreativität*. Wiesbaden: VS-Verlag.

Stehr, Nico and Marian Adolf (2015) *Ist Wissen Macht? Erkenntnisse über Wissen*. Weilerswist: Velbrück.

Stehr, Nico and Reiner Grundmann (2003) "Social control and knowledge in democratic societies," *Science and Public Policy* 30: 183–188.

Stehr, Nico and Reiner Grundmann (2010) *Expertenwissen*. Weilerswist: Velbrück Wissenschaft.

Stehr, Nico and Ulrich Ufer (2009) "On the global distribution and dissimitation of knowledge," *International Social Science Journal* 60: 7–24.

Stent, Gunther S. (1969) *The Coming of the Golden Age. A View of the End of Progress*. Garden City. New York: National History Press.

Stern, Scott, Michael E. Porter and Jeffrey L. Furman (2000) "The determinants of national innovative capacity," National Bureau of Economic Research Working Paper 7876. www.nber.org/papers/w7876.

Stewart, Thomas A. (1997) *Intellectual Capital. The New Wealth of Organizations*. New York: Doubleday.

Stigler, George J. (1980) "An introduction to privacy in economics and politics," *The Journal of Legal Studies* 9: 623–644.

Stiglitz, Joseph E. (1987) "Learning to learn, localized learning and technological progress," pp. 125–153 in Partha S. Dasgupta and Paul Stoneman (eds), *Economic Policy and Technological Performance*. Cambridge: Cambridge University Press.

Stiglitz, Joseph E. (1995) "The theory of international public goods and the architecture of international organizations," United Nations Background Paper 7. New York: United Nations.

Stiglitz, Joseph E. (1999) "Knowledge as a global public good," pp. 308–325 in Inge Kaul, Isabelle Grunberg and Marc A. Stern (eds), *Global Public Goods. International Co-operation in the 21st Century*. New York: Oxford University Press.

Stiglitz, Joseph (2000a) "Scan globally, reinvent locally," *Development and Change* 4: 8–11.

Stiglitz, Joseph E. (2000b) "The contributions of the economics of information to twentieth century economics," *The Quarterly Journal of Economics* 115: 1441–1478.

Stiglitz, Joseph E. (2001) "Information and the changes in the paradigm of economics," (Nobel Lecture): 472–540.

Stiglitz, Joseph E. ([2001] 2002) "Information and the changes in the paradigm of economics," (Nobel Lecture) *American Economic Review* 92: 460–501.

Stiglitz, Joseph E. (2005) "The ethical economist," *Foreign Affairs* 84: 128–134.

Stiglitz, Joseph E. (2007) *Making Globalization Work. The Next Steps to Global Justice*. London: Allen Lane.

Stiglitz, Joseph E. (2010) "Intellectual property, dissemination of innovation, and sustainable development," *Global Policy* 1: 237–251.

Stiglitz, Joseph E. (2012) *The Price of Inequality. How Today's Divided Society Endangers Our Future*. New York: Norton.

Stiglitz, Joseph E. (2014) "Intellectual property rights, the pool of knowledge, and innovation," NBER Working Paper 20014. www.nber.org/paers/w20014.

Stiglitz, Joseph E. (2015) "The measurement of wealth: Recessions, sustainability and inequality," NBER Working Paper 21327. www.nber.org/papers/w21327.

Stiglitz, Joseph E. and Bruce G. Greenwald (2014) *Creating a Learning Society. A New Approach to Growth, Development, and Social Progress*. New York: Columbia University Press.

Stocking, S. Holly (1998) "On drawing attention to ignorance," *Science Communication* 20: 165–178.

Stocking, S. Holly and Lisa W. Holstein (1993) "Constructing and reconstructing scientific ignorance," *Knowledge: Creation, Diffusion, Utilization* 15: 186–210.

Stone, Diana (2002) "Introduction: Global networks and advocacy networks," *Global Networks* 2: 1–11.

Storper, Michael (1996) "Institutions of the knowledge-based economy," pp. 255–283 in Organisation for Economic Co-operation and Development, *Employment and Growth in the Knowledge-Based Economy*. Paris: OECD.

Strathern, Marilyn (2005) "Imagined collectivities and multiple ownership," pp. 13–28 in Rishab A. Gnosh (ed.), *Code. Collaborative Ownership and the Digital Economy*. Cambridge, MA: MIT Press.

Strauss, Leo (1947) "On the intention of Rousseau," *Social Research* 14: 455–487.

Sturgis, Patrick, Nick Allum and Patten Smith (2008) "An experiment on the measurement of political knowledge in surveys," *Public Opinion Quarterly* 85: 90–102.

Swidler, Ann (1986) "Culture as action," *American Sociological Review* 51: 273–286.

Tan, Emrullah (2014) "Human capital theory: A holistic criticism," *Review of Educational Research* 84: 411–445.

Tangens, Rena (2006) "Tausche Bürgerrechte gegen Linsengericht. Die Wir-Wollen-Alles-Über-Sie-Wissensgesellschaft," pp. 196–205 in Grüne Akademie der Heinrich Böll Stiftung (ed.), *Die Verfasstheit der Wissensgesellschaft*. Münster: Westfälisches Dampfboot.

Teece, David J. (1977) "Technology transfer by multinational firms: The resource cost of transferring technological know-how," *Economic Journal* 87: 242–261.

Teece, David J. (1998) "Capturing value from knowledge assets: The new economy, markets for know-how, and intangible assets," *California Management Review* 40: 55–79.

Teixeira, Pedro Nuno (2014) "Gary Becker's early work on human capital – collaborations and distinctiveness," *IZA Journal of Labor Economics* 3: 12. DOI: 10.1186/s40172-40014-0012-0012.

Tenbruck, Friedrich H. (1969) "Regulative Funktionen der Wissenschaft in der pluralistischen Gesellschaft," pp. 61–85 in Herbert Scholz (ed.), *Die Rolle der Wissenschaft in der modernen Gesellschaft*. Berlin: Duncker & Humblot.

Tenbruck, Friedrich H. ([1989] 1996) "Gesellschaftsgeschichte oder Weltgeschichte," pp. 75–98 in Friedrich H. Tenbruck, *Perspektiven der Kultursoziologie*. Opladen: Westdeutscher Verlag.

Thompson, John B. (1995) *The Media and Modernity. A Social Theory of the Media*. Stanford, CA: Stanford University Press.

Thurow, Lester C. (1996) *The Future of Capitalism. How Today's Economic Forces Shape Tomorrow's World*. New York: Morrow.

Tichenor, Philip J., George A. Donohue and Clarice N. Olien (1970) "Mass media flow and differential growth in knowledge," *Public Opinion Quarterly* 34(2): 159–170.

Tomaselli, Keyan G. (2014) "Who owns what? Indigenous knowledge and struggles over representation," *Critical Arts: South-North Cultural and Media Studies* 28: 631–647.

Toulmin, Stephen (1972) *Human Understanding*. Princeton, NJ: Princeton University Press.

Touraine, Alan ([1992] 1995) *Critique of Modernity*. Oxford: Blackwell.

Toynbee, Arnold (1946) *A Study of History, Abridgement of Volumes I–IV*. New York: Oxford University Press.

Trottier, Daniel (2012) *Social Media as Surveillance: Rethinking Visibility in a Converging World*. Farnham: Ashgate.

Tsoukas, H. (1996) "The firm as distributed knowledge system: A discursive approach," *Strategic Management Journal* 17: 11–25.

Turner, Stephen (1990) "Forms of patronage," pp. 185–211 in Susan Cozzens and Thomas F. Gieryn (eds), *Theories of Science in Society*. Bloomington, IN: Indiana University Press.

Tversky, Amos and Daniel Kahneman (1974) "Judgment under uncertainty: Heuristics and biases," *Science* 185: 1124–1131.

Tywoniak, Stephane A. (2007) "Knowledge in four deformation dimensions," *Organization* 14: 53–76.

Ungar, Sheldon (2008) "Ignorance as an under-identified social problem," *British Journal of Sociology* 59: 301–326.

UNU-IHDP and UNEP (2014) *Inclusive Wealth Report 2014. Measuring Progress Toward Sustainability*. Cambridge: Cambridge University Press.

Urry, John (2003) *Global Complexity*. Cambridge: Polity.

Van den Daele, Wolfgang (1996) "Objektives Wissen als politische Ressource: Experten und Gegenexperten im Diskurs," pp. 297–326 in Wolfgang van den Daele and Friedhelm Neidhardt (eds), *Kommunikation und Entscheidung*. Berlin: Sigma.

Van der Geest, Sjaak, Susan Reynods White and Anita Hardon (1996) "The anthropology of pharmaceuticals: A biographical approach," *Annual Review of Anthropology* 25: 153–178.

Van Doorn, Niels (2014) "The neoliberal subject of value: Measuring human capital in information economies," *Cultural Politics* 10: 354–375.

Veblen, Thorstein ([1908] 1919) "The nature of capital," pp. 324–386 in Thorstein Veblen, *The Place of Science in Modern Civilisation and Other Essays*. New York: The Viking Press.

Volpert, Walter (1985) *Zauberlehrlinge. Die gefährliche Liebe zum Computer*. Weinheim: Beltz.

Von Hippel, Eric (1991) "The impact of 'sticky information' on innovation and problem-solving," Sloan School of Management, MIT, Working Papers BPS 33147 (revised).

Von Hippel, Eric (1994) "'Sticky information' and the locus of problem solving: Implications for innovation," *Management Science* 40: 429–439.

Wacquant, Loic D. (1989) "Towards a reflexive sociology: A workshop with Pierre Bourdieu," *Sociological Theory* 7: 26–63.

Wallerstein, Immanuel ([2003] 2004a) "Global culture(s). Salvation, menace, or myth?," pp. 142–150 in Immanuel Wallerstein, *The Uncertainties of Knowledge*. Philadelphia, PA: Temple University Press.

Wallerstein, Immanuel (2004b) *The Uncertainties of Knowledge*. Philadelphia, PA: Temple University Press.

Wang, Xianghong (2012) "When workers do not know – The behavioural effects of minimum wage laws revisited," *Journal of Economic Psychology* 33: 951–962.

Warren, Dennis M. (1991) "Using indigenous knowledge in agricultural development," World Bank Discussion Paper 127. Washington, DC: World Bank.

Watson-Verran, Helen and David Turnbull (1995) "Science and other indigenous knowledge systems," pp. 115–139 in Sheila Jasanoff, Gerald E. Markle, James C. Peterson and Trevor Pinch (eds), *Handbook of Science and Technology Studies*. Thousand Oaks, CA: Sage.

Weber, Max ([1904] 1922a) "Die 'Objektivität' sozialwissenschaftlicher und sozialpolitischer Erkenntnis," pp. 146–214 in Max Weber, *Gesammelte Aufsätze zur Wissenschaftslehre*. Tübingen: J.C.B. Mohr (Paul Siebeck).

Weber, Max ([1919] 1922b) "Wissenschaft als Beruf," pp. 524–555 in Max Weber, *Gesammelte Aufsätze zur Wissenschaftslehre*. Tübingen: J.C.B. Mohr (Paul Siebeck).

Weber, Max ([1922] 1964) *The Theory of Social and Economic Organization*. Edited with an introduction by Talcott Parsons. New York: Free Press.

Weber, Max ([1922] 1968) *Economy and Society*. New York: Bedminster Press.

Weber, Max ([1920] 1978) *Gesammelte Aufsätze zur Religionssoziologie*. Volume 1. Tübingen: J.C.B. Mohr (Paul Siebeck).

Weber, Max ([1911] 1988) "Geschäftsbericht auf dem ersten Deutschen Soziologentage in Frankfurt 1910," pp. 431–449 in Marianne Weber (ed.), *Gesammelte Aufsätze zur Soziologie und Sozialpolitk*. Tübingen. www.zeno.org/nid/20011442131.

Weber, Max ([1919] 1989) *Max Weber's Science as a Vocation*. Edited by Peter Lassman and Irving Velody with Herminio Martins. London: Unwin Hyman.

Webster, Frank (2014) *Theories of the Information Society*. Fourth edition (e-book). London: Routledge. VitalSource Bookshelf Online.

Wehling, Peter (2008) "Wissen und seine Schattenseite: Die wachsenden Bedeutung des Nichtwissens in (vermeintlichen) Wissensgesellschaften," pp. 17–34 in Thomas Brüsemeister and Klaus-Dieter Ebel (ed.), *Evaluation, Wissen und Nichtwissen*. Wiesbaden: VS Verlag.

Wehling, Peter (2009) "Nichtwissen – Bestimmungen, Abgrenzungen, Bewertungen," *EWE* 20: 95–106.

Weingart, Peter (1983) "Verwissenschaftlichung der Gesellschaft – Politisierung der Wissenschaft," *Zeitschrift für Soziologie* 12: 225–241.

Weizenbaum, Joseph (1976) *Computer Power and Human Reason – From Judgment to Calculation*. San Francisco, CA: W.H. Freeman.

Whatmore, Sarah J. (2009) "Mapping knowledge controversies: Science, democracy and the redistribution of expertise," *Progress in Human Geography* 33: 587–598.

White, David Manning (1950) "The 'gate keeper': A case study in the selection of news," *Journalism Quarterly* 27: 383–391.

Wikström, Solveig and Richard Normann (1994) *Knowledge and Value. A New Perspective on Corporate Transformation*. London: Routledge.

Wilensky, Harold L. (1971) *Organizational Intelligence. Knowledge and Policy in Government and Industry*. New York: Basic Books.

Wilkinson, Richard and Kate Pickett (2009) *The Spirit Level. Why More Equal Societies Almost Always do Better*. London: Allen Lane.

Williams, Raymond (1983) *Keywords: A Vocabulary of Culture and Society*. Oxford: Oxford University Press.

Wilson, Edward O. (1975) *Sociobiology: The New Synthesis*. Cambridge, Massachusetts: Harvard University Press.

Wirth, Werner (1997) *Von der Information zum Wissen. Die Rolle der Rezeption für die Entstehung von Wissensunterschieden*. Wiesbaden: Westdeutscher Verlag.

Woolgar, Steve (2002) "After word? On some dynamics of duality interrogation or why bonfires are not enough," *Theory, Culture, and Society* 19: 261–270.

World Bank (1998) *Indigenous Knowledge for Development*. Initiative led by the World Bank in partnership with CIRAN/NUFFIC, CISDA, ECA, IDRC, SANGONet, UNDP, UNESCO, WHO, WIPO. www.worldbank.org/html/aft/IK.

World Bank (1999) *World Development Report. Knowledge for Development*. New York: Oxford University Press.

World Bank (2010) "About us," go.worldbank.org/3QT2P1GNH0.

World Bank (2011) *The Changing Wealth of Nations – Measuring Sustainable Development in the New Millennium*. Washington, DC: World Bank.

World Bank (2015) *World Development Report 2015: Mind, Society, and Behavior*. Washington, DC: World Bank.

World Bank (2016a) *Digital Dividends. World Development Report 2016*. Washington, DC: World Bank

World Bank (2016b) *Digital Dividends: Main Messages. World Development Report 2016*. Washington, DC: World Bank

World Commission on the Social Dimensions of Globalization (2004) *A Fair Globalization. Creating Opportunities for All*. Geneva: International Labour Office.

World Intellectual Property Organization (WIPO) (2001) *Intellectual Property Needs and Expectations of Traditional Knowledge Holders. WIPO Report on Fact-Finding Missions on Intellectual Property and Traditional Knowledge (1998–1999)*. Geneva: WIPO.

Wright, Sarah (2005) "Knowing scale: Intellectual property rights, knowledge spaces and the production of the global," *Social & Cultural Geography* 6: 903–921.

Wright, Susan (1986) "Molecular biology or molecular politics? The production of scientific consensus on the hazards of recombinant DNA technology," *Social Studies of Science* 16: 593–620.

Wynne, Brian (1992) "Misunderstood misunderstanding: Social identities and public uptake of science," *Public Understanding of Science* 1: 281–304.
Wynne, Brian (2001) "Creating public alienation: Expert cultures of risk and ethics on GMO's," *Science as Culture* 10: 445–481.
Yeung, Henry Wai-Chung (1998) "Capital, state and space: Contesting the borderless world," *Transactions of the Institute of British Geographers* 23: 291–309.
Zhou, Yi (2015) "The tragedy of the anticommons in knowledge," *Review of Radical Political Economics*: 1–18.
Zimmerli, Walther Ch. (1999) "Management von Nichtwissen," *Bulletin. Magazin der Eidgenössischen Technischen Hochschule Zürich* 272.
Zollo, Fabiana, Alessandro Bessi, Michela del Vicario, Antonio Scala, Guido Caldarelli, Louis Shekhtman, Shlomo Havlin and Walter Quattrociocchi (2015) *Debunking in a World of Tribes*. arXiv preprint arXiv: 1510.04267.

INDEX

Abbott, Andrew 132
Abel, Günter 22
Acemoglu, Daron 209, 212–13
Adolf, Marian 152, 154, 179
Adorno, Theodor W. 177
Agnew, John 143
Akerlof, George A. 79; *The Market for Lemons (1970)* 89
Alford, Robert: *Powers of Theory (1985)* 66
Allport, Gordon W.: *The Nature of Prejudice (1958)* 118
Almquist, Alan J. 118
Altheide, David L.: *Media Logic (with Robert Snow, 1979)* 179
Antonelli, Christiano 137, 163
Appleyard, Bryan: *Brave New Worlds (1998)* 104
Aron, Raymond: *Eighteen Lectures on Industrial Society (1962)* 256
Aronowitz, Stanley 189
Arrow, Kenneth 34, 107
Atkinson, Anthony B.: *The Economics of Inequality (1983)* 212

Bacon, Sir Francis 19, 190, 238
Barnes, Barry 19; *Elements of Social Theory (1995)* 13; *The Nature of Power (1988)* 32
Barro, Robert 196, 227
Bataille, George: *The Unfinished System of Nonknowledge (2001)* 83
Bates, Benjamin 202
Beck, Ulrich 2, 27, 76, 147
Becker-Tomes model 213
Becker, Gary S. 210–11; *Human Capital (1964)* 210
Bell, Daniel 5, 27–8, 251–2, 239; *The Coming of Post-Industrial Society (1973)* 14
Bentham, Jeremy: *A Manual of Political Economy (1839)* 173
Bernal, John Desmond 161, 190
Bijker, Wiebe 103
Black, Jeremy 22–3, 143; *The Power of Knowledge (2014)* 23
Blair, Margaret M. 208, 222
Bloch, Ernst: *The Spirit of Utopia (1918)* 168

Blumenberg, Hans 1–2; *The Legitimacy of the Modern Age (1973)* 2
Böhme, Gernot 5, 41, 115, 238, 252
Boli, John 144–5
Borgmann, Albert 22, 32
Boudon, Raymond: *Education, Opportunity and Social Inequality* 219
Boulding, Kenneth 5, 23, 83
Bourdieu, Pierre 27, 130, 214–19; *Homo Academicus (1984)* 219; *Outline of a Theory of Practice (1972)* 27
Brave, Ralph 102
Brown, John Seeley 24, 147
Brzezinksi, Zbigniew 131
bureaucracy 193–6
Burke, Peter 29; *A Social History of Knowledge (2000)* 93

Calhoun, Craig: *Critical Social Theory (1995)* 219
Callon, Michel 108
Canguilhem, Georges 18
Carley, Kathleen 29
Castells, Manuel 147; *Communication Power (2009)* 179; *The Information Age (1996)* 27; *The Rise of the Network Society (1996)* 27
Cerny, Philip G. 101
Chargaff, Erwin 81, 239
Chen, Shin Horng 148, 154
Chinco, Alex 90
Cicourel, Aaron 127
Coleman, James S. 52, 215
Collingridge, David 193
common-sense knowledge *see* everyday knowledge
Comte, August 126
conceptions of knowledge: sociological 6–9, 42–4; objectivist 28; scientific 6
Condorcet, Jean-Antoine-Nicolas de Caritat, Marquis de 246
consumer 30
Cooley, James: *Social Organization (1909)* 178

Cowan, Robin 136–7, 157
Cronin, John E. 118
Crozier, Michael: *The Bureaucratic Phenomenon (1963)* 36–7
Cukier, Kenneth J. 183
capital: cultural 199; human 210–14; knowledge 214–19; symbolic 214–19

Dahl, Robert 242
Dahrendorf, Ralf 63–6
Darwin, Charles 42
Dasgupta, Samir 22
demand 109
democracy: democratic control 52; in organizations 50–4, representative 242
Dennett, Daniel C. 120
Derber, Charles 201–2
Dewey, John 78, 227–8; *Democracy and Education (1916)* 227; *The Public and its Problems (1927)* 238–9
Dierkes, Meinolf 120
DiFazio, William 189
digital media 175–6
digitization 182
discretion to create (*Gestaltungsspielraum*) 32
divisible goods 107
division of knowledge and information 88–91
division of labor 159
domination 60
Dosi, Giovanni 13, 22
Douglas, Mary: *How Institutions Think (1986)* 120–1
Downs, Anthony: *An Economic Theory of Democracy (1957)* 244
Dretske, Fred I.: *Knowledge and the Flow of Information (1983)* xii
Drucker, Peter 249–51; *The Age of Discontinuity (1968)* 249–50; *The New Society (1949)* 255; *Post-Capitalist Society (1993)* 5
Duguid, Paul 24, 147

Dunkmann, Karl 104
Durkheim, Emile 7, 124–5, 200; *The Elementary Forms of Religious Life (1912)* 13, 116; *Pragmatism and Sociology (1955)* 125; *Professional Ethics and Civic Morals (1950)* 200

Easterbrook, Frank H. 24
economic development 155
economic growth 155, 209, 252
education: educational system 215, 228; expense of education *see* New York, the State of
Einstein, Albert 42
Elias, Norbert 70, 74, 129, 151; *Über den Prozess der Zivilisation (1978)* 77
enlightenment 197
épistème (know-why) 25, 57
Ernst, Dieter 145–6
European Patent Office (EPO) 219
experts 36–37

Facebook 180
Faulkner, Wendy 21
Featherstone, Mike 145, 149
fee-rider problem 223
Ferguson, Adam 253
Feyerabend, Paul: *Against Method (1993)* 169; *The Tyranny of Science (2011)* 141
Fleck, Ludwik 75, 79; *Genesis and Development of a Scientific Fact (1935)* 94
Forey, Dominique 157; *The Economics of Knowledge (2006)* 5, 231
Foster, Kevin R. 119
Foucault, Michel 54–63; *The Archaeology of Knowledge (1969)* 57–8, 196; *Birth of the Clinic (1963)* 60; *Discipline and Punish (1975)* 60; *The Order of Things (1966)* 57
Freeman, Chris 108
French Revolution 219
Freud, Sigmund 70–2
Freyer, Hans 122
Fukuyama, Francis 106

Fuller, Stephen 144
Funtowicz, Silvio 165–6

Galbraith, John Kenneth: *The New Industrial State (1967)* 34
Gehlen, Arnold 129
genetics 102
German educational system 228
German Social Democratic Party (SPD) 48–52
Giddens, Anthony 2, 143; *The Constitution of Society (1984)* 196
Gieryn, Thomas F. 121
Ginsberg, Theo 17
global class 63–6
global knowledge 143–6, 157–64; constraints to 160; global knowledge spaces 150–1
globalization 157–8
Gouldner, Alvin W.: *The Dialectic of Ideology and Technology (1976)* 36
gouvernementalité (Michel Foucault) 55
Graber, Doris A.: *Processing the News: How People Tame the Information Tide (1988)* 96

Grandori, Anna 163
Greenwald, Bruce G. 30, 144, 220
Grundmann, Reiner 120, 165: *Experts: The Knowledge and Power of Expertise (with Nico Stehr, 2011)* 5; *The Power of Scientific Knowledge (2012)* 36
Gupta, Anil K. 135

Habermas Jürgen 103, 123, 157, 239
Hardin, Garrett 111
Hardin, Russel 117
Hayek, Friedrich August von 70–2, 146; *The Constitution of Liberty (1960)* 84; *Individualism and Economic Order (1948)* 89
Herf, Jeffrey 122
Hess, Charlotte 207, 223
Hirsch, Fred: *Social Limits to Growth (1977)* 17

Hirschman, Albert O. 107
Hobsbawm, Eric 114; *Globalisation, Democracy and Terrorism (2007)* 19
Horkheimer, Max 190–1; *Dialectic of Enlightenment (with Theodor W. Adorno, 1944)* 177
Hunter, Ian 18
Huntington, Samuel P. 145
Husserl, Edmund 136

ignorance 82–8, 120, 131–2; specified 86, 132; willful 87
indigenous knowledge *see* traditional knowledge
inequality 155; knowledge inequalities *see* distribution of knowledge; social inequality 6
information and communication technologies (ICT) 175–6, 181–5
information: asymmetric 90; definition of 31; the price of 208–10; stickiness of 109, 137–9
informationalization 183
Innis, Harold: *Empire and Communications (1950)* 180
innovations 53
Intellectual Property Rights (IPRs) 220–7
inter-nation technology trade 225–6
invisible hand 70
iron law of oligarchy 50–4

James, William F. 25, 26
Jischa, Michael F. 73, 77
Jonas, Hans 80, 104
Jünger, Ernst 122

Kant, Immanuel 3–5; *Critique of Pure Reason (1781)* 5
Katz, Lawrence 209
Keller, Evelyn Fox 106
Keynes, John Maynard 75: *General Theory of Employment, Interest and Money (1936)* 191–4
Kitch, Edmund W. 109–10
Knorr-Cetina, Karin 4

know-how 19, 39–40
knowledge: additional/incremental 28, 33–8, 203; attributes of 11–18; and authority 53–61; definition of 1, 31; distribution of 28–41, 240–7; divisibility of *see* divisible goods; enabling *see* know-how; everyday knowledge 115–121; fabrication of *see* additional knowledge; governance of *see* knowledge politics; globalization of *see* global knowledge; growth of 41–2; hidden (occult) 82; and information 21–31; lack of 79–82; mobility of 143–6; organized 123–31; ownership of 21; practical 31–33; as a public good 17, 161, 164, 199–205; scientific 47, 127; self-protection of 106–11; self-realization of 102–6; superfluous 111–12; tacit 22, 190, 136–40; traditional/local 126–31; transfer of 30
knowledge as a capacity to act 18–21
knowledge economy 64
knowledge gaps 73, 91–3, 78
knowledge of acquaintance 24–5
knowledge of pure essence (*Bildungswissen*) 15
knowledge of salvation (*Erlösungswissen*) 15
knowledge of the powerful 47–65
knowledge politics 100–12; 238
knowledge sharing 177
knowledge that produces effects (*Herrschaftswissen*) 15
knowledge-about 24–5
knowledge-guiding interest 103
Kohut, Bruce 163
Kokko, Hanna 119
Krohn, Wolfgang 19
Kroto, Harry 242
Krotz, Friedrich 178, 183
Kuhn, Thomas, 137

Latour, Bruno 165
Leighninger, Matt 247
Lemert, Charles C. 56
Lévy-Bruhl, Lucien 7
Lewontin, Richard 243
Liebknecht, Wilhelm 48–50
Limoges, Camille 37
Lindblom, Charles 31
Lipset, Martin 52, 227
Luckman, Thomas 88, 127
Luhmann, Niklas 86, 166; *Beobachtungen der Moderne (1992)* 83, 94; *Gesellschaft der Gesellschaft (1997)* 76, 255; *The Reality of the Mass Media (1996)* 176–8; *Social Systems (1984)* 48; *Wirtschaft der Gesellschaft (1988)* 169; *Wissenschaft der Gesellschaft (1990)* 2, 54
Lyotard, Jean-François 199, 204

Machlup, Fritz 23–4; *The Economics of Information and Human Capital (1984)* 14; *Knowledge and Knowledge Production (1981)* 14; *The Production and Distribution of Knowledge in the United States (1962)* 5
Manheim, Karl 7–8, 32–3, 121–4; *Ideology and Utopia (1929)* 193
market failure 90
Marx, Karl 7; *Capital (1885)* 206
Mauss, Marcel 7, 73
Mazur, Allan 37
McGeoy, Linsey 80, 83, 87
McLuhan, Marshall 180
media: architecture 180–1, logic 179; mass media 176–8; mediatization 178–85
Meja, Volker 5
Merton, Robert K. 86, 108, 120–1, 132, 195; *Social Theory and Social Structure (1957)* 81
Michels, Robert 50–4, 214; *Political Parties (1911)* 52
Mill, John Stuart: *The Spirit of the Age (1831)* 237–8
modernization 157

Moore, Wilbert 80, 85–6
Moscovici, Serge 119
Myrdal, Gunnar: *An American Dilemma (1944)* 85
myths 124–6

Nelkin, Dorothy 37
Nelson, Richard R. 39, 240
networked integration 181
Neuweg, Hans 138–40
New York, the State of 228–30
Nimkoff, Meyer F. 120
non-knowledge 72–8
Nonaka, Ikujiro 31, 136–8
Norris, Pippa: *Digital Divide (2001)* 5

Olson, Mancur: *The Rise and Decline of Nations (1982)* 244
Organisation for Economic Co-Operation and Development (OECD) 154
Orlove, Ben 132–3
Ostrom, Elinor 101, 207, 223
Oyama, Susan 29

Paras, Eric 57
Parente, Stephen 154–5
Pareto, Vilfredo 116
Parsons, Talcott 91; *The Structure of Social Action (1937)* 116
patent 219–27
Pielke, Roger A. Jr.: *The Honest Broker (2007)* 243
Pigou, Arthur C.: *The Economics of Welfare (1924)* 173
Piketty, Thomas: *Capital in the Twentieth-First Century (2013)* 155, 210
Plato 3
Poggi, Gianfranco 195
Polanyi, Michael 22, 109, 136–9, 161, 190; *Knowing and Being (1969)* 137; *Personal Knowledge (1958)* 163; *The Tacit Dimension (1967)* 138
Popitz, Heinrich 19, 92; *On the Preventive Effect of Non-Knowledge (1968)* 81–2

Popper, Karl 83, 161, 190
Porat, Marc: *The Information Economy (1977)* 27
Porter, Michael 154
Poser, Hans 83–4
Posner, Richard 220
Prescott, Edwart 154–5
Programme for the International Assessment of Adult Competencies (PIAAC) 214
Prusak, Lawrence 5
public goods 101
Putnam, Jonathan 200

Rabinow, Paul 60
rationalization 157
Ravetz, Jerome R. 76, 131, 165–6
real factors (Max Scheler) 8
Reeve, Colin 193
Rescher, Nicholas 42
Ricardo, David 211
Richta, Radovan 14, 251–2
risk of knowledge advances 53–4
Robinson, James Harvey: *The Humanizing of Knowledge (1923)* 242
Rogers, Everett M. 120
Rousseau, Jean-Jacques: *Émile, or On Education (1762)* 3
Ryle, Gilbert: *The Concept of Mind (1949)* 25, 136

Samuelson, Paul A. 108
Sarewitz, Daniel 19, 166
Scheler, Max 7–8
Schelsky, Helmut 249
Schiller, Herbert I.: *Informational Inequality (1996)* 94
Schmitt, Carl 122
Schumpeter, Joseph: *The Theory of Economic Development (1912)* 20
Schütz, Alfred 4, 69, 136
science: scientification 117, 238; scientificity 65; scientific truth 124–6; system 34

segregation 85
Sen, Armatya 81
Shannon, Claude: *The Mathematical Theory of Communication (1948)* 18
Shapin, Steven 4, 116
Simmel, Georg 2, 69, 79, 92, 129, 164; *Philosophy of Money (1907)* 124, 241
Simon, Herbert 207
Simonson, Peter: *Refiguring Mass Communication (2010)* 176
Smith, Adam 159; *The Wealth of Nations (1776)* 173
Smithson, Michael J. 83, 87
Snow, Charles Percy 77
Snow, Robert 179
Snowden, Edward 245
social conduct 25
society: information society 64, 175, 252; knowledge society 2, 14, 247–55; mass society 157; network society 10, 27, 252; post-industrial 14, 26; risk society 10, 252; work society 65
sociological relativism 4
Sombart, Werner 122
Starbuck, William H. 23, 108
Stehr, Nico 4–5, 94, 120, 152, 165, 178, 239; *The Fragility of Modern Societies* 253; *Information, Power, and Democracy: Liberty is a Daughter of Knowledge (2016)* 63, 216; *Knowledge and Economic Conduct (2000)* 34; *Knowledge Politics (2005)* 156, 244; *Knowledge Societies (1994)* 1; *Practical Knowledge (1992)* 18
Stewart, Thomas A. 21
Stigler, George J. 35
Stiglitz, Joseph E. 30–1, 70, 81, 106–7, 144, 162, 213, 221; *Making Globalization Work (2007)* 152; *The Price of Inequality (2012)* 98
Storper, Michael 108
superstition 119
supply 109
surveillance 181–5

tabular reason 57
tacitness of knowledge properties *see* tacit knowledge
Takeuchi, Hirotaka 136–8
taxation 227–30
techné (know-how) 25
Teece, David J. 35, 208
Thurow, Lester C. 199
Tichenor, Phillip 78
total institutions 80
Toulmin, Stephen 127
Touraine, Alain: *Critique of Modernity (1992)* 56–7
tragedy of the commons 111
Tumin, Melvin 80, 85–6
Turner, Stephen 92

uncertainty 75, 81
unearned income 212
Ungar, Sheldon 74, 83
United Nations 209
United Nations Environment Programme (UNEP) 133
Urry, John: *Global Complexity (2003)* 76

Van den Daele, Wolfgang 37
Venn, Couze 145, 149
Volpert, Walter 123
Von Hippel, Eric 109, 137, 163

Wallerstein, Immanuel: *The Uncertainties of Knowledge (2004)* 242

Wallman, Steven H.M. 208, 222
Warren, Dennis M. 132–6
Weber, Max 16; *Economy and Society (1922)* 190–6; *Gesammelte Aufsätze zur Religionssoziologie (1920)* 115–16; *Protestant Ethic and the Spirit of Capitalism (1905)* 160; *The Theory of Social and Economic Organization (1922)* 206
Wehling, Peter 74
Weimar Republic 122
Weingart, Peter 115
Weizenbaum, Joseph: *Computer Power and Human Reason (1976)* 123
Wilensky, Harold L. 119
Wilkinson, Richard: *The Spirit Level (with Kate Pickett, 2009)* 255
Wilson, Edward O. 105–6
Wissenssoziologie (Max Scheler) 7
World Bank 108, 135, 146–7, 209, 224
World Intellectual Property Association (WIPO) 136
World Trade Organization (WTO) 149, 220
worlds of knowledge 146–50, 164–6
Wright, Susan 111, 151
Wynne, Brian 37, 244

Yeung, Henry Wai-Chung 158

Zhou, Yi 223
Zimmerli, Walter Ch. 74